THE UNITED STATES:
A Contemporary Human Geography

P. L. Knox
E. H. Bartels B. Holcomb
J. R. Bohland R. J. Johnston

Longman
Scientific &
Technical

Copublished in the United States with
John Wiley & Sons, Inc., New York

Longman Scientific & Technical
Longman Group UK Limited
Longman House, Burnt Mill, Harlow,
Essex CM20 2JE, England
and Associated Companies throughout the world.

Copublished in the United States with
John Wiley & Sons, Inc., 605 Third Avenue, New York
NY 10158

First published 1988
Reprinted 1990, 1993

British Library Cataloguing in Publication Data

The United States: a contemporary human
    geography.
    1. Anthropo-geography — United States
    2. United States — Historical geography
    I. Knox, Paul L.
    304.2'0973   GF503

ISBN 0-582-30153-X

Library of Congress Cataloguing in Publication Data

The United States — a contemporary human geography
    Bibliography: p.
    Includes index.
    1. Anthropo-geography — United States.   2. United
States — Economic conditions.   3. United States —
Social conditions.   1. Knox, Paul L.
GF503.U57   1988   973   87-3166
ISBN 0-470-20845-7   (USA only)

Set in Linotron 202 10/11 pt Times
Produced by Longman Singapore Publishers Pte Ltd
Printed in Singapore

CONTENTS

AUTHORS

E. H. Bartels

Landscape Architect, Winthirstrasse 35, 8000 München 19, West Germany

Professor J. R. Bohland

Urban Affairs Program, College of Architecture and Urban Studies, Virginia Polytechnic Institute and State University, Blacksburg, Virginia 24061

Professor B. Holcomb

Department of Urban Studies, School of Urban and Regional Policy, Rutgers University, New Brunswick, New Jersey 08903

Professor R. J. Johnston

Department of Geography, University of Sheffield, Sheffield S10 2TN

Professor P. L. Knox

Urban Affairs Program, College of Architecture and Urban Studies, Virginia Polytechnic Institute and State University, Blacksburg, Virginia 24061

ACKNOWLEDGEMENTS

The idea for this book has its roots in the courses taught by Bryan Coates and Malcolm Lewis at the University of Sheffield in 1968. Since then, the case for a systematic approach to the human geography of the United States has been strengthened both by the increasing pace of economic and social change in the United States itself and by conceptual and theoretical developments within human geography. But translating the idea for a book into reality is never easy, and in this case the authors have been greatly assisted by the professional advice provided by the staff at Longman. In addition, thanks are due to many of our own colleagues and to successive cohorts of students who have helped us to shape and test our ideas.

We are grateful to the following for permission to reproduce copyright material:

The American Academy of Political and Social Science for fig. 7.1 (parts B & C – Harris and Ullman, 1945); American Demographics for table 1.2 (Blackburn & Bloom 1985) © January 1985; Association of American Geographers for parts of fig. 4.10 (Wohlenberg 1976b & 1976c), figs. 7.4 (Holcomb & Beauregard, 1981), 8.9 & 8.10 (Smith & Hanham, 1982), 8.11 (Cutter, Holcomb & Shatin, 1986), 9.6 (de Vise, 1973) and 9.9 (Ley, 1974); the author, T. J. Baerwald, for fig. 7.2 (Baerwald, 1984); Basic Books Inc. Publishers for table 5.5 (Bluestone & Harrison, 1982) copyright © 1982 by Barry Bluestone and Bennett Harrison; the author, J. W. Brownell, for fig. 3.3 (Brownell, 1960); Duxbury Press for fig. 9.3 (Bunge, 1975); the Editor of *Economic Geography* for fig. 2.2 (Morrill & Donaldson, 1972), part of fig. 4.10 (Wohlenberg, 1976a), figs. 5.4 (Peet, 1983) and 5.9 (Keinath, 1982); the Editor of *Growth and Change* and the author, D. L. Brown, for fig. 2.9 (Wardwell & Brown, 1980); Harper & Row Publishers Inc. for figs. 4.1 & 4.2 (Elazar, 1966) copyright © 1972 by Harper & Row, Publishers Inc., and fig. 6.1 from fig. 3.12, p. 106 of *The Human Mosaic*, 2nd Edition, copyright © 1979 by Terry G. Jordan and Lester Rowntree; Houghton Mifflin Company for fig. 3.2 (Garreau, 1981) © by Joel Garreau; JAI Press Inc. for table 5.3 (Rees, 1983a); The Johns Hopkins University Press for fig. 5.7 (Dunn, 1980), table 6.8 & fig. 6.10 (Heady, 1982) published for Resources for the Future Inc. by the Johns Hopkins University Press; Kluwer-Nijhoff Publishing for table 5.1 (Noyelle, 1983); Macmillan Publishing Co. for fig. 2.11 & table 6.9 (Bogue, 1985) copyright © 1985 by The Free Press, a division of Macmillan Inc.; McGraw-Hill Book Co. for fig. 8.8

(Harries, 1974) and figs. 9.1, 9.2 & 9.4 (Smith, 1973); the author, R. A. Murdie, for fig. 7.3 (Murdie, 1969); Oxford University Press, Inc. for fig. 3.5 (Hollon, 1966) copyright © 1966 by Oxford University Press Inc.; Prentice-Hall Inc. for fig. 3.1 from p. 118 (Zelinsky, 1973) © 1973; the author, G. Pyle, for fig. 9.5 (Pyle, 1968); Resources for the Future for table 6.2 (Clawson, 1983) © Resources for the Future 1983; Scripps Foundation for fig. 2.5 (Bogue, Shryock & Hoermann, 1957); The Southern Political Science Association for fig. 4.4 (Dye, 1984); The University of Chicago Press for figs. 2.4 (Easterlin, 1980), 7.1 (part A – Park *et al*, 1925) and 9.8 (Zorbaugh, 1929); University of Nebraska Press for table 6.3 (Luebcke, 1980), copyright © 1980 by the University of Nebraska Press; University of Washington Press for fig. 3.4 (Gastil, 1975); Westview Press for figs. 6.8 & 6.9 & table 6.6 (Gregor, 1982); John Wiley & Sons Ltd. for figs. 4.3 (Archer & Taylor, 1981) copyright 1981, and 5.1 (Conzen, 1981) copyright 1981; John Wiley & Sons Inc. Publishers for fig. 8.5 (Hartshorn, 1980), copyright 1980 John Wiley & Sons Inc.; V. H. Winston & Sons Inc. for table 6.4 (Haren & Halling, 1979).

Whilst every effort has been made to trace the owners of copyright material, in a few cases this has proved impossible and we take this opportunity to offer our apologies to any copyright holders whose rights we may have unwittingly infringed.

Paul Knox
Blacksburg, Virginia
Thanksgiving, 1986

Chapter 1

INTRODUCTION

Some time between 1890 and 1900, the US moved to the top of the world's rankings in terms of aggregate economic output. During the twentieth century, this economic power has been multiplied many times over, bringing the US to the top of the world's rankings in terms of military strength, political importance and cultural influence. By mid-century, the pivotal importance of the US in the world economy was undisputed, and the subsequent internationalization of its economic and political interests has effectively secured and reinforced this position.

What is important about these achievements to the student of the economic and social geography of the US is that they have been sustained by a tremendous *internal dynamism*. The nation's geography has been recast several times in response to the evolution of US capitalism and to the changing context – demographic, technological, political – of national economic development. The contemporary economic and social geography of the US is the legacy of this dynamism, a composite of successive shifts, dislocations and transformations that

are reflected not only in patterns of economic specialization and prosperity but also by demographic, cultural and political patterns, by the variety of ecological settings that exist in both rural and metropolitan America, and by the nature and distribution of various social problems. In this book, we describe these patterns and show how they have come about.

The geography of the US has traditionally been delineated in terms of the physiographic and economic landscapes of major sub-regions. This is the US of the Rockies, the Great Plains, the Deep South, New England, Megalopolis, and so on. But such an approach has become increasingly inadequate. For one thing, the conceptual and theoretical development of geography has come to emphasize systematic approaches at the expense of regional synthesis. More important, the actual geography of the US has meanwhile undergone significant changes as a result of demographic trends, changes in patterns of urbanization, the expansion of the role of the state and, above all, structural economic change. At the same time, however, we recognize that these changes are

Top left: Manhattan, New York City *Credit*: Paul Knox   *Top right*: Cornfield, Hamilton County, Nebraska *Credit*: USDA Soil Conservation Service   *Middle left*: Fast food strip, Norman, Oklahoma *Credit*: Paul Knox   *Middle right*: Haymond, Kentucky *Credit*: USDA   *Bottom left*: Grand Central Station, New York *Credit*: Paul Knox   *Bottom right*: New Mexico landscape *Credit*: Paul Knox

expressed in different ways in different settings. Spatial change, in other words, is complex and contingent: local variations in social, cultural, political and institutional factors constantly modify national trends and contribute to regional and sub-regional differentiation. In this book, therefore, we have adopted a systematic approach that emphasizes the imprint of successive changes that have affected the economic and social geography of the country in the period since 1945 while acknowledging the persistence of regional specificity.

The emergence of the US as a dominant component of the modern world economy was essentially due to the fact that it had vast natural resources of land and minerals, a large and – thanks to immigration – rapidly-growing market and labour force, and was big enough to breed giant corporations with large research budgets, which helped to institutionalize the innovation process in a way which European industry had never done. In short, the scale and resources of the US were coincident with the imperatives of late industrial and post-industrial capitalism. The overall strength and success of the American economy is impressive by any yardstick. With a population of 226 million, 5.1 per cent of the world's population, the US *produces* some 25 per cent of the world's coal, 30 per cent of the world's crude oil, 25 per cent of the world's copper, 15 per cent of the world's iron ore, 20 per cent of the world's timber, 26 per cent of the world's cotton, 15 per cent of the world's meat, 70 per cent of the world's soybeans, and 46 per cent of the world's maize (corn). And this pre-eminence in primary products is matched by the performance of other sectors. The US makes around 16 per cent of the world's crude steel, 25 per cent of the world's energy, and 22 per cent of the world's road vehicles. It is the base for nearly half of the world's 250 largest business corporations, each of them with an annual turnover in 1983 of $3000 million (Dunning and Pearce 1985). All this productivity means that levels of domestic *consumption* are correspondingly high. This, in turn, has helped to shape the attitudes and expectations of Americans, contributing towards a national value system that is distinctive for, among other things, its untrammelled optimism, its emphasis on consumerism, and its tolerance of waste. In

more practical terms, the capacity of the US economy to generate surplus food *and* manufactures and to provide high-order services to other nations has meant that the penetration and consolidation of overseas markets has been imperative: otherwise, output would have to be restricted and levels of living depressed. This, as much as the Japanese attack on Pearl Harbor, is what put an end to American isolationism.

It is within this overall framework that we must examine spatial differentiation. Physically, the sheer size of the nation guarantees marked variations from place to place in almost all facets of economic and social life. Table 1.1 illustrates this diversity at the State[1] level for some of the more important economic, social and demographic indicators. Note, for example, the gradients in unemployment and infant mortality, two of the most useful diagnostic indicators of economic and social well-being. Both exhibit extreme values which differ by a factor of three, with a broad spread of values between the extreme cases. Personal incomes *per capita* average out with a much shallower – but nevertheless significant – gradient, the most affluent places (Alaska, DC and Connecticut) recording income levels which are 50 per cent higher than the poorest (Mississippi, West Virginia, South Carolina). Other indicators exhibit much greater diversity: the murder rate, for example, ranges from 1.7 per 100 000 population in Montana and 2.0 in New Hampshire to 14.2 per 100 000 in Louisiana and Texas and 17.8 in Alaska.

Along with these variations, we must also recognize the marked differentiation that exists in terms of landscape and cultural traits. These dimensions of US geography are much more difficult to quantify, but they are, nevertheless, significant. Take, for example, 'MexAmerica' (see Fig. 3.2):

a place . . . that appears on no map. It's where the gumbo of Dixie gives way to the refried beans of Mexico. The land looks like northern Mexico. And the sound of Spanish in the supermarkets and on the airwaves is impossible to ignore. The news stories it produces point up the trouble Anglo

---

[1] Throughout this book, the term 'state' refers to the sovereign institution, whereas 'State' refers to a constituent unit of the US.

Table 1.1: Economic, social and demographic indicators, by State

	Total population (1983)	% Population under 5 (1983)	% Population 65+ (1983)	Infant mortality (1981)	Deaths from heart disease (1983) (per 100 000 population)	% Black (1980)	% Population with at least 4 years college education (1980)	Burglaries per 100 000 population (1983)	Murders per 100 000 population (1983)	% Non-agricultural employees in manufacturing (1983)	Female participation in the labour force (1983)	% Unemployed (1983)	Personal income per capita (1983)
N. Eng.	12 489	6.4	13.0	10.5	352.5	3.8	19.2	1 201	3.4	25.4	55.9	6.8	12 845
Maine	1 146	7.2	13.0	10.9	359.6	2.6	14.4	996	2.1	25.6	53.3	9.0	9 619
New Hampshire	959	7.1	11.6	9.7	303.2	4.3	18.2	822	2.0	27.7	59.3	5.4	11 620
Vermont	525	7.4	11.7	7.7	321.7	1.9	19.0	1 090	3.6	22.9	57.7	6.9	10 036
Massachussets	5 767	6.2	13.2	9.7	365.9	3.8	20.0	1 254	3.5	24.7	55.9	6.9	13 089
Rhode Island	955	6.3	14.1	11.8	401.2	2.9	15.4	1 332	2.7	29.2	54.4	8.3	11 504
Connecticut	3 138	6.2	12.7	12.1	330.2	6.9	20.7	1 274	4.1	27.8	55.8	6.0	14 826
Mid. Atl.	37 029	6.6	12.9	11.9	405.3	11.9	16.6	1 183	7.9	20.7	48.5	9.4	12 804
New York	17 667	6.7	12.6	12.4	412.0	13.7	17.9	1 410	11.1	17.8	47.9	8.6	13 146
New Jersey	7 468	6.5	12.3	10.7	378.2	12.5	18.3	1 237	5.3	22.6	51.5	7.8	14 057
Pennsylvania	11 895	6.6	13.8	11.9	412.4	8.8	13.6	811	4.9	24.2	47.6	11.8	11 510
E. No. Cent.	41 531	7.6	11.5	12.6	346.8	10.9	14.5	1 236	7.3	25.3	53.5	12.0	11 599
Ohio	10 746	7.5	11.6	12.3	355.1	9.9	13.7	1 156	5.6	26.1	52.0	12.2	11 254
Indiana	5 479	7.7	11.4	11.7	327.3	7.6	12.5	988	5.2	28.7	53.2	11.1	10 567
Illinois	11 486	7.8	11.6	13.9	364.8	14.6	16.2	1 214	9.7	20.1	53.8	11.4	12 626
Michigan	9 069	7.5	10.8	13.1	327.5	12.9	14.3	1 692	10.0	27.6	52.8	14.2	11 574
Wisconsin	4 751	7.7	12.6	10.4	344.5	3.9	14.8	884	2.8	26.1	58.1	10.4	11 132
W. No. Cent.	17 422	8.0	13.2	11.1	344.0	4.5	15.3	1 029	4.3	18.5	55.7	7.9	11 242
Minnesota	4 144	8.1	12.3	10.3	294.5	1.3	17.4	1 076	1.7	20.1	61.6	8.2	11 666
Iowa	2 905	7.8	13.9	10.0	363.2	1.4	13.9	916	2.3	19.5	54.1	8.1	11 048
Missouri	4 970	7.6	13.6	12.6	370.3	10.4	13.9	1 217	8.1	20.8	52.1	9.9	10 790
North Dakota	680	9.0	12.5	11.2	315.6	0.5	14.8	436	2.1	6.0	52.9	5.6	11 350
South Dakota	700	9.1	13.6	11.5	369.0	0.4	14.0	546	2.1	11.2	54.8	5.4	9 704
Nebraska	1 597	8.3	13.3	9.9	358.0	3.3	15.5	777	2.6	13.9	56.8	5.7	10 940
Kansas	2 425	8.2	13.2	11.4	342.8	5.3	17.0	1 168	5.6	18.0	55.2	6.1	12 285

Continued

Table 1.1 (*Cont'd*)

So. Atl.	38 805	7.0	12.4	13.6	331.3	20.7	15.7	1 330	9.2	19.2	53.0	8.5	11 020
Delaware	606	7.1	10.8	13.4	334.0	16.2	17.5	1 223	4.1	25.5	55.2	8.1	12 442
Maryland	4 304	6.9	10.1	12.6	300.6	22.7	20.4	1 224	8.5	12.4	57.7	6.9	12 994
District of Columbia	623	6.5	11.8	25.1	348.3	70.3	27.5	*	*	2.3	60.3	11.7	16 409
Virginia	5 550	7.0	10.0	12.5	284.9	18.8	19.1	920	7.0	18.2	56.5	6.1	11 835
West Virginia	1 965	7.3	12.8	13.0	409.0	3.3	10.4	685	4.9	15.4	38.4	18.0	8 937
North Carolina	6 082	6.9	11.0	13.1	306.7	22.4	13.2	1 190	8.1	32.8	55.4	8.9	9 656
South Carolina	3 264	7.8	9.8	16.1	288.8	30.3	13.4	1 295	9.8	30.6	53.4	10.0	8 954
Georgia	5 732	7.8	9.8	13.8	289.6	26.8	14.6	1 267	8.4	22.4	54.2	7.5	10 283
Florida	10 680	6.5	17.5	13.3	403.3	13.7	14.9	1 797	11.2	11.9	49.5	8.6	11 592
E. So. Cent.	14 946	7.7	11.8	13.2	327.4	19.5	12.1	1 082	9.6	25.1	49.6	12.3	9 056
Kentucky	3 714	7.7	11.6	12.2	349.7	7.1	11.1	977	9.8	20.8	50.8	11.7	9 162
Tennessee	4 685	7.1	11.8	12.6	323.2	15.8	12.6	1 206	8.8	27.3	51.3	11.5	9 362
Alabama	3 959	7.6	11.9	13.0	307.6	25.5	12.2	1 073	9.2	25.6	48.7	13.7	9 235
Mississippi	2 587	8.8	11.7	15.4	333.3	35.1	12.3	1 024	11.2	25.7	46.3	12.6	8 072
W. So. Cent.	25 788	8.9	10.2	12.1	288.8	14.8	15.5	1 519	12.8	15.6	53.1	8.9	11 173
Arkansas	2 328	7.7	14.1	11.9	362.3	16.3	10.8	961	7.6	27.0	48.6	10.1	9 040
Louisiana	4 438	9.2	9.6	13.7	304.8	29.4	13.9	1 293	14.2	11.5	47.6	11.8	10 406
Oklahoma	3 298	8.5	11.9	11.9	342.5	6.8	15.1	1 510	7.6	14.1	53.2	9.0	11 187
Texas	15 724	9.0	9.4	11.6	261.4	11.9	16.9	1 668	14.2	15.6	55.3	8.0	11 702
Mt.	12 331	9.3	9.7	10.4	226.4	2.3	18.8	1 411	6.5	11.9	56.1	8.6	10 864
Montana	817	8.7	11.4	10.7	288.3	0.3	17.5	908	3.7	7.8	53.9	8.8	9 999
Idaho	989	10.0	10.6	9.2	248.7	0.3	15.8	931	3.5	16.0	55.0	9.8	9 342
Wyoming	514	10.3	7.9	10.6	208.2	0.6	17.2	705	5.8	3.9	60.7	8.4	11 969
Colorado	3 139	8.3	8.6	10.0	221.7	3.5	23.0	1 532	6.4	13.6	62.0	6.6	12 580
New Mexico	1 399	9.5	9.3	9.8	158.0	1.8	17.6	1 559	8.9	7.1	49.2	10.1	9 560
Arizona	2 963	8.6	12.0	11.8	259.9	9.2	17.4	1 669	7.2	14.0	53.1	9.1	10 719
Utah	1 619	13.0	7.6	9.8	196.3	0.6	19.9	1 016	3.5	15.0	52.3	9.2	9 031
Nevada	891	7.7	9.1	11.2	221.2	6.4	14.4	2 011	12.8	5.0	62.8	9.8	12 516
Pac.	33 639	8.0	10.5	10.3	265.8	6.3	19.4	1 774	9.2	18.5	54.8	9.9	12 920
Washington	4 300	8.0	11.0	10.5	267.3	2.6	19.0	1 640	4.9	17.5	54.2	11.2	12 051
Oregon	2 662	7.9	12.5	10.9	288.2	1.4	17.9	1 746	4.1	19.3	56.5	10.8	10 920
California	25 174	8.0	10.4	10.2	270.3	7.7	19.6	1 829	10.5	19.4	54.4	9.7	13 239
Alaska	479	10.8	3.0	12.7	89.2	3.4	21.1	1 194	13.8	29.1	63.2	10.3	16 820
Hawaii	1 023	8.7	8.7	9.8	162.0	1.7	20.3	1 333	5.6	5.5	59.1	6.5	12 101

Source: Statistical Abstract of the United States 1985 (1985)

institutions have in dealing with enormous cultural strain. It's hot and dry. It has more big dreams per capita than any other place you'll ever know. Its capital is Los Angeles, but it stretches all the way to Houston. The politicians have difficulty in comprehending it, because it ignores polical boundaries. But it's there, it's there (Garreau 1981: ix–x).

Economic dynamism and spatial change

While these socio-economic and cultural patterns can certainly be seen as the product of complex interactions between resources, population, culture and politics at the local level, they must also be seen as the legacy of broader processes of change: the product of the constant reorganization of economic activity, population and landscape in response to changing market conditions not only locally but also nationally and, increasingly, internationally.

Within capitalist economies, these changes often conform to *cyclical* patterns. The most familiar of these are short-term business cycles. In the US, there were twenty-nine such cycles between 1957 and 1978, each lasting from two and a half to nine and a half years (Madison 1982); and each affecting local economies differentially, according to their particular profile of economic activity (Markusen 1985). It has been longer-term cyclical fluctuations, however, that have generally been more important in terms of spatial change. The 'Kondratieff' series of cyclical fluctuations is now widely regarded as being of particular importance in this respect. Each of these 50-year cycles consists of a long climb up from recession followed by a sharp slide into another one. During the recession period of each cycle, it seems, there have occurred exceptional clusters of new inventions, the application of which, as clusters of innovations, have triggered succeeding upswings. As this new technology is exploited, profits rise and economies expand; but when the possibilities of the new technologies are exhausted, markets become saturated and productivity flattens off, profits fall and recession begins. According to Mensch (1983), key clusters of innovations occurred around the years 1764, 1825, 1866 and 1935, to be followed

between 11 and 17 years later by a climb away from recession. The first cycle was associated with Abraham Day's discovery of smelting iron ore with coal and the mechanization of the textile industry. The second was associated with steam engines, railways and Bessemer steel; the third with oil, electricity, chemicals and automobiles; and the fourth with electronics and aerospace. According to Mensch, the fifth Kondratieff cycle should begin around 1989, and will probably be based on the likes of microchip technology, biotechnology and new energy-related technologies such as heat pumps and solar energy systems. The point about these cycles is that the ups and downs of each have been *imprinted differentially* on the geography of the US in response to the changing locational logic of each cluster of technologies.

Overlaying these changes is a further dynamic that stems from the interdependence of national economies: the 'climacteric' eclipse of core economies by emerging rivals from the periphery (Lewis 1978). The first large-scale climacteric of the capitalist era involved the relative decline of Britain and the ascent of the US, Germany, France and Russia between 1870 and 1900 as industrial growth in these hitherto peripheral nations adversely affected the price of British manufactures, precipitating *deindustrialization* in Britain and a redeployment of capital to more profitable settings such as the US. A second major climacteric cycle began around 1970, with the core nations of the world economy, now led by the US, experiencing deindustrialization while parts of the periphery – South Korea, Taiwan, Mexico, Brazil, Hong Kong and Singapore – began to ascend rapidly within the world system, creating a new category of 'Newly Industrializing Countries' (NICs) (Beenstock 1983). Once again, the important point about these cycles in the present context is that the impact has been *spatially selective*, with the social and economic reorganization associated with deindustrialization affecting each region differentially.

Finally, we must recognize the imprint of a still-broader sweep of change. In cyclical terms, this has been described in 'logistics' because of the distinctive shape of the curves of expansion and stagnation. Two such cycles have been completed, covering the feudal era (1100–1450) and the mercantile era (1450–1750). The industrial era, representing the third, is still in progress, with the emergent 'post-industrial' phase apparently representing the onset of a long period of relative stagnation in patterns of economic development (Wallerstein 1979).

Contemporary changes in the economic, social and spatial organization of the US can therefore be interpreted largely as the product of the superimposition of these cyclical changes, with the dominant influences of the current period being the international economic reorganization associated with the third logistic, the national economic reorganization associated with the second climacteric, and the incipient economic development associated with the fifth Kondratieff cycle.

One of the most far-reaching changes wrought by the unfolding of these processes has been the shift within the US away from agriculture and manufacturing employment towards *employment in services*. It is a sign of the times that neither General Motors nor US Steel has as many employees as McDonald's. Between 1947 and 1980, the service sector increased its share of total employment by about 12 per cent (to 68 per cent) and its contribution to Gross National Product (GNP) by almost 4 per cent (to 66 per cent). During the same period, manufacturing employment slipped from 32 to 24 per cent of the national total, while the contribution of manufacturing activity to GNP was maintained, thanks to higher levels of productivity, at around 24 per cent. There are, of course, exceptions to the overall trend. In contrast to the rapid expansion of computer and data processing services, engineering services, management, consulting and public relations services, the rate of expansion of radio and TV repair shops, funeral parlours and beauty shops has been sluggish; while barber shops, pool halls and drive-in theatres have actually lost business. Equally, there are some significant exceptions to the general decline in manufacturing employment, particularly among research and development (R and D) intensive industries (such as computers, industrial robots, integrated circuits and new synthetics), sophisticated assembly industries (such as communications equipment, pollution control devices and automated warehousing), and fashion-oriented industries (such as high-quality clothing, furniture and household fittings). What is important from our point of view, of course, is that these shifts have a distinctive spatial impact. In the first place, the decline in manufacturing jobs inevitably has the greatest impact on those local economies that have evolved as specialist manufacturing centres. Second, the expansion of service jobs has brought a new spatial logic that has resulted in new patterns of economic specialization.

The shift towards service employment has been reinforced by another major dimension of change: the extended *role of the state* that has come about in the postwar period in response to growing concern over social welfare (in the prosperous 1960s) and national economic well-being (in the face of the steadily increasing internationalization of the economy and intensifying international competition). As a consequence of this expanded role of the state, some aspects of regional differentiation have been attenuated (sometimes as a result of standardization, sometimes through deliberate strategic regional or macro-economic policies), while others have been introduced or intensified (sometimes as a result of the inherent myopia of bureaucratic decision-making, sometimes as a result of strategic macro-economic policies, sometimes as a result of 'pork barrel' politics, and sometimes through the incremental drift of public expenditure patterns).

A third major dimension of change has been *corporate reorganization* and *redeployment*. In response to intense competition in stagnating markets, private businesses have had to develop new strategies in order to survive: strategies that have significantly altered the fortunes of different kinds of cities and regions. The dominant outcomes have involved the *concentration* and *centralization* of economic activity. The former involved the elimination of small, weak firms in particular spheres of economic activity: partly through competition, and partly through mergers and takeovers. Centralization involves the merging of the resultant large enterprises from different spheres of economic activity to form giant 'conglomerate' companies with a diversified range of activities. As these new corporate structures have evolved, they have rationalized their operations in a variety of ways, reorganizing and redeploying their resources between different economic activities *and between different places*.

In short, the US has entered a substantially different phase in terms of *what* it produces, *how* it produces it, and *where* it produces it. In detail, these changes have prompted a complex variety of overlapping, intersecting and inter-acting spatial changes, all of them conditioned by local resources, population characteristics, political organization and the whole cumulative legacy of earlier phases of national and regional development. It is possible, however, to ident-ify some of the new effects of recent change (Fig. 1.1): the localization of industrial decline and central city poverty in the North East, the expansion of many of the metropolitan areas of the South and West, the emergence of distinc-tive innovation centres and centres of corporate control, the persistence of acute rural poverty in parts of central Appalachia and the Ozarks

and, in response to these shifting patterns of prosperity and opportunity, the emergence of major migration streams within, and into, the country.

Demographic and social change

Along with these fundamental changes in the country's economic geography, we must consider also the spatial implications of demographic change and changes in income distribution, class composition and lifestyles. Although the demography of the US is relatively stable by international standards, there are several aspects of contemporary change which are critical. The ageing of the population, for

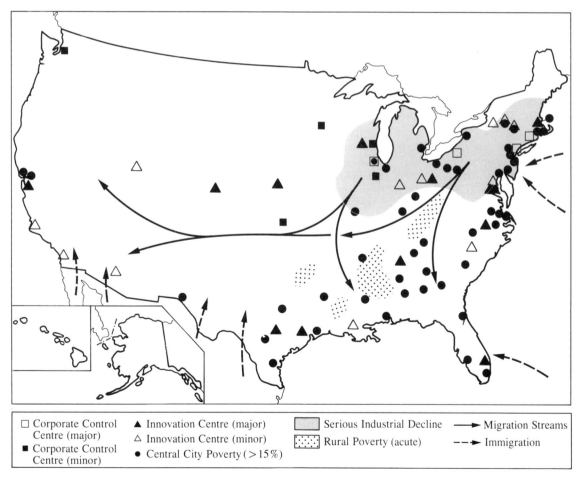

Key:
☐ Corporate Control Centre (major)
■ Corporate Control Centre (minor)
▲ Innovation Centre (major)
△ Innovation Centre (minor)
● Central City Poverty (>15%)
▨ Serious Industrial Decline
⦂ Rural Poverty (acute)
→ Migration Streams
--→ Immigration

Fig. 1.1 Some aspects of spatial differentiation in post-industrial America

example, has brought some important issues in terms of health, welfare and community politics. Moreover, patterns of vital rates have exhibited some unexpected trends. Contrary to all predictions, fertility and the rate of population growth surged upward after 1945 and then, in the early 1960s, plummeted downward in equally startling fashion. In the last 15 years, mortality rates, after a period of levelling off, have unexpectedly started to fall sharply, with especially surprising declines occurring at older ages (Easterlin 1980). These developments have had important effects on local labour markets and housing markets. Meanwhile, patterns of household formation have changed in response to changing economic circumstances and shifting social values. Americans are marrying later, deferring childbirth longer and getting divorced and remarried with greater frequency. Another important change that has been tied in to the same socio-economic dynamics has been the accelerated economic emancipation of American women, at least in terms of participation in the labour force. Immigration has also contributed a new dimension to demographic structure. The 1970s saw a surge of immigration, increasing the number of foreign-born by 4.5 million, the largest increase for any decade in US history. In the last two decades, moreover, immigration has been dominated by persons of Latin American and Asian origin. In the 1970s they accounted for over 75 per cent of all legal immigration, with Mexico, the Philippines, South Korea, Cuba, India, Taiwan and the Dominican Republic heading the list of countries of origin. In addition, illegal immigration, particularly from Mexico, seems to have increased sharply.

The interaction of these demographic changes with the economic changes outlined above has in turn brought about some important realignments in terms of *income distribution* and *class composition*. In overall terms, the growth of real disposable income *per capita* reflects the growth of the US economy: it more than doubled, from around $2200 in 1947 to over $4500 in 1982 (in constant 1972 dollars). It should also be acknowledged that the overall degree of inequality in the distribution of income has remained constant. However, recent economic and demographic trends have

conspired to produce several important shifts. Between 1973 and 1982, median family income fell from $26 175 to $23 433 (in constant 1982 dollars), with the poverty rate rising from 11.1 per cent to 15.0 per cent. By 1985, *35.3 million* Americans were officially classed as living in poverty. Among the 'new poor' were particularly large numbers of elderly, children, and female-headed households; and within these categories, blacks and hispanics were significantly over-represented (Sternleib and Hughes 1984). Meanwhile, the number of families with high incomes (>160 per cent of the US median) had risen, mainly in response to two factors: the marked increase in female participation in the labour force, and the expansion of employment opportunities for highly-skilled managers, engineers and researchers in the economy's fast-developing service and high-tech industries. The net result has been the much-publicized (but widely exaggerated) 'disappearance' of the middle classes (Blackburn and Bloom 1985). Table 1.2 shows that the middle classes (families with an income of between 100 and 160 per cent of the US median) in fact shrank from 27.4 to 23.1 per cent of all families between 1969 and 1983.

Economic and demographic changes have also contributed to changes in American *lifestyles* and *patterns of consumption*. Given the doubling of real incomes in the postwar period, Americans now enjoy high – some would say profligate – levels of consumption. Over 64 per cent of American households now own their own home, the standard suburban house consisting of a detached, four-bedroom, two- or three-bathroom dwelling standing on one-eighth of an acre lot. There is, overall, more than one car for every two people, and four private telephones for every five people. Americans consume, on average, over 100 lb (45.3 kg) of beef and more than 50 lb (22.6 kg) of chicken per person each year; and so on. As incomes have risen, so more of the 'typical' family's budget has been allocated to luxury goods, personal services and recreation; and the same economic freedom has given more and more Americans the opportunity to choose from the increasing number of lifestyles that have become available through a combination of geographical settings, family organization and patterns of consumption: from the ubiqui-

Table 1.2: Changing distribution of income class groupings, 1969–83

	1983			1969			*Per cent change (1968–83)*
	Income* (in 1982)	*Number (million)*	*Per cent*	*Income (in 1968)†*	*Number ·(million)*	*Per cent*	
Upper	>$41 456	11.4	12.8	>$46 027	5.2	8.2	+119
Upper-middle	$29 840–41 456	12.7	14.2	$32 728–46 027	9.1	14.4	+ 40
Middle	$18 426–29 840	20.6	23.1	$20 457–32 728	17.3	27.4	+ 19
Lower-middle	$11 055–18 426	16.6	18.6	$12 272–20 457	13.0	20.6	+ 28
Lower	<$11 055	28.0	31.4	<$12 272	18.6	29.4	+ 51

* Income is total family income including both earned and unearned income. A family is a group of related people living in one household, a single-person household, or each unrelated person living in a multi-person household.

† 1982 dollars.

Source: Blackburn and Bloom (1985) p. 21.

tous, family-oriented suburban exclaves and gentrified cosmopolitan enclaves to the more exclusive radical chic of parts of New York City and the environmental chic of Aspen, Colorado. However, as we have seen, the growth of incomes has been accompanied by the persistence of inequality and, recently, the spread of poverty. It follows, therefore, that the growth of consumption and the extension of lifestyle opportunities has been accompanied by the persistence of *economic hardship*. Long-term unemployment (longer than 15 weeks) in 1983 afflicted nearly 40 per cent of the country's 10.7 million unemployed. Hunger is described as a 'growing epidemic', with up to 20 million people experiencing it for some period of time each month (Physician Task Force 1985). The catalogue of economic and social problems is daunting: poor housing, high crime rates, persistent problems of illness and disease, high costs of medical care, drug abuse, environmental pollution . . . and so on (Michalos

1980a, 1980b, 1981a, 1981b, 1982; US Department of Commerce 1980). More daunting still are the rising trends associated with many of these problems. What is of special interest to the geographer, of course, is the extent to which these problems vary in intensity from place to place; whether the gradients between places are steepening or becoming shallower; and how the contours of social problems relate to other aspects of the social and economic landscape. In this book, we shall be examining these issues in some detail, looking in particular at the examples of poverty and crime (Ch. 8), before going on to summarize what it is like for different groups living in the different settings that comprise contemporary America (Ch. 9). First, however, we must come to grips with the fundamentals of the demographic, cultural, political and economic dimensions of the geography of the US (Chs 2 to 5, respectively), and establish the character of both rural and metropolitan America (Chs 6 and 7).

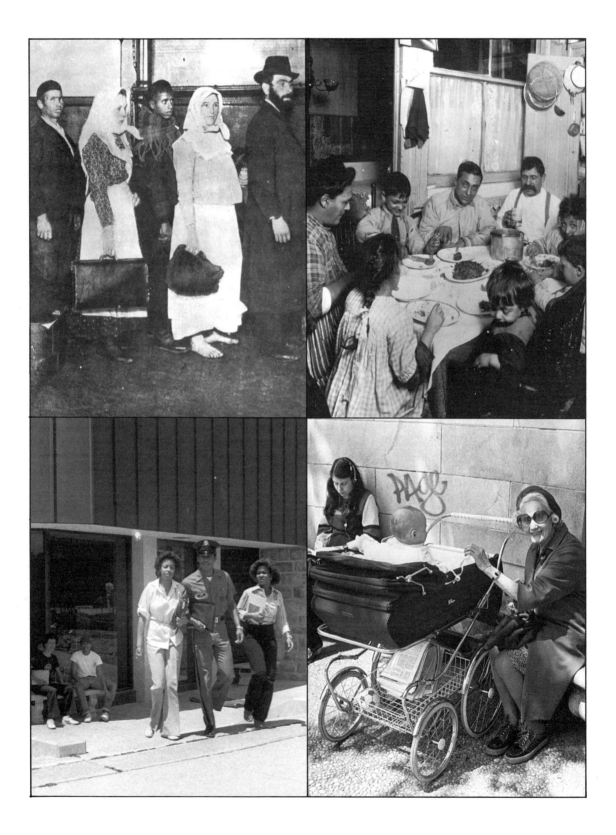

Chapter 2

POPULATION GEOGRAPHY OF THE US

A nation's population is its most fundamental resource. The size, composition and distribution of population both respond to and initiate change in the economic, social and cultural structure of a society. The complexity and interdependence of demographic responses and initiatives to other aspects of life make it difficult to decide where to begin to unravel the linkages. We have chosen to begin with an appraisal of the population structure of the United States not because it implies some type of demographic determinism, but because the dynamics of the nation's population provide a reference point for understanding those forces which have shaped the social and economic landscape of the country.

Both the history of demographic change and current growth trends in the US share some commonalities with the advanced industrial nations of Western Europe. Certain aspects of US geography and development have, however, altered its demographic history and population geography to the extent that it is distinctive from other industrialized nations. Three factors are particularly important here.

First, the *industrialization* of North America occurred *later* than in most Western European nations. Once begun, however, the transformation from an agrarian to an industrial nation moved rapidly: within half a century the economic transformation had been completed. As a result, the demographic restructuring associated with industrialization was compressed within a shorter period of time.

Second, the availability of *cheap land* for agricultural settlement on the western edge of permanent settlement continued until the end of the nineteenth century and led to over a century of continuous, extensive frontier migration. Urban labour markets had to compete for population against the attractiveness of inexpensive, western agricultural land. Such competition was not present in Europe during the course of its industrialization. The competition forced industrialists to turn to sources other than white, rural Americans to fulfil the labour requirements of industrialization. The eventual reliance on foreign immigrants and then on blacks for a labour force has had a significant and long-lasting impact on the social geography of the nation.

Finally, since its earliest days as a colony, the

Top left: Nineteenth-century immigrants arriving at Ellis Island *Credit*: US National Park Service, Statue of Liberty National Monument   *Top right*: Immigrant family in Boston *Credit*: US National Park Service, Statute of Liberty National Monument   *Bottom left*: (no title) *Credit*: Virginia Tech Photographic Labs.   *Bottom right*: (no title) *Credit*: Jon Crispin Photography, Ithaca, New York

US has always had a large non-white *minority population*. Initially, blacks and, to a lesser extent, American Indians, were the major groups; but more recently Hispanics and Asian Americans have become large, visible minorities in the social fabric of the country. Social conflict, racial tension and discrimination have frequently been the consequences of the nation's multi-national, multi-racial population, but each group has enriched the cultural and economic character of the country and its individual regions. The minority populations have created a social geography that is unique to the US.

Census geography of the US

Before proceeding further, it is important to outline the basic census geography of the country. The United States Bureau of the Census collects and distributes population statistics in a regional hierarchy (Bureau of the Census 1982a). At the top of the hierarchy are four census regions – East, North Central, South and West. These four are further subdivided into nine census districts (Fig. 2.1) which are aggregates of States. These in turn are aggregates of counties or their equivalents. States are the principal geographic units used when greater regional detail is required, while counties are used to examine intraregional variations.

In addition to this regional hierarchy, population data are reported for a variety of urban and rural classifications. Rural and urban are place-of-residence concepts in the lexicon of the US Census Bureau. Persons living in urbanized areas or in places of 2500 or more that lie outside urbanized areas are classified as urban. All others are rural residents. Urbanized areas

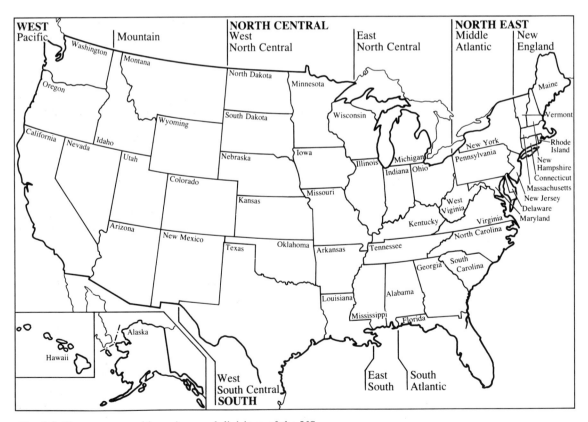

Fig. 2.1 Census geographic regions and divisions of the US
Source: US Bureau of the Census (1983), Fig. 1, pp. 1–5

consist of cities of 50 000 or more and the surrounding 'built-up' area. A density criterion of 1000 per square mile is used as the standard for determining the boundaries of the built-up fringe of urbanized areas.

The Census Bureau in 1960 introduced the concept of the Standard Metropolitan Statistical Area (SMSA) for enumerating the larger urban centres in the country. Since its inception, the SMSA has become one of the most widely utilized census concepts. It is used extensively by businesses for marketing analyses and by the federal government (e.g. for allocating money to cities).

As originally conceived, a SMSA was a county with a central city of 50 000 or more and any adjacent counties which were functionally linked to the central city. Functional linkage was based primarily on commuting, shopping and communication patterns. After the SMSA was introduced it became the official means of differentiating between metropolitan (SMSA counties) and non-metropolitan (counties outside SMSAs) areas. In 1980 the Bureau modified the metropolitan concept slightly by adding size differentiations and by changing the name to Metropolitan Statistical Area (MSA). Four categories of MSAs were recognized – classes A, B, C and D. These consist of places greater than 1 million, 250 000 to 1 million, 100 000 to 250 000, and 50 000 to 100 000 respectively.

Each of the concepts used by the Census Bureau measures a different and non-comparable aspect of urbanization. Non-metropolitan, for example, has come to mean 'rural' to many, but non-metropolitan counties may include cities of up to 50 000. Also, SMSAs may encompass farmers since rural residents are defined as those who do not live within the immediate boundaries of the central city or its suburbs.

Growth and change: stages in the population geography of the US

In 1980 the population of the US was over 226 million, making it the fourth most populated country in the world behind China, India and the USSR. With an annual growth rate of slightly over 1 per cent, the US is grouped with a number of other industrialized countries, most of them in Western Europe. that are at the low end of the demographic growth spectrum.

To understand the contemporary geography of the US population, some historical perspective is necessary. The emphasis in this chapter is on recent population trends and distributional dynamics, but an historical account of the nation's population geography, albeit brief, provides a context for understanding more recent trends as well as a basis for understanding the relationships between the country's population geography and economic and social development. The inclination here to attach pre-eminence to historical events must be tempered with the realization that in the US demographic trends have changed significantly within a short time period. In the mid-1960s, for example, demographers and geographers considered the important distributional issues in the country to be accommodating substantial population increases within the nation, integrating large numbers of immigrants into ever-expanding metropolitan areas, stabilizing the growth of the largest metropolitan areas in the country, and reducing the large net flow of people moving out of the South into northern and western States. In the 1980s the issues became the lower fertility rates, the reduced national growth, the out-migration of urban residents to non-metropolitan counties, the loss of population in the nation's largest cities, and the net loss of migrants from the northern to southern and western States (Beale and Fuguitt 1981).

The demographic history of the nation can be subdivided into four distinctive periods which correspond roughly with major shifts in the economic structure (see Ch. 5).

- colonial America to 1870s – the agrarian period;
- 1870s to 1940s – the industrializing period;
- 1940s to 1960s – the postwar boom period;
- 1960s to present – the modern period.

As with all historical categorizations, the dates are approximations marking transitional periods from one stage to another. The four do, however, represent periods in the nation's history in which population dynamics were consistent for extended periods of time.

For our purposes the last two stages are discussed jointly because the modern period can best be understood in the context of the postwar boom period, and because the modern period represents such a relatively short time span. Its brevity, in fact, raises the question of whether it represents a major break with the past or simply a brief anomaly within the postwar boom period.

The agrarian period

The federal government began a regularly scheduled census of population in 1790, but analyses of population dynamics in the agrarian period are hindered by the absence of reliable data and by the ever-expanding size of the country. Despite enumeration problems, a reasonably accurate count of the nation's population was possible in 1790. At that time approximately 4 million people resided within the US and the territories under its control (US Bureau of the Census 1976). For the next 70 years growth fluctuated greatly, but averaged approximately 3 per cent annually.

The demography of the agrarian period was dramatically altered by the industrialization of the nation's economy, but two distributional patterns emerged that had long-lasting effects. The first was the westward movement of population. The second was the importation and subsequent growth of the black population in the American South.

Westward expansion of territory and population was a major theme in the politics and demography of the nation from its inception as a colony (Zelinsky 1973). Manifest Destiny, the belief that the nation was pre-ordained to incorporate all lands between the Atlantic and Pacific Oceans, was a dominant theme in the national culture for much of the nineteenth century. Territories purchased, as with the Louisiana Purchase or the Gadsen Purchase, or obtained as spoils of war, as with the Mexican War, provided the nation with an enormous reserve of cheap land which eventually was sold or given to those adventurous enough to move westward into the frontier lands. The availability of cheap land coupled with the periodic discovery of gold or silver were powerful magnets pulling people westward, and the pace of frontier migration continued to grow throughout the agrarian period. The westward movement of population and fascination with the American West has continued into the present day. The lure of cheap land and gold or silver has been replaced by the temperate climate, the lifestyle, and the employment opportunities in California and other Pacific coast States, but many Americans still see the West as the land of opportunity and the 'good life'.

In 1619 the first indentured, *black servants* were brought to the Virginia colony. Initially this importation was loosely regulated by colonial governments, and blacks were able to purchase their freedom much like other indentured servants brought to the colonies as labourers. However, by 1700, slavery had been institutionalized, and blacks were legally defined as chattel rather than as persons with basic human rights.

Blacks became concentrated in the South as slavery became institutionalized in the plantation economy of that region (see Ch. 6). With the growth and geographic expansion of the plantation economy, the number of blacks forced into slavery and shipped to the US increased dramatically throughout the eighteenth century. From 1750 to 1800 it is estimated that as many as a million slaves were brought to the country, primarily from West Africa. As settlement moved West, slavery followed and large concentrations of blacks became distributed throughout the South by 1850 (Fig. 2.2).

By 1870, blacks were primarily a southern population phenomenon. In northern communities, they rarely constituted more than 5 per cent of the population. In contrast, in the South the proportion of blacks exceeded 80 per cent in some counties, and over 95 per cent of the blacks in the nation were located in southern States. This concentration remained high until the beginning of the twentieth century when out-migration of blacks from the South began in earnest.

The industrializing period

The 1870s are an important decade in the nation's history. Not only was territorial expan-

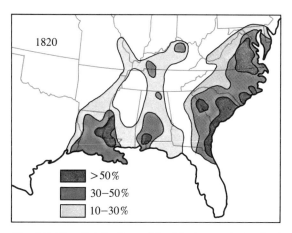 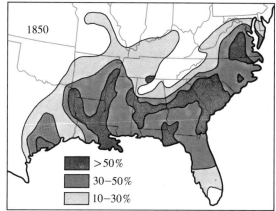

Fig. 2.2 The distribution of the black population in the South, 1820 and 1850
Source: Morrill and Donaldson (1972), p. 6

sion ending, but industrialization was beginning to restructure the nation's economy.

The effects of industrialization on the growth of the nation's population were far-reaching. The most important of these were:

- a decline in the growth rate of the nation's population;
- a sharp decline in mortality by the early twentieth century followed by a continuous but slower decline through the rest of the period;
- a slow but steady decline in fertility throughout the period; and
- a large, yearly influx of foreign immigrants until 1921.

Growth trends

When the nation's growth rate began to decline in the late 1800s, the decline initially was sporadic (Table 2.1). In general, the fluctuations *corresponded closely with changes in the volume of immigration which in turn varied with national economic conditions*. The rate of natural increase remained fairly constant during the first three decades of industrialization, averaging approximately 15 per 1000 until 1910. Immigration, however, varied substantially, ranging from years when it accounted for almost 40 per cent of the nation's total population growth to years when it was responsible for less than 17 per cent (Table 2.1).

After 1910 the nation's growth rate declined steadily, except for a brief spurt in the early 1920s. The decline reached a climax in the depression years of the 1930s when fertility dropped to its lowest point in the nation's history to that date and international net migration was near zero.

Mortality and fertility

Changes in natural increase rates between 1870 and 1940 were a function of differential time lags in the way that mortality and fertility responded to the forces of industrialization and urbanization. As in Europe, mortality declined more rapidly than fertility and, consequently, growth rates remained high during the early stages of industrialization. Only after fertility began to respond to forces which lowered family size did the rate of growth begin to diminish.

The death rate declined for all age groups, but the most dramatic reductions were in infant mortality. In 1915 (reliable national figures on mortality are not available for earlier periods) the infant mortality rate was 100 per 1000. By 1940 it had been reduced by over 50 per cent to 47 per 1000 (US Bureau of the Census 1976). Reductions in mortality among older Americans were mainly a function of reduced deaths from infectious diseases, but rates of mortality decline for older cohorts were not of the magnitude of those for infant mortality. Between 1915 and 1940, for example, the death rate among middle-aged Americans (ages 35–44) declined by only 37 per cent, while for

Table 2.1: Average growth rate of population by component of change – 1870–1980 (per thousand per year)

Period	Rate of growth	Net immigration rate	Per cent of growth	Natural increase rate
1870–1875	25.5	6.7	26.1	19.0
1875–1880	18.3	3.4	18.6	15.0
1880–1885	25.4	10.1	39.7	15.9
1885–1890	19.9	5.8	29.1	14.7
1890–1895	20.1	4.5	22.3	14.8
1895–1900	16.3	2.8	17.1	12.4
1900–1905	18.5	6.0	32.4	12.4
1905–1910	19.8	6.9	34.8	13.0
1910–1915	17.5	5.3	30.3	12.8
1915–1920	10.5	1.1	10.4	9.9
1920–1925	16.9	3.6	21.3	13.7
1925–1930	12.5	2.0	16.0	10.9
1930–1935	7.0	–0.4	–5.7	7.3
1935–1940	7.2	0.2	2.8	7.0
1940–1945	10.6	.5	4.7	10.3
1945–1950	15.6	1.3	8.3	14.6
1950–1955	16.9	1.2	7.1	15.6
1955–1960	17.0	1.8	10.6	15.2
1960–1965	14.5	1.9	13.1	12.8
1965–1970	10.6	2.2	20.7	8.6
1970–1975	10.6	1.7	16.0	6.8
1975–1980	10.4	2.2	22.0	6.2

* The sum of the components does not exactly equal total increase because the net immigration rate refers to alien arrivals less departures, and thus includes some non-migratory movements.

Sources: The data for the table were taken from Easterlin (1980), Table 4.A.1 and the *Statistical Abstract of the United States 1982*.

the elderly (65–74) the decline was only 13 per cent (US Bureau of the Census 1976).

Mortality began to decline in the late nineteenth century and continued to fall well into the postwar period. However, the reductions were episodic. The death rate would drop rapidly for several years, usually in response to the eradication or control of specific pathogens. A period of stable death rates would follow, and this would in turn eventually be broken by yet another medical or public health innovation, initiating another fall in mortality (Fig. 2.3).

The decline in mortality was concurrent with industrialization, but mere coincidence of time does not provide an explanation for the sharp reductions. Analysis of data from individual communities indicates that mortality remained high during the initial stages of industrialization and in fact increased slightly until the 1890s or 1900s when it began to decline (Meeker 1972; Florin 1971). The decline began well *after* urbanization and industrialization had advanced.

In cities, the externalities accompanying industrialization at first created serious health problems:

During the nineteenth century, the circumstances surrounding the Industrial Revolution brought on an explosive aggravation of many pathological states with a resulting deterioration of the general health, especially among the labouring classes. Within a few decades, millions of men and women migrated from rural districts into mushrooming industrial cities where they had to live under physiologically deplorable and totally strange conditions (Dubos 1968: 72).

In writing about the environmental degradation accompanying industrialization in American as well as in European cities, Dubos has vividly portrayed the consequences of development

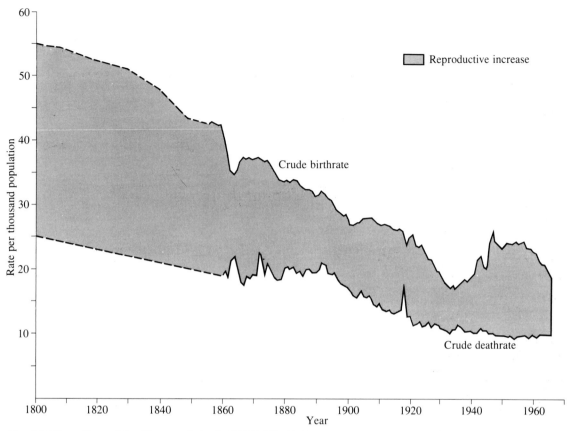

Fig. 2.3 Mortality and fertility trends in the US, 1850–1980

surpassing the infrastructure capacity of the urban environment. In most cities, sanitation systems were poorly developed, pollution was extensive, water supplies were always in danger of contamination, and residential crowding resulted from inadequate housing. All were conducive to the easy and rapid spread of disease. Urban health care delivery systems were fragmented and poorly developed; consequently, many residents in poorer neighbourhoods had poor access to adequate care (Bohland, Shumsky and Knox 1985).

The *decline in mortality* was in fact due to factors initiated by the restructuring of the economy but it lagged behind the initial, rapid expansion of urban America. These factors included:

- changes in the practice of medicine;
- genetic changes in the virulence of disease organisms;

- diffusion of public health programmes;
- a general uplifting of family levels of living (Meeker 1972).

Of the four, new public health initiatives and improvements in the level of living were the more important (Meeker 1972; Easterlin 1980).

The poor environmental and health care conditions of the industrial city eventually gave rise to public health programmes which had their origins in 1850 with the Shattuck report on sanitation in Massachusetts. However, only after conditions in cities had become so intolerable did States take the initiative to institute public health programmes in cities. Humanitarian reasons were frequently cited for the adoption of public health programmes, but economic considerations were often paramount. Unhealthy conditions in cities wreaked havoc on the supply of labour, and since an elastic labour supply was essential to industrial capitalism, it was in the best interest of the owners of industry to ensure a healthy and viable labour force (Rosen 1958). Consequently, many industrialists who earlier had thought public health programmes contradictory with private enterprise began to lobby for their adoption.

Levels of living rose when the wealth generated by industrialization became more widely distributed within American society. Social institutions such as labour unions, professional organizations, and populist political parties helped distribute the benefits of industrialization more broadly. This set into motion a number of changes, including improved access to health care, heightened educational levels, better nutritional intake, upgraded housing quality, and improved personal hygiene, that eventually reduced the risk of death to rural and urban residents alike.

Mortality eventually declined rapidly as a result of these factors, whereas *fertility* declined more slowly (Fig. 2.3). In 1880 the birth rate per 1000 stood at 35.2, while in 1940 it was 19.4, a decline of less than 50 per cent (US Bureau of the Census 1976). Declines in fertility as with mortality were a result of social and economic forces set into motion by industrialization. Urban living created a social and economic context which made reduced family size and delayed marriage rational behaviour for the city resident. The forces for change included higher economic costs of having large families in cities, depreciation of the value of child labour for city families, new ethnic populations (many of which had lower fertility levels than resident Americans), greater social mobility among urban residents, and increasing participation of women in the urban labour force (Potter 1965).

Lower fertility was not, however, confined just to cities; reductions were also evident in rural America at this time. In some regions, rural/urban fertility rates were comparable, and in others rural counties actually had lower rates than cities. The reductions in rural fertility suggest that urbanization was not the sole reason for the changes in fertility behaviour that occurred in conjunction with the industrialization of the economy. For example, reductions in the availability of good arable land for farming, particularly in the eastern States, are cited as being important in reducing rural fertility (see Hareven and Vinovskis 1978 for a summary of studies of rural fertility in the period). But, though it is true that the social movements responsible for reductions in fertility were not confined to the industrial city, most of them originated in the cities and then quickly diffused to rural America. Among the movements thought to be most significant were general improvements in education, particularly with respect to women; changes in the income status of most Americans; and increased involvement of women in the labour force (Wells 1985).

Immigration

Immigration has always been important to population growth in the US but its importance transcends numbers or growth rates. The US may not have always been the 'melting pot' characterized in Zangwill's play of the same name (Zangwill 1909), but the rich 'stew' of its pluralistic society created a cultural diversity whose influence on the nation's social geography is still readily apparent.

The size, composition, and geography of the nation's immigrant population has changed from one period to another. The changes have, it should be noted, always been steeped in controversy and politics: defining who is not an indigenous American has always been a tricky exercise, susceptible to isolationist and protectionist sentiments. These sentiments, when coupled with severe fluctuations in the economy, explain why the nation opened its doors to the poor and downtrodden of the world, only to slam them shut when fear of losing economic status or paranoia over cultural contamination came to dominate politics.

This schizophrenia over foreign immigration was very apparent in the industrial era. Foreign immigrants filled the reservoirs of the urban labour market, making economic growth possible. Yet many Americans feared the employment and cultural consequences of having nearly 1 million immigrants enter the country annually. Consequently, immigration increasingly became an issue at the forefront of both national and local politics. At the local level, big city political machines, such as Tammany

Hall in New York, traded patronage and social welfare benefits for the votes of the immigrants. Vestiges of 'machine' politics in industrial cities remained through the 1960s until the death of Richard Daley, Mayor of Chicago, signalled the final curtain on a century of an urban political system predicated on foreign immigration. At the national level, concern over foreign immigration stemmed from the numbers involved and from the nationality of the 'new' immigrants. From 1890 to 1910 over 12 million immigrants entered the country, accounting for about one-third of the nation's growth. In some local communities the contribution of immigration was even more spectacular. In industrial cities such as Milwaukee, New York, Chicago and Detroit, foreign immigrants and their immediate descendants accounted for over 75 per cent of the cities' population by the turn of the century (McKelvey 1973).

The immigration totals for the 20-year period are spectacular, but the yearly volumes fluctuated wildly in response to economic cycles. Demand for immigrants increased in periods when industry was expanding and declined when the economy softened. In the depression years of the 1890s, for example, the immigrant flow was below 300 000 per year, while in 1907 over 1.2 million immigrants entered the country.

Immigration declined sharply in the mid-1920s after the passage of the Immigration Act in 1920 which placed an overall ceiling of 150 000 per year and set quotas for each country. Pressure from both labour unions (which were concerned about the effect of immigration on wage and employment levels) and from nationalistic groups such as the American Protective Association and the Daughters of the American Revolution (who voiced concerns about the impact of immigration on American society and its values) led to passage of the legislation.

The industrialization that stimulated and sustained foreign immigration also forced a change in the *spatial pattern of immigrant origins and destinations*. Prior to industrialization, the period Bogue (1985) called 'Old Northwest European Migration', the majority of immigrants came from northern or western European nations (Fig. 2.4) and initially settled primarily in eastern States. However, as the

railroad network expanded, a greater proportion moved west to agricultural lands in Michigan, Minnesota and Wisconsin. By 1890 these States surpassed northeastern States in the number of foreign born in their population (Ward 1971).

The immigrants of the industrial era, Bogue's 'Intermediate Migration Period', came primarily from eastern and southern Europe. The shift in origins was in response to events external to the US as well as to the restructuring of the American economy. Australia and Canada were becoming new areas of settlement for immigrants from the British Isles, industrial development in Germany and Sweden enabled many potential immigrants to remain at home, and political turmoil and religious persecution in eastern Europe, particularly towards Jews, forced many to flee and seek new opportunities. Also, the labour requirements of an industrializing America were more compatible with immigrants from eastern and southern Europe, who were more willing to accept the low wages and poor working conditions associated with the early factory system than were those from countries such as Great Britain which had industrialized earlier (Ward 1971).

The majority of immigrants in the industrial era, then, settled in cities in eastern and Midwestern States. By 1910, eastern States again had the largest number of foreign immigrants, and the ethnic diversity and numerical dominance of foreign-born residents that came to characterize the social geography of the nation's industrial cities was well established (Radford 1981). It should be emphasized that throughout the period of industrialization neither the South or the West attracted large numbers of immigrants. In the West, Chinese were brought into the country as a cheap source of labour to build railroads and to work in mines, but aside from the indigenous black population, the South remained a bastion of WASPS (White, Anglo-Saxon, Protestants).

Distributional patterns and processes

As the nation's population grew, important regional variations in growth became evident. Internal migration began to be restructured, foreign immigration was channelled into a few regions, and regional differences in fertility and

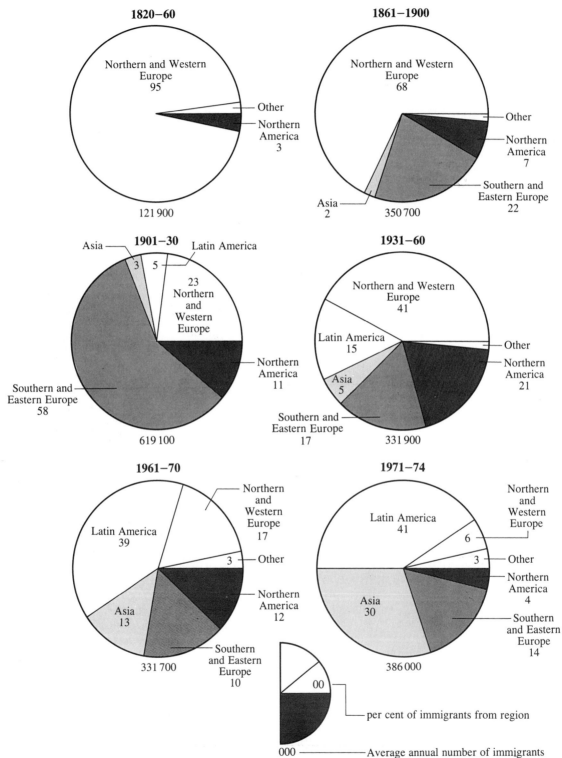

Fig. 2.4 Changing patterns of immigration to the US, 1820–1975
Source: Easterlin (1980), Fig. 4.10

mortality emerged. The significant distri-butional trends of the industrial era were:

- significant growth in urban America;
- the beginnings of urban decentralization;
- a concentration of population within the industrial core of the nation;
- a redistribution of the black population from the South to the North.

With industrialization, the nation increasingly became more *urban*. By 1880, eastern and Midwestern States recorded over 50 per cent of their population in cities. In 1920 the nation had over half of its population classified as urban for the first time. Industrialization was not only accompanied by rapid urbanization, but the growth in urban America was concen-trated in large cities. Between 1860 and 1910 the total population increased by 193 per cent, while the urban population grew by 575 per cent and cities of 100 000 or more by 669 per cent (Pred 1965). Growth occurred throughout the entire urban system, but particularly in the larger cities until 1930 and the onset of the Great Depression. With the collapse of urban labour markets during the depression, urban growth slowed and losses were recorded in a number of cities.

The rapid growth of urban America up to 1920 was attributable to natural increase, foreign immigration and rural to urban migra-tion. Foreign immigrants were the principal component of growth for many of the larger industrial cities in the East and Middle West. Rural to urban migration was, however, an important component of growth, particularly after 1920. Reliable data on internal migration during this period are scarce, but 'the large proportion of "new immigrants" from abroad with urban destinations was probably no greater than among native-born Americans who migrated after about 1875' (Ward 1971: 58). The migration of rural residents to urban America generally occurred within the immediate region, for inter-State migration actually declined during the industrializing period.

Although inter-regional migration declined, manuscript census data for particular cities indicate that mobility among urban residents was extremely high, with the overall turnover of the urban population approaching 55 per cent (Allen 1977). By comparison, the rate in the 1980s is only 20 per cent. The high mobility evident among urban residents suggests a time of 'geographic restlessness' brought on by the newness, diversity and rapid growth of cities (Radford 1981). The growing importance of rural to urban migration, the slowing of inter-regional migration, particularly involving rural to rural moves, and the high mobility rates among urban residents quite aptly characterizes what Zelinsky called the 'late mobility tran-sitional phase' in a country's evolution towards modernization (Zelinsky 1971).

The high rates of residential mobility partially reflect the beginnings of the *suburban-ization* process. According to Muller, 1888 marked a turning point in the history of the American city. It was then that the electric streetcar was first adopted for intra-urban transportation (Muller 1981). The availability of the automobile to the cities' middle classes in the 1920s accelerated the suburbanization process. By the beginning of the postwar period, suburbs had become an integral part of the population geography of the nation, and the urban sprawl which came to characterize Amer-ican cities was well underway. Indications of the trend towards horizontal development are found in the decline in metropolitan density gradients during this time (Mills 1970).

Regionally, the nation's population was still concentrated in eastern and Midwestern States during the period, although the westward migration of large numbers continued unabated. By 1920 over 60 per cent of the nation's urban population lived in the 'urban core', an area roughly bounded by lines connecting the cities of New York, St Louis, Milwaukee and Boston. The States within this core accounted for 53 per cent of the nation's total population at that time. The size of this population concentration created a market area which further encour-aged the agglomeration of economic activities and assured the growth of population in the region (see Ch. 5).

After 1920, the concentration of population in the industrial/urban core began to decline as growth shifted ever westward. As inter-regional migration increasingly became the mechanism for population redistribution, movement to the West and South eroded the dominance of the core. Surprisingly, even with the tremendous economic growth and urban development in the

Table 2.2: Net migration by region and race: 1900–70 (in thousands)

Race	1960–70	1950–60	1940–50	1930–40	1920–30	1910–20	1900–10
White							
New England	214	−47	−105	−23	−190	−53	−84
Middle Atlantic	−617	−159	−714	−139	−59	−205	−182
E.N. Central	−578	178	−218	−102	283	−303	−487
W.N. Central	−643	−857	−932	−568	−708	−444	−475
S. Atlantic	1873	1189	465	282	−158	51	−101
E.S. Central	−128	−845	−571	−241	−391	−374	−342
W.S. Central	−264	−292	−397	−335	10	−63	437
Mountain	317	549	70	37	−153	156	364
Pacific	2103	2970	2402	1090	1274	629	869
Nonwhite							
New England	92	70	25	5	7	12	8
M. Atlantic	654	472	387	166	342	170	85
E.N. Central	418	521	494	108	324	201	46
W.N. Central	40	37	35	20	41	44	10
S. Atlantic	−476	−542	−424	−175	−509	−162	−110
E.S. Central	−568	−620	−485	−122	−181	−248	−110
W.S. Central	−223	−295	−336	− 50	−61	−46	50
Mountain	8	8	20	6	−1	10	5
Pacific	462	324	284	43	37	18	14

Source of data: Bogue (1969) p. 782 and Bowles, Beale and Lee (1977) Part 7.

industrial States, they were net exporters of people (Table 2.2). Urban growth was due mainly to high rates of natural increase, large numbers of foreign immigrants, and rural to urban movement from within a region rather than between regions.

By 1940 the migration patterns of the industrial period had become well imprinted on the demographic landscape of the country (Fig. 2.5). Areas with sizeable net migration surpluses were primarily in the West, in Florida, and in metropolitan areas along the mid-Atlantic coast and in the Middle West. In contrast, rural areas in general, and particularly in the South and the Central Plains, experienced net migration losses. But aggregate migration figures for the period mask an important component of *inter-regional migration* which began at the turn of the century and which came to dominate south to north movements in future decades. The movement initiated a change in the social geography of the industrial city that was to have long-lasting and far-reaching consequences. As

we saw earlier, prior to 1910 black Americans were almost exclusively a southern minority. After 1910 southern blacks began to migrate to the industrial cities of the north. The movement began slowly, but with restrictions placed on foreign immigration, blacks soon became a major component of the labour force in northern industrial cities, and in doing so they restructured the country's social geography (Fig. 8.5). The magnitude of the movement is evident in contemporary regional distribution of blacks. In 1980 only 53 per cent of the black population lived in southern States, while New York and California had the largest black populations of any States.

The migration of *blacks* out of the South was in response to a number of factors. Mechanization of southern agriculture and reductions in cotton production decreased the demand for agricultural labour in the South (see Ch. 6), while limits on immigration created a labour vacuum in the northern industrial cities (Morrill and Donaldson 1972). Political and social

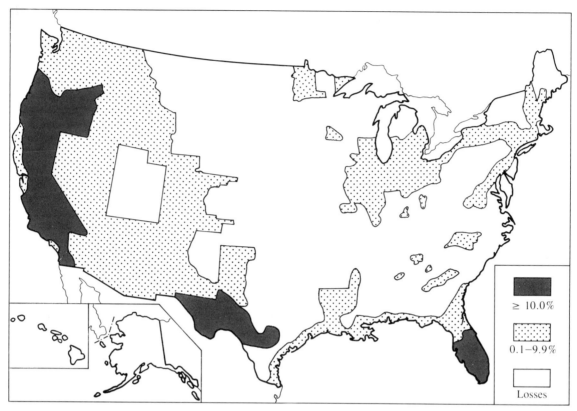

Fig. 2.5 Net migration rates 1935–40, generalized by State Economic Regions
Source: Bogue, Shryock and Hoermann (1957), p. 40

conditions in the South also encouraged blacks to leave. Organized violence against blacks, discrimination in education and in employment opportunities, disfranchisement, poor housing and meagre social services pushed many blacks out of the South in the hope of finding a better life to the north (Davis and Donaldson 1975).

It was during the early stages of inter-regional black migration that 'the first generation ghettos in northern cities were formed' (Rose 1971). Although most blacks encountered discrimination, both *de facto* and *de jure*, upon relocating in the North, and most were less well off than the whites in the northern cities, conditions there were generally better than those which they had left. Black migration continued and information networks between origins and destinations developed which led to the formation of well-defined channels of movement between southern and northern counties. Blacks from southern Atlantic coastal States

like the Carolinas moved primarily into cities in the Northeast; those from Midsouth States like Alabama, Mississippi and Tennessee tended to migrate to Midwestern cities; while blacks in States on the western edge of the South moved westward and became part of the large black communities in cities like Los Angeles or Oakland (Davis and Donaldson 1975).

The importance of blacks to labour markets in northern cities and to population growth in industrial States is evident from the migration figures in Table 2.2. Without the migration of southern blacks, industrial States would have experienced negative net migration rates for much of the twentieth century. The impact of net losses through inter-State migration undoubtedly would have seriously impacted labour markets in the North, forced a restructuring of wage levels and altered the level of industrial output.

Postwar and modern periods

The population dynamics of the postwar and the modern periods differ in a number of important ways. The 'explosion' of growth in the postwar boom period was accompanied by a continued concentration of urban growth in the industrial regions of the North. This contrasts with the demographic stagnation and regional and non-metropolitan redistribution of population that characterize the modern period. These trends are clearly linked to economic forces in the nation although the nature of these interlocking relationships is not clearly understood.

Clearly, . . . population growth within an ebullient economy fed the flame of general business vigor in the first post-World War II generation. But one of the major questions of our times is to define the impact of the phenomenon in the midst of relative stagnation. The demographics of affluence, from a market perspective, are very different from the results given a relatively fixed pool of wealth. And it is the latter which defines the governing circumstances of America since the 1973 energy crisis (Sternlieb, Hughes and Hughes 1982: xiv).

Growth trends

The postwar rate of population growth represents a major demographic event in the country's history. It was not simply that an earlier trend of decline had been reversed, which was important, but that high growth rates were sustained for so long, over 25 years. Beginning in the late 1940s, the nation's population grew at annual rates in excess of 1.6 per cent, which would have amounted to a doubling in 40 years. It was not until the early 1960s that the growth rate began to subside. However, once the reduction began, the country entered an extended period of declining growth rates. Throughout the 1970s and into the 1980s, the annual increase hovered around 1 per cent (US Bureau of the Census 1982a). The 1960s, in retrospect, represented a period of transition between the high growth rates of the immediate postwar period and the lower rates of the 1970s.

The dramatic shifts in national growth after World War II are generally attributed to significant changes in fertility. However, increases in foreign immigration, including illegal or un-documented immigraton, and reductions in mortality also contributed to the accelerated growth. The net effect of the three has not only been to change growth rates dramatically but also to change the age and ethnic composition of the population.

Fertility and mortality

The major demographic phenomena shaping America after 1940 have been the *baby boom* and the *baby bust* (Sternlieb, Hughes and Hughes 1982). The disparity between the boom and the bust can be seen in the fertility rates for the postwar and the modern periods. Between 1955 and 1959 the fertility rate (the average number of births in a year to females in the age group 15–45 year), was always in excess of 3.5. In 1976 it was 1.76 and had risen only slightly to 1.82 by 1981 (Bogue 1985). The enormity of the postwar baby boom has meant that although the fertility rate has been below replacement level (2.1) since the early 1970s, the US population will continue to experience growth through natural increase well into the twenty-first century because of the large number of women born during the boom who will be in the childbearing cohorts until then.

The radical upswing in fertility represented by the baby boom took public officials and demographers by surprise. In the 1920s, public officials had expressed concern that the country's birth rate would fall below the replacement level by the 1940s or the 1950s at the latest. Their forecasts proved false.

The effects of the postwar baby boom on the population composition, social organization and economy of the nation have been widespread. The passage of the 'baby boomers' through different lifecycle stages has, in most instances, required reallocations of resources and new social policies. When the cohort reached school age, for example, the demand for teachers, new schools and curriculum reform led to major capital investments in the country's educational system. To accommodate record enrolments, colleges and universities had to invest heavily in new structures and staff. With the ageing of the cohort, the size of the labour force (ages 16 to 64) increased by 46 per cent between 1960 and 1980, and when the heightened demand for housing presented itself, it created significant inflationary pressure on housing costs. When the cohort retires the financial solvency of the existing national retirement system and of Medicare, the national medical programme for the elderly, will be severely strained (Russell 1982).

The *reasons* for the prolonged period of high fertility after World War II are not understood. The initial increase in fertility was partially in response to delays in family formation and reductions in family size occurring in the depression years. Birth rates had begun to rise prior to World War II as marriages and families delayed by the depression were formed. The disruption in formation of families caused by the war forestalled the momentum towards increased fertility only temporarily, for after the war, the birth rate quickly reached 26.5 per 1000, a rate higher than any since 1920. While the delays in family formation caused by the Depression certainly contributed to the immediate postwar fertility boom, the prolonged period of high fertility was closely linked to the strong surge in the economy in the two decades after the war: the growing economy created a context which was conducive to family formation and increased family size.

Once fertility began to *decline* in the early 1960s, it continued steadily downward until the early 1980s when a slight increase was evident. Explanations for the long and continuous downward trend in fertility vary, but birth control innovations and social movements seem most important. The introduction of the contraceptive pill in the 1960s, changes in female status and in sex roles, and the increased participation of women in the workforce have all caused major changes in attitudes about family formation, the appropriate age for beginning a family, and family size (Westoff 1977).

Changes in the structure and composition of the American *family* in fact represent one of the most significant demographic events of the *modern period*. Between 1960 and 1980 the percentage of households consisting of married couples declined from 74.3 to 60.9 per cent, while the number of single women who never married increased from 19.0 to 22.4 per cent (Sternlieb, Hughes and Hughes 1982). These adjustments in adult living arrangements have been paralleled by reductions in the number of

children per family, 1.46 in 1963 to 1.10 in 1978 (Trees 1981). The changes in family composition and size are more pronounced in urban America, but significant regional variations do not exist (Bogue 1985). Thus, while the implications of these changes on the urban labour force, service delivery and the social structure of the city are manifold, no major regional effects can be expected.

National fertility trends mask important differences among subdivisions of the population. When large enough, these differences can lead to changes in the relative size of populations groups. Historically, fertility in the US has varied by socio-economic status, educational levels, occupation, ethnicity and race (Bogue 1969). As a group, the *non-white* population has typically had higher fertility than the white population, largely because of disparities in economic conditions. This higher fertility, along with declining mortality and increased immigration among non-whites, has caused the non-white growth rate to exceed the rate for whites by at least 1 per cent per annum since 1950 (Fuchs 1980).

Even more striking than the non-white fertility rates are those of the *Hispanic* population. In 1981, Hispanics accounted for 9 per cent of all births in the country although they constituted about 6 per cent of the population (US Bureau of the Census 1982a). Because Hispanics are concentrated in the American Southwest, the effect of the high fertility on the population composition of that region is substantial. In Texas and California, for example, over 25 per cent of all births in 1983 were by women of Spanish origin (*American Demographics* 1984). These high fertility rates, coupled with the immigration of Mexicans, have made the Hispanic group one of the fastest growing minorities in the country and a majority population in many areas in the Southwest.

While not as dramatic as the fertility boom and bust cycles of the postwar and modern periods, *mortality* rates also displayed distinctive temporal cycles. After World War II and until the 1950s, mortality declined quite steadily as the assault on infectious diseases continued. By the end of the 1950s, however, deaths caused by infectious diseases had been reduced to a point where further reductions only marginally influenced the overall death rate, and so the rate stabilized. A sharp decline in mortality after 1970 resulted from significant reductions in deaths caused by heart disease (a 2.1 per cent decline per annum in deaths between 1965 and 1980) that were attributed to changes in lifestyle (e.g. reductions in the prevalence of smoking) and new technologies for treating severe heart problems (Easterlin 1980).

The *ageing* of the American population has been one of the important consequences of mortality and fertility cycles in the postwar and modern periods. Reductions in mortality have prolonged life in the US and increased the number of persons in the older age categories. However, it has been changes in fertility which have had the greatest impact on the proportion of the population in the elderly age groups. In 1980, 11.3 per cent of the population was 65 years of age or older, compared to 8.1 in 1950 (US Bureau of the Census 1982b). The economic and social implications for a nation of having a large proportion of its population outside the labour force and drawing retirement benefits are countless. Moreover, in the US, as in the UK and other Western European nations, older persons have tended to become concentrated in particular types of environments, particularly those which offer recreational and other amenity opportunities (Warnes and Law 1984; Cribier 1982; Graff and Wiseman 1978). For these communities, the impact of an ageing population on the social services, tax base and local economy has been substantial (Longino and Biggar 1982; Monahan and Green 1982; Lee 1980). As the number of retirees increases and new retirement areas emerge (Rowles, Hanham, and Bohland 1985), the impact of a large resident or temporary population of older Americans will be felt by a greater number of communities within the country.

Immigration

Immigration ebbed during the Great Depression. It increased steadily after World War II until by the 1970s it was again responsible for nearly 20 per cent of the nation's annual growth. The increase in immigrant numbers was in response to the acceptance of many refugees after World War II and the Vietnam War, to growth in the US economy immediately after World War II, and to the abolition of the quota system in 1965. The increased percentage of national growth attributable to immigration, however, was due not so much to increases in immigration as it was to reductions in fertility after 1960.

The composition of the immigrant population in the postwar and modern periods differed from that in the industrial period. The majority of recent immigrants are from Latin America and Asia (Fig. 2.4). Since 1950 at least 70 per cent of all immigrants to the country have been from these two continents. Precise totals are impossible to determine, however, because of the large number of undocumented migrants, many of whom originate from Mexico or other Latin American countries.

As in previous decades, destinations for recent immigrants are concentrated in a few States. Three-quarters of them have settled in only six States: California (23.3 per cent); New York (16.7 per cent); Texas (8 per cent); Florida (8 per cent); Illinois (6 per cent); and New Jersey (6 per cent) (Immigration and Naturalization Service 1978). This geography contrasts sharply with the pattern for the industrial period when southern and western States were seldom destinations for immigrants.

While the national origins and regional destinations of immigrants have changed since World War II, most still choose to live in urban areas upon entrance into the country. The new minorities have created neighbourhoods different in composition, but analogous in function to the ethnic neighbourhoods associated with the early industrial cities. Cuban, Vietnamese, Haitian, Dominican and Cambodian neighbourhoods are now elements of the social mosaic of many American cities, replacing or supplementing the older ethnic residential concentrations of past immigrants.

Many Asian and Latin American immigrants have been admitted as refugees and unfortunately do not possess marketable skills. With the decline in the demand for unskilled labour in central cities, many new immigrants have found it difficult to secure employment. Many remain unemployed or under-employed for extended periods and must rely on social services for support. Tension between the older urban minorities and the new immigrants has occurred because the former see their employment opportunities and social service benefits threatened by the new arrivals.

The Immigration Act of 1965 stressed the importance of educational and occupational skills for entrance. Consequently, the occupational and educational levels of immigrants have changed significantly (Fallows 1982). At the turn of the century, only 1 per cent of the immigrant population was in a professional occupation, whereas in 1966 the figure was over 25 per cent (Easterlin 1980). In 1980, Korean immigrants, for example, were more than twice as likely as native Americans to have a college degree (Robey 1985).

The emphasis on labour skills and education has raised the issue of selective immigration, the so-called 'brain-drain'. The issue has been hotly debated as to its impacts on both the US and the originating countries, but no simple solutions appear to exist. Unless origin quotas are set or completely open admission is granted, neither of which appears to be desirable or politically feasible, it is difficult to envision an immigration policy that could eliminate selective migration and not discriminate against members of specific occupations or classes.

Viewed from a larger perspective, the brain-drain is the consequence of uneven development in the world. It is the inevitable result of the integration of developing nations into the international market and of an economic system that permits flows of human capital without regard to the consequences for the developing countries (Glasser 1978). As the US extends its corporate structure into developing countries, a flow of foreign management and research personnel back to the management core within the US will continue unless some constraints are placed on such movement either by the US or by developing countries, or unless greater resources and personnel are exported

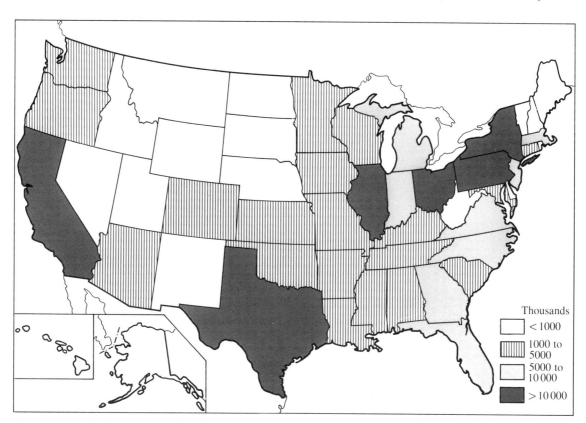

Fig. 2.6 Distribution of population, by State, 1980

to developing nations to assist them in achieving higher levels of living.

Regional population patterns

The population distribution that evolved in the industrial era has maintained much of its structure until the present time. Differentials in regional growth rates have begun to reshape that geography in recent years, but the pattern which evolved prior to 1940 has endured for much of the postwar and modern period. The largest number of people are still in States in the old industrial region (Fig. 2.6). Florida, Texas and California stand out as the major exceptions.

The *density* of population across the nation still shows the clear imprint of the industrial/urban transformation (Fig. 2.7). The high-density counties are primarily in the old industrial core, moderate densities occur in most counties east of the Mississippi River,

while the West, despite its long history as a net importer of population, has remained a region of lower density. The pattern of low density in the West is broken only by the higher densities associated with the metropolitan counties. Only in southern California and in Oregon and Washington from the Willamette Valley to Puget Sound can extended areas of moderate to high density be found.

As noted above, the demographic dynamics of the modern period have begun to make some significant changes in the distribution that has for so long characterized the nation's population geography. It would be erroneous, however, to assume that the current regional growth trends did not have antecedents. The regional growth trends of the postwar period foreshadowed those which were to occur in the 1970s and 1980s. The only difference has been in the magnitude and scale of the trends (Sternlieb, Hughes, and Hughes 1982).

The most striking distributional characteristic

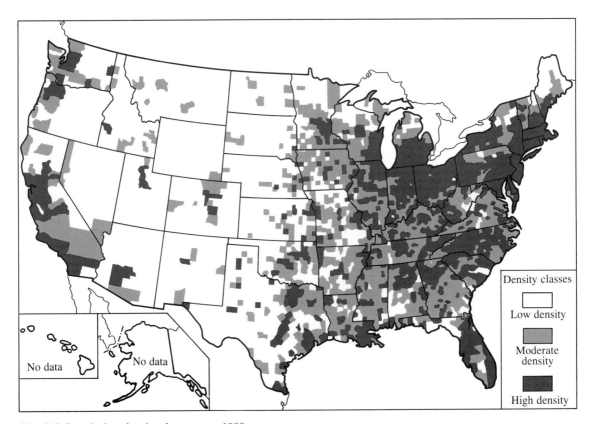

Fig. 2.7 Population density, by county, 1980

Table 2.3: Regional population growth pattern: 1940-80

	Population (thousands)					Numerical change 1940-80				Percentage change 1940-80			
	1940	1950	1960	1970	1980	1940-50	50-60	60-70	70-80	1940-50	50-60	60-70	70-80
Northeast Region	35 977	39 478	44 678	49 061	49 135	3 501	5 200	4 383	74	9.7	13.2	9.8	0.2
New England	8 437	9 314	10 509	11 847	12 348	877	1 195	1 338	501	10.3	12.8	12.7	4.2
Middle Atlantic	27 539	30 164	34 168	37 213	36 787	2 625	4 004	3 045	- 462	9.5	13.3	8.9	-1.1
North Central	40 143	44 461	51 619	56 590	58 866	4 318	7 158	4 971	2 276	10.8	16.1	9.6	4.0
E.N. Central	26 629	30 399	36 225	40 263	41 682	3 770	5 826	4 038	1 419	14.2	19.2	11.2	3.5
W.N. Central	13 517	14 061	15 394	16 328	17 183	544	1 333	934	855	4.0	9.5	6.1	5.2
South	41 668	46 197	54 961	62 813	75 372	4 529	7 764	7 852	12 559	10.8	16.5	14.3	20.0
South Atlantic	17 823	21 182	25 959	30 679	36 959	3 359	4 777	4 720	6 280	18.8	22.6	18.2	20.5
E.S. Central	10 778	11 477	12 050	12 008	14 666	699	573	758	1 858	6.4	5.0	6.3	14.5
W.S. Central	13 065	14 538	16 951	19 326	23 747	1 473	2 413	2 375	4 421	11.2	16.6	14.0	22.9
West	14 379	20 190	28 053	34 838	43 172	5 811	7 863	6 785	8 334	40.4	30.9	24.2	23.9
Mountain	4 150	5 075	6 855	8 290	11 373	925	1 780	1 435	3 083	22.3	35.1	20.9	37.2
Pacific	10 229	15 115	21 198	26 548	31 800	4 886	6 083	5 350	5 252	47.8	40.2	25.2	19.8
Total	132 165	151 326	179 311	203 302	226 546	19 161	27 985	23 991	23 244	14.5	18.5	13.4	11.4
Per cent of national growth in South/West						53.9	55.8	61.0	89.9				

of the postwar era was the consistency in *regional growth rates* (Table 2.3). The highest growth rates were in the East North Central, South Atlantic, Mountain and Pacific divisions, while the West North Central and East South Central divisions had lower growth rates. Although growth percentages in the West remained high throughout the period, the rate actually declined between 1940 and 1970, going from 40.4 to 24.2 per cent. It should be noted that throughout the postwar period the two regions which comprise the Sunbelt, the West and South, had high percentage increases, and in the South these percentages had begun to increase, albeit moderately, after 1950.

Although regional growth patterns of the postwar boom era were a precursor to those in the 1970s and 1980s, the magnitude by which the patterns intensified came as a surprise to public officials. Rarely do demographic trends strike a responsive chord with policy makers and the popular media, but the 'Frostbelt/Sunbelt' population redistribution has received considerable attention from both. The interest and controversy over Sunbelt/Frostbelt stems from the fact that

(a) migration has become a more important and more highly visible component of population growth or decline in many localities as fertility has fallen to near replacement levels, and (b) some dramatic and largely unanticipated changes in migration patterns occurred causing policy planners, researchers, and others to reassess reasons for moving and locational preferences of individuals (Long and Frey 1982: 1).

The dramatic change in the structure of inter-regional migration has resulted in an appreciable decline in the population growth rates of States throughout the Northeast and North Central regions, except for the West Central division which historically has had low growth (Table 2.3). In the Northeast the loss of population in the Middle Atlantic division was particularly alarming to public officials because of the number of major industrial cities in the region.

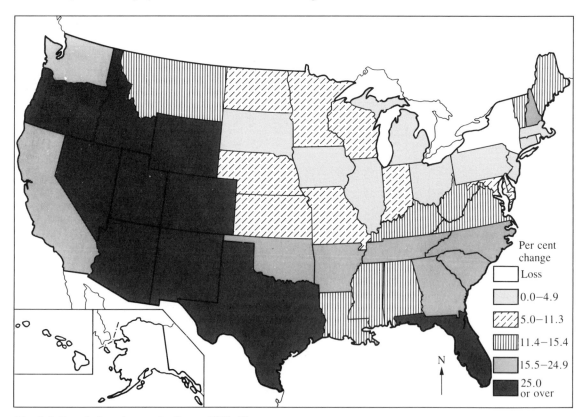

Fig. 2.8 Population change, by State, 1970–80

In contrast to the depressed growth in the North and East, in the South and the West high growth rates became ubiquitous (Table 2.3). One important difference in the growth patterns in the South in the modern period was that in the postwar period, growth had been confined principally to the South Atlantic division, while in the other divisions growth was below the national rate. After 1970, the East South Central and West South Central divisions also experienced rapidly expanding populations.

In the West, high growth rates persisted in both divisions, although in the Pacific the percentage continued to decline. Within the Sunbelt, population growth has not been uniform at the State scale (Fig. 2.8). As measured by percentage change, growth was greatest in southern States such as Florida, while in the West, Nevada, Arizona, Washington, Utah and Wyoming had the highest percentage increases.

Percentages depict only one dimension of the distribution of growth. Many western States have relatively small populations, making small increments appear as large growth percentages. For example, the 64 per cent increase in Nevada's population represented only an additional 310 000 persons, whereas Michigan's 4.2 per cent increase represented over 375 000 new residents.

A different growth dimension is evident when one considers the proportion of the nation's total growth located in a State. Although growth is still highest in the South and West (Fig. 2.9), the concentration of population growth within States is quite striking. Sixty per cent of the nation's growth in the 1970s was concentrated in just five States: California, Texas, Florida, Arizona and Georgia. At the other extreme, two States, Rhode Island and New York, and the District of Columbia had absolute losses in the decade.

During the first half of the 1980s, growth continued to be focused on the South. The region as a whole had a positive net migration balance with the Northeast, Midwest and West, although the net balance was not as great as it

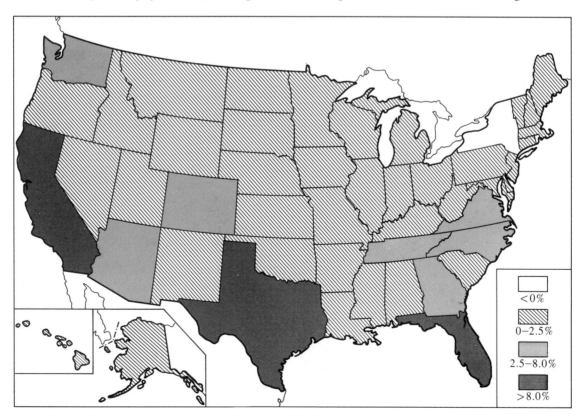

Fig. 2.9 Contribution to national growth, by State, 1970–80

had been in the previous five-year period (Kasarda *et al.* 1986). Within the South, growth was concentrated in a few States. For example, between 1980 and 1983 over *half* of the nation's growth was concentrated in just three States: California, Florida and Texas. In the same period, absolute population losses were recorded in four Midwestern States–Indiana, Iowa, Michigan and Ohio–and in the District of Columbia (US Bureau of the Census 1984). These losses represented an important shift in the geography of population decline, away from the Mid-Atlantic and New England States to those in the western portion of the old industrial core. All these shifts, as we shall see (Ch. 5), were closely related to the changing economic organization of US space. Whether the losses in the old industrial States will continue is problematic in the light of recent contractions in the energy market. Declines in the fortunes of energy-related industrial activities may make southern States less attractive and the older industrial States may well find that the early 1980s represented the bottoming-out of their population decline.

Distribution of minority population
Subsumed within the overall population growth and distributional trends of the postwar and modern period are the spatial dynamics of the nation's minority populations. While the numbers for minorities are smaller, their distribution has always been relevant to the country's social geography. The importance of any one group tends to be magnified because most minorities are regionally concentrated. As a result, national minorities constitute regional majorities in many areas.

The two largest minority populations in the nation in 1980 were blacks and Hispanics, but the fastest growing is the Asian American population. Of the three, blacks are the largest, constituting 11.7 per cent of the population in 1980. Hispanics, a minority based on linguistic rather than racial attributes, are smaller in number, 6.4 per cent of the population in 1980, but their rate of growth is much higher than that for blacks. On the other hand, Asian Americans, usually considered to be mostly Chinese, Japanese, Filipino, Asian Indian and Southeast Asian, constituted only 1.6 per cent of the population, but grew by 142 per cent

between 1970 and 1980 (Bouvier and Agresta 1985).

All three minorities, along with other racial or ethnic groups, display considerable spatial variations in the proportion of the total population they represent (Table 2.4). Most minority groups are now concentrated within cities, but each has a distinctive regional geography. American Indians, for example, are prevalent in southwestern States such as Oklahoma, Arizona and New Mexico; Asian Americans are concentrated in California, Hawaii, New York, Illinois and Washington; while Mexican Americans are most numerous in the borderland States, i.e. those along the international border with Mexico (Table 2.4). The distinctive nature of the distributions can be traced to historic factors which influenced their initial settlement, the recent geography of international immigration, and inter-regional migration.

As we noted earlier, for much of their history *blacks* were primarily a southern, rural minority. Through time the black population has become concentrated in large metropolitan areas. With the 'white flight' to the suburbs, blacks became the majority population in the central cities of many SMSAs. Some suburbanization of blacks occurred, but at rates considerably below those for whites. As a result, the proportion of blacks living in the urban fringe declined continuously from 1900 to 1950 (Muller 1981). Since 1950 the number of blacks living in suburban America has increased, albeit slightly, with the greatest growth occurring in the 1970s. During the last two decades a change in their distribution within the metropolitan system has begun. The percentage of blacks who lived in central cities declined slightly (58 to 56 per cent), while the proportion in suburbia increased from 16 to 21 per cent between 1960 and 1980 (Long and de Are 1981). At the same time the black percentage of the suburban population increased from 4.7 to 6.1. The reasons for this change in black metropolitan geography are not totally clear. In part, the growth of the black middle class has led to suburbanization, but the movement of many suburban whites to non-metropolitan counties or more remote suburban counties has enabled blacks to move into housing in the older, inner suburban ring of

Table 2.4: State minority populations (per cent of the total population)

State	Black	Hispanic	Japanese	American Indian native	Chinese	Other Asian
Alabama	26.0	0.8	0.04	0.2	0.04	0.2
Alaska	4.0	2.0	0.4	16.0	1.0	1.3
Arizona	3.0	16.0	0.2	6.0	0.3	0.4
Arkansas	16.0	0.8	0.3	0.4	0.1	0.2
California	8.0	19.0	1.0	0.8	1.4	3.0
Colorado	4.0	12.0	0.3	0.6	0.1	0.5
Connecticut	7.0	4.0	0.1	0.1	0.1	0.4
Delaware	16.0	2.0	0.1	0.2	0.2	0.4
Florida	14.0	9.0	0.05	0.2	0.1	1.6
Georgia	27.0	1.1	0.1	0.1	0.1	0.3
Hawaii	2.0	7.3	25.0	0.3	5.8	16.0
Idaho	0.3	3.9	0.3	1.1	0.1	0.2
Illinois	14.7	5.6	0.2	0.1	0.2	1.0
Iowa	1.4	0.9	0.03	0.2	0.1	0.3
Indiana	7.6	1.6	0.04	0.1	0.1	0.2
Kansas	5.3	2.7	0.06	0.06	0.1	0.4
Kentucky	7.0	0.7	0.03	0.1	0.03	0.2
Louisiana	29.4	2.3	0.03	0.3	0.1	0.2
Maine	0.3	0.4	0.03	0.4	0.04	0.2
Maryland	22.7	1.5	0.1	0.2	0.3	1.0
Massachusetts	3.8	2.4	0.07	0.1	0.4	0.3
Michigan	12.9	1.7	0.06	0.4	0.1	0.4
Minnesota	1.3	0.8	0.07	0.9	0.1	0.4
Mississippi	35.0	1.0	0.02	0.2	0.1	0.2
Missouri	10.4	1.0	0.02	0.2	0.1	0.3
Montana	0.2	0.1	0.33	4.7	0.04	0.2
Nebraska	3.0	1.8	0.09	0.6	0.07	0.3
Nevada	6.3	6.7	0.29	1.7	0.4	1.0
New Hampshire	0.4	0.6	0.04	0.2	0.09	0.2
New Jersey	12.6	6.7	0.13	0.1	0.31	5.4
New Mexico	1.8	36.6	0.10	8.0	0.10	0.3
New York	13.7	9.4	0.84	0.2	0.1	4.3
North Carolina	22.4	1.0	0.05	1.1	0.05	0.4
North Dakota	0.4	0.6	0.03	3.1	0.04	0.2
Ohio	10.0	1.1	0.05	0.1	0.09	0.3
Oklahoma	6.8	1.9	0.07	5.6	0.08	0.4
Oregon	1.4	2.5	0.32	1.0	0.3	0.6
Pennsylvania	8.8	1.3	0.04	0.1	0.1	0.4
Rhode Island	2.9	2.1	0.05	3.0	0.2	0.3
South Carolina	30.4	1.1	0.04	0.2	0.04	0.3
South Dakota	0.3	0.6	0.04	6.5	0.04	0.2
Tennessee	15.8	0.7	0.04	0.1	0.1	0.2
Texas	12.0	21.0	0.07	0.2	0.2	0.6
Utah	0.6	4.1	0.37	1.3	0.2	0.3
Vermont	0.2	0.6	0.04	0.2	0.06	0.2
Virginia	18.9	1.5	0.10	0.2	0.2	0.9
Washington	2.6	2.9	0.64	1.5	0.4	1.2
West Virginia	3.3	0.7	0.02	0.1	0.05	0.2
Wisconsin	3.9	1.3	0.05	0.6	0.09	0.2
Wyoming	0.6	5.1	0.13	1.5	0.08	0.2
District of Columbia	70.2	2.8	0.13	0.1	0.4	0.5

communities. This 'spillover' effect is not universal, nor does it display regional characteristics, but along with other forces it appears to have set into motion the decentralization of the urban black population (Long and de Are 1981). How long and extensive that process will be is a question to be resolved during the next two decades.

In part because of conditions in northern cities, a major turnaround has occurred in the migration of blacks. Migration from the South to northern industrial cities has diminished. For the first time since the movement of blacks out of the South began, the South was not a net exporter of its black population in 1980 (Table 2.5). Only in the East South Central division was the net migration for blacks negative. In contrast, in the industrial areas of the nation net losses in the non-white population were evident for the first time since the turn of the century. The return migration of blacks to the South emerged in the 1970s as a new factor shaping the geography of the nonwhite population in the country (Long and Hansen 1975; Campbell, Johnson and Stangler 1974). The number of blacks returning South does not match the totals for whites moving to the Sunbelt, but it does represent a significant departure from the historic pattern. Black migrants to the South represent a very self-selected group. They are younger and better educated and less likely to be poor than those already living there (Robinson 1986). Morever, many blacks returning South are choosing to live in cities. These migrants plus the southern blacks who are moving to southern metropolitan centres have caused the black population in cities such as Atlanta and Houston to grow at rates in excess of those for northern cities.

The *Hispanic* concentrations in the American Southwest are a function of American territorial expansion and of the geography of recent international immigration. When the US claimed vast western territories from Mexico after the war of 1848, the foundation for today's Hispanic distribution was laid (Nostrand 1970). The historic core of population has been intensified and the distribution of Hispanics expanded in large measure from immigration, primarily from Mexico (Table 2.4).

The importance of immigration to the continued expansion of the Hispanic regional geography has a dimension which makes it unique in the annals of the nation's population geography. A large number of Mexicans entering the country are *illegal* or undocumented immigrants. Accurate data on illegal immigration are difficult to obtain, but it is believed that the vast majority of illegal immigrants, approximately 50 per cent, come from Mexico, while another 25 per cent are from other Central or South American countries (Slater 1985). Estimates place the annual total from Mexico at between 100 000 and 300 000, or approximately 3–10 per cent of the total yearly growth rate of the US (Heer 1979). Proximity to the US, a lengthy common border that is impossible to adequately patrol, the availability of jobs for 'illegals', and the large and increasing differential in development between the US and its southern neighbour are the principal reasons for Mexico's pre-eminence.

Most illegal immigrants from Mexico are young males and are unskilled in non-agricultural occupations. Movement into the US is clearly related to economic conditions, but it is usually a spontaneous move rather than the result of long-range planning. Most stay in the US temporarily, although they may return several times within their lifetime. Also, despite claims to the contrary, most undocumented immigrants make few demands on local social service systems (Jones 1982).

The largest proportion of undocumented

Table 2.5: Net migration by census division: 1975–80

	(in thousands)	
	White	*Black*
New England	–110	3
Middle Atlantic	–1016	–63
East North Central	–876	–27
West North Central	–102	–1
South Atlantic	1303	211
East South Central	253	–7
West South Central	1002	66
Mountain	787	24
Pacific	926	113

Source: US Bureau of Census, *Gross Migration for Counties: 1975–1980*. US Department of Commerce 1984.

immigrants choose to reside in California (50 per cent), New York (11 per cent) and Texas (9 per cent) (Slater 1985). The destinations are even more concentrated for Mexican undocumented immigrants, 55 per cent in California and 23 per cent in Texas (Jones 1982). Border States have the largest number of Mexican–American residents because information networks are well developed there, the social/cultural milieu is supportive, job opportunities and wages are more attractive, the legal climate is more favourable, and illegal immigrants find it easier to become invisible within the communities (Jones 1984).

A definite channelization of immigrant flow exists between Mexico and the US. Illegal immigrants who reside in Texas, for example, come primarily from northeastern states within Mexico, usually along the border with Texas. In California, the majority of the immigrants come from the west central area of Mexico rather than border states because the latter in this region are sparsely populated. The linkage between origins and destinations has been influenced by early railroad patterns that connected these areas and by immigration which occurred under the Bracero programme (Jones 1984). Under the Bracero programme, initiated in the early 1940s because of a labour shortage in the American southwest, Mexican farm labourers were allowed to enter the US as seasonal, migrant workers and to work on farms in the region. The connections established with this programme are still used by illegal migrants to obtain information about jobs and accommodation.

A number of sizeable Hispanic concentrations occur outside the core area of the southwestern borderlands in the central city areas of large metropolitan centres such as New York or Chicago. Although Hispanics are not as urbanized as blacks, their rate of growth in urban centres is higher. These concentrations of Hispanics outside the borderlands are the result of the inter-regional migration from them, and of the diversity within the Hispanic minority. Hispanics include persons from Mexico, Puerto Rico, Cuba, Spain, or any other nation in Latin America. Thus, in New York the majority of Hispanics are from Puerto Rico, while in Florida most are from Cuba. These concentrations have no historic ties to the major concentrations within the southwestern States.

Regional growth processes

Since 1940, regional growth differentials have been primarily due to inter-regional migration. With the regional restructuring of the economy, inter-regional migration has been responsible for most of the distributional changes described in the preceding sections. Regional variations in fertility and mortality still exist, but their influence on regional growth differentials are not as important as in earlier periods. Regionally, *fertility* rates have been converging over the longterm; but a shorter cycle of divergence has occurred with the downturn in national fertility rates (O'Connell 1981).

Regionally, *mortality* rates have been converging. Regional variations in mortality still exist, however, because of

- differences in the geography of high-risk populations, the compositional effect;
- differences in the geography of high-risk environments, the environmental effect; and
- differences in proximity to disease hosts, the contagious effect.

The most important of the three is the compositional effect. When, for example, age, race and social economic status are held constant, little geographic variation in mortality or morbidity exists at the regional level (Sauer 1974). The same associations occur at the urban scale as Pyle and Rees, for example, found disease mortality within the city of Chicago to be associated with poverty status and race (Pyle and Rees 1971; see also p. 243).

Environmental effects are more difficult to validate because most deaths today have multiple causes. While rural/urban differences in mortality were evident in the industrial period, urban and rural mortality rates have since been converging (Palen and Johnson 1983). This is true not only for crude death rates, but it also seems valid for specific disease mortalities, such as cancer (Greenberg 1981).

Migration

Three migratory movements have been important in the postwar and modern periods:

- inter-regional migration;

- metropolitan-non-metropolitan migration;
- intra-metropolitan migration, i.e. residential mobility.

Metropolitan–non-metropolitan movements are discussed later in this chapter, but it should be emphasized that inter-regional and metro–non-metro migration are part of the same relocation decision for many migrants. The out-migration from inner cities of the North and Midwest, for example, includes a sizeable number of people who are relocating to non-metropolitan counties in southern or western States. With a highly mobile population, distinctions between small-scale and large-scale migration become blurred, and it is difficult to separate regional redistributive and metropolitan decentralization effects.

Between 1940 and 1970 some adjustments in *inter-regional migration* patterns occurred, but the basic structure of migration remained similar to that which existed in 1920 (Table 2.2). The two western divisions, Pacific and Mountain, remained regions with large net surpluses. The two census divisions which

contained industrial States, the Middle Atlantic and East North Central divisions, had net surpluses, but this was due primarily to the large number of blacks migrating from the South. States in the deep South (the East South Central and West South Central divisions) and in the Plains region (the West North Central division) had negative net migratlon throughout most of the postwar period.

Inter-regional migration in the 1970s and 1980s broke from the pattern established in the postwar boom period (Table 2.5). The West still had a large net surplus of migrants, but all three census divisions in the South recorded sizeable net positive balances for the first time. In fact, the ratio of net to gross migration (net/gross × 1000) was higher for the South than for the West (265 vs. 233). All the divisions in the North Central and the Northeast regions lost population by migration after 1970. As a region, the Northeast had negative balances with all other census regions, while the North Central only showed a positive net balance from the Northeast (Fig. 2.10).

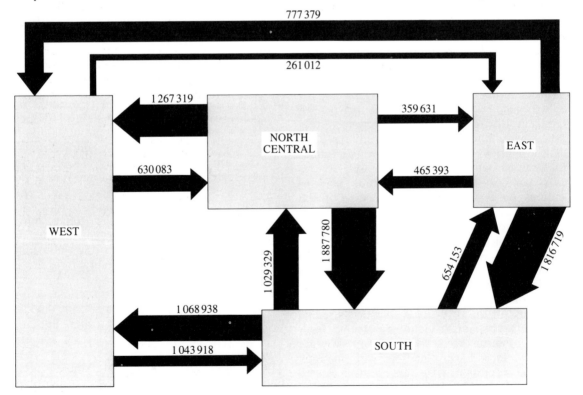

Fig. 2.10 Regional migration flows, 1975–80

In the 1980s the migration pattern of the 1970s has persisted generally; however, some new trends have emerged which may be indicative of a new realignment. The salient new trends are:

- An increase in the movement to the South, but a decrease in the likelihood of movement to the West.
- A decrease in the attractiveness of the East South Central division to migrants, creating two divisions of high growth in the South separated by an area of slower growth.
- Increased attractiveness of the Northeast as a destination for inter-regional movers.
- A decline in the proportion of inter-regional migrants residing in the East North Central division.
- A slowing of growth due to migration in the Pacific division, but the converse in the Mountain division of the West (Rogerson and Plane 1985).

These readjustments in inter-regional migration were in response to further realignments in economic activities and employment markets. High wages and land costs in California have prevented the State from continuing as the locus of national growth, while further reductions in employment in the 'smokestack' industries in the East North Central division have accelerated out-migration from the area. In contrast, in the Northeast recent gains in high-technology industries have stemmed the population losses (Rogerson and Plane 1985).

Attempts to model and to *explain* inter-regional migration in the postwar and modern periods have emphasized employment and labour force conditions (Greenwood 1975, 1981). Early formulations of inter-regional migration theory argued that in-migration to a region was primarily a function of an expanding labour market, i.e. increasing employment opportunities, labour deficits and high wage levels, but that the relationships between out-migration and origin area economic conditions were less clear (see Shaw 1975; Clark and Ballard 1980; Greenwood 1975).

The view that migration responds to regional differentials in wages and employment opportunities is consistent with neoclassical economic theory which views labour migration as a means of achieving equilibrium in regional economic growth. For the individual, migration can be a response to changes in employment opportunities that result from locational shifts in economic activities (Kuznets 1964). At the regional or urban scale, if in-migration continues, a labour surplus develops, wages are depressed, in-migration is reduced, and population growth slowed (Greenwood 1981).

Empirical studies of net migration indicate that migrants do respond to labour market conditions (Greenwood 1975; Shaw 1975), but the structure of inter-regional migration is more complex. For example, in the neoclassical model out-migration should be inversely correlated, or at least uncorrelated with in-migration. Yet correlations between in- and out-migration are typically positive and very high (Gleave and Cordey-Hayes 1977; Bohland, Rowles and Hanham 1985). Population turnover is high in growth counties, contrary to the push–pull view of migration. High turnover exists because people use migration as a means of achieving occupational mobility, i.e. moving in and out of metropolitan centres which offer employment opportunities (Clark 1982b).

Neoclassicists view inter-regional labour force migration as a *long-run* population equilibrium process which is not responsive to short-term changes in a region's economy. Accordingly, we would expect some temporal lag between economic restructuring and population redistribution. However, labour migration within the US has been shown to be quite volatile and responsive to short-term changes in the national economy when those changes lead to shifts in a region's share of national production (Clark 1982a; Clark and Ballard 1980; Ballard and Clark 1981). It is this quick locational response by labour to changes in the spatial structure of the nation's economy that has caused regional growth rates to react more rapidly to economic change than had been anticipated.

Finally, although much of the migration to the South and the West from Northeast and North Central States has been labour force movement stimulated by the expansion of the regions' economies (see Ch. 5), decisions based on non-economic factors have also been important in shaping recent migration patterns. The increased importance of amenities in people's migration decisions has made the West and South more attractive destinations for many Americans. A warm climate (particularly after the widespread adoption of air conditioning) and lower living costs have become increasingly important to many persons seeking to relocate. Amenities are particularly important to elderly persons who are now more likely to relocate upon retirement because improvements in private and public sector retirement programmes give them the financial security necessary to undertake long-distance relocation. The importance of elderly migration to growth areas in Florida, Arizona and Texas, and other southern States is well documented (Graff and Wiseman 1978; Rowles, Hanham and Bohland 1985). In addition to increased amenity migration, Mincer (1978) has argued that changes in family structure have increased the volume if not the direction of migration. The reduction in marriage rates among the young, the increase in divorce, and the larger proportion of childless marriages make members of the labour force more mobile and able to respond more quickly to new regional allocations of employment opportunities.

Metropolitan/non-metropolitan growth

By 1920 the US had become an urban society demographically. The urban population continued to grow during the Depression, albeit at a slower rate, but it accelerated with the postwar economic boom.

Postwar urban growth was largely a function of migration which had three separate and distinctive components: (1) hinterland migration; (2) channelized migration; and (3) interurban migration (Roseman 1977). Hinterland migration consisted of migration to cities from the surrounding non-metropolitan areas in which typically a distance decay trend was evident. Well-defined channels of migration between cities and more distant non-metropolitan areas comprised the second stream. The channelization of migration was in response to information networks established by prior migrants (Roseman 1977). Inter-urban migration, the movement between metropolitan areas, constituted the major share of metropolitan migration in the postwar period. The importance of inter-urban migration continued through the modern period: approximately 67

per cent of migration in 1980 was between metropolitan areas.

In the first two decades of the postwar period, migration between SMSAs was directed upward in the urban hierarchy. Larger SMSAs and their central cities experienced higher positive net migration than smaller places. However, with time this trend began to reverse. By the 1960s the migrants to metropolitan America were electing to live in the smaller communities on the urban fringe, not in central cities, as suburban America increasingly became the choice of new metropolitan residents.

During the postwar period the inevitability of metropolitan growth seemed assured as long as the national economy was expanding. This viewpoint was jarred in 1980 when the census revealed that between 1970 and 1980 the proportion of the population living in cities remained almost constant (73.5 per cent versus 73.7 per cent), and the proportion living in the larger SMSAs (250 000 or more) declined from 67 to 65.8 per cent. Growth had become concentrated in the smaller towns and cities and in counties lying outside the metropolitan centres of the country (Beale 1975; Long and de Are 1980). The trend was almost universal across the country. Non-metropolitan counties grew more rapidly than metropolitan counties in the majority of the nation's regions (Table 2.6). The growth of the rural population was not as high as that for non-metropolitan counties, but it was comparable to the rate for the urban population (11.1 per cent versus 11.6 per cent), and the number of rural residents in 1980 was the largest it had been since 1870.

This reversal in metropolitan/non-metropolitan growth represents one of the demographic characteristics differentiating the postwar and modern periods. Considering that after 1940 the rural population in several regions had declined by as much as 36 per cent, and that the net loss in population in non-metropolitan counties exceeded 2 million as late as the 1960s, it is not surprising that many public officials and population analysts were surprised and somewhat sceptical of the early reports of the reversal. However, when the 1980 census confirmed that non-metropolitan America had indeed undergone a 'turnaround', and that the nation's population geography was undergoing

Table 2.6: Growth of metropolitan and non-metropolitan counties in the United States by census division: 1960–80

Census division	Metro			Non-metro		
	Per cent of region's population 1980	Per cent change 1960–70	Per cent change 1970–80	Per cent of region's population 1980	Per cent change 1960–70	Per cent change 1970–80
New England	76.6	12.6	1.0	23.4	13.3	16.5
Mid Atlantic	87.7	9.2	–2.7	12.3	6.6	11.7
East North Central	78.1	12.7	1.9	21.9	5.7	9.8
West North Central	53.3	14.6	5.6	46.7	–2.3	4.9
South Atlantic	70.4	25.9	20.8	29.6	3.2	19.6
East South Central	51.9	11.9	13.9	48.1	0.8	15.1
West South Central	70.4	21.0	26.3	29.6	1.3	15.4
Mountain	63.1	34.1	41.3	36.9	30.5	38.8
Pacific	89.4	27.0	18.6	10.6	10.9	30.7

Source: Statistical Abstract of the United States, 1981.

an important transformation, scepticism turned to inquiry as reasons for and the impacts of the transformation were sought.

The dramatic turnaround in non-metropolitan growth should not overshadow the realities of the nation's current population distribution. *Three-quarters* of the nation's population still lived in metropolitan counties in 1980, and in the South metropolitan counties grew more rapidly than non-metropolitan counties. Also, data for the early 1980s indicated that growth in metropolitan America had again surpassed that in non-metropolitan counties. Between 1980 and 1984 the metropolitan population increased by 5.0 per cent whereas non-metropolitan growth was only 3.8 per cent. What is even more striking is that central cities within metropolitan areas–especially those in the Northeast and Midwest–grew more rapidly than non-metroplitan counties (Engels and Forstall 1985). This urban population comeback has been attributed, in part, to recent weaknesses in rural economies (see p. 181), together with the reductions in services and increased costs imposed on rural areas as a result of airline and telephone deregulation.

The distribution of metropolitan growth
Two sets of conflicting spatial trends have char-acterized the geography of metropolitan growth in America in the postwar and modern periods: concentration/redistribution and centralization/decentralization. Concentration and centralization dominated throughout the early decades of the twentieth century although redistributive and decentralization effects had been evident at the end of the nineteenth century. Throughout the ending decades of the industrial era and into the postwar period, population continued to be concentrated in a few regions but in decentralizing cities. In the modern period, however, redistribution and decentralization have come to dominate the shaping of the nation's metropolitan geography.

The concentration of the urban population in the industrial core continued well into the postwar period; since then it has been progressively *redistributed* throughout other regions. The convergence in regions' levels of urbanization accelerated after 1960 when a number of the larger metropolitan centres in the industrial core experienced substantial losses in population, while cities in the South and West increased their populations substantially (see Fig. 7.4). Of the two regions, it is in the South where urban growth has been greatest since 1970. The fact that the South is now becoming the locus of metropolitan growth is indicative of the magnitude of the restructuring of the nation's urban system. It was not until 1950 that over 50 per cent of the population of the South resided in urban centres, yet by 1980 it had become the focal region for the nation's urban growth.

Individual examples of this restructuring abound. The New York SMSA, for example, lost over 850 000 residents in the 1970s; Cleveland over 150 000 and Philadelphia over 100 000. Conversely, Dallas added 600 000; Atlanta 435 000; and Miami 360 000. Yet, perhaps no city exemplifies the new urban America better than does Houston, Texas. An annual growth rate of 3.8 per cent in the 1970s lifted the city into the elite of the country's urban hierarchy. Between 1970 and 1980, almost a million new residents were added to the city's metropolitan population. Although some its growth occurred because of the annexation of suburban communities, most was due to in-migration which was stimulated by growth in the local economy. Over 92 000 new manufacturing jobs were created in Houston in the 1970s. Popularized in Country and Western songs like 'Detroit, Michigan', 'refugees' from Frostbelt States like Michigan, Illinois, Indiana and Ohio moved to Houston when the city's economy was booming during the energy crisis in the 1970s. Many were to find, however, that when the energy industry entered a recession after 1980, unemployment and hard times were not confined to the Frostbelt industrial cities.

It should not be concluded, however, that the old industrial cities are subject to irreversible decline. Despite losses in population, the older urban core still contains the bulk of the nation's urban population. Six of the nation's ten largest cities are located in the core and, after a decade of decline, States and metropolitan counties in the Northeast are beginning to show net migration surpluses instead of negative balances. Nevertheless as capital investments continue to stimulate industrial development in the South, and the 'smokestack' industries find their market share further eroded by foreign competition, many cities in the old core will continue to struggle with economic and population stagnation.

Decentralization of the urban population began late in the nineteenth century, but after 1940 it became a dominant force in shaping urban America. Growth in the suburban rings accelerated while the growth of central cities stabilized and eventually declined after 1940 (Fig. 2.11). From 1940 to 1970 the growth rate between cities and suburbs differed by 20 per cent even though many central cities grew at moderate to high rates after the war (Muller 1981). Between 1960 and 1980, differences in central city/suburban growth within metropolitan America had a distinctive regional pattern.

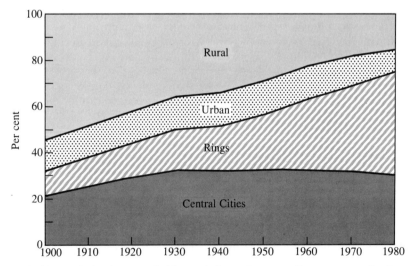

Fig. 2.11 Per cent of US population in central cities and rings of metropolitan areas, and urban and rural portions of non-metropolitan areas, 1900–80
Source: Bogue (1985), Fig. 3.9a, p. 130

Table 2.7: Per cent change in metropolitan centre city/suburban populations by region: 1960–80

| Region | Per cent change in population | | | |
| | 1960–70 | | 1970–80 | |
	Centre city	Suburban ring	Centre city	Suburban ring
Northeast	−1.9	19.2	−7.3	13.5
North Central	−0.3	26.8	−4.4	23.3
South	11.2	35.6	18.2	69.0
West	18.0	37.1	19.3	34.5

Source: US Bureau of Census 1972.

In the Northeast and North Central regions, central city losses increased and suburban growth began to slow. In the West, growth in both the suburbs and central cities remained high although suburban growth had begun to slow slighly in the 1970s. It has been in the

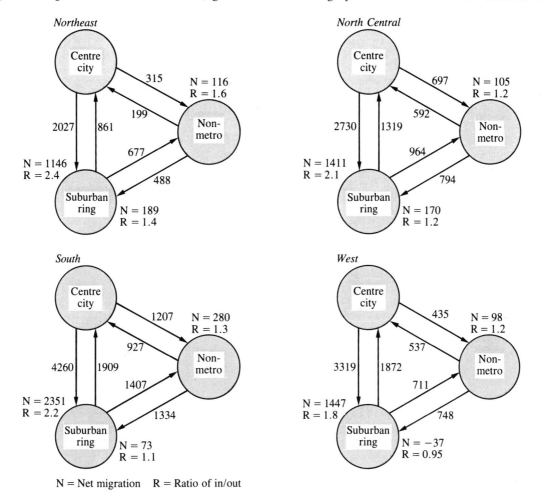

N = Net migration   R = Ratio of in/out

Fig. 2.12 Migration flows between centre city, suburban rings and non-metropolitan areas (in thousands), 1975–80

South that decentralization within the metropolitan area has continued at an expanded pace (Table 2.7). The differentials in suburban/central city growth in the South are in part a function of increases in the number of metropolitan counties in the decade, but net migration balances between central cities, suburban communities and non-metropolitan counties also have played a major role. In the South the flows in and out from both central city and non-metro counties were more heavily biased towards suburbs than was true in the other regions (Fig. 2.12). The net migration balance between central city and suburb in the South exceeded 2.3 million in the 1970s, and suburban net losses to non-metropolitan counties were surpassed by central city losses to non-metro areas by a ratio of 3 : 1. As a consequence of these flows, suburbanization in the South has occurred at rates in excess of those associated in the earlier periods of suburban expansion in the industrial cities of the North.

Decentralization has led to fundamental changes in the urban hierarchy. Since 1960, growth increasingly has become concentrated in the smaller and medium-sized cities on the fringe of larger metropolitan centres and in non-metropolitan counties (Roseman 1977). In the three decades from 1950 to 1980, the proportion of the population in cities of 1 million or more has declined steadily. In contrast, in the less populated cities (10 000 to 50 000) the proportion of the total population has increased every decade (Table 2.8).

Despite a century of decentralization, speculation that central cities will undergo a renaissance and attract a larger segment of the metropolitan population has increased, fuelled by the gentrification of inner-city neighbourhoods (Long 1980). Initially, it was believed that the energy crisis would reduce commuting and stimulate a resurgence of central city growth. However, the impacts of higher energy costs on commuting have had minimal effects

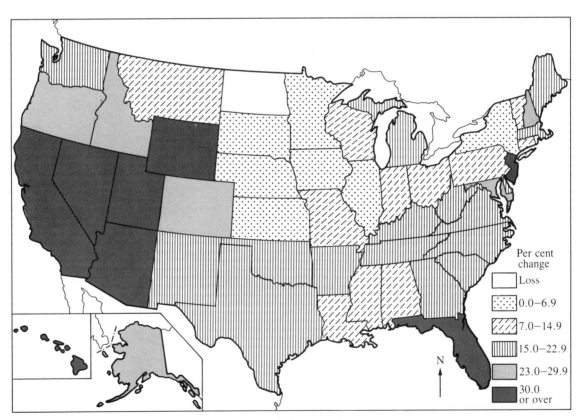

Fig. 2.13 Change in non-metropolitan population, by State, 1970–80

Table 2.8: Changes in urban population by size of place: 1960–80

Size of place	1980		1970		1960	
	Per cent of total population	Change in per cent (1970–80)	Per cent of total population	Change in per cent (1960–70)	Per cent of total population	Change in per cent (1950–60)
1 million +	7.7	-1.5	9.2	-0.6	9.8	-1.7
500 000 to 1 million	4.8	-1.6	6.4	0.2	6.2	0.1
250 000 to 500 000	5.4	0.3	5.1	-0.9	6.0	0.6
100 000 to 250 000	7.5	0.5	7.0	0.5	6.5	0.1
50 000 to 100 000	8.7	0.5	8.2	0.5	7.7	1.8
25 000 to 50 000	10.3	1.5	8.8	0.5	8.3	2.5
10 000 to 25 000	12.2	1.7	10.5	0.7	9.8	2.0
5 000 to 10 000	6.8	0.4	6.4	0.9	5.5	0.1
2 500 to 5 000	4.1	0.1	4.0	-0.2	4.2	-0.1
Places of less than 2 500	0.6	0.2	0.4	0	0.4	0
Other urban	5.6	-2.0	7.6	2.1	5.5	0.6

on centralization/decentralization trends. Other factors such as the growing incidence of two-paycheck families, childless families and the growth-limiting policies of suburban communities have probably been more important in making central-city living more attractive to residents of metropolitan America (Long and Frey 1982).

Non-metropolitan growth
The magnitude of the growth in non-metropolitan counties reported in the 1980 census surprised both demographers and public officials. Sceptics had initially viewed non-metropolitan growth as a minor aberration, but census data confirmed it to be substantial and widespread geographically. Non-metropolitan counties increased their population by 25 per cent between 1970 and 1980. In five of the nine census districts, non-metropolitan growth rates exceeded those for metropolitan counties (Table 2.6). States in the South and the West had the highest percentage changes in their non-metropolitan populations (Fig. 2.13). The North Central and Northeast regions had smaller increases in non-metropolitan population, but non-metropolitan growth was responsible for most of the overall population increase in both regions. In fact, in the Mid Atlantic States, without the increases in non-metropolitan counties, States would have recorded absolute losses (Table 2.6).

The growth of population in non-metropolitan America was so striking because it contrasted with earlier growth patterns. Non-metropolitan counties have always grown in population even when people were leaving in large numbers to urban America because natural increase rates were so high. When

fertility declined and rural/urban differences in birth rates converged, the growth gap between metropolitan and non-metropolitan counties expanded because migration became the principal growth mechanism (Long and Frey 1982). Therefore, to understand the reversal in non-metropolitan growth, we must understand the reasons for the change in metropolitan–non-metropolitan (metro–non-metro) migration behaviour.

Migration between metro and non-metro counties is not independent of inter-regional movements, and the interdependences vary by region. Inter-regional migration to the South and West, for example, involved a large number of people who moved from metropolitan to non-metropolitan counties. In contrast, in northern States non-metropolitan migrants came primarily from metropolitan counties from within the region (Table 2.9).

The magnitude and the broad geographic distribution of the changes in metro/non-metro net migration raises questions about the validity of existing theories of migration behaviour, and the ability of traditional models to explain this new movement. Were there shifts in the motivations prompting migration, or were old motives simply recast in the new spatial structure of the nation's economy?

Past surveys of the labour force have found employment and other work-related factors to be the principal *reasons* for migration (Lansing and Muller 1967; Shaw 1975). However, studies of movers to non-metropolitan counties indicated that the 'usual emphasis on economic determinants of migration may be less applicable for this migration' (de Jong and Humphrey 1976: 536). In their survey of movers to non-metro counties, Williams and Sofranko found

Table 2.9: Non-metropolitan net worker migration by region and metropolitan–non-metropolitan place of work: 1970–75

Origin of migrants	Net migration (000s)			
	Northeast	North Central	South	West
From all areas	39	−68	88	114
From metropolitan areas within the region	43	5	3	52
From metropolitan areas outside the region	−6	−51	78	44
From non-metropolitan areas outside the region	2	−22	7	16

Source: Wardwell and Brown 1980.

that the importance of employment consider-ations depended on the origin of the migrant. For those coming from metropolitan counties, employment reasons were cited by 35 per cent of those of working age. However, for those originating from non-metropolitan counties, employment considerations were cited by 56 per cent (Williams and Sofranko 1979). A more detailed analysis of non-metro migration decision-making by Roseman and Williams found that environmental quality issues were the main reason people chose to leave metropolitan areas, while social ties were the principal reason migrants selected a non-metropolitan county in which to settle (Roseman and Williams 1980). As Goldstein argues, an 'emphasis on quality of life as opposed to more strictly economic considerations seems to be assuming increasing importance as a motivation both in the decision to move and in the choice of residence' (Goldstein 1976: 424). However, economic considerations are still very important to many, particularly those coming from other non-metropolitan areas who relocate in the countryside.

Research (McCarty and Morrison 1977; Long and Frey 1982; Long and de Are 1980; Beale 1977; Williams and Sofranko 1979) has ident-ified a number of factors or attributes associated with positive net migration in non-metropolitan counties including:

- Proximity to metropolitan centres.
- Dispersion of economic opportunities, including extraction activities, to non-metro-politan counties.
- Changes in the American lifestyle.
- Expansion of public institutions in non-metropolitan counties.
- Movement of urban elderly to rural retire-ment areas.
- Growth in the importance of rural rec-reational areas.

Movement to non-metropolitan counties was initially thought to be simply an expansion of the urban fringe, in part because this was consistent with the prevailing views and trends about decentralization and the expansion of metropolitan influence. Fringe movement accounts for some, but certainly not all or even most of the non-metropolitan net migration surplus (Sternleib, Hughes and Hughes 1982).

Counties adjacent to SMSAs had higher rates than the more remote ones at the beginning of the decade, but many counties remote to urban centres also experienced positive net migration. According to Zelinsky, 'the economic-cum-metropolitan sprawl strategy collapses when we confront those hundreds of remote, thinly settled and emphatically bucolic counties' (Zelinsky 1977: 176). Moreover, as Morrison and Abrahams (1982) noted, migration to non-metropolitan counties on the urban fringe does not necessarily indicate that migrants are simply expanding their commuting fields and remaining tied to the metropolitan employment market. In some non-metro fringe counties, the commuting time of movers was actually reduced because residential relocation was accompanied by a change in the location of employment (Morrison and Abrahams 1982).

The relocation of industry to rural America (Ch. 5) has encouraged migration to non-metropolitan counties. This is true for those industries moving in response to labour costs as well as those which are tied to the extraction of resources. Energy-related economic growth was particularly important in western States where the extraction of energy resources occurred at accelerated rates in the 1970s. After the boom town exuberance and population growth associated with energy development, however, people in these communities have had to face the realities of a world surplus of oil and a recession in energy-related industries. As a consequence, many communities born of the energy boom have seen their population and economic hopes plummet in the 1980s as rapidly as they rose in the 1970s.

Economic factors alone do not account for the increased in-migration to non-metro coun-ties, as the surveys have shown. Lifestyle changes and reorientation of the motivations prompting migration have made non-metro-politan counties more attractive. The trend towards early retirement, which has increased the migration potential of the elderly, has led to greater amenity-related migration. Conse-quently, counties which have recreational resources or lower living costs have attracted elderly migrants (Bohland and Treps 1981). The importance of recreational resources is not confined to the elderly. Younger migrants are also moving to counties whose major attractions are the availability of recreational resources, for example, water-based resources (Hart 1984).

Whether non-metropolitan counties will continue to attract new residents at the rates evident in the mid-1970s is questionable. Most migration is still between metropolitan counties. Also, recent research indicates that non-metropolitan migration had begun to slow by the late 1970s (Richter 1985). And, as we have seen, in the first years of the 1980s metropolitan growth rates again surpassed those for non-metropolitan counties. Unfortunately, as Zelinsky has noted, the absence of any theoretical framework for explaining non-metropolitan migration and growth makes prediction precarious (Zelinsky 1980). Whether non-metropolitan migration continues at the same pace, accelerates or diminishes will depend in great measure on the structure and geography of future national economic growth. Whatever transpires, it is apparent that the decade of growth in non-metropolitan America has slowed the expansion of the metropolitan growth and has changed the demographic and social character of rural America (Ch. 6).

What does the future hold for US population growth?

Will the distributive processes of the 1970s continue through the 1980s and into the 1990s? Or, alternatively, will the growth of southern and western States stabilize and the in-migration to non-metropolitan counties abate and eventually succumb to a resurgence of urban growth and geographic expansion of metropolitan America? The absence of general population theory coupled with the lack of comprehensive empirical studies from other advanced industrial nations makes forecasting a hazardous activity. Vining and Strauss (1977) argue that the recent redistribution and decentralization of population represent a *clear break* with the past and should continue. What distinguishes the current trends from past events is that population dispersion has been occurring at all scales. For much of the twentieth century, population dispersal occurred at

the regional and State scales but not at the county or local scales. At the local scale, population was becoming concentrated through the urbanization process. The trends of the modern period break from this pattern because dispersion is evident at all geographic scales. Since a similar pattern has appeared in Western Europe and in Japan, it may be characteristic of nations in the later stages of industrialization and modernization and, if so, it should continue in the US for several decades (Vining and Strauss 1977).

In commenting on future regional growth in the US, Jackson and his colleagues (1981) emphasize that no single growth model is appropriate for the nation as a whole. Regions will exhibit very different future growth patterns. According to their projections, States in the East South Central, West South Central and Mountain census regions will experience rapid growth into the 1980s and 1990s. The combination of low wages, elastic labour supply, energy resources and attractive amenities in these regions make growth highly probable. The rate of growth in Pacific and South Atlantic States, two areas of very high growth in the 1970s, will decline. In South Atlantic States, rising wage levels and declining birth rates will cause the decline. Some growth will continue, however, because of the migration of elderly into the region. In the Pacific region, the scale of in-migration in the last 20 years has caused the labour supply to exceed demand; however, because wage levels are high, industrial development will not respond readily to the labour surplus. Eventually, therefore, there will be less incentive for labour migration into the region (Jackson *et al.* 1981). The reductions in inter-regional migration into the region in the first years of the 1980s indicate that growth is already beginning to slow (Rogerson and Plane 1985).

The future for most Mid Atlantic and East North Central States, the heart of the old industrial core, does not appear to offer any reasonable hope for renewed growth, unless major changes occur in the economic climate. The downward spiralling of oil prices after 1983 may constitute such a change. If the comparative advantage of southern and western State is *not* radically altered by changes in the energy market, population in the Mid Atlantic and

East North Central States will stabilize only when the labour supply and the wage levels have reached a point where industrial reinvestment occurs. Neither condition appeared on the immediate horizon at the beginning of the 1980s, and the absolute losses in population in the first half of that decade suggest that population stabilization has yet to take place.

Some resurgence of population growth is predicted for the old industrial States of New England, and the agricultural States in the West North Central region. Growth in either would be particularly noteworthy because both have had recent histories of low growth or population losses. Future growth in the two will occur for very different reasons. In New England, new investments have in fact already taken place because of favourable labour conditions (Jackson *et al.* 1981).

The accuracy of regional growth predictions is of course problematic. Remember the errors of those who worried about continued urban growth, the concentration of population in the Eastern States, rampant fertility, and the depopulation of rural counties! Unforeseen shifts in world economic relations, in the nation's economic condition, and in the structure of employment opportunities can quickly change migration patterns and alter growth scenarios. It does appear, however, that the 1970s will not be an anomaly in the demographic history of the country, but rather the period that ushered in new and important changes in the structure and distribution of the nation's population.

Chapter 3

CULTURE AND ENVIRONMENT

An understanding of the relationship between cultural attitudes and the physical and socio-economic environment of the US requires, first of all, an examination of the baggage of memory which the explorers and early settlers brought with them from the Old World. Although many of the preconceived notions of Europeans about the newly discovered continent were disproved, certain basic beliefs persisted and became firmly fixed in the consciousness of the nation, to the extent that they can be referred to as the collective images or social myths of America (Smith 1950; Watson 1976).

The combination of fact and fiction that was to provide the impetus for exploration and to become a factor in the development of the country can be found as early as 1493 in the letter of Columbus to his benefactor in Spain. This record of contact between western civilization and what was viewed by Europeans as a virgin continent spares no superlatives in describing the natural beauty and lushness of the scene:

All these islands are extremely fertile and this one [Hispaniola] is particularly so. It has many large harbours finer than any I know in Christian lands, and many large rivers. All this is marvellous. The land is high and has many ranges of hills, and mountains incomparably finer than Tenerife. All are most beautiful and various in shape, and all are accessible. They are covered with tall trees of different kinds which seem to touch the sky (Cohen 1969: 116).

Top left: De L'Isle's L'Amerique Septentrionale, Paris, 1700 *Credit*: Library of Congress, Washington, DC *Top right*: A view of Savannah as it stood on the 29th of March, 1734 drawn by P. Gordon *Credit*: Library of Congress, Prints and Photographs Division, Washington, DC *2nd left*: New York farm circa 1800, from Turner, O. *History of the Holland Purchase*, Buffalo, New York, 1850 *Credit*: Smithsonian Institute, Washington, DC   *2nd right*: Washington's Mount Vernon: the Big House *Credit*: Elizabeth Heekin Bartels *3rd left*: Montana: the Rocky Mountains *Credit*: Elizabeth Heekin Bartels *3rd right*: The Rush for the Promised Land over the Border in Oklahoma, undated and unsigned view of the beginning of the Oklahoma land rush on April 22, 1889, from *The Graphic*, May 11, 1889 *Credit*: Cornell University, Ithaca, New York, Olin Library *Bottom left*: Abilene in its Glory, unsigned and undated view of Drovers Cottage at Abilene, Kansas, circa 1870, drawn by H. Worrall, engraved by Baker and Co., Chicago, from McCoy, J. *Historic Sketches of the Cattle Trade of the West and Southwest*, Kansas City, 1874 *Credit*: Cornell University, Ithaca, New York, Olin Library *Bottom right*: New York City: Manhattan and Central Park *Credit*: Elizabeth Heekin Bartels.

Though Columbus was convinced that he would find the fabled riches of the East, he discovered only simple villages populated by native West Indians. Nonetheless, he felt compelled to write that most of the 'many and great rivers' contained gold and, therefore, he was one of the first promoters of the image of America as a land of enormous wealth and boundless natural resources.

Subsequent explorations fostered this idea and, at the same time, perpetuated the illusion that the lands discovered were merely stepping-stones on the route to Cathay. Cartographers often depicted a navigable waterway leading westward as if it were a fact, rather than a product of wishful thinking; and with no conception of the geographical extent, the sheer, intractable vastness of the continent, the explorers and their backers believed for some 200 years in the existence of this Northwest Passage or Buenaventura River (Watson 1967, 1969; Allen 1976).

In 1584, Captain Arthur Barlowe described the land of Virginia in language that is reminiscent of Columbus. He found the shore 'so full of grapes, as the very beating and surge of the Sea overflowed them, of which we found such plentie, as well there as in all places else, both on the sand and on the greene soile of the hils . . . that I thinke in all the world the like abundance is not to be found.' (Barlowe 1584, reported in Marx 1964: 37). This report, along with countless others, used images of 'fecundity, growth, increase and blissful labor in the earth' to express the 'master symbol' or myth of America as a great garden (Smith 1950: 123).

America as a New Eden

The myth of America as a garden or, in keeping with the Judeo-Christian traditions of Europe, a New Eden, has played a major role in prompting the waves of immigration described in Chapter 2. Of course, the interpretation of the garden myth has been modified over time: the earthly paradise of the seventeenth century became the agrarian landscape of the eighteenth, and this, in turn, became the landscape of technological progress in the nineteenth. However, each version was founded on the belief that America is endowed with unlimited resources and, despite the warnings of twentieth-century advocates of controlled growth and development, the Great American Cornucopia is still portrayed as overflowing. In fact, this image so dominates the imagination that government policies aimed at belt-tightening are considered antithetical to the American way of life.

To return, however, to colonial times, it can be seen that the myth of the garden appealed to both the materialistic and the idealistic aspirations of the early settlers and that both of these attitudes left their imprint on the physical landscape, as well as on social and political institutions. The promise of a better life across the Atlantic implied that risk would be rewarded by material gain; and this idea of profit as a primary motivating factor in the settlement of America is best represented by the successive quests for gold: including the search for the cities of Cibola in the 1500s and the California Gold Rush of 1849. For the majority of Europeans the wealth of the continent was there for the taking; nature existed not to be admired and praised, but to be plundered and exploited.

The promise of material reward, ranging from the dreams of gold of the Spanish Conquistadors to the more humble yearnings of the pioneer farmer for a few hundred acres of land and a good plough, was counterbalanced by the promise of spiritual reward. The view of the New World as (potentially) an earthly paradise can be found in the histories of the Puritans of New England, the Quakers of Pennsylvania, the Mormons of Utah, and also in the utopian communities of various peripheral religious sects, such as the Shakers of Hancock, Massachusetts, and the Inspirationists of Amana, Kansas. Although espousing radically different philosophies, the various groups shared the belief that the spiritual and moral environment could be improved through the creation of a certain kind of community. The vision of a New Zion or a City of Brotherly Love was to be realized by communitarian effort and each group formulated a specific plan, in keeping with its utopian goals, for structuring the physical and social environment. The discrepancy between the vision and the reality, however, was often enormous; and while some groups abandoned or modified their original programme in order to survive, others, notably the Mormons, were able to successfully provide for both the temporal and spiritual well-being of their members (Hayden 1976).

Thus, two juxtaposed conceptions of what the Great American Garden had to offer contributed to the founding of the nation and to the emergence of a national consciousness. The utopian aspirations were equivalent to the desire to improve or reform the physical/social environment, in order to attain certain group goals. On the other hand, the desire for material reward resulted in a philosophy of individual gain which viewed nature as a raw material to be shaped, first by the axe, and later by the machine, to meet the needs of this acquisitive new breed, the American.

Two views of nature: the American Indian and the European

If Ralph Waldo Emerson was correct in observing that the views of nature held by any group of people seem to 'determine all their institutions' (Emerson 1856: 548), then the European view, which objectified nature and separated it from man, forms an important part of the American intellectual legacy. This view was diametrically opposed to that of the American Indian which, characteristically, considered nature and man a unity: 'The American Indian is of the soil, whether it be of the region of forests, plains, pueblos or mesas. He fits into the landscape, for the hand that fashioned the continent also fashioned the man for his surroundings' (Chief Standing Bear 1933, reported in Babcock 1965: 199). This quality of being 'of the soil' can be seen in the Cliff Palace of Mesa Verde, which consists of a compact mass of geometric shapes fitted into the ledge of a canyon wall. A comparison of Mesa Verde, where the man-made forms reflect the landscape, and Mount Rushmore, where the landscape literally reflects the face of man, is revealing. The geomorphic style of town building of the Pueblo Indian can also be contrasted with the gridiron layout of towns built by white men. For the most part, the use of the gridiron reflects an expedient approach to planning – towns appearing overnight, first as a reaction to a new and hostile environment, and then as a result of speculative real estate interests. These towns, which became ubiquitous throughout America (Reps 1965), are essentially different from those of the Pueblo, whose organic growth reflects the evolving social conditions of a homogeneous population (Scully 1975).

Cronon points out the initial fallacy in the European notion that the New World was 'virgin land,' unorganized and unformed by human hands (Cronon 1983). Indians had lived on the continent for thousands of years prior to the white man's arrival and had modified the land according to their needs and the requirements of the particular ecosystems. New England settlers, inspired by the vision of a land of plenty, where labour and enterprise could be quickly realized as profit, regarded the Indians, who moved from place to place in order to take advantage of seasonal variation and minimize their impact on the land, as lazy savages and, therefore, undeserving of the fruits of the garden.

Above all, the conflict between the two ways of living and of using the land was centred on the concept of property ownership: 'What the Indians owned – or more precisely, what their villages gave them claim to – was not the land but the things that were on the land during the various seasons of the year' (Cronon 1983: 65). In contrast, the colonizing Europeans believed that remaining sedentary and 'improving' a fixed and bounded area entitled them to ownership of the land itself, thus superseding the tacit claims of the Indian population. As Cronon indicates, the European view of land as a commodity and the belief in the right of acquisition through improvement provided the justification for the 'European ideology of conquest' (Cronon 1983: 53).

In retrospect, it can be argued that the American Indian's respect for the ecological processes of specific geographical regions, such as the Great Plains and the Great Basin, allowed for a far more appropriate use of the land than did the white man's ideology of conquest. It was not until the second half of the nineteenth century that attention was focused by whites on conservation and management of

Cliff Palace, Mesa Verde, Colorado: The pueblo is situated underneath a ledge in the canyon
wall. *Copyright*: The Author: EHB

the land, and then only after exploitative agricultural practices had resulted in disastrous environmental conditions (for example, soil depletion in the South and the erosion of the Great Plains).

Not only was the potential contribution of the American Indian to a better understanding of the physical environment disregarded, but the Indian came to be viewed as an obstacle in the path of the 'manifest destiny' of the white man to conquer and control the continent. Congressman Francis Baylies wrote in 1823:

The swelling tide of our population must and will roll on until that mighty ocean interposes its waters, and limits our territorial empire . . . To diffuse the arts of life, the light of science, and the blessings of the Gospel over a wilderness, is no violation of the laws of God; it is no invasion of

Mount Rushmore National Memorial in the Black Hills of South Dakota: The head of President Washington is as high as a five-storey building. *Copyright*: Photograph by Robert Harding Picture Library, London

the rights of man to occupy a territory over which the savage roams, but which he never cultivates . . . (Baylies 1823, reported in Robertson 1980: 72).

The journalist Horace Greeley, who originated the phrase, 'Go West, young man', echoed this sentiment when he wrote: 'These people [the Indians] must die out. There is no hope for them. God has given this earth to those who will subdue and cultivate it, and it is vain to try to struggle against his righteous decree' (Greeley, reported in Babcock 1965: 8).

Thus, the white settlers and their descendants interpreted the call to 'subdue and cultivate' the earth as a sacred mission: only when the wilderness, and by extension the Indian, are obliterated can God's will be done. The myth of America as a garden is in keeping with this war on wilderness, for the garden image implies a cultivated state which can be attained only by clearing and 'improving' the land.

America as a 'howling wilderness'

The accounts of Columbus and Barlowe, which purported to find a ready-made paradise in the new, unspoiled land, can be viewed as part of the promotional literature that was to flood Europe. The illusion fostered by these reports, of finding an Arcadia where the sun always shines and the natives are always friendly, was shattered, however, against the reality of settlement in an oftentimes inhospitable environment. If the garden did not pre-exist, then it would have to be forcibly shaped out of the wilderness which was its antithesis.

This theme has been examined by historians, such as Henry Nash Smith (1950), Leo Marx (1964), Roderick Nash (1967) and John Stilgoe (1982), who demonstrate that for the inhabitants of the Old World, and thus for the first settlers of North America, the wilderness was not only a physical place, but also a *state of mind*. It was the alien and uncontrolled chaos of Nature located just beyond the cultivated fields of the agricultural communities. A seventeenth-century observer wrote that the New World at the time of settlement was: 'A waste and howling wilderness/Where none inhabited/But hellish fiends, and brutish men/That Devils worshiped' (Wigglesworth 1662: 83). Because of this equation of wilderness with an environment of evil, where all vestiges of moral behaviour, of organized and responsible action have disappeared, the first settlers fought against the wilderness for spiritual, as well as physical, survival. Conquering the wilderness meant ensuring the triumph of virtue.

According to Marx, 'to describe America as a hideous wilderness is to envisage it as another field for the exercise of power. This violent image expresses a need to mobilize energy, postpone immediate pleasures, and rehearse the perils and purposes of community' (Marx 1964: 43). This clearly identifies the Puritan viewpoint which placed the righteous citizen securely within the stockade and the lost soul 'in the heart of the deep wilderness, still rushing onward with the instinct that guides mortal men to evil' (Hawthorne 1835: 83).

It is easy to understand the psychological insecurity of the first settlers, confronted as they were by both the challenge and the threat of life in an untamed land. The urge to conquer and destroy that this attitude engendered can be seen in William Faulkner's *The Bear*, which describes the Mississippi bottomland of the 1880s as a microcosm of 'that doomed wilderness whose edges were being constantly and punily gnawed at by men with plows and axes who feared it because it was the wilderness'. Old Ben, the hunted bear, is, likewise, 'the epitome and apotheosis of the old wild life which the little puny humans swarmed and hacked at in a fury of abhorrence and fear' (Faulkner 1942: 229).

Frontier America: shaping the wilderness

The battle against the wilderness did not stop at the Appalachian frontier, but pushed on to the Ohio, the Wabash and the Mississippi Rivers. In 1811, barely a million people lived in the trans-Appalachia territory, but within 20 years their numbers had quadrupled. Nathaniel Southgate Shaler commented that 'the settlement of the Mississippi Valley is the first instance in history of the reduction of a wilderness in a single lifetime' (Shaler 1894, reported in Brown 1948: 536). The annexation of trans-Mississippi territories during the course of the nineteenth century (the Louisiana Purchase of 1803, the First Mexican Cession of 1848, and the Gadsden Purchase of 1803), along with federal land policies aimed at encouraging settlement (the Homestead Act of 1862, the Timber Culture Act of 1873, and the Desert Land Act of 1877), assured the steady movement of the frontier westward.

Already in 1784, when Virginia ceded its lands west of the Ohio River to the newly formed national government, there was a public clamour for land to be sold or granted to individuals. In order to dispose of the lands of the Old Northwest Territory, which were approximately twice the size of France, it was necessary to establish a national land policy, or method of parcelling the unknown and unsurveyed area. The resulting Land Survey Ordinance of 1785, which was based on a proposal by Thomas Jefferson, specified that the western lands be neatly laid out in rectangular townships, each 10 square kilometres (6 square miles). This geometric scheme was eventually applied on a smaller scale to mark off individual lots, the effect of which can be viewed as one flies over more than three-quarters of the present area of the continental US and looks down upon the chequerboard arrangement of farmlands and the orthogonal layout of roads and fences.

According to Daniel Boorstin, the American land pattern 'is a relic of the young nation's need to make a commodity of its land, and hastily to map and sell it, even before it was explored or surveyed'; and, as such, 'it is one of the first examples of the peculiar importance of packaging in America' (Boorstin 1965: 245). This method of dividing up vast areas of land to facilitate a quick sale did not allow for variations in the terrain. Parcels were made of the public domain regardless of topography, soil quality, proximity to water etc.; and thus

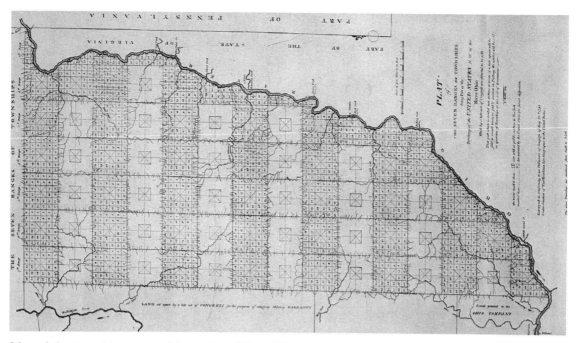

Map of the townships surveyed in eastern Ohio, 1796: the 'packaging' of America. *Copyright*: Plat of the Seven Ranges of Townships being part of the Territory of the United States N.W. of the River Ohio which by a late act of Congress are directed to be sold, drawn by M. Carey after surveys by T. Hutchins, engraved by W. Baker, published by M. Carey, Philadelphia, 1976. William L. Clements Library, University of Michigan, Ann Arbor, Michigan.

the suitability of a section of land for a particular use was not considered. Despite various problems connected with the land apportionment policies of the federal government, the land acts did precipitate a mass movement into the Northwest Territory as shown by the fact that more than two-thirds of Minnesota was settled by homesteaders.

By the end of the nineteenth century, the US had disposed of approximately 461 million hectares (1.14 billion acres) of public land, in order to raise money directly by sale or indirectly by encouraging settlement. In the case of the Homestead Act, as well as the opening of the Oklahoma Territory in 1889, the lands were essentially given away by the federal government. John Steinbeck in *East of Eden* records the race of the pioneer farmer and immigrant to stake a claim:

When people first came to the West, particularly from the owned and fought-over farmlets of Europe, and saw so much land to be had for the signing of a paper and the building of a foundation, an itching land greed seemed to come over them. They wanted more and more land – good land if possible, but land anyway . . . The early settlers took up land they didn't need and couldn't use; they took up worthless land just to own it (Steinbeck 1952: 12).

The first step in taking possession of a new homestead was to clear the land of trees, rocks, hills or whatever obstacles stood in the way; and this was accomplished with what one observer deplored as 'wanton savagery' and 'unthinkable ruthlessness' (Boissevain 1882, reported in Billington 1981: 202). The land was then planted year after year with the most profitable crop, and when the soil was finally depleted, the next step was to move on to the cheap, unspoiled lands to the west. As long as these lands were plentiful, the careless destruction of irreplaceable natural resources, what James Fenimore Cooper in *The Prairie* called 'the madness of their waste' (Cooper 1826: 786), could continue.

The frontier spirit: shaping the American character

David Lowenthal, in commenting upon the American's urge to conquer the wilderness and fill the vast emptiness of the continent, writes:

To the Elizabethans, America was simply a vision; to the settlers that vision was a challenge requiring action. Action became so strong a component of the American character that landscapes were often hardly seen at all; they were only acted on. Immediate necessity made a mockery of mere contemplation. To wrest a living from the soil, to secure frontiers against hostile forces, seemed to demand full attention. Appreciation of the landscape itself, apart from its practical uses, was disdained as pointless and effete (Lowenthal 1968: 72).

Josiah Royce, who wrote in 1886 of the conquest of California, noted that the 'feverish endeavor' on the part of the frontiersman 'to ruin the landscape' was not solely an expression of his materialistic outlook, but 'because mere nature is, as such, vaguely unsatisfactory to his soul, because what is merely found must never content us . . . Hence the first desire is to change, to disturb, to bring the new' (Royce, reported in Boorstin 1973: 245). Thus, Royce identified a frontier spirit or mentality, which can be further described as a restless pursuit of novelty and of new frontiers on which to act out the adventure of conquest and settlement.

To European observers, Americans seemed to be constantly on the move, hastily building up a farmstead, only to abandon it when new lands were opened to the west. This nomadic lifestyle was facilitated by the invention in the 1830s of the balloon frame, a type of construction which could be easily dismantled and transported and which, therefore, was very different from the permanent, traditional structures of the Old World (Lowenthal 1976; Billington 1981).

The historian Frederick Jackson Turner did much to advance the idea that the westward movement of the frontier, what he termed 'the frontier experience', was the single most important factor in determining the American character and in differentiating it from the European. The Turner thesis stated: 'American social development has been continually beginning over again on the frontier. This perennial rebirth, this fluidity of American life, this expansion westward with its new opportunities, its continuous touch with the simplicity of primitive society, furnish the forces dominating American character' (Turner 1920: 2–3). While Turner emphasized the positive aspects of American social development, the rugged individualism and self-reliance which he praised also had their negative side. The frontier sense of personal freedom and independence, when combined with the illusion of unlimited land to be claimed and fortunes to be made, resulted in the careless and uncontrolled carving up of the landscape without regard to the preservation of its natural beauty or its natural resources. The mobility and impermanency which were characteristic of the frontier experience went hand in hand with an acceptance of wastefulness; and this attitude has been handed down to the 'throw away society' (Toffler 1970) of contemporary America.

Although the frontier era was essentially over by the end of the 1800s when shocked Americans discovered that the physical expansion of the nation did, indeed, have limits, the concept of ever new frontiers has not died. It has become an integral part of the American character and has proved as durable as the image of the cowboy riding into the sunset. Throughout the twentieth century, the definition of the frontier as an unexplored region has been continually revised and expanded to meet the realities of an age in which it is believed science and technology provide the means for realizing the American Dream.

Rural America: the agrarian myth

In 1782, when J. Hector St John de Crèvecoeur wrote his *Letters from an American Farmer* extolling the virtues of rural life, nine out of ten Americans were farmers and the consensus was that agriculture would remain the principal undertaking of the nation and the basis of its prosperity for years to come. As we have seen, the steady march westward of the frontier during the nineteenth century was assured by the understanding that 'Uncle Sam had a farm for everyone' and by the conviction that, in transforming the wilderness into a rural landscape, the nation was fulfilling its 'manifest destiny'.

The equation of the rural landscape that was being hewn out of the wilderness with the garden myth is an obvious one. The garden, represented by the cultivated field and pastureland of the farm, is located, according to Marx (1964), in a 'middle landscape' somewhere between the opposing forces of civilization and wild nature. This is the locus of health, of freedom and of moral values, for, as Thomas Jefferson stated, 'Those who labor in the earth are the chosen people of God' (Jefferson 1787: 164).

Jefferson believed that private ownership of land – farmland, that is – is necessary for individual freedom and, by extension, that it is only the free individual who is able to be an active and effective participant in the process of forming and maintaining a democratic society. His adherence to the ideal of the middle/rural landscape can be seen in his *Notes on the State of Virginia* (1787) and in the policies of the new government which he helped to shape. The Land Survey Ordinance of 1785, with its proposal to divide the landscape into equal agricultural parcels, was in many respects a utopian scheme in that it provided 'the blueprint for an agrarian, equalitarian society' (Jackson 1970). After the war of 1812, Jefferson modified his view that America would and should remain a nation of virtuous farmers, exporting raw materials to Europe and importing manufactured goods, and admitted that manufacturing centres were needed to free the country of foreign domination and to ensure economic prosperity.

The technological and scientific advances made during the nineteenth century transformed agriculture from a small-scale family operation based on the Jeffersonian model into a large-scale business enterprise. Bonanza farming, which was introduced in the late 1870s in North Dakota and Minnesota, was characterized by large investments in land and capital, mechanization and hired management, and was thus 'not in the least concerned with the development of the rural community; with the family

farm as a way of life; or with the long-range productivity of the soil: it was a process for producing wheat in commercial quantities' (Jackson 1972: 52). The decline of the farm population, which corresponded with the rise in agricultural productivity, became evident after the Civil War and has continued into the 1980s (see Ch. 6). In 1930, 25 per cent of all Americans lived on a farm, as opposed to 2.5 per cent today. Though the number of farmers has been steadily dwindling, the rural population, on the whole, has been increasing, to the extent that the population growth rate in non-metropolitan counties is 60 per cent greater today than it is in large cities and suburbs. The renaissance of rural areas during the 1980s, along with the current revival of interest in the cultural trappings of country living, reflect the continued search for the Arcadian 'middle landscape'. Thus Charles Little, editor of *American Land Forum*, can write: 'the beautiful dream of pure country persists. It persists because it is ingrained in our politics, in our history, and maybe even in our genes' (Little 1984: 83).

Industrial America: the 'Spirit of Progress' and the age of the 'iron horse'

The shift from a nation of farmers to a nation of manufacturers, which had been completed by the end of the nineteenth century, had far-reaching consequences for the physical and cultural landscape (Giedion 1969). It is no exaggeration to say that industrialization changed the face of America: it contributed more than any other factor to the growth and development of the nation's cities, to the invention of new building types such as the assembly line factory, and to the creation of regional-scale transportation landscapes.

Though the proponents of an agrarian America may have had misgivings about the changes wrought by the Industrial Revolution, the nation, as a whole, enthusiastically welcomed the new technology and the associated economic profits. In effect, the 'Frontier Spirit' which had played such an important role in carving the first homesteads out of the wilderness was replaced by the 'Spirit of Progress'. The optimistic, individualistic frontiersman was ready to place his faith in the machine, confident that it would assure national unity and prosperity, and that America would never duplicate the 'satanic mills' of industrial Europe.

Perhaps the most vivid symbol of progress in nineteenth-century America was the steam locomotive. After its introduction from England in 1829, it became an American passion, rivalled only by the American love affair with the automobile in the twentieth century. By the end of the 1800s, one-half of the world's railroads were in the US; and with tracks spreading from coast to coast, the country could finally refer to itself as a 'continent-nation'. Indeed, the new form of transportation proved to be ideal for America with its vast, unsettled inland empire. Faster, cheaper and more dependable than roads or canals, the railroad expedited the movement of goods and people and provided access to markets. Not only did it act as a transporter, but also as a colonizer, opening up new areas for population growth, extending agriculture into vast areas inaccessible to water transportation and stimulating the development of inland cities (White 1976; Stilgoe 1983).

Essentially, the railroad companies, which were granted millions of hectares of western land by both State and federal governments as an inducement to cross the continent, acted as land companies. Texas, for instance, eventually made gifts to railroads of over 13 million hectares (32 million acres), or one-sixth of the State. Land grants to railroad companies included not only the right of way but, in the usual federal grants, alternate sections of 260 hectares (640 acres) on either side of the tracks. The railroad then sold this land to settlers, especially the immigrants streaming in from Europe, at a handsome profit. The promotional campaigns of the railroad companies, which included opening real estate offices in foreign countries and providing easy credit, were nothing short of fantastic.

Realizing that town development and company profits went hand in hand, the railroads, through 'associates', built hundreds of towns, each of which was advertised as the site of a great and splendid metropolis. In fact, many of the claims proved to be bogus; and, on arrival, the weary traveller might find what Charles Dickens discovered in Cairo, Illinois: 'a hotbed of disease, an ugly sepulchre, a grave uncheered by any gleam of promise; a place without one single quality, in earth or air or water, to commend it' (Dickens 1890: 249). Though all places were not as bad as Cairo, the regular use by the railroad companies of a standard gridiron plat bisected by the tracks and centred on the station contributed to the monotonous and makeshift character of most of the railroad towns.

Nonetheless, the role of the railroad in opening up territory in the West should not be underestimated. The tracks and their accompanying telegraph wires cut a linear swath through the vast expanse of the Great Plains and many of the lone outposts along the way eventually did become active and prosperous centres for the distribution and processing of goods from the surrounding farmlands. By aggressively promoting the settlement of areas popularly considered to be uninhabitable, the railroad helped to dispel the myth that the prairie was a barren wasteland, unsuitable for agriculture and, thus, it was a major force in moving the frontier westward.

Urban America: the 'city wilderness'

In the East, the combined effects of improved transportation, rapid industrialization and increased immigration transformed cities, such as New York, Philadelphia and Boston, into major urban centres which dominated the surrounding countryside. In the latter part of the nineteenth century, streams of new immigrants from industrialized Europe were lured by the promise of jobs and brighter prospects, not on the declining farms of the eastern seaboard, nor on the frontier of the Wild West, but in the factories of the growing metropolises. This is shown by the fact that in the century from 1790 to 1890, the total population of the US had grown sixteen times, while the urban population grew 139 times.

This phenomenal urban growth, especially after the Civil War, was not without consequences for the physical and social environment of the city (Schlesinger 1971; Warner 1972). Despite the soaring skyscrapers and the gleaming bridges, the American city was soon beset with many of the problems which had plagued the industrial centres of Europe. The prosperous look of Fifth Avenue and Wall Street were just part of the picture; behind these facades were the slums and sweatshops where 'the other half' (Riis 1890) lived and worked in overcrowded, unsanitary and hazardous conditions. Although Walt Whitman wrote of the exhilarating qualities of urban life in his poems celebrating the dynamism of New York City, Upton Sinclair portrayed Chicago as a jungle and vividly described the chaotic and perilous life of immigrants living in the 'wilderness of two-story tenements that lie "back of the yards"' (Sinclair 1905: 31).

While the seventeenth-century Puritan view equated town life (civilization) with virtue, the nineteenth-century view considered the city to be the repository of social evils. In the twentieth century, the exploded city, or megalopolis, has perpetuated this idea. It is perhaps stretching a point to say that the Los Angeles Freeway has something in common with the woods outside of seventeenth-century Salem, Massachusetts. Nonetheless, it is necessary to identify in the contemporary landscape the place where traditional beliefs and civilized behaviour are perceived to be threatened. As we saw in Chapter 2, recent disaffection with urban living has been indicated by census statistics showing a significant shift in population from metropolitan to non-metropolitan areas.

A new view of nature: Thoreau's legacy

In the nineteenth century, anti-urban sentiment, coupled with enthusiasm for the ideas of the Romantic Movement, produced a change in the attitude towards nature, and specifically towards the Great American Wilderness. By the end of the 1800s, many of the more privileged inhabitants of large east coast cities were actively seeking out remote wooded areas in which to escape the pressures of urban life. A sojourn in a rustic Catskill cabin, for example, allowed the vacationer to recall pioneer days without actually experiencing the dangers and hardships of the times.

It was not necessary, however, to go quite so far away from town, for the *suburb*, whose development had been facilitated by improved railroad and streetcar service, and whose continued existence would be assured by the automobile, offered an alternative to city living. Andrew Jackson Downing commented in 1848 in 'Hints to Rural Improvers':

Hundreds and thousands obliged to live in the crowded streets of cities, now find themselves able to enjoy a country cottage, several miles distant – the old notions of time and space being half annihilated; and these suburban cottages enable the busy citizen to breathe freely, and keep alive his love for nature, till the time shall come when he shall have wrung out of the nervous hand of commerce enough means to enable him to realise his ideal of the 'retired life' of an American landed proprietor (Downing 1848, reported in Schmitt 1969: 5).

Although Downing often referred to the 'rural landscape', the nineteenth-century romantic suburb was, in fact, a compromise between a genuinely rural life and an urban one (Scully 1955). It was an answer to Emerson's lament: 'I wish to have rural strength and religion for my children and I wish facility and polish. I find with chagrin that I cannot have both' (Emerson 1844: 506). Riverside, Illinois, designed by F. L. Olmsted and Calvert Vaux in 1869 with graciously curved, tree-lined streets and umbilically linked to Chicago by railroad, offered, theoretically, the best of both worlds to those who could afford it. The plan, which became a model for the nineteenth-century suburb, was successful in striking a balance between demands for privacy and the need for a sense of community. Though the term 'bedroom community' has been used pejoratively to describe the contemporary suburb, the continued preference of the middle class for this kind of living is evident in the post-World War II trend towards the suburbanization of America and subsequent decline of the central city (see Ch. 7).

For those nineteenth-century urbanites who were unable to retreat to the mountains or to the romantic suburb, the next best opportunity for experiencing the refreshing effects of nature was the *public park*. Although the history of the park movement in America has been well-documented (Fein 1968, 1972), it is important to make a few points concerning the relationship between the public park, the city and the ideal of American democracy. In the view of Olmsted, who designed New York's Central Park in 1858, and his colleagues:

America was called upon to demonstrate in physical terms innovative responses to the social problems of industrializing and urbanizing nations. The nation had to prove that a democracy organized in the eighteenth century to meet the needs of a rural population could still retain the basic elements of a Jeffersonian ideology with the new forms required of urban living (Fein 1972: 18).

Olmsted believed that the role of the park was not only to provide relief from oppressing urban conditions by introducing a country-like atmosphere into the city ('rus in urbe'), but also to act 'in a directly remedial way to enable men to better resist the harmful influences of ordinary town life and to recover what they lose from them' (Olmsted 1881, reported in Jackson 1972: 217). Thus, the park, by providing the antithesis of urban conditions, would contribute to the reform of the social and moral environment. In essence, the tired worker, given the chance to enjoy the natural scenery of the urban park, would become the virtuous citizen of democratic America which Thomas Jefferson had envisioned.

The late nineteenth-century appreciation of nature, especially on the part of those living and/or working in the city, was not limited, however, to the joys of a stroll in Central Park or even to a weekend at a mountain resort. With the awareness that the frontier was drawing to a close, that 'the Wild West is tamed, and its savage charms have withered' (Parkman 1892: ix), came recognition and celebration of the *natural beauty* and sublimity of the wilderness. The new view of nature in the wilds was influenced by the Transcendentalist philosophy and the Romantic imagination and also, at a popular level, by a growing nationalist sentiment. 'Nature served Americans as an ideal type of tradition, older than the human past, untainted with human follies and crimes, and uniquely American in its scenic grandeur' (Lowenthal 1976: 102). Thus, the scenic wonders of the West were viewed by Americans as morally superior to the architectural monuments of the Old World. Henry David Thoreau expressed this idea when he wrote in his essay 'Walking' of 1862: '. . . ever I am leaving the city more and more, and withdrawing into the wilderness . . . I must walk toward Oregon, and not toward Europe' (Thoreau 1862: 603–4).

Thoreau, who recorded his withdrawal from society to the woods outside Boston in his book *Walden* (1854), led an intellectual revolution with profound consequences for the American environment. He announced a new age of thinking when he declared: 'The West of which I speak is but another name for the Wild, and what I have been preparing to say is, that in Wildness is the preservation of the World' (Thoreau 1862: 609). The concept of preserving wilderness and of thereby preserving mankind, which was so radically opposed to the views of the settlers and pioneer farmers, soon gained support from other intellectuals. Among them was George Perkins Marsh, the Father of American Conservation, who introduced a new justification for preservation when he indicated the scientific value and utility of wilderness (Lowenthal 1976).

Government views: wilderness preservation and environmental quality

Various members of government opposed to the uncontrolled economic exploitation of land and natural resources also spoke out in favour of preserving wilderness areas. As a result, legislation for the world's first national park, Yellowstone, was signed in 1872 by President Grant. This park was followed by Sequoia and Yosemite, among others, and by State parks, such as the Adirondack Forest Preserve. Subsequently, legislation was enacted to provide for more effective management of these public lands, including the establishment of the National Park Service in 1916. As a result of increased awareness of the value of wilderness as part of the national heritage, new criteria have been developed for determining which lands should be preserved:

It is useful to remember that the concept of a system of places and structures to embrace the national patrimony is a relatively new idea. In the beginning the primary object was to set aside the greatest of the majestic 'wonders' of the nation. Today that concept embraces a wide spectrum of resources – natural, historical and recreational – that taken together share a remarkable similarity to the geographical and ethnic pluralism of our culture (Dickson 1983).

The movement to preserve wilderness culminated in 1964 with the establishment of a National Wilderness Preservation System. Although this legislation fell short of preservationists' expectations, it did indicate government recognition of the need to end wholesale destruction of the natural environment by keeping a portion of the nation forever wild. Legal recognition of wilderness, however, did not end the controversies between development and preservation interests, as the past 20 years indicate. For example, in 1980 President Carter signed an Alaska land bill creating over 42 million hectares (104 million acres) of national parks, conservation areas and wildlife refuges. This ended a 4-year debate, between conservationists, backed by the Carter administration, and the State government, allied with timber, oil and mining interests, over how to use the extensive federal landholdings in Alaska. The steady progress made during the 1970s in the protection of wilderness and wildlife was reversed, however, by the Reagan administration: in 1983, Secretary of the Interior James Watt decided to remove 325 780 hectares (805 000 acres) of Bureau of Land Management public lands in Alaska from protected status as wilderness areas.

The 1982 proposal of the Reagan administration to dispose of approximately 14 million hectares (35 million acres) of public land (an area the size of Maine, New Hampshire and Massachusetts combined) throughout the country by sale to private real estate interests and developers proved to be very controversial. Though 162 million hectares (400 million acres) of parks, wilderness areas and miscellaneous lands designated by Congress were exempt, this proposal still raised fundamental questions about how America should manage its landholdings. The administration argued that the federal government owns too much property

(altogether 300 million hectares (740 million acres), or 32.7 per cent of the land in the US, most of which is west of the Mississippi) to effectively oversee and that the sale of underutilized land would produce revenue and benefit the taxpayer. Opponents, such as the American Wilderness Society, argue that 'American history has demonstrated that the public is not well served, in the long run, by turning over commodity lands to private interests. The aim of business is short-run profits, not long-run preservation – and experience has shown that conservation of resources is critical to maintaining a high standard of living – or living at all' (Stoler 1982: 31).

The questions concerning the private use of public lands, whether through purchase or lease (for example, the lease of the US outer continental shelf for offshore oil drilling), which the Reagan administration raised 'go to the very heart of democracy and the national character . . . Should a government dedicated to the principle of private property own more than half of Utah, Idaho, Oregon and Nevada and nearly 75 per cent of Alaska?' (Beck *et al.* 1983: 23). Carl Pope, Political Director of the Sierra Club, believes that the trend towards the 'privatization of America' reflects Reagan's belief in a 'frontier-style capitalism' and points out that 'the frontier society to which Reagan often refers was one in which all people pursued their own interests, with minimal concern for the risks involved, the impacts on their neighbors, or the needs of the future' (Pope 1984: 51–4).

During the past 25 years concern has been expressed not only for the conservation of public wilderness areas and natural resources, but also for the quality of the human environment in general (O'Riordan 1976). The 1969 National Environmental Policy Act (NEPA), one of the most important and comprehensive environmental measures ever passed by the government, requires that all federal proposals significantly affecting environmental quality be subject to review. In addition, the Act states that 'Congress recognizes that each person should enjoy a healthful environment and that each person has the responsibility to contribute to the preservation and enhancement of the environment'.

The effectiveness of NEPA and of subsequent environmental legislation has been undermined to varying degrees by conservative political and economic interests and, as a result of the 'oil crises' of the 1970s, by those favouring a self-sufficient America in terms of its energy production. This is evidenced by the 1973 decision of President Nixon to approve the Trans-Alaska Pipeline, despite his misgivings that environmental standards might have to be relaxed.

During the 1980s, the Reagan administration has consistently pledged to take all necessary steps to protect the American people from the health hazards associated with toxic waste and air pollution while, at the same time, making drastic cutbacks in the funds and staff of the federal agencies responsible for environmental control. Clearly, Reagan has stressed the initiative of individuals/private enterprise over that of government with regard to the regulation of environmental standards.

Cultural regions: homogeneity versus diversity

Implicit in the foregoing discussion of cultural attitudes affecting the use and misuse of the physical environment is the notion that these attitudes are representative of a national ethos. Of course, there have been regional variations in outlooks and self-perceptions which have evolved during the nation's history and which distingush one region from another. What are these regions and how have they been described by the cultural geographer?

Traditionally, it has been most convenient to divide the country into four parts: the Yankee North and the Confederate South; the settled (colonial) East and the frontier (trans-Appalachian) West. Clearly, this emphasizes an historical view of America and lumps together vast areas of the US whose boundaries and subdivisions need to be identified. Zelinsky (1973) further defines the major traditional culture areas as New England, the South, the Midland, the Middle West and the West (Fig. 3.1). In the case of the West, which accounts for roughly half of the coterminous US, he admits difficulties in arriving at an adequate cultural classification and questions whether a genuine, single, grand Western culture exists.

Zelinsky's 'Doctrine of First Effective Settlement' is based on the tenet that the culture areas of the US are European in origin, 'the result of importing European colonists and ways of life and the subsequent interaction among and within social groups and with a novel set of habitats' (Zelinsky 1973: 117). The traditional region is defined primarily by the culture of the people who first settled the area and secondarily by those cultures dominating later periods of settlement. In addition, Zelinsky defines a second class of culture area, the 'voluntary region', which has replaced 'the traditional spatial and social allocations of individuals through the lottery of birth . . . by a process of relative self-selection of lifestyle, goals, social niche and place of residence' (Zelinsky 1973: 111). These newly formed voluntary regions are superimposed on the older set with little functional connection; and viewed together they amount to a 'new geometry of culture' (Zelinsky 1973: 112).

Running counter to the attempts of geographers, including Gastil (1975), Watson (1963, 1979), Hart (1972) and Rooney et al. (1982), to refine the definition of culture areas within the US are claims that the social and cultural environment of America has become increasingly homogeneous, as a result of highly sophisticated transportation and communication technologies which have altered traditional perceptions of time and space (Webber 1964; Toffler 1970). As we point out in Chapter 6, the products and technology of urban America are found everywhere in the rural landscape: the satellite dishes that sprout like mushrooms across the American countryside are indicators of the far-reaching influence of mass media on the daily life of rural residents from coast to coast.

In 1967, Herman Kahn predicted that any study of the US in the year 2000 would focus on three megalopolitan regions, outside of which he presumed few people would live (Kahn 1967). In his view, the areas from Boston to Washington (Boswash), Chicago to Pittsburgh (Chipitts), and San Francisco to San Diego (Sansan) would define the cultural atti-

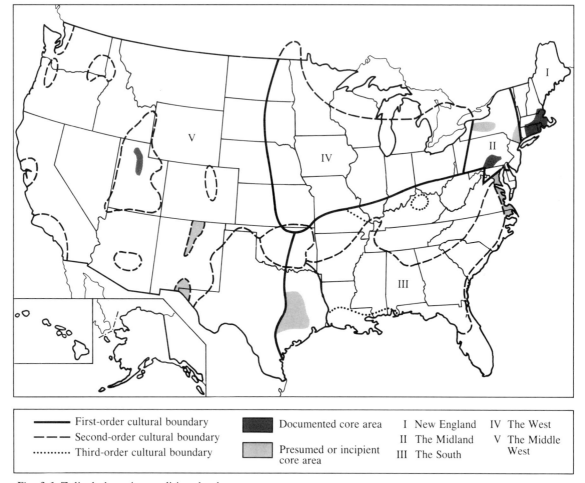

Fig. 3.1 Zelinsky's major traditional culture areas
Source: Zelinsky (1973), p. 118

tudes and perceptions of the entire nation. The accuracy of Kahn's prediction has been questioned, however, in view of recent trends towards the decentralization of business and politics (Naisbitt 1984). In writing of the post-industrial/information society of the 1980s, Naisbitt points out that 'Americans are spreading out to small towns and rural areas and leaving the old industrial cities as decaying monuments to a past civilization. As we decentralize, we diversify and tend to stress our differences instead of our similarities' (Naisbitt 1984: 104). In rejecting the notion that the US is a homogeneous nation, Naisbitt points to social indicators, such as variations in attitudes

towards abortion and homosexuality, and he identifies a new economic regionalism based on energy as a key commodity.

The study of regionalism: the vernacular landscape

According to Michael Steiner, 'regionalism implies both the systematic study of areal variations and the sense of identity that persons have with a portion of the earth which they inhabit' (Steiner 1983: 432). The interest of intellectuals in the study of regionalism was particularly pronounced during the Great

Depression when such influential works as *The Great Plains* (1931) by Walter Prescott Webb and *American Regionalism* (1938) by Howard Odum and Harry E. Moore were published. Steiner relates the search during the 1930s for 'regional order, certainty, and security in the indigenous, the communal, and the past' to the 'desire for a sense of place in a perilously dislocated world' (Steiner 1983: 434). Thus, the economic insecurity of the times produced a need for place-identity and rootedness within an historical tradition, which was in direct opposition to the heretofore unchallenged belief of Americans in progress and its guarantee of a bright and shining future. In attempting to identify with a sense of place, Americans developed an attachment to the land and an appreciation of folklore and local customs.

Cultural geographers interpreted this as a call to discover the true, primal America underlying the political and corporate divisions and to create 'a vernacular vision of American regionalism' (Steiner 1983: 431). Howard Odum and John K. Wright, among others, eschewed the standard classifications of regional theory and sought out the rich mosaic of vernacular landscapes as they existed 'in the minds of countless ordinary folk' (Wright 1947: 10). This work has been continued by geographers such as John Fraser Hart, Wilbur Zelinsky and Terry Jordan. Jordan, who has mapped and analysed the major vernacular regions of Texas, defines the perceptual/vernacular region as 'the product of the spatial perceptions of average people' and, as such, they are 'composites of the mental maps of the population' (Jordan 1978: 293).

With this in mind, Zelinsky has attempted to define North America's vernacular regions through an analysis of the frequency of selected regional and locational terms in the names of enterprises, as listed in telephone directories (Zelinsky 1980). Likewise, Hale has identified vernacular regions by the frequency with which place names appeared, using a survey (Hale 1984). Few of the names compiled by Hale, such as the 'little Egypt' region of Illinois, appear in standard atlases; nonetheless, they are well-known to the local residents.

The efforts of geographers to understand vernacular regions have been aided by studies which focus on particular aspects of the socio-cultural environment, including language (Mencken 1936), diet (Trillin 1978), music (Ford 1971; Carney 1980) and religion (Smith 1984). Smith's demographic analysis of the differences in moral views and political ideology among religious denominations, for example, provides basic information for the study of the influence of proportionally dominant groups on the attitudes and character of specific regions. In addition, a number of informative studies have focused on aspects of the built environment, such as vernacular architecture and settlement patterns, and have attempted to discover the regional characteristics of building types and construction techniques. These include Trewatha's study of farmsteads (1948); Glassie's study of barns as indices to early cultural identity (1968); and Hart's studies of field patterns (1968) and fences (Hart and Mather 1957). Kniffen (1965), in examining folk housing as a key to diffusion, identifies three principal culture hearths: New England; the Mid-Atlantic, centring on southeastern Pennsylvania; and the lower Chesapeake, centring on Tidewater Virginia. Through extensive field investigation and identification of regional housing types, he traces the westward movement of settlers from the source areas, beginning around 1790 and continuing until the mid-nineteenth century. In so doing, Kniffen shows that even the lowliest corn-crib can be a significant factor in describing cultural and vernacular regions.

A reference of studies dealing with the vernacular landscape would not be complete without mention of the works of J. B. Jackson (1972) and of the various literary observers who have hit the road in search of America, including Jack Kerouac (1957), John Steinbeck (1962), Studs Terkel (1980) and William Least Heat Moon (1982). These writers have provided an invaluable record of the personal histories, thoughts and dreams of the common folk on the backroads and 'blue highways' of America.

Classic cultural regions

Raymond Gastil (1975) defends the hypothesis that it is useful to divide the country into cultural regions, while noting that the boundaries given to regions vary from study to study, depending on what the author wishes to analyse. Though exact borders may differ, most geographers agree that a rigid adherence to State lines contributes to spurious ideas about cultural variation. As Garreau says of his definition of the 'nine nations' of North America: 'There are sharp differences in history, attitudes toward the land, prejudices, economics, and futures among these nations, and it's how these differences come together that defines their boundaries' (Garreau 1981: 66) (Fig. 3.2).

In the following examination, the designation of five 'classic' cultural regions (patterned on those of Zelinsky) is used in order to give an overview of the historical development, key landscape features, and values and attitudes

Fig. 3.2 Garreau's 'nine nations' of North America
Source: Garreau (1981)

towards the environment of areas which have been recognized and referred to throughout the nation's history. A knowledge of these classic cultural areas will be helpful in understanding regional responses to social and economic trends.

New England

Zelinsky divides the New England region into two parts: the northern zone comprised of Maine, Vermont and most of New Hampshire; and the southeastern, nuclear zone comprised primarily of Massachusetts, Connecticut and Rhode Island. During the century of expansion after the American Revolution, the latter subregion, with the Boston metropolitan area at its hub, vigorously exported its ideas along with its native sons to New York, northern New Jersey, northern Pennsylvania and much of the Upper Midwest, thus giving a strong New England character to these areas.

Traditionally, New England has exercised a powerful influence, disproportionate to its relatively small size, on the social and cultural life of the entire nation. As de Tocqueville commented in 1864: 'The principles of New England spread at first to the neighboring States, then passed successively to the more distant ones; and at length they imbued the whole Confederation. They now extend their influence beyond its limits over the whole American world' (de Tocqueville 1864: 33). Van Wyck Brooks has described the far-reaching cultural impact of the literary figures who contributed to the 'flowering of New England' from around 1815 to 1865. In essence, these writers believed that 'New England was appointed to guide the nation, to civilize it and humanize it' (Brooks 1936: 528); and this moralistic view of the region's role as 'a beacon lit upon a hill' (de Tocqueville 1864: 33) can be traced from the founding of the colony to contemporary times.

According to John Winthrop, Governor of Massachusetts Bay from 1630 to 1649, the Puritan settlers had entered into a covenant with the Almighty and had been assured of His blessing in founding a 'City upon a Hill', on which the eyes of all people would be fixed (Winthrop 1629: 5). Establishing a new colony was viewed as a divinely ordained mission and was synonymous with creating a model community, where truth – as the Puritan fathers saw it – would prevail over the moral chaos of the surrounding wilderness. As the affairs of daily life and of government were inseparable from religious convictions, Puritan New England represented 'a noble experiment in applied theology' (Boorstin 1958: 3).

The organization of the physical environment was also viewed by the Puritans as an expression of God's will. An anonymous essay of 1638, entitled 'The Ordering of Towns', described the ideal Puritan landscape of compact towns, each arranged to mirror a divinely sanctioned social hierarchy. Land should be assigned such that 'every man may have his due proportion, more or less according to his present or apparent future occasion of employment, and so the mean ones not be neglected' (reported in Stilgoe 1976: 4). At the centre of the ideal plan was the meetinghouse, representing the moral authority of those men of 'great estate' who were to guide the community. The houses of the townspeople were situated in a tight ring around the meetinghouse, proximity ensuring the safeguard of society's moral fibre; and beyond this were rings of common and private fields for planting and grazing.

Though no New England town replicated the neat, concentric scheme proposed in this essay, the ideal of nucleated village-farm units was adhered to, by and large, during the early period of settlement, when nearness to one's neighbour and communal endeavour were necessary for survival. 'So great was the diligence and industry of the New-England planters,' wrote Hannah Adams, 'that they had already settled [by 1642] fifty towns and villages . . . had furnished themselves with comfortable dwelling houses, had laid out gardens, orchards, cornfields, pastures, and meadows, and lived under the regular administration of their own government and laws' (Adams 1805, reported in Watkins 1976: 39).

The eighteenth-century New Englander, no longer content with the restrictive size of the originally assigned freeholds or with the concept of communally tended fields, sought to break away from the traditional settlement pattern. 'Husbandmen wanted larger and larger lots, both of arable and of meadow land, and they wanted to live on them to better supervise the livestock and crops and to avoid the long walk from the nucleus of houses. Most of all, however, they demanded an end to common fields and to relying on joint effort because innovation rewarded them with greater profits' (Stilgoe 1982: 47). Thus a growing individualism combined with the spirit of free enterprise to challenge the traditional forms of land apportionment and the communal control envisioned by the founders.

The original goal of establishing an agrarian community proved impossible to realize given the shallow, rocky soils of New England, and so the more individualistlc Yankee farmers began moving west shortly after the Revolution in search of fertile land. This exodus resulted in the decline of rural New England (Jackson 1972). As more farms were abandoned, the forest (two-thirds of which had been cleared by the 1830s) began gradually to re-emerge; and it is this second- or third-generation woodland, with its derelict stone fences, which has become associated with the image of New England.

Just as the nineteenth-century Bostonian had come to view the forest in terms of its scenic qualities, so countless vacationers today – the 'Summer People', the 'Leaf Freaks', *et al.* – continue to seek out picturesque backdrops which recall a pre-industrial past. It should be noted that New England, which is heir to the ideas of Thoreau and G. P. Marsh, has a liberal record with regard to environmental issues, and this has been viewed sceptically by other parts of the country as indicative of an elitist – Eastern – view of nature.

Of course, the cultural landscape of New England is not adequately represented by a bucolic view of stone fences and sugar maples. Mercantilism and manufacturing flourished during the nineteenth century in the Boston area, and it was in river towns, such as Waltham and Worcester, that the first factories were built. Lowell, Massachusetts, the country's first factory town, was begun in 1822 and remained a major textile centre for over a century. The original social organization and physical layout of the town epitomized the paternalistic tradition of New England: the factory owner had a moral obligation to provide for the needs of the workers and of the community. Thus, Lowell can be viewed as a

socio-economic experiment in creating a unique living and working environment – another model community on which the eyes of all people would be fixed. However, the philanthropic ideals which governed Lowell proved to be the exception. More typical of the new type of manufacturing town was Lynn, Massachusetts, with its cheap housing for the newly arrived immigrants and its dirty, coal-powered factories.

However, not only did the New England environment lack soils suitable for agriculture, it also lacked the raw materials, particularly iron ore and coal, necessary for new forms of twentieth-century industry. This, among other reasons, accounts for the decline of manufacturing in New England over the past hundred years and the consequent economic plight of many former mill towns, such as North Adams (Mass.) and Manchester (N.H.). How then has New England continued to be a viable and, for many, desirable place to live?

First of all, despite the region's social and economic problems, it is still perceived as having a monopoly on the nation's educational institutions (Harvard College founded 1636) and on its humanistic traditions; and this accounts for a certain sense of cultural and moral superiority. In addition, New England, though restricted in size and natural resources, has been able to capitalize on its primary physical asset, the scenery and the historical associations it evokes, to attract tourism and the second-home industry. To the list of small towns and villages where the region's history and traditions have been preserved (Sturbridge Village, Shaker Village) one can now add Lowell, which in the late 1970s was revitalized or 'recycled' as an Urban Cultural Park. Paradoxically, in preserving remnants of the early industrial landscape, New England has shown itself to be in the vanguard. In fact, a case can be made that 'New England is rapidly transforming itself into North America's first truly twenty-first-century, postindustrial society, and, as such, it is again a land of pioneers' (Garreau 1981: 19).

The South

The South has been operationally defined as the eleven ex-Confederate States, including

Oklahoma, with parts of the border States of Kentucky, West Virginia, Maryland and Missouri sometimes included in the definition. Much recent discussion has centred on whether Florida and Texas, in view of their tremendous economic growth and influx of new immigrants (Hispanic and Mexican), belong to the heart of Dixie.

The uniqueness of southern folk culture and its separateness from mainstream America have been studied by a variety of scholars, among them Olmsted (1860), Odum (1936), Cash (1941), Hart (1967) and Reed (1972, 1982). More than any other classic culture region, the South has been distinguished by a strong sense of regional identity, viewed by Reed as an ethnocentric attachment to place. Zelinsky notes: 'The South has been so distinct from the non-South in almost every observable or quantifiable feature and so fiercely jealous of its peculiarities that for some years the question of whether it could maintain political and social unity with the non-South was in serious doubt' (Zelinsky 1973: 122).

The need to protect a peculiar institution, slavery, from outside forces regarded as hostile to the southern way of life and the consequent experience of war, defeat and reconstruction enforced regional ties. As a popular song reminded the Confederate soldier: 'We are a band of brothers, and native to the soil,/Fighting for the property we gained by honest toil;/And when our rights were threatened, the cry rose near and far/Hurrah for the bonnie Blue Flag that bears a single star!' (McCarthy 1861, reported in Commager 1973: 555).

Watson (1976) points out that the marked cultural and political differences between the North and the South cannot be attributed to the condition of the native soil, *per se*. More significantly, they are the result of the way in which specific geographical conditions were perceived and the imprint of these perceptions, or 'mental images', on the landscape. The belief that the climate was hard on the white race was frequently used to explain, if not justify, slavery. In fact, the plantation proprietors shunned physical work because of an attitude towards manual labour which distinguished the landed gentry of the South from the industrious, public-spirited Puritans of New England. While the Puritan, in breaking

away from the Church of England, emphasized community endeavour and self-governance, the southern gentleman sought to perpetuate English traditions and institutions, in particular the feudal manor system. As we indicate in Chapter 4, the South continues to be dominated by a 'traditional culture' with roots in the plantation-based agricultural system. The political legacy of the South is inherently conservative and paternalist, based as it is on the rule of a one-party elite determined to maintain the status quo of white/Anglo-Saxon supremacy and to defend, sometimes through the private use of force, the traditional values of the South.

During the eighteenth century, the southern aristocracy accumulated large landholdings, averaging 2000 hectares in 1732, and, in so doing, established a system of autonomous plantations based on the use of slave labour and the production of a single cash crop. The focus of the plantation, each of which was a small world unto itself, was the 'Big House' of the master, subordinate to which were a number of outbuildings for farming and basic services and, of course, the slave quarters. Mount Vernon and Monticello, the homes of Washington and Jefferson, respectively, are two examples of prestigious Tidewater plantations that accommodated slavery: 'The pattern of land subdivision, the siting and arrangement of buildings in the landscape, the circulation between rooms in the big house, the garden and the quarters . . . all indicate a grappling with the peculiar institution and its social implications' (Anthony 1976: 17). The basic characteristics of the plantation were also influenced by local building traditions and the requirements of the cash crop, and thus vernacular differences can be found, for example, between the South Carolina rice and the Louisiana sugar cane plantations. However, the romanticized image of the Big House with its white columns has come to represent the hierarchical and racist social structure of the ante-bellum South.

The accessible location of the eighteenth-century plantation along the navigable tidewaters assured the direct contact of the plantation owner with the European market and, in so doing, undermined the need for centralized port towns. In addition, the small subsistence farms of a yeoman class of independent farmers, many of whom were formerly indentured servants, were scattered irregularly across the back country, with only a church or a cross-roads store to mark a meetingplace and, therefore, did not contribute significantly to the creation of villages or towns. As indicated, Jefferson approved of this diffused pattern of settlement in that it assured a rural way of life.

The plantation system, however, proved to be ecologically destructive because of poor agricultural practices, particularly the reliance on mono-cropping (Ch. 6). Instead of reinvesting in the land, as was common in European agricultural societies, the Southerner simply abandoned the old, worn-out fields in favour of the cheap lands to the west. Stilgoe, in commenting on the scene of desolated farms to be found in the South at the end of the eighteenth century, writes:

. . . the fear of that blighted landscape spreading over the fertile, virgin land coveted by westward-moving northerners sparked strident criticism throughout the pre-Civil War years. Outsiders focused their anger on abused slaves and eroded, abandoned fields, but the very alienness of the southern landscape unnerved them more. Even Pennsylvanians unaccustomed to villages or nucleated towns wondered at abandoned plantations and acres of brush (Stilgoe 1983: 77).

Despite the progressive deterioration of the southern garden, the South continued to be a society of agriculturalists, with wealth and land concentrated in the hands of a few, while the North converted to meet the needs of the Industrial Age. In 1850 the South, with about 40 per cent of the US population, was producing less than 14 per cent of the manufactured goods. After the Civil War, which devastated the economy and the countryside, King Cotton was enthroned once again, thus contributing to the further depletion of the soil. The large plantations were divided up between tenant farmers and share croppers, who eked out a meagre existence from the exhausted land.

The history of the South since the Civil War has been basically one of trying to catch up to the rest of the country in terms of economic growth and development. In the past 25 years the South has begun to shed its image of being predominantly poor and rural, as testified to by Atlanta, Georgia, which grew from a hilltop railroad station in the 1830s to a city of nearly 22 000 in 1870, and which today boasts a booming downtown with a glittering array of the latest in corporate architecture. In addition, southern whites, though still distinguished from the rest of the country by diet, accent, and the religious uniformity of the 'Bible Belt', have done much to overcome the stereotype of the uneducated, intolerant 'cracker'. In fact, the changes in the social and physical landscape of the South have been so pronounced that some interpret this as a trend towards the 'Americanization of Dixie':

the South and the nation seem to be in many ways imitating the worse in each other, exporting vices without importing virtues; there is no spiritual or cultural or social balance of payments. The South is becoming more urban, less overtly racist, less self-conscious and defensive, more affluent – and more uncritically accepting of the ways of the North. And the North, for its part, seems more overtly racist than it had been; shorn of its pretensions of moral innocence, it is exhibiting many of the attitudes that once were thought to be the exclusive possessions of white Southerners (Egerton 1974: 18–19).

Nonetheless, clear indications have also been noted of the cultural intactness of the South, its ability to endure and persist as a distinctly perceived cultural region, despite the pressures of mass society (Reed 1972). A good example of this is provided by country music, with its distinctive instruments (dulcimer, fiddle, banjo, guitar), lyrics (sentimental, chauvinist, individualistic, anti-urbane) and singing style (nasal). Though the 'country pop' of Chet Atkins, Floyd Cramer, Johnny Cash, Loretta Lynn and Merle Haggard and the 'country rock' of Alabama, Carl Perkins, Willie Nelson, Waylon Jennings and Jerry Jeff ('Up Against the Wall Redneck Mother') Walker have successfully been exported to the rest of the nation, country music in general – from the 'traditional' variety revived recently by the Front Porch String Band to the 'singing cowboy' music of Gene Autry and Tex Ritter, the 'honky tonk' of Ray Price and Buck Owens, the 'bluegrass' sound of the Blue Grass Boys, the 'western swing' of Asleep at the Wheel and the Original Texas Playboys, and the more recent country pop and country rock – is a 'major cultural element' in the South (Carney 1980), reflecting, maintaining and projecting the region's image of itself.

The Mid-Atlantic

The Mid-Atlantic region is composed of New York, New Jersey, Pennsylvania and the northern parts of Maryland (the Baltimore area) and Delaware (the Wilmington area); and thus it is the last of the classic culture regions to fall within the original thirteen colonies. Zelinsky says of the Mid-Atlantic: 'As both the name and the location would suggest, [it] is intermediate in character in many respects between New England and the South. Moreover, its residents are much less concerned with, or conscious of, its existence' (Zelinsky 1973: 128). In addition, Zelinsky indicates the problem of identifying this region on the basis of 'first effective settlement', as it was characterized from early colonial times by its ethnic diversity.

Shortly after colonization by William Penn and his Quaker associates, the southeastern Pennsylvania subregion around Philadelphia became the locus of a flourishing agricultural society consisting of large, independent farms. This situation was in contrast to New York, where a system of feudal land tenures established by the Dutch and continued by the English made obtaining land difficult and, in so doing, held up the settlement of the northern hinterland. By the mid-eighteenth century, Philadelphia and New York were established as the social and economic centres of their respective subregions and as major port cities for the trade and commercial activities of the colonies. In 1817 work began on the Erie Canal connecting the Hudson River at Albany to Lake Erie at Buffalo. This opened upstate New York to settlement and provided New York City with a direct link to the lands west of the Appalachian frontier. With a strategic location at the end of a major east–west transportation route for shipping and passenger travel, New York City soon displaced Philadelphia as the largest and wealthiest city in the country, thereby gaining a primacy it never lost (Gastil 1975).

Indeed, New York maintained a grip not only on the economy of a rapidly industrializing nation, but also on its social and cultural life.

Although the New Yorker's view of the city as the focal point of the nation (or centre of the universe) is often resented by non-New Yorkers, the importance of the city in setting trends and marketing an image should not be underestimated. The lifestyle and mentality of the New Yorker, along with the physical environment of the city, are certainly not representative of the nation as a whole. However, the image of the Statue of Liberty against the New York skyline has come to stand for the American Dream: the promise of a land of plenty assured by the twin agents of Democracy and Progress.

By the end of the nineteenth century the Mid-Atlantic region had become the industrial heartland of the nation. Pennsylvania, once an agricultural oasis, became the centre of the iron and steel industries, and the eastern part of the State was dotted by mining and manufacturing towns, such as Scranton and Allentown. Western Pennsylvania was dominated by Pittsburgh, the epitome of the new order of industrial cities, with the immigrant factory worker at one end of the socio-economic scale and the giants of industry, such as Andrew Carnegie, at the other.

The Manufacturing Belt

Pittsburgh is, in fact, a border city between the Mid-Atlantic region and the Midwest, and the argument can be made that here the traditional approach to regionalization breaks down. More informative are studies which consider the Mid-Atlantic and the part of the Midwest including Ohio, with its concentration of industrial cities (Cleveland, Columbus, Cincinnati, Akron, Dayton, Toledo and Youngstown), and the areas around the Great Lake cities of Detroit, Chicago, Gary and Milwaukee as part of the 'Manufacturing Belt' (see Ch. 5). The economic success of iron and steel industries in the Manufacturing Belt attracted immigrants from Europe and blacks from the rural South, all of whom, theoretically, came together in the urban melting pot. This economic region, though not without agricultural areas, is characterized by its cities which, by the standards of the nation, are relatively close together, densely populated, and ethnically and racially mixed.

The economic decline of the nation's smoke-stack industries during the 1970s, and the concurrent boom of high-tech industries in the southern and western States, have had a significant impact on the cities of the Manufacturing Belt. Once viewed as the sturdy backbone of America's industrial development and economic prosperity, cities such as Gary, Cleveland, Buffalo and Trenton are now associated with the dirt and decay of an ageing industrial apparatus. The economic plight of these cities, of course, is reflected in the social environment. As Garreau points out, the Manufacturing Belt/Foundry 'is still struggling with its historic role as the integrator of wildly different personalities and cultures and ethnic groups, and there is no assurance that the sociological battles that it has been assigned will end in victory' (Garreau 1981: 65). Thus, a region which, historically, has been the hearth of America's technological prowess has had to face an uncertain, if not bleak, future.

In an effort to revamp the region's image as the 'Rustbelt' of America, the older manufacturing cities have undertaken programmes to revitalize deteriorated downtowns and modernize outdated facilities. This has required a renewed commitment of political will and of public faith, which can be illustrated best by the 'I Love New York' promotional campaign – a direct response to the threatened bankruptcy of the city in the 1970s. Other cities have attempted to polish up grimy downtown areas through the partnership of public funds and private enterprise (see Ch. 7). Detroit's Renaissance Center was also intended by its planners to be a symbol of economic resurgence; however, in light of the auto industry's financial woes, it appears now to be rather pretentious.

More typical of the area is Hamtramck, Michigan, which was devastated when Chrysler shut down its Dodge plant in 1980 throwing 2925 people out of work. The smaller steel-making cities have a similarly grim story to tell: in 1977, Campbell Steel Works closed its Youngstown, Ohio, plant eliminating 10 000 jobs; in 1982 Bethlehem Steel closed in Lackawana, N Y, near Buffalo eliminating 7300 jobs; and US Steel announced plans in 1984 to close down operations in such renowned Big Steel locations as Gary, Indiana, Fairless and Homestead, Pennsylvania, and the South

Works in Chicago. It is these secondary cities of the Manufacturing Belt which have been particularly hard hit and which, taken together, present a distressing view of a landscape in decline. While major cities, particularly New York and Chicago, have been able to retain their positions, consolidated during earlier phases of economic development, as important 'control centres' for business and finance (see Ch. 5), the smaller cities of the Mid-Atlantic and the industrial Midwest seem to have been passed by, much as were the New England mill towns of the early twentieth century.

Thus, the changing economic geography of the US has called into question the cultural identity of a region whose characteristics are so strongly linked with its historic role as industrial heartland and economic backbone of the nation. Uncertain of its place in the national economy and defensive in regard to the rise of the Sunbelt, the region is labouring to adapt itself to new technologies and market conditions and, in so doing, to create a vigorous new image of itself.

The Midwest

While much of the Midwest has been classified, along with the Northeast, as part of America's Manufacturing Belt, a strong case can be made for its definition according to psychological rather than economic criteria for, as Brownell (1960) has indicated, this section of the country can stand as a region only in a cultural sense. According to Zelinsky, 'Everyone within or outside the Middle West knows of its existence, but no one seems sure where it begins or ends. The older apex of the eastward-pointing equilateral triangle appears to rest in the vicinity of Pittsburgh, and the two western corners melt away somewhere in the Great Plains, possibly southern Manitoba and southern Kansas' (Zelinsky 1973: 128). In terms of its historical geography, the Midwest, and specifically the Upper Ohio Valley, can be viewed as a funnel which brought together the people and cultural traits of the three eastern hearth areas, with New England and the Mid-Atlantic particularly influential in the settlement of the Upper Midwest (as divided by the forty-first parallel) and the South in the Lower (Zelinsky 1973).

Jackson ascribes the first wide usage of the

term 'Midwest' to define the territory between the Appalachians, the Ohio to the south and the Mississippi to the west to the period after the Civil War. He further notes:

It had from the start far more than a geographical significance; it meant the heartland of the United States, the moral and social epicenter of the nation. With half the population, more than half of its agricultural activity, and a proud record of having given more than its share of wealth and men to the Union cause, the Midwest had entirely outgrown its frontier status and had acquired an exhilarating sense of its own identity (Jackson 1972: 58).

This sense of regional identity, which is strongly related to the image of the Midwest as a mediator between the extremes of Eastern and Western culture, has persisted in the minds of Midwesterners. On the basis of responses to a questionnaire sent to postmasters of 536 communities selected along several arbitrary radii extending for hundreds of miles in all directions from Chicago, a city universally accepted as Midwestern, Brownell has identified a central core:

Outlined by county boundaries, it spreads over all or nearly all of Ohio, Indiana, Illinois, Wisconsin, Minnesota, Iowa, Missouri, North Dakota, South Dakota, Nebraska and Kansas. It also includes the greater part of Michigan and significant portions of Oklahoma. The cultural region contains approximately 20 per cent of the land area of the continental United States lying largely in the Mississippi River drainage basin (Brownell 1960: 82) (Fig. 3.3).

Hart (1972) indicates an important division of the urban/industrial Midwest, that is the part

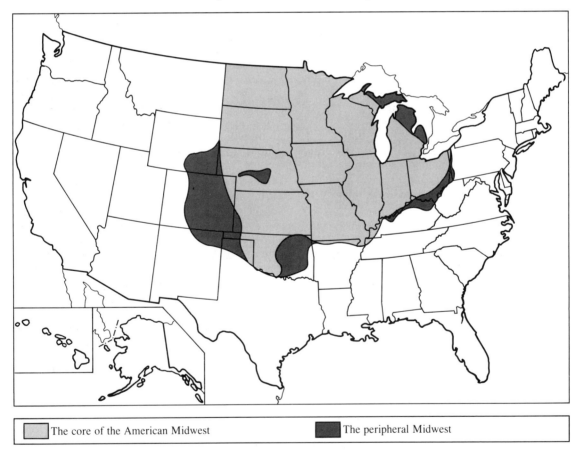

| | The core of the American Midwest | | The peripheral Midwest |

Fig. 3.3 Brownell's definition of the cultural Midwest
Source: Brownell (1960), p. 83

that lies within the Manufacturing Belt. The Indiana–Illinois line divides the area into an eastern district dominated by Detroit and the automobile industry and a western district dominated by agriculturally related industries such as food processing and manufacturing of farm machinery. In fact, the western district can be viewed as an enormous farm service centre meeting the needs of the prosperous agricultural areas of the Midwest. These include America's Dairyland (Michigan and Wisconsin) and the Wheat and Corn Belts (Minnesota, Illinois, Kansas, Nebraska and the Dakotas).

As we shall see, the Midwest, which is favoured with climatic and soil conditions ideally suited for grain and livestock production, has developed into one of the world's richest agricultural areas. The development of new farm technologies after the Civil War enabled settlers to take advantage of the extremely fertile, but tightly packed and poorly drained, soil of the prairie and, as a result, this vast, flat expanse of grassland became part of the realization of a Great American Garden. We shall also see that the image of the 'typical' American farm is based on the Midwestern stereotype of relatively small-scale, family-operated farmsteads, despite the fact that the traditional character of farming in the Midwest has been radically changed by agribusiness. Likewise, it is the image of the cheerful, prosperous and predominantly rural, small towns of the Midwest, such as the Winesburg, Ohio, of Sherwood Anderson, which is associated with the region and with the 'real' America, despite the economic realities of the urbanized Midwest described in the preceding section.

The persistence of these images, in view of the changes wrought in the cultural and physical landscape of the Midwest during the twentieth century, indicates how strongly the region has come to be associated with a traditional set of values. While the Land Survey Ordinance of 1785 left its imprint on the agricultural landscape of the Midwest, the Jeffersonian notion of a virtuous agrarian society left its imprint on the minds of Midwesterners, who believe that they, alone, are most true to the beliefs and standards of the Republic. This adherence to oldtime virtues is alternately admired as representative of the best in America and disdained as a form of provincialism by those outside the region.

The West

Although there have been disagreements concerning where the West really begins, the 100th meridian (or any longitudinal line between 96 and 100) is often used as a starting point. The lands west of this line have been divided into various subregions, according to the viewpoints of respective geographers. Zelinsky divides the western US into four major tracts that reveal genuine cultural identity: the Upper Rio Grande region, the Mormon region, Southern California, and Central California. Of these, the Southern California region is the most spectacular 'not only in terms of economic and population growth, but also for the luxuriance, regional particularism and general avant-garde character of its swiftly evolving cultural pattern'; and, as such, it is 'the outpost of a rapidly approaching post-industrial future' (Zelinsky 1973: 132). Gastil (1975) divides the West into the following cultural regions: Rocky Mountain, Mormon, Interior Southwest, Pacific Southwest, Pacific Northwest, and parts of the Central and Upper Midwest (Fig. 3.4). In all studies there seems to be agreement that the Mormons who, under the leadership of Brigham Young settled in the Great Basin in 1847, were unique in their ability to adapt to environmental constraints and to maintain cultural separateness and that the Mormon region of Utah today is the most homogeneous of all American cultural areas (Meinig 1965).

The use of the 100th meridian as a dividing line between East and West is not as arbitrary as it may seem. West of the meridian, the average rainfall is less than 51 centimetres (20 inches) and therefore the climate in this part of the US, except for a strip along the Pacific shore from northern California to southern Alaska, ranges from semi-arid to arid. In addition, the 100th meridian roughly marks a change in physical geography: the low-lying prairie lands east of the line give way to the high plains, which rise to over 610 metres (2000 feet).

It was the Great Plains region of the West that constituted the major portion of the Great

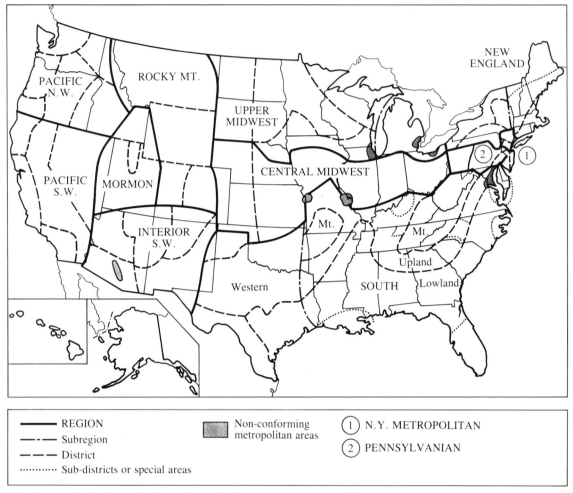

Fig. 3.4 Gastil's cultural regions
Source: Gastil (1975), p. 29

American Desert, so named in 1820 by the explorer, Stephen H. Long. Originally, the myth of a Great American Desert included the area from the Mississippi Valley to the eastern slope of the Rockies, and thus included portions of the more humid prairie states of Kansas, Nebraska, Oklahoma and Iowa, which today are part of America's Wheat Belt. The illusion that much of the American interior consisted of a vast desert was due, in part, to the scarcity of trees on the Great Plains, which suggested to those from the forested eastern part of the country that the soil was barren (Webb 1931). Edwin James, the geographer of

the Long expedition, did not hestitate to conclude that the region 'is almost wholly unfit for cultivation, and of course uninhabitable by a people depending upon agriculture for their existence' (James 1819, reported in Brown 1948: 552).

Though the geographic knowledge provided by future explorations eventually pushed the boundary of a desert region further west, the Plains were still considered in the 1850s as something to get across on the way to more promising areas, such as the Oregon Country. In fact, they were viewed as worthless enough to be assigned to the Indians as part of the resettlement process. Thus, the agricultural frontier bypassed the vast interior of America for the Pacific coast.

The development of the cattle industry, which began when the grasslands of the Great Plains were found to be suitable for raising livestock, is the history of ruthless exploitation of the public domain. The practices of the open range, where cattle roamed freely on unfenced public land, led to overgrazing, especially in areas contiguous to water supplies, and consequently to the destruction of the protective plant cover. This problem was finally addressed in 1934 with the passage of the Taylor Grazing Act, which closed the public domain and provided protection for millions of hectares of grassland.

The invasion of agriculture on to the cattleman's turf began with the invention of the chilled steel plough, the first instrument capable of breaking through the tough prairie sod. The use of barbed wire fences by farmers, beginning in 1874, changed the land-use patterns of the Plains by cutting up the open range and restricting the movement of cattle. The attempts of farmers to transform the Great American Desert into the Great American Garden did not succeed, however, until the end of the nineteenth century with the development of dry farming methods and drought-resistant crops and, in particular, with the establishment of interstate irrigation projects.

The actual desert region of the US has been defined by Hollon (1966) as including the arid western portion of the Great Plains, the Rocky Mountain region and the Great Basin (Fig. 3.5). The heart of this American desert includes: Montana, Wyoming, Colorado, New Mexico, Arizona, Utah, Idaho, Nevada, southern California and southwestern Texas; and it is in these States, more than in any other, that water is a political and economic issue. According to Garreau, the entire region of MexAmerica in the southwest corner of the country is obsessed with two basic questions: 'Where will the water come from to allow industry to expand, food to be grown, and subdivisions to be built? And where will the power come from to keep the climate and the immense distances at bay?' (Garreau 1981: 221).

Despite the lack of water in the Southwest,

this area is surpassing the rest of the country in economic growth and its two major cities, Houston and Los Angeles, are world leaders in such fields as energy, electronics, aerospace, construction and finance. The cities of the Southwest have a brand-newness in common, reflected in their flashy architecture, sprawling character, and devotion to the air-conditioner and the automobile. Los Angeles, with a population of almost three million within 805 square kilometres (500 square miles), is called a city but 'is, in fact, an immense post-urban process, the tentative validation of a concept New York only hints at and Cleveland or Des Moines doesn't dare to express' (Gold 1981: 25). The Southwestern cities have had to pay the price, however, for such phenomenal growth and development. Foremost among their urban ills are pollution, with Los Angeles leading the way as the 'Smog Capital' of the country, and crime, with Houston competing for the title of 'Murder Capital'. What sets these places apart from up-and-coming cities in other regions is the distinct blend of Mexican and American cultures, which is especially evident in language and lifestyles.

The Northwest, which includes Utah, Colorado, Idaho, Wyoming, Montana, Washington and Oregon, epitomizes most of the ideas and images of the frontier West. The western ranching subculture of this area, 'the source of America's most powerful and pervasive myths of freedom, democracy, romance and brutality, still retains much of its traditional character' (Robbins 1984: 82). However, it is a region convulsed with the changes brought about by a shift in land ownership from family-owned ranches and farms to large, corporate, absentee-owned parcels, as well as by high interest rates, rising land prices and a slumping livestock market.

With its extensive ranch and farmlands, its generous endowment of national parks and its low population density, this is still a region of wide open spaces and spectacular vistas. The natural beauty of the region is threatened, however, by the abundance of its resources: coal and oil vital to energy production, and metals and minerals necessary for twentieth- and twenty-first-century industries. Vast acreages of the rural West have now been over-

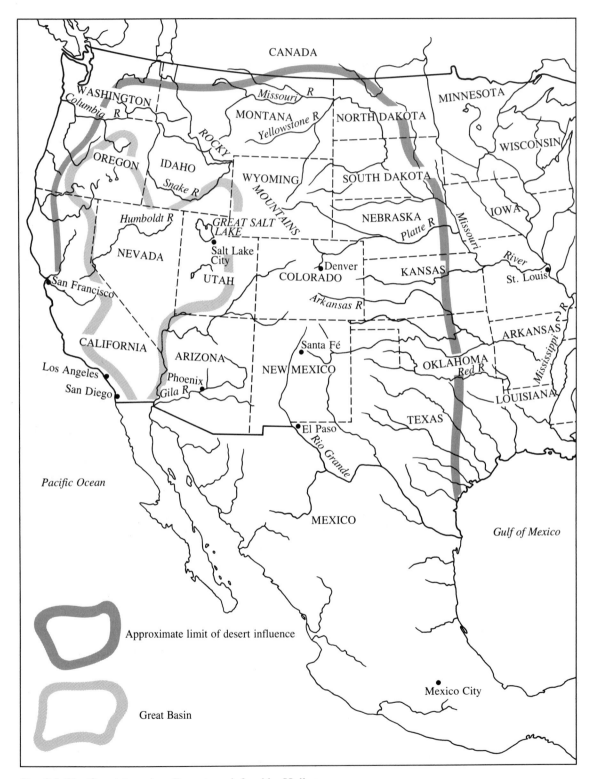

Fig. 3.5 The Great American Desert, as defined by Hollon
Source: Hollon (1966), p. 2

taken and radically altered by strip-mining operations; and State and local governments, in what is known as the Sagebrush Rebellion, are attempting to gain more control of these reserves from the federal government, which owns and controls the vast portion of resource-rich land, to sell or lease to corporations. According to a 1983 report for the Western Governors' Conference, approximately 2400 square kilometres (1500 square miles) of ranch-land in the Rocky Mountain States will be removed from production by the year 2000. Michael S. Clark of the Northern Lights Institute, a non-profit group which has studied the social and political issues related to development of the region's natural resources, has commented:

If ranch land in the West is used solely as a cheap source for coal, or as tax havens and playgrounds for the rich, this nation will lose one of its most valuable assets – an accumulated knowledge that has been built up over the past 100 years by ranch families who see this region as their home, ranching as an integrated way of life and the future as something they can pass on in a concrete way to their children and grandchildren (reported in Robbins 1984: 84).

Indeed, the future of this region will be determined largely by the outcome of debates over resource development and conservation.

Alaska

Though both Hawaii and Alaska, by virtue of their isolated locations, unique ethnic origins and relatively late statehood, do not fall into the definition of *classic* culture areas, they along with major subregions, such as the Mormon district, need to be identified as an important part of the cultural geography of the US. The remainder of this study will deal briefly with Alaska, whose history dramatically illustrates the old battle between frontier-style development and environmental conservation.

When Alaska was acquired from Russia in 1867, the 152 million hectare (375 million acre) purchase was believed to consist largely of a frozen wasteland referred to as 'Seward's Icebox' or 'Seward's Folly' after the Secretary of State who arranged the purchase. The Klondike Gold Rush of 1898 raised hopes that Alaska might provide the nation with more

than salmon and sealskins; however, the boom was short-lived. Up until statehood was declared in 1958, fishing, hunting and forestry were the major sources of income, and formed the basis of a subsistence economy for many natives and homesteaders. This pioneer way of life, seen as a last opportunity to live out the frontier dreams of rugged individualism and self-reliance, attracted an influx of twentieth-century settlers from the forty-eight States. Nonetheless, Alaska remained underpopulated, as shown by the fact that in 1976 there were 400 000 residents of a State one-fifth as large as the coterminous US. Also, it is important to point out that less than 1 per cent of Alaska is privately owned, with the bulk divided among the State, the native tribes and the federal government, which operates the lion's share.

The 1968 report of the Atlantic Richfield Company, which confirmed opinions that enormous reserves of oil exist beneath the north-eastern Alaskan shore around Prudhoe Bay, reversed the popular image of Alaska as an arctic wilderness of little economic value (O'Riordan 1976). With oil and mineral companies lining up for development rights, it became necessary first to settle long-standing claims of the State and of Alaskan natives to extensive portions of the federally controlled lands. The Alaskan Native Claims Settlement Act of 1971 gave 16 million hectares (40 million acres) and $1000 million to approximately 60 000 natives composed of Eskimos, Indians and Aleuts, who established corporations to hold and invest the new wealth. John McPhee says of this historic legislation:

. . . it not only changed forever the status and much of the structure of native societies; it opened the way to the Trans-Alaska Pipeline, which is only the first of many big-scale projects envisioned by development-minded Alaskans and, like a jewel cutter's chisel cleaving a rough diamond, it effected the wholesale division, subdivision, patenting, parcelling, and deeding out of physiographic Alaska (McPhee 1976: 18).

Though there is some disagreement within the State concerning the extent of development which should be allowed in the future, Alaskans, by and large, agree that they, rather than the federal government, should control the State's natural resources. The pro-development interests have been frustrated in the past (for example, delays in the building of the Trans-Alaska Pipeline in the 1970s) by national conservation groups which have brought pressure on Washington to restrict the sale and use of Alaska's resource-rich lands. The Alaska National Interest Land Conservation Act of 1980, whose provisions strictly govern the use of about one-third of the State, has been bitterly protested by Alaskans resentful of the interference of 'outsiders'. This has produced a tension in Alaskan society comparable to the divisiveness caused in frontier days by such matters as grazing and water rights. It is the tension of 'preservation versus development, of stasis versus economic productivity, of wilderness versus the drill and the bulldozer' (McPhee 1976: 79); and, as such, it is a significant factor in the scramble for land in a region once characterized by an awesome sense of spaciousness.

Conclusion

In conclusion, it is interesting to note that both environmentalists, who advocate setting aside large portions of undeveloped land for conservation purposes, and pro-development interests, who believe that it is unfair to lock up land which could provide needed revenues and energy resources, claim to be anticipating the needs of coming generations. The issue of nuclear power highlights the controversial nature of providing for America's future. The history of the nuclear power industry shows that the postwar faith in the seemingly boundless potential of technology for improving the standard of living and, by extension, the quality of life, caused America to leap into the Nuclear Age without fully considering the possible consequences. Accidents, such as those at the Brown's Ferry reactor (1975), which gave birth to the anti-nuclear movement, and at Three Mile Island (1979), which intensified opposition, make clear that a simplistic view of progress is a dangerous one.

Back in the eighteenth century that quintessential farmer, St. John de Crèvecoeur, defined Americans as a 'race of men, whose labours and posterity will one day cause great changes in the world' (Crèvecoeur 1782: 43). Although the prophecy undoubtedly has been fulfilled, the US is now in a position where it must question the nature of these changes in order to set responsible goals for the future. In so doing, the basic attitudes outlined in this chapter, among them the belief that technological progress is inevitably beneficial and that an affluent society can afford to be wasteful, must be examined in terms of their effect upon the physical and social environment of America.

Chapter **4**

THE POLITICAL ORGANIZATION OF US SPACE

The study of any modern society is substantially incomplete – indeed, fatally flawed – if it ignores the manifold and key roles of the state. Even in the US, with its strong belief in the capitalist system and the unfettered operation of market forces, the state is one of the largest institutions. It employed some 16 million civilians in 1983 (there were 2.1 million in the military), and total government expenditure was $1360 billion (UK = $1.3 billion) (60 per cent by the federal government, 18 per cent by the States, and 22 per cent by local governments): some 42.5 per cent of the Gross National Product.

Although simple statistics such as those quoted above give a quantitative impression of the extent of state activity, they do not reveal the full extent of the state's role in American society. Clearly, in terms of the geography of the country, such a large employer and spender must make decisions that affect virtually all aspects of local economic and social environments, and thus individual life chances; the geography of 'what the state does, where'. But this is not all. The state undertakes many roles within society that influence its geography not simply through the provision of job opportunities or the expenditure of state grants, but also by its implication in the manipulation of individual rights and freedoms associated with the ownership and use of land, and by its participation in the creation and maintenance of society's ideology.

To study the activities of the state, it is necessary therefore to appreciate what it is and why it fulfils its various roles, which involves a theoretical understanding. This is necessary for the study of any particular state, but it is not sufficient. The theory of the state, as currently developed, is not a predictive theory in the sense that applies to, say, central place theory or von Thünen's agricultural land use theory. It indicates *what* the state must do, but cannot say *how* it will do it: the former are general imperatives but the latter are contingent upon specific interpretations by people with the relevant decision-making power at the appropriate time and place (Johnston 1982a; Clark and Dear 1984). Such individuals do not operate in a vacuum, but rather in the cultural context within which they have been socialized. Different cultures – including regional cultures – have developed their own separate ideologies of the state and state action, which influence how decisions are made within the state apparatus.

To understand the political organization of US space, therefore, it is necessary to appreciate, first, the nature of the state as a theoretical concept and, secondly, local interpretations of how the state should be operated. These two topics are the subject of the first sections of this chapter. Given that context, the remainder of the chapter illustrates the state in action. Two themes are stressed. The first is the political manipulation of space (a fundamental resource in American society, as we have seen) for economic, social and political goals. The second is 'space in the political process', illustrating how the geography of the country and its component parts is deeply implicated in the activities of governments.

The nature of the state

The state comprises a set of institutions, created to promote and oversee activities within the territory over which it exercises *de jure* sovereignty. It is necessary to the operations of society, and the nature of its institutions reflects the form of the society. For the study of the state in the US, one need focus on only one type of society and state (although it must be recognized that the details of the American state, as they were established after the Declaration of Independence, reflected a reaction against the states typical of northwestern Europe at that time).

American society is dominated by the capitalist mode of production. The term 'mode of production' refers to the ways in which surplus is produced and used within a society; a surplus is production extra to that which is retained by the producer, and the destination and use of the surplus determines the rate and nature of growth and change within the society. The capitalist mode of production is one in which

capital – either money or credit, fixed productive investments (e.g. machinery), or stocks of goods and materials – is central to the creation of a surplus. The capital is owned by individuals, who buy the labour power of others and set it to work on other resources (also privately-owned) to produce an increase in capital; the return on the investment is the difference between the price paid for the labour and the other factors of production (all of which are ultimately the product of labour) and the price received from sale of the output. Without a surplus, or the potential for one, investment in production will not be forthcoming, labour will be underused, consumption will fall and the economy will be in decline. If growth is to occur, more commodities must be produced, more productively, and then consumed (for a full outline, see Harvey 1982).

The nature of this mode of production creates tensions within the society between the two major classes of individuals, the employers of labour, who wish to exploit it to the maximum extent (i.e. to make the surplus as large as possible), and the owners of labour, who wish to receive as large a proportion of the selling price as they can. Such tension is broken down into a large number of separate antagonisms between employers and their employees. The conflicts that it invokes threaten the stability of the society. (Note that whereas the employees are individuals, the employers may not be. In the early stages of capitalism, most production units were owned by individual employers. Today, capitalism is dominated by large corporations and institutions in which ownership is diffuse but management is centralized. The goal of managers is to make profits for their 'employers', the shareholders in most cases, who may include many employees. Despite this organizational shift, however, the goal of capitalism remains the same – so that, paradoxically, some employees may have shares in the firms for which they work and with whom they are in conflict.)

Progress in the capitalist mode of production is not continuous. As we have seen (Ch. 1), it is characterized by a series of cycles of alternating expansionary booms and contracting crises. The crises come about because of production and labour surpluses (Taylor 1985).

Obtaining a surplus requires greater efficiency in production, which in a technologically-advanced society involves replacing labour by machines. Greater efficiency means greater production, and the potential that this cannot be consumed: because of market saturation and also because, as less labour is used in production, the same processes that advance productivity also remove some of the capacity to consume (because labour is being displaced; labour – if paid – can consume, but machinery cannot). Each sector of the economy passes through such crises, which are countered by the redeployment of capital and labour into other sectors (which probably means other places too). If many sectors are in crisis contemporaneously, then redeployment is difficult. The result is a general crisis, which can only be surmounted by devaluation: of capital (through monetary inflation), of commodities, and of labour.

In such an unstable system, institutions are needed that might provide some stability. There are two major functions for such institutions. The first is to provide an environment in which the capitalist goals can be pursued with some confidence by the many investors – large and small – who wish to be involved in the buying and selling, for profit, of commodities and labour power. For example, trade involves contracts and money. Those entering them will want to be sure that the other partners will honour the terms. But it is in nobody's individual interest to honour contracts, and the only way to ensure that they do is to have an accepted body which oversees contractual obligations and ensures that they are met, and which guarantees the value of the money involved. Similarly, a technologically-advanced industry wants trained workers. But it is in no one employer's interests to provide the many years of basic education – at cost – when educated workers can then be 'poached' in the labour market, by employers who have not met training costs. A separate institution, financed by all, is needed which provides the trained work force.

These two examples illustrate the need for institutions separate from the investor class, which meet the requirements of that class as a whole. Such institutions are part of, or stimu-

lated and subsidized by, the state. Their power to raise money, by taxation, and to spend it, in the general interest of the capitalist system, is accepted, because they apparently favour no group or set of institutions within the capitalist class. Similarly, it is recognized that the state should raise money to provide a variety of other functions which underpin capitalist success (Smith 1984). A physical infrastructure is a good example of this. No individual investor will put large sums of money into a freeway, because the returns will come in only slowly and – as the history of the railroad system shows – can be undercut by other freeway providers. But freeways are needed, and capitalists are prepared to pay (reasonable) taxes in order to get them provided by the state – so long as everybody else pays too.

The state, then, is a set of institutions which act as *promoters of accumulation*. These oversee the operations of business, to ensure fair dealing. They guarantee a stable currency; they provide a physical infrastructure; they produce a satisfactory labour force – in terms of skills and health, for example; and they regulate the use of scarce resources, such as land. In short, they underpin capitalist success.

However, in promoting capitalist accumulation, the state is promoting a mode of production based on the exploitation of labour Its success inevitably contains the seeds of its problems: it promotes policies which can eventually lead to overproduction and crisis; and it promotes capitalist growth, which exacerbates class tensions. With regard to the former, it must constantly tune its policies and promote new developments to avoid crises. With regard to the latter, it must seek to ameliorate the potential conflicts. This it does by containment policies, which seek to win apparent concessions for labour and yet at the same time promote within labour the ideology of capitalism – the benefits to be gained from enterprise, and the need for redeployment, for example. Thus the second major function of the state is to act as the *legitimator of capitalism*. Again, this function – part of which involves the police function – can only be undertaken by a set of institutions that is empirically separate from capital, otherwise it would not be accepted as legitimate by the labouring population.

The state in capitalist society, then, is a set of institutions necessary to the continued existence of that society; without it, anarchy would probably prevail, capitalist success would be very doubtful and investment withheld, and conflict would be rife, between and within all sections of society. The implication that with a state none of these will occur should not be drawn, however. Without a state – or some similar set of institutions – failure is almost certain; with one, success is not guaranteed, but is more likely.

The argument so far is that *a state is needed*; nothing has been said about the territory over which its sovereignty extends. Theoretically, a single state for the whole capitalist mode of production is possible. This is unlikely to happen, however, because space is an impediment to the flows that characterize a capitalist economy. Thus a state will be needed to organize the mode of production in a given area – to protect the interests of those within the area against those outside and, indeed, to guarantee them certain monopolistic privileges. In certain circumstances, employers and employees may combine, through the state, to advance common interests against the members of another state.

The state, then, is a political set of institutions, established to pursue economic and social policies in a given territory, over which it has sovereign power (Mann 1984). The extent of its territory may be inherited, from a pre-capitalist mode of production, for example; and it may seek to change this in its dealings with other states.

The state is a cohesive force in capitalist society, therefore, a territorial alliance of interests which are in competition and yet have some common goals. Within the territory of most states there are local territorial alliances, or potential alliances, either within one of the major groupings (employers and employees) or combining members of both, who seek 'protection' against the residents of other areas. To promote their interests, they may be able to achieve some measure of local political autonomy, being granted institutions that serve the interests of a spatially-defined segment of the society, within the context of the national state, which is the only body with sovereign power.

The state in the US

The previous section provides a rationale for the state in general terms, and not for the state in the US alone (for a full treatment of these topics, see Greenberg 1983). It indicates the *necessity* of the state in capitalist society. This must not, however, be interpreted as an argument regarding the form of the state. The nature of the state institutions and how they operate is in no way predetermined. There are many ways in which the interests of capitalist accumulation can be advanced, the whole system legitimated, and relationships with other states conducted. More importantly, the chosen ways will reflect particular situations in time and space. History in a capitalist system does not repeat itself; the context for decision-making is always new, so that although lessons can be learned from roughly comparable previous situations, political decision-makers within state institutions are always reacting to a new set of pressures.

The operation of the state, therefore, is a human process involving individuals reacting to situations, not in any mechanistic stimulus–response sequence but in ways peculiar to themselves. Such individuals do not operate in vacuums, of course. They are socialized into a cultural context, which predisposes them to identify certain issues as more important than others, to evaluate these in certain ways, and to propose certain types of solution. The state is thus a part of the *culture* of a country. It has a certain form and *modus operandi* because these seemed sensible when they were established and which, once created, have structured subsequent developments and decision-making. Again, those future developments are not determined. At any one time, the individuals operating the state may decide that radical alterations are needed (decisions that may at least in part be pressed on them by outside interests); the probability of such radical decisions is slight, however.

Within a general appreciation of the nature of the roles of the state, therefore, the study of a particular society requires a focus on the form of the state there. Only by understanding what particular form has been created, and why, is it possible to understand how the state acts. Throughout, however, it is necessary to realize that the state is a body of individuals reacting to the imperatives of the economic system and to the pressures of the members of society for concessions from the system.

The cultural context of the American state

The American state was created in a revolution against another state – the British. Some of its characteristics reflect the nature of its predecessor, for many of its institutions were retained. Others reflect the reactions to the British state and attempts to create a superior set of institutions – attempts whose nature reflected the cultural origins of those involved.

Three basic elements to American political culture can be identified. (This section draws heavily on the work of Elazar 1966.) The first is the culture of *individualism* (sometimes termed privatism), which is very largely a 'minimal government' culture. Primacy within economy and society is placed on the individual, who is to be allowed to make personal decisions rather than have them made, often anonymously, by a distant state. In economic terms, this is the culture of the marketplace, of unfettered capitalist competition. In social terms, it is the culture of personal responsibility and self-direction; success is a product of individual effort. And in political terms it is the culture of individual responsibility, with political representatives, office-holders and employees being individually accountable to the electorate.

Under the individualistic, *laissez-faire* culture the state is accepted as a necessity to ensure order in economic and social affairs. But its role is a minimal one, and it must intrude on personal decision-making as little as possible. When it intrudes it does so according to the tenets of the *moralistic culture*, which promotes the concept of government for the common good. The American state serves the US population as a whole, not segments within it. It is something that all should participate in, and its goal should be to build consensus, not promote conflict. Thus the moralistic culture discourages polarization within society. Decisions within the state are made pragmatically, not in the context

of some guiding principles which motivate the group currently most powerful within the state (Vile 1976). Politics is public service, not the pursuit of sectional goals. As a consequence, political decision-makers are open to discussion, debate and pressure, and respond accordingly; therefore, no one body of opinion need have permanent control of the state, if the decision-makers can be persuaded of the validity of a shift.

The third cultural element is *traditionalistic*, which has roots in the pre-capitalist era; there is some ambivalence towards the *laissez-faire* market economy and a stronger belief in beneficent elite rule. The assumption is of a fixed social structure in which the relatively small group at the peak of the hierarchy sees its role as undertaking the functions of government in order to ensure maintenance of the existing social order. It is, then, inherently conservative and paternalist.

These cultures are to some extent in conflict, both among themselves and with the imperatives of a capitalist society. The individualistic and the traditionalistic conflict, for example, in the degree to which they promote individual self-advancement and the role of the politician as an individual. And the traditionalistic and the moralistic conflict in that the former is ideological and conservative whereas the latter is pragmatic and liberal. The individual may conflict with the role of the state in a capitalist society in that he or she resents state controls – many of which may be introduced for moralistic reasons. (In the ideology of capitalism, things done 'for the common good' are also things done to protect the existing order, which is built on exploitation.) The traditionalistic may conflict with the necessary role of the state, because it sees 'concessions' to labour – granted to ensure legitimation – as attacks on the existing order.

The relative importance of these cultures, and those socialized within them, will vary from time to time. It also varies, according to Elazar, from *place to place* within the US (Fig. 4.1). The South, for example, is dominated by a traditionalistic culture, the direct lineal descendant of the plantation-based agricultural system; it spread westwards from that core, with the advancing frontier, into the newer States of Oklahoma and

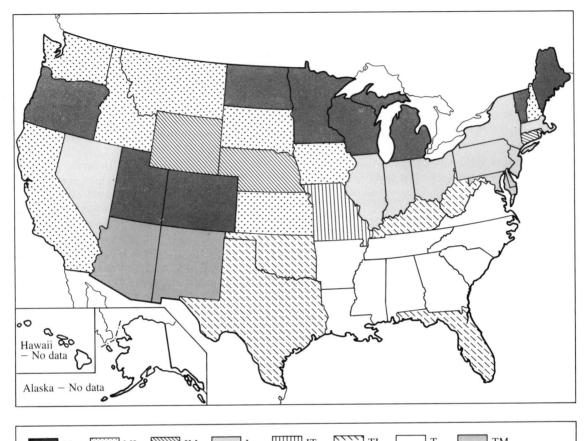

M = MORALISTIC
MI = MORALISTIC/INDIVIDUALISTIC
IM = INDIVIDUALISTIC/MORALISTIC
I = INDIVIDUALISTIC

IT = INDIVIDUALISTIC/TRADITIONALISTIC
TI = TRADITIONALISTIC/INDIVIDUALISTIC
T = TRADITIONALISTIC
TM = TRADITIONALISTIC/MATERIALISTIC

Fig. 4.1 The dominant political culture, by state. The terms are described in the text
Source: Elazar (1966), Fig. 4, p. 108

Texas, New Mexico and Arizona. Further north, in Missouri, it met and mingled with a dominantly individualistic culture, typical of the northeastern States. Here, the major social goal of immigrant groups, largely from Britain and northern Europe, was individual advancement; the political culture reflected this (and no doubt accounted for the early industrialization of these areas). Further north, the moralistic culture dominated – in New England, where it was the descendant of the communal organization of the early Puritan settlers, and the Great Lakes States where many of the initial settlers were communally organized around strong religious bases. This orientation spread westward with the frontier; it dominated in Utah (associated with the Mormon settlement). Colorado and Oregon, but elsewhere it emerged with the individualistic culture spreading from the northeastern States, producing a hybrid western culture.

The form of the state

This cultural mix was extremely influential in the creation of the institutions of the US. The individualistic culture favoured minimal government, and feared a central power; the moralistic favoured community (or local) politics, with central power only as and when this was necessary to the overall public good; and the traditionalistic favoured a form of government which protected the interests of the elite and minimized the power of the mass. The compromise between these, worked out in the 1770s and the 1780s and in place ever since, involved two major elements: a constrained central state, constitutionally limited in its powers and countered by a federal system of States with defined rights; and a tripartite separation of power within the state – between President, Legislature and Judiciary. The latter also incorporated a compromise with regard to elections: within the Legislature, the House was to be elected by the people, and the Senate by the constituency for the State legislatures (which was defined in and by the States; only since 1913 has the Senate become a popularly-elected chamber): the Senate contained an equal number of representatives of each State, whereas representation in the House was to be proportional to population. The President was to be elected by State-appointed electors (again, their selection by popular ballot was not required by the Federal Constitution; that it now happens – by custom and not by law – reflects the decline of the traditionalistic culture); and the Judiciary was to be nominated by the Executive but confirmed by the Senate.

This format is repeated, with minor variations only, in all of the States. These vary substantially, however, in their attitude to local government and the devolution of power away from the centre. In the original New England States, for example, there is a strong tradition of local government, reflecting the settlers' origins and their strong moralistic/community orientation. Countering this, in the South there is a strong centralist tendency, reflecting the traditional culture and its 'fear of rule by the masses'. Elsewhere, the general trend favours localism, in accord with the individualistic and moralistic cultures. The need for a central presence is accepted, however, in order to serve the general good. As Elazar's map (Fig. 4.2) shows, the centralist tendencies are stronger in the newer, western States, as well as in the South.

In the States and in the federal government, however, the founding fathers and their immediate successors were unsure whether the separation of powers, the Constitutional protection of States' rights, and the encouragement of local government were sufficient to protect the people from tyrannical rule; the monarchical tyranny of Britain could readily be replaced by an American legislative tyranny. And so the original Constitution was extended in 1791 by the ratification of the first ten Amendments, generally known as the Bill of Rights. These included: the freedom of religion, speech, the press, assembly and right to petition the government for redress (Amendment I); the freedom to bear arms (Amendment II); the freedom from search without duly issued warrant (Amendment IV); the right not to be deprived of life, liberty or property without due process of law, to have just compensation for any public requisition of private property, to trial by jury, and to decline to be a witness against oneself (Amendment V); the right to be represented in a trial by jury (Amendment VI); and the absence of excessive bail and fines, and of cruel and unusual punishments (Amendment VII). Three further Amendments extended these rights to all American residents: slavery and involuntary servitude were abolished (Amendment XIII, 1865); States were denied the right to deprive citizens of life, liberty or property without due process of law, were prevented from passing laws abridging citizen rights and immunities, and were not to deny citizens the equal protection of the laws (Amendment XIV, 1868); and the right to vote could not be abridged, by State or the US, on grounds of race, colour or previous slavery (Amendment XV, 1870). (The last of these was extended in 1920 – Amendment XIX – to cover sex; poll taxes were ended in 1964 – Amendment XXV; and discrimination by age, for all over eighteen, was made unconstitutional by Amendment XXVI in 1971.)

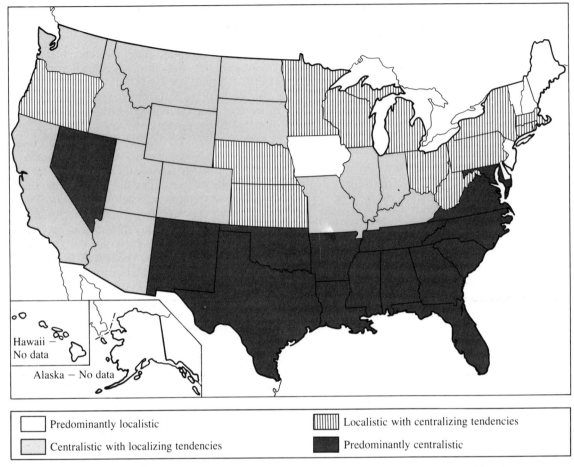

Fig. 4.2 The dominant political culture, by State, with regard to relations between state and local governments
Source: Elazar (1966), Fig. 8, p. 187

Legend:
- Predominantly localistic
- Centralistic with localizing tendencies
- Localistic with centralizing tendencies
- Predominantly centralistic

The operation of the American form of government

The Americans in the late eighteenth century provided themselves with a republican form of government, so structured that any one group within society could not readily take complete control, and organized so as to protect the individual liberties and property rights of citizens. This structure has now been in place for more than 200 years. In detail, it has evolved with the society that it serves, for it has been called upon to promote a booming industrial capitalist economy and to legitimize that economy, and the social system that it has bred, to its population.

Elections and the creation of governments

In a republican, democratic format, governments are elected by the people. Initially, the founding fathers and their supporters – many of them drawn from the traditionalistic political culture – feared what popularly-elected governments might do and constrained the possibilities by restricting the franchise. Increasingly, the franchise was widened, and eventually universalized. (In theory at least. Although all adult males, including blacks, have had the franchise for more than a century, much was done to prevent certain groups – especially blacks – from registering as voters. Many of these practices have been deemed unconstitutional, but even in 1984, only 68 per cent of the population aged 18 and over had registered as electors, and the turnout at the 1984 Presidential election was only 53 per cent of the potential electorate – 74 per cent of the registered electorate.)

Despite the individualistic political culture within the US, it was not long before groups organized themselves into political parties which would promote candidates for office who favoured certain policies and would seek to form a government of like-minded individuals. It was in Washington that the first parties were established, around the two main factions that represented the polarization of opinions over Alexander Hamilton's financial policies; these were the Republicans and Federalists (the latter was later replaced by the Whig and Democrat factions). Initially, only in federal politics were parties active, and State politics remained individualistic.

Power is obtained through electoral systems by winning votes. For the Presidency, a majority of votes must be won in sufficient States to ensure a majority in the Electoral College. (Each State is allocated votes in the College according to the number of Representatives that it sends to the federal Congress, plus two for its two Senators. Thus College votes are distributed roughly in accordance with population; currently California has forty-seven and New York thirty-six, whereas Wyoming and other small States have only three each. It is possible to win the Presidency with a bare majority of votes in only the fifteen largest States.) For the legislature, a majority of seats

must be won in each House; the grouping with such a majority is then entitled to a majority of the seats, plus the all-important chairmanship, on every Committee, giving it, and the individuals involved, immense power over the nature and progress of both legislation and budget appropriations. Such voting majorities could be forced by individual candidates in the case of the Presidency and by coalitions of members, created after the elections in which they stood as individuals, in the Congress. Despite the individualistic ideology, however, a party system has developed. For more than 150 years, American politics have been dominated by two parties only (not necessarily the same two); the single-member constituency, plurality electoral system encourages this, but it is not a necessary consequence.

Parties seek to mobilize blocks of votes around particular interests. In many societies, the cleavages so created reflect the basic socio-economic divisions within the society. This is not so in the US, however, where most of the party systems have been organized on sectional (or regional) rather than socio-political grounds. (A socialist party, allied to the working class, has never developed as a major political presence, for example; no socialist party has won more than one million votes in a Presidential election: Bennett and Earle (1983).) The period from the end of the Civil War to the end of World War II has been characterized by Archer and Taylor (1981: 35) as the era of the 'politics of sectional dominance'. The various sections of the country initially had very different interests in the major areas of federal policy. In the 1840s and 1850s, for example, the interests of the three main sections were characterized by Billington (1960: 353; see Archer and Taylor 1981: 77) as:

	West	South	Northeast
Disposal of public lands:	Low price	High price	High price
Tariffs:	Protectionism	Low tariff	High tariff
Federal investment in infrastructure:	Federal building	None	Federal building

The task of the parties was to try and build coalitions from two of these separate interest groups to ensure Congressional majorities and

Presidential election success. (Such coalition building via agenda-setting limits electoral choice: as Schattschneider (1960) expresses it, 'all organization is bias'.) During the era of sectional dominance, at least three such systems were in operation; in all three, a common feature was the Democrat Party hegemony of the South, a consequence of its establishment there after the Civil War defeat as the party that would uphold the 'white supremacy' traditionalistic ideology, despite the loss of the institution of slavery.

The first of these party systems produced a period of Democrat Party success, anchored in its southern stronghold and with some vote-winning in neighbouring western and southern States, though the party only won the Presidency in 1884 and 1892. After 1896, the Republican Party created a successful coalition of conservative northern and progressive western interests, confining the Democrats to the South. And then, from 1928 on, a new coalition was formed – focused around F. D. Roosevelt – of conservative southern and northern liberal Democrats. Since 1948, this coalition has occasionally collapsed; in 1948 and 1968, Strom Thurmond and George Wallace respectively split the southern vote, standing as 'white supremacist' independents against the liberal (i.e. northern) Democrat campaign; in 1960, the candidacy of a Roman Catholic (Kennedy) introduced a disturbance to the normal pattern of voting; and in 1968 and 1972, the conservative Republican candidate (Nixon) was more popular than the liberal Democrats (Humphrey and McGovern) in the South. Carter re-established the Democrat coalition of Roosevelt in 1976 and 1980 and Mondale maintained it in 1984 (Archer 1985; Archer *et al.* 1985) but current evidence suggests a much increased volatility in Presidential voting behaviour; people are more inclined to vote on the particular issues of the time and less ready to remain loyal to a sectional party.

This partisan dealignment of recent years is clear in voting at Congressional as well as Presidential elections. Until the 1960s, there was a very strong tendency for voters to support all of a party's candidates at the various elections being held contemporaneously – for President, Senator, Representative, State Governor, State Senator etc. Thus a popular Presidential candidate was able to get other members of his party elected 'on his coat-tails' (this assumes that people made their voting decision on the Presidential candidate). Today, the coat-tails phenomenon is much weaker and ticket-splitting is common.

That the residents of blocks of contiguous States – the sections – have tended to vote together during the past century is illustrated by Archer and Taylor's (1981; see also Archer *et al.* 1985) factor analytic studies. For the period 1872–1980 they have been able to characterize each State's voting according to its degree of southernness, northernness, westernness and uniqueness. Figure 4.3 illustrates the outcome. The dominance of the three blocks is clear, in a pattern that overlaps substantially with the map of political cultures derived by Elazar.

Until the recent period of dealignment, this pattern of Presidential and Congressional voting was matched by the political composition of the State Legislatures and Executives. A major feature of the latter has been the Democratic hegemony in the South where, in some legislatures, the Republicans have failed to win a single seat. (As a consequence, as Key (1949) showed in his classic study, the most important elections have been the primary elections to determine the Democrat candidate. Because there are no ideological issues to separate candidates within a party, the individualistic culture is strong at this level and candidates tend to perform best in their home areas.) Countering this, there are no States where there is a corresponding Republican hegemony. Dye (1984) has recently categorized States according to their political complexion in the period 1950–80, using two variables: inter-party competition, defined by the size of the winning party's margin in gubernatorial elections; and voter turnout. The twenty most competitive States ranked in the top half (of all fifty) for smallness of winning margin and level of turnout in at least 25 of the 30 years, and the twenty labelled non-competitive were similarly in the bottom half; for ten States only, there was no consistency in their ranking (in some years there were small margins and high turnouts, but not consistently so). His map of those groupings (Fig. 4.4) has much in common with Elazar's (Figs. 4.1 and 4.2); non-competitive States are almost all in the region

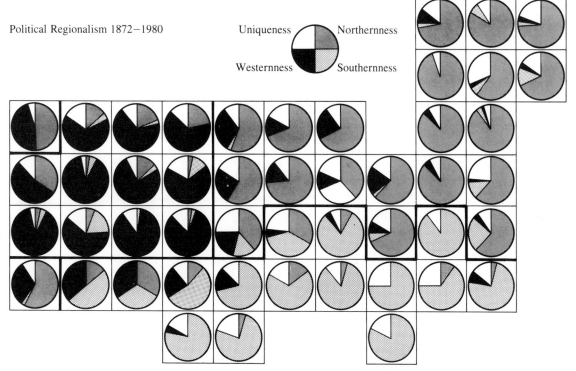

Fig. 4.3 The regional pattern of voting for President over the period 1872–1980. The forty-eight conterminous States are portrayed in an equal-area cartogram, with the thicker lines representing the major regional boundaries
Source: Archer and Taylor (1981), Fig. 3.1, p. 106

of the traditionalistic political culture, for example.

Local government

There is a very large number of local governments in the US. Most States have two types of multi-purpose local government: counties, which cover the entire State territory; and municipalities, which provide separate government for incorporated areas with a minimum population and density (as specified in State Law). In addition, twenty-one States have townships, subdivisions of counties which provide a few relatively minor services. Nearly every State has a mosaic of school districts, providing the public junior and high schools, and there are also many single-purpose special

districts, most of them created for an *ad hoc* purpose (fire protection, for example, and the operation of an airport) and serving a territory that is not contiguous with any other. The vast majority of these local governments have revenue-raising powers, most of them reserved to property taxes only.

All local governments in the US are overseen by elected members, and many of the officers are elected too. In some, elections are contested by parties, and local politics are controlled by the party 'machines'. Many of these, especially in the northeast, have the reputation of being run to favour particular interest groups; in large cities, a coalition of big business interests with ethnic minorities has been common, with the powerful individuals in the latter 'delivering' the needed votes in return for patronage and other benefits. The machines were linked to particular parties – usually the

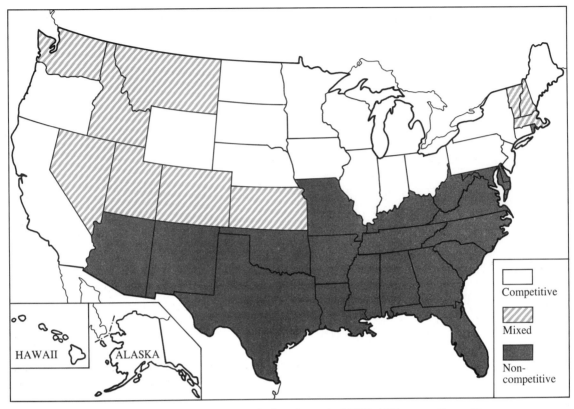

Fig. 4.4 The classification of State governments during the period 1950–1980, according to Dye
Source: Dye (1984), Fig. 1, p. 1103

Democrats – but operated no political ideology other than a pragmatic approach to personal and group interests.

The nature of machine politics, and the frequent correlation of these with corruption in the mind of the electorate, offends the individualistic and moralistic political cultures of many Americans. To counter this, during the twentieth century attempts have been made, largely led by the middle classes, to depoliticize local government. It has been argued that local government should be run on business-like grounds for the general good, so parties should be banned and local government handed over to responsible individuals (an interesting combination of the moralistic, individualistic and, to a lesser extent, traditionalistic cultures). The movement – known as *reform* – has been very successful and about half of American municipalities now have 'reform' governments. Most of these debar political parties from participating in local elections and government – only individuals can contest seats, as individuals. They also operate 'at large' rather than ward-based electoral systems, thereby preventing minority groups concentrated in certain parts of the territory from winning seats. Many have legally-imposed limits on their tax-raising powers, and extra taxes or loans can only be raised after voter approval has been obtained in a referendum. (This limitation is one reason for the multiplication of special districts.) And they also have provision for popular initiatives, whereby a portion of the electorate can require a referendum on an issue, the results of which are binding on the local government, or 'recall' an elected representative before his or her full term is complete.

The party and the member

Although nearly all members of the federal and State Legislatures are elected as members of a particular political party (Nebraska is an exception to this; parties are debarred from the State Assembly), this does not mean that the individualistic culture is submerged. For most elected members, party is a convenient stepping stone to power rather than ideological base, and loyalty – in terms of voting records – may be very slight. There are party whips, and loyalty to the party may be sought – usually in return for political benefits – but once in Congress or Assembly the elected member is free to operate very much as an individual.

This freedom allows the elected member to pursue particular interests. Some at least of these will be related to winning votes in the next election; this may involve obtaining benefits for constituents and for sponsors who will donate much-needed funds for the next campaign. Thus American politics, as described below, is *very much the politics of place*.

The political manipulation of American space

Space is a resource which is manipulated within society for a combination of economic, social and political reasons. Other chapters in this book illustrate economic and social manipulations – of the market for land, for example, and with regard to the creation of residential patterns. Here the focus is on political manipulation – involving some arm of the state. Three brief case examples are given, one of manipulation solely for economic goals, one for socio-economic purposes, and the third for political ends. Common to all three is the involvement of one element in the American state apparatus which is frequently ignored in geographical analyses – the judiciary. The American courts exist, *inter alia*, to interpret the Constitution and to adjudicate on disputes that involve constitutional issues. Their rulings – especially those of the Supreme Court – have had an important bearing on a variety of aspects of spatial manipulation (Johnston 1984; Clark 1985).

Removing the barriers to commerce

As outlined above, the creation of a federal form of government in the US was undertaken as part of the system of checks and balances introduced to prevent the development of a centralized, highly powerful state apparatus. The concept of federalism, according to Wheare (1953: 53), involves two levels of government – State and federal – which 'are not subordinate to one another, but coordinate with each other'. There is a constitutional division of powers so that

each government is autonomous in at least one
defined area of political activity; each government
is the final authority with its defined sphere of
activity; each level of government is directly
accessible to citizens; each level derives sovereign
powers from the Constitution, and is not
dependent on the other; and neither level can
change the relationship unilaterally, so that States
exist in their own right (Reagan 1982: 8)

All of these elements of a federation are clearly specified in the US Constitution: Article 1, Section 8 lays out the duties and powers of the Federal Congress, and the Tenth Amendment says that 'The powers not delegated to the United States by the Constitution, nor prohibited by it to the States, are reserved to the States respectively, or to the people.'

Despite these safeguards, it is widely accepted that the States' rights are now of little value and that the federal government has become an all-important central power: as Reagan (1982: 11) expresses it, 'the only aspect of State government that is beyond the reach of Washington is the very existence of the States with their present boundaries.' Further, the Tenth Amendment no longer provides an obstacle to the extension of the central power, which has created a 'nationally dominated system of shared power and shared functions' (Reagan 1982: 145).

Why has this come about, with the removal of spatial differentiation within the US? Clark has argued that it represents the role of the state as promoter of accumulation: 'For many merchants and traders at the turn of the nineteenth century, spatial integration was considered to be a necessary condition for national economic growth' (Clark 1981: 1199). In short,

State borders impeded the free movement of capital and commodities. Capitalist reproduction requires both free and rapid movement and a unified monetary system.

The so-called Commerce Clause of the Constitution (Article 1, Section 8, Sub-Section 3) gives Congress the power 'To regulate Commerce with foreign Nations, and among the several States, and with the Indian Tribes.' This has been used by the judiciary, in a series of landmark cases, to limit State power and therefore to prevent the development of spatial monopolies with protection from outside competitors. In an 1824 Supreme Court judgment (*Gibbons* v. *Ogden*), for example, Congress was recognized as having the power to regulate all inter-State commerce; in 1871 the Court ruled that Congress could regulate an intra-State boat because it was carrying inter-State trade, and in 1914 (*Houston and Texas Railway* v. *United States*) it extended such regulations to railroad rates; in 1937, it gave Congress power to regulate labour relations because of their impact on inter-State commerce (*Virginia R. Co.*, v. *System Federation*); and in 1942 it gave Congress powers to regulate agricultural production (*Wickard* v. *Filburn*). Some of the relevant Supreme Court judgments were based on the Fourteenth Amendment, which was passed to promote individual freedoms. The results were the removal of the legal barriers to free circulation, providing uniformity of regulation of commerce, and furthering federal intervention in all aspects of production and exchange. The Constitution has been used to enforce economic homogeneity in the States, to encourage maximum national economic growth irrespective of its spatial location.

The erection of barriers: local government

Whereas the Constitution has been used to remove any effective barriers to circulation in the economic sphere, it has, somewhat paradoxically, also been used to support the creation of other barriers erected to protect the interests of individuals and groups. These barriers are the boundaries of local governments.

The US, as pointed out above, has a large number of separate local governments. Although these are not sovereign bodies or autonomous, and exist and operate solely with the agreement of their superior governments (the States), their existence is very much protected in the national, anti-centralist ideology. (Perhaps not surprisingly, fragmentation is least in the SMSAs in the South.) Recently, a range of Supreme Court judgments has bolstered this protection, indicating that only State action can remove the autonomy that they have *de facto*, if not *de jure*.

Local governments exist to provide services paid for very largely by local residents through property taxes. In an urban agglomeration with a single local government covering the entire built-up area, the nature, level and distribution of services would be decided by an administration representing the population as a whole, as would the level of taxation. On the other hand, if the agglomeration were divided into a large number of separate authorities, then these could vary in the service/tax 'portfolios' which they offer the consumer-residents; as Tiebout (1956) argued in a classic paper, this variety would allow residents to 'shop around' and select the local government whose policies most closely conformed to their desires.

Tiebout's free market model of metropolitan local government does not conform to reality, however, because it assumes freedom of choice in where to live (see Whiteman 1983). For a variety of reasons, this does not exist. In part, this is because the powers available have been used by residents to promote their self-interests and to avoid contributing to the welfare of others. Local governments are financed through tax income, largely property tax income. With regard to the payment of taxes, all but the highly altruistic wish: (1) to pay as little as possible; (2) to free-ride on others; and (3) to avoid paying for services which others benefit from. The tax income is used to provide services. However, many would prefer that services were paid for by the users rather than through the taxation system; only for widely-used services (police, education etc.) is there general support for contributions, and even with these the free-rider/subsidy-avoidance requirements hold. The existence of separate local governments allows at least some groups within American society to opt out of contributing to the costs of services, because they live beyond the boundaries of the relevant taxing authority.

One group of property taxpayers who are relatively mobile and able to choose where to locate are non-residential land users – industrialists, office and shopping centre developers etc. Traditionally, these were located in the city centres, where property tax bills were high to pay for the costs of running a high-density, increasingly obsolete set of public services, for welfare and other payments to the poor, and so on. In separate suburban municipalities, on the other hand, most of the costs could be avoided. If the industries occupied separate municipalities, then their taxes would not be used to provide services for their employees, who live in other municipalities. Suburbanization could mean lower tax bills.

Exactly the same arguments apply to residential land uses; escape from the central city could mean escape from paying taxes to subsidize the poor living there. In this, the escape could be enhanced if the poor could be prevented from escaping too. The residents of small suburban municipalities have found that they can do this, through the use of the land-use zoning powers devolved to municipalities in most States. By careful control of housing densities (mainly by minimum lot size regulations; minima as high as one dwelling per hectare (2.5 acres) are not uncommon) and by excluding apartments, trailer homes and other land uses/users likely to have a negative impact on the local social and economic milieu, property values have been raised to such a level that the poor, and in particular the black poor, are excluded from much of suburbia.

Whereas for non-residential land users the main benefits of suburbanization are low tax bills, especially in municipalities zoned almost exclusively for such uses, for residential users, especially the most affluent, the fiscal advantages are combined with means of ensuring neighbourhood socio-economic exclusivity. The latter brings with it a further advantage, crucial to many affluent white families. As already noted, public education is provided in most States through a network of school districts whose basic finance comes from the local property tax and whose school board has considerable autonomy over various aspects of service provision. In the central cities of large metro-

politan areas, school district and city council boundaries coincide and annexation by the latter is accompanied by growth of the former. In the suburbs this is not so, and the separate school districts established when the area was rural are retained. Thus the exclusive suburban municipalities are parts of exclusive school districts; taxes paid to the latter do not go towards the costs of educating the poor who live elsewhere in the metropolitan area, and the local school milieu is strongly supportive of socio-economic class norms. Furthermore, blacks are excluded from the local schools, so that a move to suburbia means a move away from the possibility of racially integrated schools ('white flight') and from the associated bussing of students.

The mosaic of many separate overlapping governments in suburbia was promoted by Tiebout as presenting democratic choice. In fact, it is used to promote the interests of particular groups within society, largely to the benefit of the already affluent. Inequalities in service provision, in tax bills and in neighbourhood characteristics are institutionalized, and municipal boundaries are important social dividing lines. This promotion of inequalities via the local government system, and therefore involving the State, has been challenged through the Courts, in most cases invoking the Fourteenth Amendment with its promise of equal protection for all. However, the Courts have in most cases ruled that discrimination by wealth is not unconstitutional so that only explicit racial discriminatory policies can be challenged successfully. Even so, the impact of the latter is limited. Most blacks live in the central cities; most suburbs are white. To achieve racially integrated schools it would be necessary to combine central city and suburbs into single school districts, but the Supreme Court has not been prepared to sanction such an invasion of local democracy. Suburban municipalities are 'tight little islands' (cf. *Warth v. Seldin* 1976) and the Courts and the State governments are prepared to accept the exclusionary policies operated to protect the fiscal and social advantages enjoyed by the island residents. (This is being challenged in some States, notably New Jersey, where the judiciary has interpreted municipalities zoned exclusively for low-density, high-value developments as unconstitutional: Johnston 1986.)

The map of local governments is constantly changing, and the changes that come about are only a small proportion of those that are proposed. Many municipalities wish to expand their territories, for example, and promote annexation plans – involving either unincorporated land or other municipalities adjacent to their borders. The goal of an annexation is usually fiscal, for the government/residents of an expanding municipality will not want to annex land which will be a net drain on the local exchequer. Thus land suitable for either industrial–commercial or high-value residential uses (or already containing them) will be favoured because of the relatively high land values involved, whereas low-status residential areas will be much less attractive. Since, in most States, annexation only occurs with the consent of the owners of the land concerned, the expanding municipality must offer an attractive tax/service package. If it is successful, the outcome may be a very odd-shaped extension, along a main road say, producing not only a very fragmented local government map but also a very complicated one.

Manipulating space for political ends: malapportionment and the gerrymander

Most American politicians, including all members of the Federal House of Representatives and of the lower house of each State Assembly, are elected from single-member constituencies. For their parties, it is important – in order to gain a majority in the legislature with the political power that this brings, especially in the committee systems which handle most of the detailed business and which allow the operation of pork-barrel politics (see below, p. 98) – that their members are able to win sufficient seats.

There are many ways to win electoral support and then to retain it. Voters must be persuaded that it is in their interests to support a particular candidate/party. Given that a certain level of support is relatively guaranteed, then a variety of means can be used to try and retain a seat once it has been won. Two of these involve the manipulation of space through the

definition of constituencies.

The first of these manipulative procedures is *malapportionment* which involves the creation of constituencies that differ substantially in their numbers of electors. The smaller a constituency's electorate, the smaller the number of votes needed to win it. Thus, for example, in a State with 4 million residents and ten Congressional districts, it could be to the advantage of the party in power in the State Legislature (all districting for federal and State elections is handled by the State Legislatures, plus the Governors, and hence controlled by the party in power there) to create a number of small districts in parts of the State where its supporters are in a majority – perhaps six with an average population of 200 000 – counterbalanced by large districts where the opposition have majority support – four with an average population of 700 000. In this way, the effectiveness of its own votes is increased, whereas many of its opponent's votes are wasted (it needs only 100 001 votes to win the small districts but 350 001 to win the large; a party with only 600 006 voters out of 4 million could then win a majority of the seats).

The second method of manipulating constituency boundaries is *gerrymandering*, named after Governor Elbridge Gerry of Massachusetts who created a salamander-shaped district. In this, the boundaries of districts are carefully drawn to ensure that a majority of them contain a majority of the relevant party's supporters. This could involve either 'stacking' all of the opposition's voters in a minority of the districts, or 'cracking' its voters by making them a substantial minority in most districts.

Both malapportionment and gerrymandering have been widely practised and have been the source of much concern, especially among those substantially disadvantaged. Gerrymandering was the first to be practised explicitly, but it was malapportionment that was successfully challenged and overthrown. By the middle of the twentieth century, many States displayed substantial malapportionment, not so much because of explicit design but rather because constituency boundaries were not revised to keep pace with changing population distributions. The depopulating rural areas were advantaged, and the vested rural interests in the State Legislatures were not prepared to redistrict and hand over power to the burgeoning urban areas. Thus by 1962 in Tennessee the ratio of the population of the largest to the smallest district for the Legislative Assembly was 18 : 1, whereas for the State Senate it was 5.2 : 1. (This was far from an extreme case; in Georgia for the State Senate the ratio was 99 : 1.) These disparities were the basis for a challenge – brought under the Fourteenth Amendment – in the classic 1962 Supreme Court case of *Baker* v. *Carr* which led to what became known as the 'reapportionment revolution'. Malapportionment has now been outlawed by the Courts (Johnston 1979a).

Gerrymandering has not been similarly outlawed, however, in part because there is no accepted objective standard against which any scheme can be evaluated, unlike the situation with malapportionment for which population equality, and the degree of allowed variation, can be readily defined. Thus it is still open to political parties to draw up boundaries, within the size constraints, that represent a gerrymander – as suggested by the 1983 proposals for Congressional districts in New Jersey (Fig. 4.5). Only in one aspect of gerryman-

Fig. 4.5 The proposed Congressional districts for the State of New Jersey. These were produced to meet the 'equality of population' requirement set down by the Supreme Court, and on average differed by only 0.1384 per cent from the average population. The population of the largest was 527 472 and the smallest 523 798. The proposal was rejected by the Supreme Court, not because it was a clear attempted gerrymander but because it was shown that an even smaller deviation could have been achieved with a minor change in the allocation of municipalities to districts

dering have the Courts been prepared to intervene. In some States, constituency boundaries have been drawn to minimize the number of districts in which black voters form a majority. The Courts have ruled that this is against the equal protection afforded to blacks under the Fourteenth Amendment, and have required redistricting schemes which give blacks a majority in the number of districts relative to their percentage of the state population: this is known as *affirmative gerrymandering* (Grofman et al. 1982).

Space in American political processes

The focus in the previous section was on the political manipulation of space for individual and group ends, within the context of the capitalist system. Here the focus shifts to the role of space in political processes, with particular reference to the geography of public spending.

Governments provide a variety of goods and services for the residents of their territories. Some of these goods and services are known as *pure public goods* and are provided equally for all residents, wherever they live within the national territory; further, those residents are unable to opt out of 'consuming' the relevant good (a collective term for goods and services). The best example of pure public goods is national defence which, in theory at least, provides blanket coverage for the entire US so there is no geography to its provision.

Most public goods fall into one of two other categories. *Impure public goods* are those which are in fixed locations, such as public parks, and provide greater benefits to nearby residents than to people living further away. The spatial distribution of benefits around the location may take a variety of forms. The most common are: (1) the tapering distribution, whereby the benefits available decline with distance from the location, because the further they live from it, the less able people are to use the facility provided there (health care facilities are used most by those living nearby, for example); and (2) the cellular distribution, whereby the service is available only to the residents of a defined territory within which it is located (some municipalities have libraries but others

do not, for example). Finally, there are the *impurely distributed public services*, which are not provided equally but are allocated spatially so that some areas, and their residents, benefit more than others. It is with this last type, with better schools in some areas than others, for example, or better levels of street repair, and with the political processes involved in the 'impure' distributions, that the brief examples in the remainder of this section refer to.

The pork barrel

In the federal Congress, in the State Legislatures, and in some county and city councils, each of the elected members represents a defined constituency – a State for a US Senator, a Congressional district for a US Representative, and a ward for City Councilman. All members of federal and of most State legislatures are elected on a party label. They will wish to be re-elected and will therefore benefit from party support. In addition, however, members will seek to win favour with the electorate by showing that they are representing them successfully; one way of demonstrating this is by winning political benefits. This is known as *pork-barrel politics*, defined by Ferejohn (1974: 2) as 'a few powerful senators and congressmen . . . able to treat the public purse as a development fund for their states or districts'.

This apparent ability of members to influence the flow of public money – i.e. to distribute public goods impurely so as to benefit the people who, hopefully, will vote for them at the next election – reflects the decentralized nature of much American political decision-making, as illustrated here by the federal Congress. There, spending decisions are enacted via a budget, presented to Congress by the President, debated by the House and the Senate, and finally a compromise is agreed upon by all. The budget proposes spending under programmes already agreed by the Congress, so what the President is doing is suggesting how much should be spent, given that some spending has been agreed. Although it is Congress as a whole which makes the final decision (which the President can veto; the Presidential veto can be over-ridden only by a two-thirds majority of *both* houses), the details are discussed in a range of standing Committees and Sub-Committees. Thus, for example, issues relating to national defence are discussed in the Armed Services Committees, and the budget for the agreed programmes is discussed by the Defense Sub-Committees of the Appropriation Committees. Membership of the relevant Sub-Committees and Committees should allow congressmen substantial control over the allocation of funds, which they can exercise in their own interests. Within those Committees and Sub-Committees, greatest power resides in the members of the majority party, and within each party it resides in the more senior members.

According to this presentation of the operations of Congress, individual congressmen should seek to represent the interests of their constituents, and thus to further their re-election chances, by obtaining positions on Committees and Sub-Committees which allow them to manipulate the allocation of relevant public benefits. The outcome should be that money is directed to the States and districts represented on the relevant decision-making bodies.

The first part of this hypothesis is readily substantiated, for the evidence of congressmen seeking, and obtaining, 'pork-barrel-oriented' Committee positions is clear. For example, the House and Senate Agriculture Committees are responsible for determining federal policy with regard to agricultural subsidies and other programmes of immense benefit to farmers, and the relevant Sub-Committees of Appropriations (Agriculture, Environmental and Consumer Protection) decide on the levels of spending on each programme. (The Agriculture Committees are subdivided: the House Committee, for example, has Commodity Sub-Committees on Cotton, Rice and Sugar; Livestock, Dairy and Poultry; Tobacco and Peanuts; Wheat, Soybeans and Feed Grain. Members of the Committee will want to be on Sub-Committees that can be used to further their pork-barrel interests.) The geography of representation for agriculture in 1985 illustrates the position very well (Fig. 4.6). On the two Agriculture Committees and the two Appropriations Sub-Committees together there was only one member representing a New England State

(a Senator from Vermont) and the industrial States of the Northeast were substantially under-represented; not surprisingly, the congressmen from the agricultural States dominated. And then in the Sub-Committees of the House Committee (Fig. 4.7), the special interests of particular groups of States are clearly represented.

Not all congressmen are able to obtain coveted Committee positions – their party may have no vacancy there, or there may be others from their home State already allocated to them. And so they must serve elsewhere, and will then bargain with the members of other Committees to obtain desirable benefits (this is known as log-rolling). In addition, the parties need members for the Committees that carry few potential pork-barrel benefits – Government Operations, Judiciary, and Rules, for example; in general, these Committees are dominated in the House by Representatives from the larger States, which can 'afford' a member on such a Committee because the size of the State's delegation ensures its full representation on the 'pork-barrel' committees (Johnston 1980).

Despite this clear evidence of Committee assignments following the pork-barrel instincts of congressmen, the evidence that they are able to manipulate the budget to their constituents', and their own, ends is much less convincing. There is a great deal of anecdotal evidence, but detailed statistical analyses rarely provide overwhelming support; congressmen, it seems, obtain privileged positions on Committees, boast of this and of their ability to represent their constituents accordingly, but fail to 'deliver the goods', at least on a wholesale basis. Part of this is because their freedom of action is limited: much of any year's budget is fixed by previous decisions (known as incrementalism), so that it is only at the margins that congressmen can influence the geography of spending. This was indicated in a careful analysis by Ferejohn (1974) of spending in major public works projects on rivers and harbours undertaken by the Corps of Engineers. He looked only at new projects and found that in 1967 the States represented on the relevant Committees gained on average 0.819 new projects, compared to 0.032 for the States not represented. Within the Committees, members

Member of
the House
Committee on
Agriculture

Member of
the House
Committee on
Appropriations,
Sub-Committee
on Agriculture,
Rural
Development
and Related
Agencies

Fig. 4.6 States represented on the Agriculture Committees and the Agricultural Sub-Committees, 1985

■ Member of the Senate Sub-Committee on Agriculture, Nutrition and Forestry

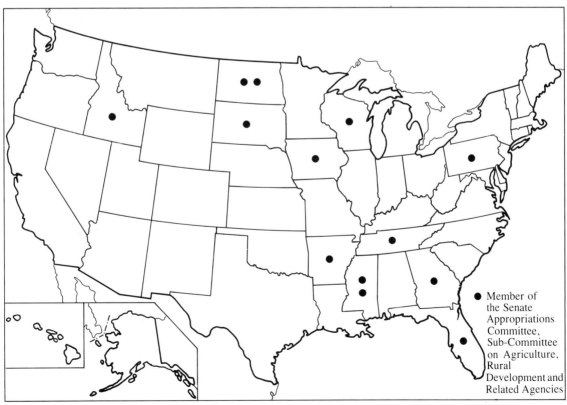

● Member of the Senate Appropriations Committee, Sub-Committee on Agriculture, Rural Development and Related Agencies

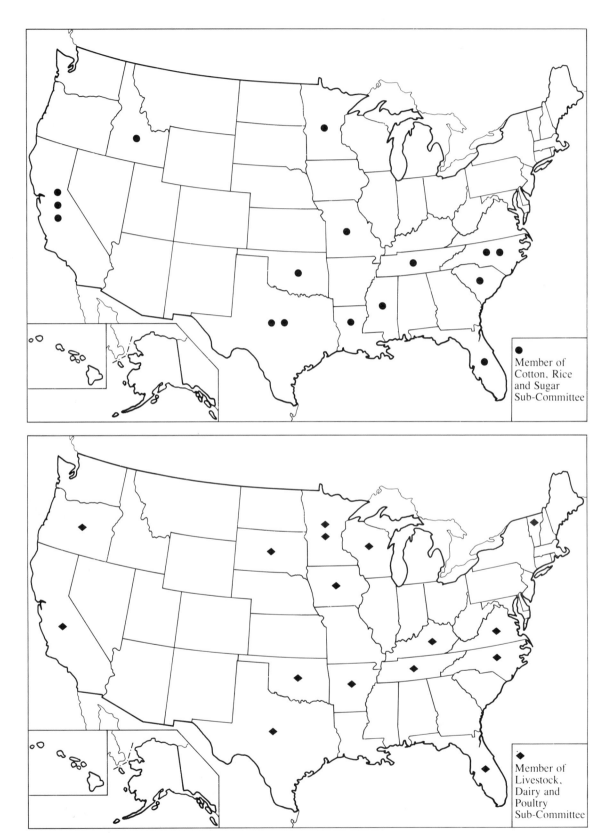

Fig. 4.7 States represented on the Commodity Sub-Committees of the House Committee on Agriculture, 1985

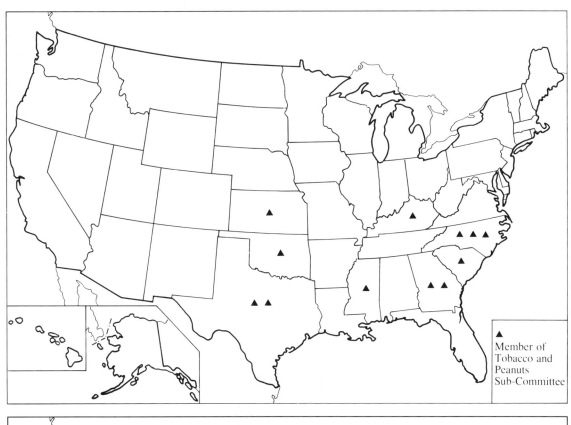

Member of
Tobacco and
Peanuts
Sub-Committee

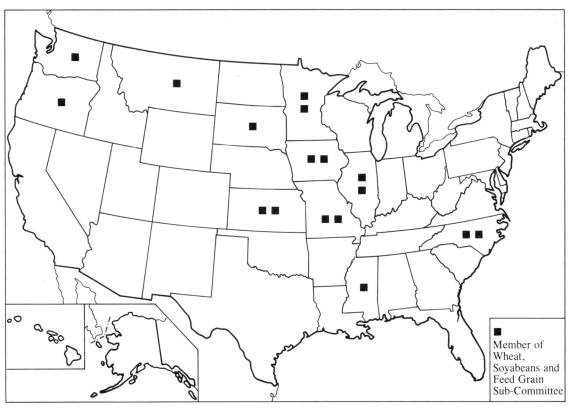

Member of
Wheat,
Soyabeans and
Feed Grain
Sub-Committee

of the Public Works Committee (the programme setters) were better able to serve their home States than were members of the relevant Appropriations Sub-Committees, the senior members of the Committee were best able to win pork-barrel benefits, and Democrats (the majority party) were more successful than Republicans.

Ferejohn's findings indicate the pork-barrel process very clearly, as do several others (reviewed in Johnston 1980). Many do not, however, and the statistical links between representation, spending and re-election are generally weak (Archer 1980, 1983). Rundquist (1983: 410) suggests that 'a policy-maker's ability to provide political benefits is contingent on whether some other policy-maker needs his or her support and is willing to trade political benefits to get it'. He argues that one policy-maker (A – a congressman in the present

context) will offer benefits to B (i.e. allow B pork-barrel benefits from a programme), if the programme favoured by A is thought to face serious opposition; in that context A will seek B's support, assuming that B is unlikely to support the programme unless he or she is induced to and that offering B pork-barrel benefits will win support for A's policy. This argument, he claims, accounts for the research findings that whereas pork barrelling has been clearly identified in the context of relatively small programmes (as a percentage of the total budget) it has not been discerned in the large programmes, such as military contracts. This is because the latter need wide support because of their expense; Committees and Sub-Committees can promote their own interests with small programmes but with the large ones a majority of members are interested (if they don't get some benefits, their credibility is

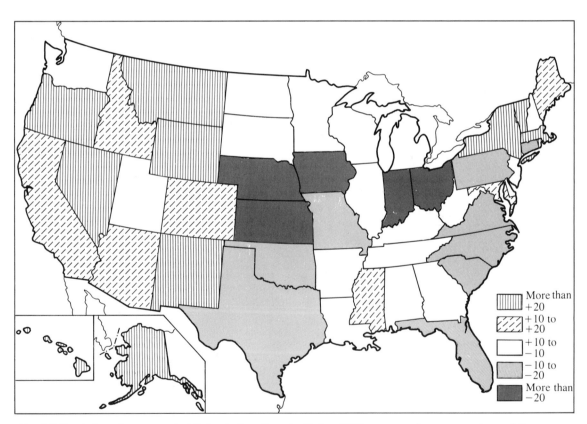

Fig. 4.8 Deviations from expected federal allocations to States, 1978, expressed as a percentage of the estimated allocation according to State population
Data compiled from Copeland and Meier (1984)

weak), and so a minority cannot benefit themselves without facing a challenge on the floor of the House. If widespread support is required, virtually every member must be offered some of the benefits, so the pork barrel is only relevant (nationally, though not locally) with small programmes.

Given that most congressmen will obtain at least one position on a Committee or Sub-Committee handling small programmes with which pork barrelling is possible, then all will win some benefits, and overall the geography of public spending will show no bias reflecting a geography of political power. Copeland and Meier (1984: 17) have suggested that as a consequence Congress operates two norms: (1) that 'everyone should receive a reasonable share whenever practical'; and (2) that when this is not practical, everyone (i.e. every congressman) should benefit from some programmes. The result will be equal shares in

the overall pattern of public spending – it should be highly correlated with the distribution of population. Their analyses show this ($r^2 = 0.95$ for 1978). Nevertheless, there are variations, as Fig. 4.8 shows. The States which received well 'above-average' shares in 1978 were almost all either in the West (where the federal government owns much land) or in the Northeast; the exceptions were Maryland (much of which is suburban to Washington DC) and Mississippi (which is among the poorest). Most of the major 'losers' were either in the South or in the Midwest. The States in the latter have for long complained of poor treatment in the federal allocation of money (see Murphy 1971), especially given their above-average contributions to the federal exchequer via taxation (Johnston 1980). Residents of the southern States pay less in taxes per capita, and so most of these States are net beneficiaries overall (Fig. 4.9).

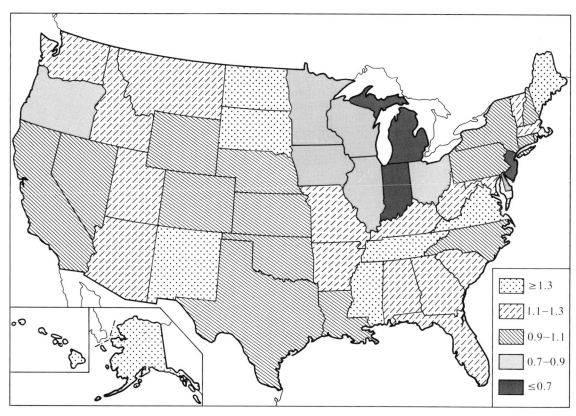

Fig. 4.9 Net flows to and from States, 1979. The ratios are of federal funds received during the fiscal year 1979 divided by federal taxes paid, so that a ratio greater than 1.0 indicates a net outflow

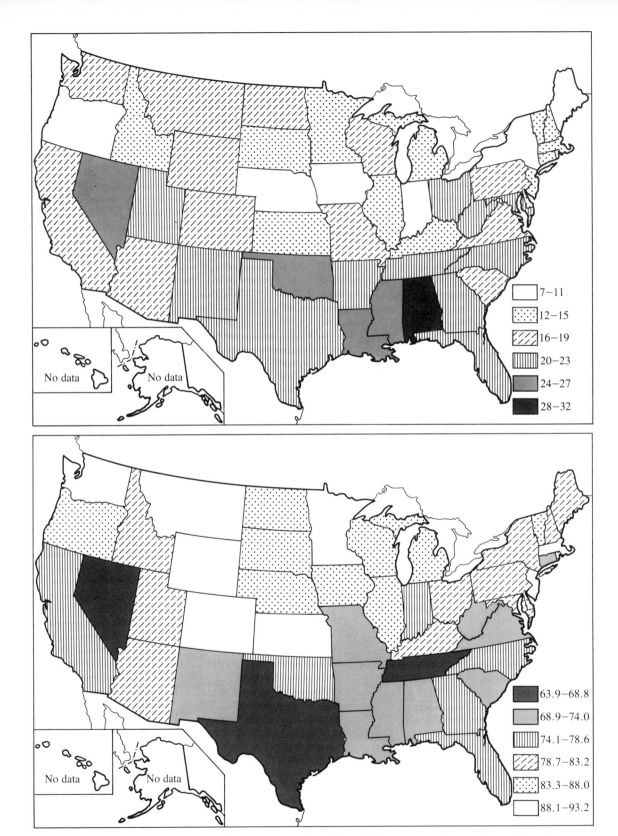

Fig. 4.10 The geography of the AFDC programme, 1972–73: (A) States assessed according to the stringency of the eligibility criteria applied (the higher the index, the greater the stringency); (B) the percentage of applications approved; (C) the monthly spending, largest amount, to meet basic needs for a family of four; and (D) the percentage of a State's families living below the poverty line but lifted above it by receipt of AFDC payments

Sources: Wohlenberg (1976c), Fig. 1, p. 383; (1976a), Fig. 2, p. 257 and Fig. 4, p. 261; (1976b), Fig. 1, p. 442

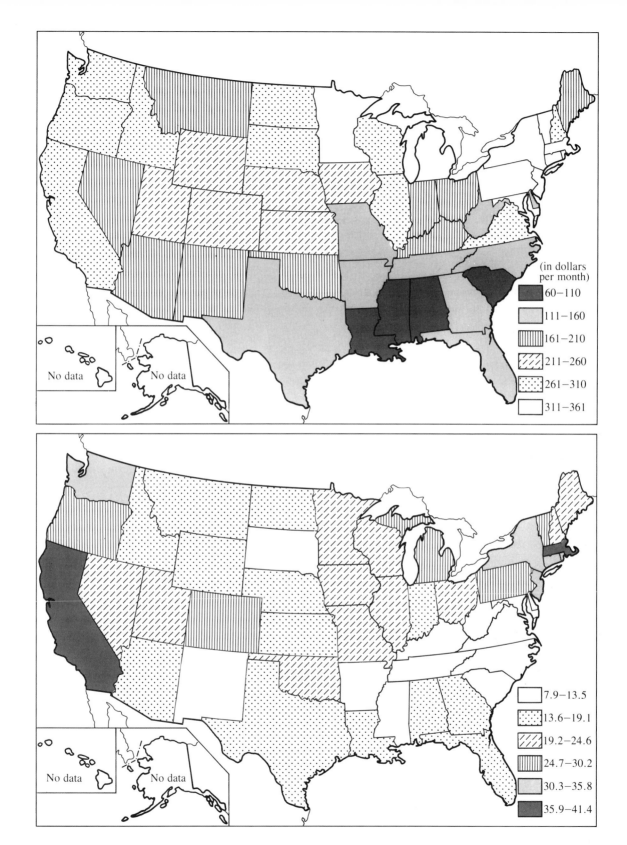

(in dollars per month)

■	60–110
▨ (light gray)	111–160
▥ (vertical lines)	161–210
▨ (diagonal lines)	211–260
▨ (dotted)	261–310
□	311–361

No data   No data

□	7.9–13.5
▨ (dotted)	13.6–19.1
▨ (diagonal lines)	19.2–24.6
▥ (vertical lines)	24.7–30.2
▨ (light gray)	30.3–35.8
■	35.9–41.4

No data   No data

State governments and welfare programmes

The preceding discussion has outlined how representatives of a particular district within a territory can seek to benefit their constituents via the geography of public spending. This can operate at any scale, in local governments as much as in the federal government. Local governments (including State governments) also have autonomy to decide how much they will spend on a particular programme, thereby providing a geography of local action.

The geography of spending on a particular type of programme should reflect three sets of factors. The first comprises *needs*: the greater the need for a certain service, the greater its provision should be. The second comprises *resources*: the richer the authority, the greater its provision should be. The final comprises *political dispositions*: if the population of the area and the government representing it are favourable to a certain type of programme, then spending is likely to be greater than where they are not in favour. These three sets interact, especially with regard to welfare state programmes. Needs and resources are usually negatively related, for example, in that places with substantial demands for welfare programmes are usually those with relatively weak tax bases. On the other hand, needs and political dispositions should be positively related: the greater the need, the more likely this is to be high on the political agenda.

Many analyses, almost all at the State government level, have sought to demonstrate the validity of this general model, particularly the political disposition variable. In general, it has been suggested, and at least partially verified, that those who operate the political system – State government politicians and bureaucrats – should be most responsive to needs in *marginal* States, where a lack of response could mean a loss of power. Spending on welfare state programmes, then, should be greatest where (a) needs are greatest, (b) resources are greatest, and (c) the political realities demand a response. Johnston (1980) has shown, in line with this, that in 1972 the States with substantial Democrat control (mainly in the South) spent on average about $80 less per capita on educational services than did the more marginal States, and their monthly welfare payments were significantly lower too.

Such analyses suggest that there is a clear geography not only of State spending on welfare programmes but also of policy success. Many welfare programmes have been promoted by the federal government, which offers financial inducements to State governments to operate them. The degree to which the States take up these inducements should reflect their political dispositions. the needs that they face, and the local resources at their disposal. But there is no uniformity of treatment.

One of the largest federal–State welfare programmes in recent decades has been the *Aid to Families with Dependent Children* (AFDC) programme, aimed mainly at poor, one-parent families. Within this, the States determine the eligibility criteria, and Wohlenberg (1976a) has shown that in general the southern States have the most stringent criteria (Fig. 4.10A); some States, for example, excluded only applicants with liquid assets of $1000 or more, whereas others excluded those with any such assets. The States also differed in their acceptance rates as a consequence (again, the southern States stand out, approving the lowest percentages of applications: Fig. 4.10B), in the cost of living standards that they applied (Wohlenberg 1976b), and thus in the monthly payments that they made (Fig. 4.10C; note again the position of the southern States). The result was a clear geography of AFDC effectiveness (Fig. 4.10D); in the southern States it was least effective in lifting poor families above the poverty line (Wohlenberg 1976c).

The maps in Fig. 4.10 suggest a geography of welfare spending in line with the expectations regarding political dispositions. The AFDC programme was not very effective in raising large percentages of families above the poverty level in the block of non-competitive States in the South, for example (compare Figs 4.4 and 4.10D). This suggests that the political geography of State government, itself a consequence of political cultural variations, has strongly influenced policy operation and effectiveness. Although needs are great in the South, political dispositions are not inclined to meet them, because the Democrat Party is so securely entrenched in power. However, the southern States are also poor, the federal payments cover only part of the costs of operating AFDC programmes, and it may be the absence of resources, as much as the lack of political mobilization of demand, which produces the poor southern performance (Johnston 1980).

These analyses do not take full account of the variations in political culture within the US. As stressed earlier in this chapter, the parties differ very substantially between regions in their ideological base: the northern Democrats are relatively liberal on welfare state programmes whereas the ultra-conservative southern Democrats are strongly opposed to them, largely because they see the main beneficiaries as blacks (Cowart 1969). Thus, further analyses have investigated the political dispositions in terms of both party control and the presence of black recipients (Johnston 1983). These showed: (1) that average payments declined as the percentage of blacks in the population increased; (2) that average payments increased as per capita incomes increased; and (3) that average payments were lowest in the non-competitive States. Thus the greater the resources the greater the payments, but the greater the probability that blacks would benefit; and the firmer the Democrat Party control, the lower the payments.

In summary

The federal government must act to preserve, protect and help guarantee the future of American capitalism . . . continually responsive to the many problems, tensions, and contradictions thrown up by the dynamic processes of the capitalist economy (Greenberg 1983: 345).

This chapter has provided a foundation for understanding the political element in the contemporary geography of the US. The institutions of the state are necessary to the operations and are built on tensions among the many different interest groups within society. Without the state, the legitimation of the capitalist system would be seriously under threat, and the prospects for continued accumulation dim.

The state is necessary to American economy and society, therefore – just as it is to any other (capitalist or not). But its detailed form is not determined. The state is a set of institutions created by individuals and groups in response to perceived situations, and continually modified as the situations change – in part, because of state actions. How the situations are perceived, and what the sensible response to them is identified as, reflects the individuals concerned. These operate in cultural contexts, within which they have been socialized: their perceptions and decision-making are constrained by those contexts, which provide the environment that enables individual action. Capitalism is a mode of production created and maintained by individuals operating as free agents, but within the confines of their cultures which provide the parameters for action.

The cultural context of the state in America is an amalgam of several influences, each of which is more important in some parts of the country than in others. Thus the political geography of the US and the geography of the state – how it is organized, what it does, and how – reflect the political–cultural geography. In seeking to understand what the state does where, therefore, we must appreciate not only the general theory of the state in capitalist society but also how that theory has been interpreted locally. The state is deeply implicated in the geography of the US; understanding that requires careful study of the political cultures.

Chapter 5

THE ECONOMIC ORGANIZATION OF US SPACE

In just over six generations, the US economy has evolved from a relatively minor outpost of the European economic system into the world's largest and most powerful economic force. At the same time, it has changed radically in its nature and organization. Since the subsistence economies of native Americans were edged aside by a variable mixture of frontier farming and colonial mercantilism, the continual adjustment and evolution of the economy has resulted in a remarkably rapid transition through independent mercantilism to industrial capitalism and on to the advanced form of capitalism which now not only characterizes the US economy but also forms the leading edge of the world economic system.

Meanwhile, the economic landscape of the US itself has been transformed by the successive imprint of mercantilism, industrial capitalism and advanced capitalism. During each of these major phases of development, new resources, new technologies and new types of business organization were exploited against the constraints and contradictions imposed by the legacy of previous phases of development. As these changes shifted the margins of profitability in different kinds of enterprise, so the pattern of economic activity was altered, recasting the structure of employment opportunities and overwriting the economic landscape with new elements of settlement and infrastructure. In some regions, and for certain periods, these changes were superimposed one on the other. In other cases, the imperatives of profitability excluded whole regions from particular aspects of change. In short, each phase of economic development has impacted in different ways and to different degrees in different regions. The present economic geography of the US must, therefore, be seen in the light of the spatial evolution of the economy. The first part of this chapter accordingly reviews the template of economic development established during the phases of mercantilism and industrial capitalism. Attention here is focused on the growth of the urban system, the

Top left: Harvesting wheat, Washington State *Credit*: United States Department of Agriculture   *Top right*: Abandoned store, Appalachian coalfields *Credit*: Paul Knox   *Middle left*: Manhattan, New York *Credit*: Paul Knox   *Middle centre*: The pickling line at US Steel's Irvin Plant *Credit*: US Steel Corporation   *Middle right*: Computer storage files *Credit*: IBM Corporation   *Lower left*: Blast furnace at US Steel's Pittsburgh plant *Credit*: US Steel Corporation   *Lower right*: Robotics section of General Motors assembly line *Credit*: General Motors Corporation

evolution of the transport system, and the emergent pattern of regional economic specialization, with particular emphasis on the rise of the Manufacturing Belt between New England and the Upper Midwest. In subsequent sections, we examine the spatial implications of the postwar era of advanced capitalism and of the increasing influence of government on urban and regional development. The concluding section of the chapter outlines the overall outcomes in terms of contemporary patterns of economic specialization and prosperity and describes the recent trajectory of particular groups of cities and regions in relation to one another.

The evolution of the urban system

The history of US urbanization is in great measure also the history of the development and evolution of the US economy. Under all three major phases of economic development – mercantilism, industrial capitalism and advanced capitalism – cities have played a central role in facilitating, expressing and conditioning the nation's economic affairs. Borchert (1967) suggests that the evolution of the US urban system can be interpreted in terms of the interaction of three factors: the pattern of *resources*, major *technological innovations* (especially innovations in transportation and communication), and *movements of population*. Thus:

Major changes in technology have resulted in critically important changes in the evaluation or definition of particular resources on which the growth of certain urban regions had previously been based. Great migrations have sought to exploit resources – ranging from climate or coal to water or zinc – that were either newly appreciated or newly accessible within the national market. Usually, of course, the new appreciation or accessibility came about, in turn, through some major technological innovation (Borchert 1967: 324).

Other important influences on long-term change in the urban system include political independence, the complementarity of regional resource bases, and processes of circular and cumulative growth; the emphasis given to each,

though, varies according to different theoretical orientations (Conzen 1981; Pred 1966, 1977, 1980; North 1966; Vance 1970). There is general agreement, however, that there were several distinctive phases in the evolution of the urban system and that each phase was characterized by a distinctive set of economic activities, transport and communication technologies, and methods of commercial and industrial organization. Moreover, it is generally recognized that the major turning points in the evolution of the system occurred around 1790, 1835, 1875 and 1920.

Colonial origins: the urban system to 1790

The closed, localized, subsistence economies of native American Indian communities could not sustain urban development of any kind, so that the first towns and cities in the US were those that were established as part of the colonial expansion of European mercantile capitalism. Located along the Atlantic seaboard in bays or estuaries, and on the navigable reaches of the Connecticut, Hudson, Delaware and Savannah rivers, these settlements acted as *gateway ports*: control points for the assembly of staple commodities for export, for the distribution of imported manufactured goods, and for the civil administration of the new territories (Johnston 1982b). For some time, each of these gateway ports, from Boston in the north to Savannah in the south, operated quite independently, drawing on their immediate hinterlands for hides and staple crops and engaging in diverse ocean trading patterns.

As colonization proceeded and the number of gateway ports increased, there developed an embryonic hierarchy of settlements. Those with more prosperous and/or more accessible hinterlands or with larger and more established local markets or administrative functions became larger and more developed in terms of their range of urban services. Meanwhile, there developed a system of lateral connections between ports, with coastal shipping providing a feeder service which facilitated the rationalization of transatlantic routes. The net result was that a few cities – Boston, New York, Philadelphia, Baltimore and Charleston – were able to establish themselves as major entrepôts. Salem (Mass.), Providence (R.I.) and Newport (R.I.) were able to achieve the status of second-ranking entrepôts, while the more important of the smaller ports included Portsmouth and Newburyport (N.H.), New Haven and New London (Conn.), Annapolis (Md.), Norfolk (Va.), Savannah (Ga.) and New Orleans (La.). In addition, the larger hinterlands of the major entrepôts were able to support an array of smaller settlements – emergent *inland gateways* which acted as bulking points and provided central place functions for the frontier agriculturalists. By the time of the Revolution in 1776, the most notable of these were Hartford, Middletown and Norwich (Conn.), Albany (N.Y.), Lancaster (Pa.) and Richmond (Va.).

1790–1835: independent mercantilism and the sail and wagon epoch

Political independence stimulated the development of the urban system in several ways. First, independence from Britain and national political integration under a federal system provided an important stimulus for economic links to be forged between the component parts of the old colonial system. Second, it meant that a much greater proportion of mercantile investment was financed by American capital, with the result that less of the profits were 'leaked' back to the European metropolitan system. Third, it stimulated a remarkable proliferation of government functions at all levels, consequently stimulating the growth of hundreds of towns. Finally, the territorial expansion of the US stimulated the westward extension of the urban system by making much larger potential hinterlands available. In 1783, when the US finally achieved independence from Britain, its land area totalled 2.27 million sq km, or about one quarter of its present size. This was almost doubled by the Louisiana Purchase of 1803, while the addition of Texas, Oregon and the territories acquired from Mexico in 1846 extended the US land area to nearly 7.68 million sq km: thirty-five times the size of Britain.

Urban and economic development in this period was based on a combination of frontier agriculture and mercantilism. Both, however, were constrained by the relatively primitive transportation system of the 'sail and wagon' epoch (Borchert 1967). Foreign commerce began a long decline in its contribution to urban growth, so that the most vigorous development occurred in areas of westward expansion: the drift-covered valleys and plateau surfaces of western New York, the Ontario Plain, the Mississippi Valley, the Bluegrass and the Nashville Basin, the timber-rich areas of plentiful water power in the Adirondacks and northern Appalachia, and the anthracite areas of northeastern Pennsylvania. The most striking growth of all, though, occurred in the gateway cities located at strategic points along the inland waterways that linked the new western lands with the major centres of the Atlantic seaboard. New Orleans grew particularly rapidly in the first two decades of the nineteenth century because of its situation at the mouth of the Mississippi system and the comparative advantage of water-borne transport over the primitive turnpike network. The extent of this advantage is illustrated by the fact that European goods destined for Cincinnati were shipped inland via New Orleans and the Mississippi rather than overland through one of the east coast ports.

East coast merchants, however, were not content to let the lucrative trade from western and southern hinterlands slip from their grasp. Their response was the intensive development of their common immediate hinterlands, tapping the waterways of the Great Lakes and the Hudson, Ohio and Mississippi river systems with networks of canals. As a result, New York gained an early dominance which has never been seriously challenged, while two major regional wholesaling alignments emerged roughly at right angles to the coastal axis of entrepôts. One of these stretched from New York up the Hudson and the Erie Canal (opened in 1825) to the eastern Great Lakes, where Buffalo and Detroit emerged as major inland gateways. The other reached across the mountains from Philadelphia and Baltimore to Pittsburgh and the Ohio Valley, where Cincinnati and Louisville were the most important gateways. Further west, St Louis also emerged as a major gateway, with its location at the confluence of the Missouri and Mississippi allowing it to tap its own hinterland to the west while capitalizing on the trading routes both to the east and to the south.

Meanwhile, the urban system was becoming increasingly *differentiated* in terms of economic functions. Manufacturing began to contribute to the growth of the leading eastern mercantile centres, while some specialized industrial towns – Albany, Lowell, Newark, Ploughkeepsie, Providence, Springfield and Wilmington – emerged in the more heavily populated and intensively developed northeast; and Cincinnati began to specialize in hog processing, thus acquiring the dubious distinction of 'Porkopolis'. This differentiation reflects the increasing integration of the urban system, to the extent that, by 1835, it could be conceived of as a more or less independent economic system. Nevertheless, long- distance transport retained expensive, and the fundamental organization of mercantilism remained focused on individual gateway cities, articulated through dendritic systems of waterways. Thus the economic landscape of independent mercantilism can best be described as a *mosaic of resource regions*, with each region dominated by a few major centres and each rather different in its detailed pattern of settlement. Conzen (1981), for example, points to the contrasts between the intensive, three-tier central place subsystems which developed within the immediate hinterland of Philadelphia, the radial central place network which centred on Cincinnati, the failure of smaller towns to emerge at all in the plantation-dominated economy of the South, and the proliferation of specialized manufacturing towns and villages throughout eastern Massachusetts.

1835–75: industrialization, expansion, realignment and differentiation in the 'iron horse' epoch

The process of transition from mercantilism to industrial capitalism accelerated strikingly during the late 1830s and early 1840s. In part, this was the result of the diffusion of industrial technology – particularly the wider industrial application of steam and the accompanying changes in the iron industry – and methods of industrial and commercial organization from the hearth of the industrial revolution in north-western Europe. In addition, the demand for foodstuffs and other agricultural staples, both in the US and abroad, stimulated the growth of industrial capitalism as farmers sought to increase productivity through mechanization and the use of improved agricultural implements. Increasing agricultural productivity, in turn, helped to sustain the constantly growing numbers of immigrants, thus allowing them to be channelled into industrial employment in America's mushrooming cities.

The development of the railroad system was central to the evolution of the new economic order. Within a few years of the initiation of work on the first railroad – the Baltimore and Ohio – in 1828, there had emerged a series of regional rail networks, each converging at ports on the inland waterways that penetrated the extensive agricultural potential of the Interior Plains. Initially, therefore, the railroads were complementary to the waterways as competitive long-haul carriers of general freight. By the end of the period – the 'iron horse' epoch (Borchert 1967) – the railroad network had not only realigned the urban system but also extended it to a continental scale. In 1869, the railroad network reached the Pacific when, at Promontory, Utah, the Union Pacific railroad, building west from Omaha, met the Central Pacific railroad, building east from Sacramento; and by 1875 intense competition between railroad companies had begun to open up the western prairies as far as Minneapolis–St Paul and Kansas City. The significance of this has been stressed by Hamilton (1978: 26, emphasis added):

Not only did this permit American enterprise to exploit fully the commercial advantages and scale economies of large, diversified natural resources and of the revolutionary technologies evolved in those decades, but it generated rapid, large-scale functional and spatial concentration of finance and management unimpeded by world events, creating a *trans*continental business mentality. Wide spatial separation of major resources, cities and markets, and adjacency to the easily-penetrated Canadian economy all induced mental thresholds for thinking '*inter*continental' once imported resources and markets overseas became a necessary ingredient to sustain business activity at home, especially during and after the Second World War.

In short, the railroad can be seen as the catalyst which allowed a regional economy to develop into a continental economy which stood poised to become the leading component of the world economic system.

Meanwhile, the spatial organization of the US economy was *realigned* by the development of the railroad system. Once Ohio, Indiana and Illinois began to be criss-crossed by feeders to the Ohio Valley routes of the Pennsylvania and Baltimore and Ohio railroads, increasingly large quantities of agricultural commerce were siphoned off directly to the north east. Similarly, the westward thrust of railroads such as the Chicago, Burlington and Quincy into northern Illinois, southern Wisconsin and eastern Iowa allowed large quantities of corn and wheat to be moved directly eastwards rather than being shipped by water via St Louis and the Lower Mississippi. As a result, New Orleans lost a good deal of its trade and, further disadvantaged by the outcome of the Civil War, thereafter functioned more as a higher-order central place than as a major gateway city (Lewis 1976). The westward extension of the railroads also affected the relative fortunes of the inland gateway cities. Buffalo and Louisville, for instance, slowed their rate of growth and came to rely increasingly on more diversified regional functions, while St Paul and Kansas City grew rapidly to become major wholesaling depots. It is also important to note that the development of improved transportation networks led to adjustments in spatial organization within the Northeast, where fierce competition between the railroads and water-borne transport (which led to a fall in freight rates from between 30 to 70 cents per ton-mile at the beginning of the century to less than 5 cents per ton-mile in 1850), coupled with equally fierce rivalry between neighbouring cities, led to a marked increase in intra-regional trade (Pred 1980). This, in turn, helped to lay the foundations of what was to become the Manufacturing Belt, as the two major east–west wholesaling alignments (New York/Buffalo/Detroit and Philadelphia/Pittsburgh/Cincinnati/Louisville) began to merge into a larger subsystem which included Chicago, Milwaukee and a number of other urban newcomers.

At the same time, the entire system became increasingly *differentiated* as the industrialization of the economy created new kinds of specialist town. Thus emerged a variety of specialist mining towns – mainly in Appalachia – and a whole series of specialist manufacturing towns based on the water-power resources of the Fall Line in New England and along the eastern margins of the Appalachians. The production of agricultural machinery, meanwhile, became a specialty of some Midwestern towns – notably Racine (Wisconsin) and Moline (Illinois), where J. I. Case and John Deere respectively established large plants. The new spatial division of labour associated with industrialization also made for differentiation and specialization in established cities. Thus, for example, Jersey City emerged as a specialist wholesale terminal, Rochester specialized in office and optical equipment, and Washington, DC became established in the role of federal administrative centre. The economic base of most of the longer-established cities became more diversified as manufacturing establishments and service industries were opened to serve local markets while the very largest (including the mushrooming Chicago and San Francisco), with more local capital, bigger markets, larger pools of skilled labour, and a high degree of nodality in relation to newspaper, postal and telegraphic services, were able not only to expand and diversify their economic base but also to become the major control centres of industrial activity for the entire continent.

1875–1920: industrial location within the urban system

As industrial capitalism gathered momentum and transport and communications networks became both more extensive and more efficient, the shape and character of the urban system increasingly came to be determined by spatial variations in the *costs of production*. Patterns of urban and economic growth were influenced by the logic of economies of scale, the relative pull of markets and raw materials, the development of localized economic linkages, the multiplier effects of industrial employment, the creation and diffusion of technological innovations, and accessibility to sources of capital through the emerging banking system (Conzen 1977; Pred 1966). It was in this period that the template of *regional economic specialization* was established and the nation's economic core – the Manufacturing Belt – was consolidated.

At the same time, the entire urban system expanded as immigration continued to fuel the growth of existing cities, the infilling of settled areas, and the colonization of the few remaining frontier regions. Conzen (1981) estimates that over 1300 new urban places appeared between the censuses of 1880 and 1910, doubling the total number and representing twice the rate of expansion that had occurred during the 'iron horse' epoch. Many of these new settlements were the result of the commercialization of the remaining agricultural land resources of the West – the Texas and Oklahoma Prairies, the Colorado piedmont, the Wasatch piedmont, the Central Valley and Southern California, and the Puget Sound/Willamette lowland – and the exploitation of major mineral deposits, such as the copper at Butte, the lead and zinc of southwestern Missouri, and the iron ore around Lake Superior. The escalating demand for coal, meanwhile, resulted in a cluster of boom cities on the Western Pennsylvania coalfields, in the area between Pittsburgh and Lake Erie, and on the rich bituminous deposits of West Virginia and eastern Kentucky. Following the Civil War and Reconstruction and the extension of regional accessibility conferred by the development of the railroad system (from just over 48 500 fragmented kilometres of track in 1860 to over 257 000 integrated kilometres by 1890 (Meyer 1983), new towns such as Birmingham, Jacksonville, Memphis and Houston emerged in the South to provide regional central place functions; and for the same reasons most of the older towns – Savannah, Charleston, Mobile and Nashville, for example – revived to become regional hubs. The railroads were even more influential in the expansion of settlement in the Great Plains, where company officials, working in collaboration with grain elevator companies and lumber dealers, literally dictated the pattern and design of lower-order central places (Hudson 1979).

It would be misleading, however, to convey the impression of unmitigated urban growth. The changing logic of industrial location worked to the disadvantage of manufacturing towns at historic water-power sites along the Fall Line, while the continued expansion of east–west wholesaling chains based on the railroads ensured the relatively sluggish growth of St Louis and Louisville together with many of the smaller towns on the great waterways. Furthermore, inertia and conservatism among the leading entrepreneurs of some of the older mercantile cities resulted in a failure to invest in more profitable industries such as iron and steel, machinery and machine tools, leaving the local economy to depend on slower-growing industries such as printing and publishing, confectionery, clothing and furniture which relied heavily on local rather than regional or national markets. And in the South, urban development was undoubtedly retarded (central place functions notwithstanding) by the combination of absentee ownership of industrial activity and a freight-rate system which required southern producers to pay more for shipping their manufactures a given distance than their northern competitors. Thus the period between 1875 and 1920 saw not only the expansion of the urban system and the establishment of the pattern of American regional economic specialization but also the origins of *uneven urban and regional economic development.*

The Manufacturing Belt and regional economic specialization

Although there is some debate as to the underlying processes (Lindstrom 1978; Meyer 1983; Muller 1977; North 1961), it is generally agreed that the fundamental pattern of regional economic specialization had emerged by 1920, dominated by a national economic heartland which de Geer (1927) dubbed the Manufacturing Belt (Fig. 5.1). As we have seen, the lineaments of the Manufacturing Belt, in the form of a set of wholesaling alignments and urban subsystems with an incipient industrial base, was already in existence by the 1870s. What happened during the late nineteenth century was that the territorial expansion of the

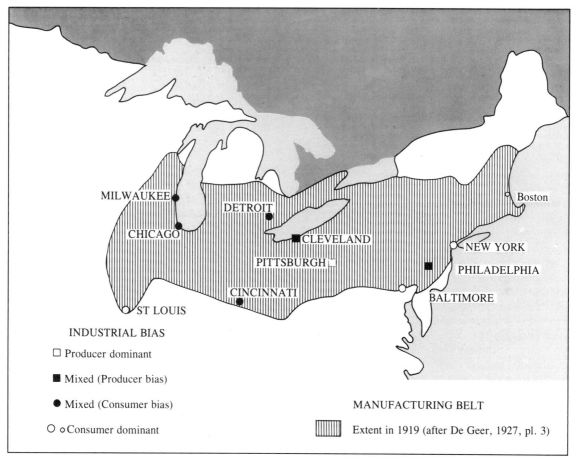

Fig. 5.1 The Manufacturing Belt in 1920
Source: After Conzen (1981), Fig. 9.13, p. 340

Manufacturing Belt was halted and its cities became both more *specialized* and more *closely integrated* with one another. In essence, the consolidation of the Manufacturing Belt as the national economic heartland was the result of initial advantage. With its large markets, well-developed transport networks and access to nearby coal reserves, it was ideally placed to take advantage of the general upsurge in demand for consumer foods, the increased efficiency of the telegraph system and postal services, the advances in industrial technology and the increasing logic of scale economies and external economies which characterized the late nineteenth century. The net effect was twofold.

First, individual cities beginning to specialize as producers were able to gear themselves to national rather than local markets:

Between 1870 and 1890, advances in milling technology and concentration of ownership supported the emergence of Minneapolis as a milling center. Furniture for the mass market centralized in fewer, larger plants using wood-working machinery. . . . The rise of national brewers between 1880 and 1910 is an example of national market firms encroaching on local–regional firms. The brewers in Milwaukee and St. Louis achieved economies of scale in manufacture, used production innovations such as mechanical refrigeration, and capitalized on distribution innovations made possible by the refrigerated rail car and an integrated rail network (Meyer 1983:160).

Similarly, fruit and vegetable canning and men's clothing emerged as specialties in Baltimore, musical instrument manufacture and men's clothing in Boston, meat packing, furniture manufacture and printing and publishing in Chicago, coachbuilding and furniture manufacture in Cincinnati, textile manufacture in Philadelphia, and glass and iron and steel in Pittsburgh. In smaller cities, specialization was often much more pronounced, as in the production of foundry and machine-shop products in Albany/Troy, Fort Wayne, Paterson and Taunton, iron and steel and coachbuilding in Columbus, furniture in Grand Rapids, distilled liquors in Peoria, agricultural implements in Springfield, and boots and shoes in Worcester. Overall, there emerged a three-part segmentation of the Manufacturing Belt (Fig. 5.1), with a heavy bias towards consumer-goods production in the mercantile-oriented ports of Baltimore, Boston and New York, a producer-goods axis between Philadelphia and Cleveland, and a western cluster of rather less specialized consumer-oriented manufacturing cities.

Second, this specialization provided the basis for increasing commodity flows between individual cities, thus binding the Manufacturing Belt together. These linkages, in turn, generated important multiplier effects through the intermediary functions of wholesaling, finance, warehousing and transportation, thus adding to the cumulative process of regional industrial growth (Pred 1977) and increasing the region's comparative advantage in terms of further industrial growth. These advantages meant that the Manufacturing Belt was able to attract a large proportion of any new industrial activities with large or national markets, and this in turn stifled the chances of comparable levels of industrialization in late-developing regions. As a result, the Manufacturing Belt did not extend westwards much beyond Minneapolis/St Paul and St Louis or southwards beyond Cincinnati and Baltimore.

This does not mean, of course, that other regions did not become industrialized. Rather, it was the scale and the intensity of industrialization which differed: later-developed regions were able to support an array of locally-oriented manufacturers, together with some nationally-oriented activities based on particular local advantages or raw materials; but they were rarely able to attract manufacturers of producer goods *for the national market*. Furthermore, it is clear that the increasing integration of the national economic system made for a significant degree of regional specialization (Niemi 1974). The most important features to emerge during the late nineteenth century were as follows:

- The rise of textile production in Georgia and the Carolinas: by 1900, South Carolina exhibited a greater degree of specialization in textile production than any other State in the Union, while the dominance of textile production in North Carolina was only exceeded in Rhode Island and New Hampshire.
- The rise of iron and steel production in Alabama, Tennessee and West Virginia.
- The increased emphasis on food manufacture – mostly sugar refining – in Louisiana.

The overall economic geography of the country in 1900 is illustrated by Fig. 5.2, which shows for each State the two most dominant industries in terms of their contribution to total manufacturing value added. At this level of generalization, the most striking feature is the extensive zone of specialization in food processing which extended from Kentucky through the Midwest to the Great Plains. Among the more important second-order manufactures in this zone were tobacco products (Kentucky and Missouri), transportation equipment (Kansas) and printing and publishing (North Dakota, South Dakota and Oklahoma). Equally striking is the dominance of food and lumber processing in the zones to the north (Upper Midwest) and south (Texas and the Lower Mississippi region). To the east, textile production accompanied by the manufacture of machinery and leather goods dominated New England; textiles with tobacco and lumber products dominated Georgia and the Carolinas; and primary metal production with non-electrical machinery and lumber products were the mainstay of Ohio, Pennsylvania, West Virginia and Alabama. Vermont, Virginia and Florida are conspicuous as eastern inliers of less 'advanced' mainstays: lumber processing with stone products, food processing and tobacco processing respectively.

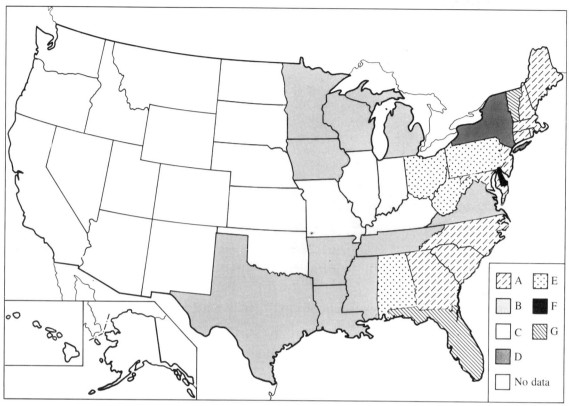

Fig. 5.2 Dominant manufacturing activities in 1900. A = Textiles/other; B = Food/lumber; C = Food/other; D = Apparel/food; E = Primary metals/other; F = Transportation equipment/leather products; G = Lumber/other
Based on data in Niemi (1974), Table 10, pp. 36–40

The inter-war years: growth and depression

If the template of American urban and economic geography had been established by 1920, the full details of industrial capitalism were etched in between 1920 and 1940, when the arrival of *truck and automobile* transportation and the acceleration of the *functional integration* of the economy triggered a further series of shifts and adjustments. As Borchert has pointed out, the mass production of the internal combustion engine

. . . put the farmer in an automobile and thus encouraged the centralization of urban growth at the larger, diversified centers in all the commercial farming regions. But also, by putting the farmer on

a tractor, it multiplied the land area he could work alone, initiated a revolution in family farm size, and sped the urbanization of much of rural America. In addition, air passenger transport helped to encourage centralization of the national business management function in a few cities, and the auto stimulated the decentralization of most metropolitan functions (Borchert 1967: 305–6).

Another consequence of the transition from steam to internal combustion was the relative decline of coal and railroad centres and, conversely, the rapid growth of metropolitan areas in the oilfields: from central Kansas through Oklahoma to western Texas, along the western Gulf Coast, and in southern California. In more densely populated metropolitan sub-regions, the development of highway networks induced the appearance of hundreds of satellite cities and dormitory towns and precipitated the process of metropolitan decentralization in which the entire structure of American cities was to be reorganized (Ch. 7).

Road and air travel, along with improvements in electronic communications, also increased the capacity and efficiency of the economy and facilitated the functional integration of both business and regions at an intoxicating pace. The 1920s were the 'New Economic Era', and the liberal reactions to industrialism which had characterized the Progressive Era before World War I were quickly edged aside by consumerism and boosterism. It was the larger companies based in the major metropolitan centres which were best placed to exploit the increased capacity and efficiency of the economic system. A flurry of company mergers just before the war had transformed the business structure of the US, resulting in a relatively small number of very powerful corporations which now stood poised to dominate the economy. By 1920, John D. Rockefeller's Standard Oil Company was providing paraffin for street lighting, asphalt for roads, lubricating oils for machinery, and petroleum for trucks and cars. One third of all jobs and nearly one half of the country's production was accounted for by just 1 per cent of all firms:

The Captains of Industry were clearly in charge. Across the country, territorial communities watched effective control over local production slip out of their grasp. Political power came to focus on the national level of territorial integration which, for the time being, effectively bounded the operation of most businesses (Friedmann and Weaver 1979: 22).

But the New Economic Era fostered some serious problems. Mechanized agriculture became so 'over-productive' that the selling price of a bushel of wheat plummeted from $1.82 in 1920 to 38 cents in 1932; while the industrial market became unstable as a result of a labyrinth of holding companies which had been created with 'watered' stock. In October 1929 the stock market collapsed, initiating the Great Depression in which millions of workers lost their jobs. Because of the regional division of labour which had emerged over the previous 50 years, some areas suffered particularly acute

social and economic problems, the intensity of which is best conveyed by novels such as Steinbeck's *The Grapes of Wrath* (1939). There were two consequences of the Great Depression which had important outcomes for the subsequent evolution of the spatial organization of the US economy. First, it drew attention to the inherent unevenness of regional development under industrial capitalism. In the South, concern over the region's economic and political dependency on the metropolitan core in the northeast spawned both the backward-looking Southern agrarians and the more liberal-minded New South movement. Elsewhere, concern over regional economic problems found expression in the Regional Planning movement, which had its roots in European ideas on utopian communities, resource conservation, municipal socialism and 'balanced' regional development. Second, the ideology of free enterprise came to be seriously challenged. Although President Hoover still felt morally obliged to pursue a policy of non-intervention in the 'natural' workings of the business system as late as the third year of the Great Depression, American voters preferred the idea of government intervention to provide relief, reform and recovery. Thus Franklin Roosevelt was elected to the presidency in 1932, not only introducing the New Deal programmes of progressive interventionism and the first real experiments in regional planning but also initiating a general expansion in state activity which was to gain increasing momentum until 1980 and which remains a major influence on the geography of economic and social well-being.

Development under advanced capitalism

Since World War II, the American economy has entered a substantially different phase: not simply in *what* it produces but also *how* and *where* it produces. This phase is sometimes referred to as 'late capitalism', 'corporate capitalism' or 'monopoly capitalism' as well as 'advanced capitalism'. Its principal characteristics follow from some of the trends which had been observable during the inter-war period of mature industrial capitalism: (a) a shift away from agriculture and manufacturing industries and towards service activities in the use of labour and capital (but not in terms of output), (b) a trend towards oligopoly as larger and more efficient corporations drive out their competitors and diversify their range of activities, and (c) an international redeployment of capital by large corporations in response to changing factor costs and the search for new markets. As in previous phases of economic development, the spatial outcomes of these organizational trends have been heavily conditioned by changes in transport and communications technologies. In this latest phase, the most significant developments have been the construction of the Inter-State Highway system (see p. 196), the growth of regional and subregional airports capable of handling large passenger and cargo jets, and the emergence of advanced telecommunications technologies.

A new economic context

Together, these trends and developments represent a new context for the spatial reorganization of the US economy. It is important, therefore, to identify the major processes involved in the postwar transition to advanced capitalism and to establish the associated changes which have occurred in the overall structure and performance of the economy.

Sectoral change

The sectoral shifts which characterize advanced capitalism stem from the cumulative interaction of several processes. One of the origins of the expanded role of the service sector can be traced to the specialization inherent to industrialization, the result of which was not only to stimulate trade but also to generate new opportunities for employment and investment in trade-related services: transportation, communications, utilities, wholesaling (distribution services); and services which enable firms to maintain their specialized roles: marketing, advertising, administration, finance and insurance (producer services). On the other hand, the increased productivity of agriculture and manufacturing which resulted from mech-

anization, automation and improved business organization has meant that fewer people are required to produce a given amount of goods. Meanwhile, the market for some basic manufactured goods has become saturated, leaving consumers free to spend a larger proportion of their incomes on various personal services (consumer services), thus making, in turn, for increased investment opportunities in the service sector. Market saturation in the manufacturing sector has also encouraged firms to seek ways of making existing products more cheaply or, better still, of developing new products to market, thus creating another kind of producer service: scientific research and development (R and D). Finally, a large number of service jobs has been created in the public sector as federal and local governments have expanded their range of activities and responsibilities in response to the increasing complexity of American economic and social organization (Stanback *et al.* 1981).

The magnitude of these shifts can be illustrated with a few basic statistics (Table 5.1). Thus it emerges that the manufacturing sector accounted for less than one quarter of all employment in 1980, compared with almost one third in 1947. But, because of higher productivity, it was able to sustain its relative contribution to the Gross National Product (GNP): about 24 per cent. The service sector increased its share of total employment by about 12 per cent and its contribution to GNP by almost 4 per cent over the same period. As Table 5.1 shows, however, there were in fact substantial differences in the performance of different *types* of services. Contrary to the popular view of retail and consumer services as a driving force in the postwar economy of the US, they have not, in fact, grown very rapidly. Rather, it has been producer services, public sector services and non-profit services (mainly higher education and certain aspects of health care) which have contributed most to the expansion in service sector employment. Of these, producer services and non-profit services also increased their relative contribution to GNP, while public sector services, although employing more people, contributed less. Similarly, the overall decline of employment in the manufacturing sector encompasses a considerable diversity of performance, with some indus-

Table 5.1: Changing structure of employment and output, 1947–77

	1947		1969		1977	
	Employment	GNP	Employment	GNP	Employment	GNP
Agricultural, extractive and transformative	43.39	37.38	35.09	35.99	31.60	32.81
Agriculture	4.31	5.57	1.74	3.06	1.90	2.87
Extractive and transformative[a]	39.08	31.81	33.35	32.93	29.70	29.94
Manufacturing	32.27	24.53	27.66	25.60	24.10	24.18
Services	56.61	62.68	64.91	64.03	68.40	66.09
Distributive services	13.54	13.36	10.97	15.00	11.36 –	16.51
Producer services	6.06	15.50	10.03	18.26	11.96	20.12
Retail services	12.57	11.06	13.00	9.78	14.18	9.89
Mainly consumer services	7.67	5.47	5.75	3.35	4.99	3.11
Non-profit services[b]	2.61	2.67	4.67	3.58	6.34	4.04
Government and government enterprises	14.16	14.62	20.48	14.07	19.57	12.43
	100.00	100.00	100.00	100.00	100.00	100.00

[a] Includes mining, construction, and manufacturing.
[b] Public education (grade school and State colleges) is included in government.

Source: Noyelle (1983), Table 8.1, p. 119

tries – electronics, computing machinery, chemicals and plastics, aerospace production and scientific instruments, in particular – exhibiting a pronounced growth in employment opportunities while others have contracted at a much faster rate than that of the manufacturing sector as a whole: primary metals, food processing, textiles, apparel and lumber processing (Bureau of Industrial Economics 1980).

Corporate giants and the urge to merge

In every industry, there are limits both to the extent to which productivity can be increased and to the extent to which consumers can be induced to purchase more. As competition to maintain profit levels becomes more intense, some firms will be driven out of business while others will be taken over by stronger competitors in a process of *horizontal integration*. Furthermore, the chances of new firms being successful tend to be retarded as the larger corporations draw on economies of scale to edge out smaller competitors by price cutting. But even giant corporations cannot forestall market saturation indefinitely; and they are particularly vulnerable to unforeseen shifts in demand. A common corporate strategy has therefore been to indulge in *vertical integration* (taking over the firms which provide their inputs and/or those which purchase their output) in an attempt to capture a greater proportion of the final selling price. Alternatively (or in addition), *diagonal integration* (taking over firms whose activities are completely unrelated to their own) offers the chance to gain access to more profitable markets. The net result is the emergence of a diminishing number of increasingly powerful conglomerates.

This is what happened in the US after World War II. Spearheaded by the large corporations which had emerged – mainly through horizontal mergers – in the 1900s, Big Business began to exert an increasing influence on economic life. Horizontal mergers became relatively less important after the introduction of antitrust legislation (the Celler Kefauver Act) in 1950, but vertical and diagonal integration proceeded at unprecedented rates, generating around 1000 mergers per annum by the mid-1950s and over 3000 per annum at the peak in the late 1960s (Scherer 1980). As a result, the fifty largest companies increased their share of the total value added in manufacturing from 17 to 24 per cent in the 30 years after 1947; and the largest 200 increased their share from 30 to 44 per cent. Similar trends have occurred in the service sector, where the control of variety stores, department stores, car rental firms, motion picture distribution and data processing has become particularly concentrated and centralized.

International redeployment

Overseas investment by American enterprise began in the nineteenth century, and since 1914 it has remained fairly steady at around 4 per cent of GNP. But before World War II most of this investment was directed at obtaining raw materials – principally oil and minerals – for domestic manufacturing operations. Directly after the war, however, large US firms began to use direct foreign investment as a means of penetrating foreign consumer markets through local production operations. Initially, the focus of this investment was Western Europe, where the Marshall Aid program, NATO rearmament and the US military presence in West Germany provided useful information feedback and points of entry to an expanding consumer market. In addition, the establishment of the US dollar as the world's principal reserve currency at the 1944 Bretton Woods Conference facilitated the takeover of foreign industries by US corporations, and many of them soon began to penetrate other expanding markets, such as Latin America. In this process, mergers and acquisitions were again an important mechanism, so that many of the large US corporations became transnational corporations, taking full advantage not only of overseas markets and raw materials but also of advanced technologies and special skills. By 1970, almost 75 per cent of all US exports and 50 per cent of US imports were transactions between the domestic and foreign subsidiaries of transnational conglomerates.

Bulova Watch provides a clear example. Bulova now manufactures watch movements in Switzerland and ships them to Pago Pago, in American Samoa, where they are assembled and then shipped to the United States to be sold. Corporation President Harry B. Henshel said about this arrangement: 'We are able to beat the foreign competition

because we *are* the foreign competition' (Bluestone and Harrison 1982: 114).

By 1978, over 30 per cent of the overall profits of the 100 largest US corporations and banks were derived from their overseas operations (*Business Week* 1979).

In the 1970s, however, the pre-eminence of US firms came to be threatened: (a) by the growing competition of goods produced with cheap labour by a few fast-growing Third World nations (Taiwan, Mexico, Hong Kong, South Korea etc.) and (b) the increasing penetration of European and Japanese multinationals into American markets after the collapse of the Bretton Woods accord in 1971. In response, US transnational corporations have begun to restructure their production processes, eliminating the duplication of activities between domestic and foreign-based facilities and reorganizing the division of tasks between them (Storper and Walker 1984). Effectively, this has meant a further redeployment of capital, bringing Third World nations into the production space of US corporations in order to benefit from lower labour costs and withdrawing from locations where unskilled and semi-skilled labour is more expensive (i.e. North America and northwestern Europe) while retaining existing facilities which require high inputs of technology or skilled labour. Thus 'During the 1970s GE (General Electric) expanded its worldwide payroll by 5000, but it did so by adding 30 000 foreign jobs and reducing its US employment by 25 000. RCA Corporation followed the same strategy, cutting its US employment by 14 000 and increasing its foreign workforce by 19 000' (Bluestone and Harrison 1982: 6).

Changes in occupational composition

The transition of the economy into advanced capitalism has been accompanied by some important changes in the composition of America's labour force. To begin with, the shift away from agriculture, manufacturing and construction has resulted in a substantial decrease in blue-collar employment and a commensurate increase in white-collar employment. Moreover, it seems that white-collar employment itself has been increasingly dichotomized between professional and managerial jobs on the one hand and routine clerical jobs on the other (Noyelle 1983). Within the manufacturing sector, meanwhile, advances in technology and automation have begun to polarize employment opportunities between those for engineers/technicians and those for unskilled/semi-skilled operatives. The differential growth of different kinds of service activity has also altered the structure of the labour market. Retailing and consumer services, for example, have been dominated by part-time jobs and 'secondary jobs': jobs in small firms or the small shops or offices of large firms, where few skills are required, levels of pay are low, and there is little opportunity for advancement (Gordon 1979); and the trend has been accentuated by the penetration of large capital in areas once confined to small businesses, resulting in a greater standardization and a marked lowering of skill requirements (as in fast-food chains). Government services, on the other hand, tend to have increased the pool of 'primary jobs' (jobs with higher levels of pay and security). It should also be noted that the sharp rise in oil prices after the 1973 OPEC manoeuvres contributed significantly to the growth of secondary jobs during the late 1970s. Suddenly, many businesses had to concentrate on saving energy and this created, temporarily, large numbers of low-paid jobs such as installing insulation and stripping the paint from airliners in order to increase their mileage.

The aggregate effect of all these changes, according to some observers, is a tendency towards the erosion of the intermediate segment of the labour market, with increased numbers of higher-qualified, higher-paid employees on the one hand and of employees in 'secondary jobs' on the other (Edwards, Reich and Gordon 1975; Stanback and Noyelle 1982). The evidence on earnings seems to support this, though it should be borne in mind that the data also reflect changes in inflation and the age and sex structure of the available labour force at different times (Sternlieb and Hughes 1984). Between 1960 and 1975, 54 per cent of the jobs created were in the lower-earning (less than 80 per cent of the average for all workers) segment and 35 per cent were in the upper-earning (more than 120 per cent of the average) segment. As a result, the pro-

portion of low-paid workers rose from 32 to 38 per cent of the workforce, the proportion of high-paid workers rose from 32 to 34 per cent, while the intermediate earnings segment fell from 36 to 28 per cent.

Changes in the organization and composition of the labour force reflect these occupational trends. Thus the proportion of the non-agricultural workforce in trade unions fell from over 35 per cent in 1950 to less than 25 per cent in 1980 (though within this overall decline there was a marked increase in public sector unionization, from around 12 per cent to nearly 20 per cent). Meanwhile, the expansion of higher-paid managerial, professional and technical jobs has been associated with a tendency for young Americans (especially white males) to stay on at school and college. Coupled with a general decrease in the age of retirement, this created a large gap in the labour market, allowing more women to participate in the labour force. Between 1947 and 1980, the female participation rate shot up from just over 30 per cent to well over 50 per cent. A large proportion of this increase has been absorbed by the expansion of part-time jobs, 'secondary' jobs and routine clerical jobs in the service sector, though significant numbers of women have been able to penetrate job markets in all sectors and in all occupational classes (Oppenheimer 1970; Freeman 1980).

The performance of the economy

In overall terms, the American economy performed very well from the late 1940s until the early 1970s. In contrast to the century before World War II, real output and unemployment remained fairly stable and GNP grew steadily each year. Real disposable income per capita rose from just over $2200 (in constant 1972 dollars) in 1947 to over $3800 in 1972. The 1960s were particularly prosperous, with economic growth averaging over 4 per cent per year, thus expanding the GNP by 50 per cent over the decade. Despite the chronic inflation which characterized the period, the average family enjoyed a real increase of over 30 per cent in its disposable income. These were the years of Galbraith's Affluent Society (Galbraith 1958).

Since the early 1970s, however, economic growth has averaged only about 2 per cent per year. Productivity in the private business sector, having increased at around 3.3 per cent per year up to 1970, fell away to 1.3 per cent per year during the 1970s. 'By 1979, the typical family with a $20 000 income had only 7 per cent more real purchasing power than it had a full decade earlier. Ten years had brought a mere $25 more per week in purchasing power for the average family' (Bluestone and Harrison 1982: 4). By 1980, the US had slipped to tenth position in the international league table of per capita GNP behind Switzerland, Sweden, Denmark, West Germany, Luxembourg, Iceland, France, the Netherlands and Belgium (though the US has been able to maintain its leading position in terms of GDP per capita measured via Purchasing Power Parities – the internal domestic purchasing power of each local currency). Unemployment, having fluctuated around 4.5 per cent until the early 1970s, had almost doubled by 1975, but levelled off at around 7 per cent in the early 1980s. Meanwhile, the rate of inflation tripled, from around 2.5 per cent per year in the 1960s to nearly 7.5 per cent per year in the 1970s. In 1971, the US economy moved into a negative trade balance with the rest of the world for the first time this century; and repeated the performance in 12 of the next 14 years.

The reasons for this downturn in the economy are not entirely clear. The rise in oil prices in 1973 as a result of the OPEC cartel has been cited widely as a major cause, but the evidence is inconclusive (Denison 1979). Other important contributory factors, it has been suggested, include the changing demographic composition of the labour force, the ability of some labour unions to obtain wage increases in excess of productivity increases, and the extra costs imposed on industry by government legislation to protect the physical environment and the health and safety of workers; but the search for explanations has extended the list to include everything from American industry's reduced R and D effort since the mid-1960s to bad weather, poor harvests and the disappearance of anchovies off the coast of Peru (Mansfield 1982; Reischauer 1981). What is clear, however, is that the downturn in the US economy represents an unprecedented setback with serious – but as yet unspecified – implications for a wide range of industries, social

groups and communities (Castells 1980; Glickman 1983; Magdoff and Sweezy 1981).

Spatial adjustment under advanced capitalism

The spatial implications of the transition to advanced capitalism have still to be fully established. It is clear, however, that it has involved complex and often cross-cutting processes of reorganization and adjustment, resulting in simultaneous trends towards, on the one hand, decentralization and, on the other, concentration/consolidation. In addition, the new 'high-technology' industries of advanced capitalism have begun to gather momentum, thus adding the possibility of an entirely new dimension to the economic landscape.

Decentralization: metropolitan, urban–rural, regional and international shifts

The dominant trend in the spatial reorganization of the American economy under advanced capitalism has been towards decentralization, and it can be identified at four different scales: metropolitan, urban–rural, regional and international. The longest-established of these is at the *metropolitan* scale, involving the exodus of industry and employment from central cities to suburban areas throughout the US. Gordon (1984) points out that such movement can be traced to the early decades of the twentieth century, suggesting that the major reason was employers' desire to sidestep the increasing militancy of labour in central city neighbourhoods. Suburban locations have also been attractive to industry because of the availability of larger tracts of relatively cheap land. With the widespread availability of trucks and automobiles after World War I, the process of decentralization accelerated rapidly, creating a new urban form (Ch. 7). Residential decentralization provided labour supplies which further encouraged the suburbanization of many kinds of economic activity, thus creating a mutually reinforcing process which has in turn been sustained by certain locational disadvantages of central city areas. A major factor here has been the higher taxes which central cities

Table 5.2: Annual costs and income of a specified manufacturing plant in alternative locations within the Atlanta metropolitan area, 1977

Annual cost and income per employee	Establishment locations		
	New plant in suburbs	New plant in central city	Existing plant in central city
Annual sales	$40 000	$40 000	$40 000
Annual costs			
Payroll	10 000	10 000	10 000
Materials	16 800	16 800	16 800
Capital costs and debt service	3 300	3 400	3 200
Local taxes	600	1 300	1 250
Other operating costs	6 900	6 900	6 900
Net annual income before state and federal taxes	2 400	1 600	1 850

Source: US Department of Housing and Urban Development 1980, Table 3–13, pp. 3–15

have had to levy in order to maintain their more extensive range of municipal services. Table 5.2 illustrates the implications of such tax differentials for a typical manufacturing establishment in the Atlanta metropolitan area, presenting estimates of the annual costs and income per employee in three locations: a new suburban plant, an existing 20- to 30-year-old plant in the central city, and a new plant in the central city. Overall costs are shown to be highest for manufacturers in a new plant in the central city, and lowest for a new plant in the suburbs. Overall, annual costs vary by as much as $800 per employee, and *most of the differences stem from the different rates of local taxation*. The net effect has been a marked difference in the rate of growth of employment between central city and suburban areas throughout the US, with central cities experiencing substantial absolute losses of employment in manufacturing, construction, transportation, communication and public utility industries, together with strikingly inferior rates of employment growth in wholesale and retail trade, finance, insurance and real estate (Table 5.3).

In recent years the process of employment decentralization has spread outwards, penetrating much of non-metropolitan America and

contributing to the non-metropolitan population gains described in Chapter 2. This *urban–rural* decentralization is the product of the same kind of cost and demand factors that were responsible for the economic growth of suburban and satellite communities. Advances in transport and telecommunications systems have greatly reduced the need for manufacturing, wholesaling and even office establishments to locate near large urban centres, enabling firms to take advantage of spatial variations in production costs or to locate in amenity-rich environments (Estall 1983: Rees 1983a; Sternlieb and Hughes 1977). Empirical studies have shown that the main attractions of non-metropolitan locations have been the availability of relatively low-cost labour, inexpensive supplies of easily-developed land, lower levels of local taxation, and low levels of unionization and labour militancy (Haren and Halling 1979: Kale and Lonsdale 1979). Because low-cost labour also tends to be less skilled, these attractions have been greatest to firms in relatively labour-intensive industries such as apparel, textiles, fabricated metals and electronics.

An important mechanism in the whole process of urban–rural decentralization has been the functional and locational reorganization of large corporations in response to the

Table 5.3: Employment change in central and suburban counties of large metro areas, 1970–76

	Suburban counties (fringe of large metropolitan)		Central counties of large metro areas (1 000 000 or more pop.)	
	Per cent change	Absolute change	Per cent change	Absolute change
Number of counties	123	123	48	48
Total employment (full and part-time)	16.74	1 364 475	1.57	459 355
Agriculture (total farm)	16.02	9 218	12.13	7 652
Agricultural services, forestry, fisheries, etc.	26.32	8 290	32.23	17 577
Mining	12.14	3 376	26.84	21 800
Construction	2.31	9 614	(−)13.80	(−)157 742
Manufacturing	(−)0.37	(−)7 307	(−)10.05	(−)661 296
Transportation, communication and public utilities	13.59	47 268	(−) 7.45	(−)146 932
Wholesale trade	47.79	146 179	2.17	41 017
Retail trade	26.96	338 782	5.44	215 132
Finance, insurance, real estate	44.29	111 847	5.52	109 736
Services	35.71	426 019	13.98	762 061
Total non-manufacturing	22.22	1 371 782	4.95	1 120 651

Source: Rees 1983a, Table IX.1, p. 245

imperative of maintaining profit margins in the face of diminishing productivity and overseas competition (Peet 1983). One outcome has been the location of *branch plants* (dealing with standardized, routine production processes) in non-metropolitan areas while corporate headquarters and more complex functions are maintained in large metropolitan areas, often in a different region. This can also be interpreted in terms of the *product-cycle model* of industrial location, which postulates that products evolve through three distinct stages in their life-cycles and that each stage tends to take place in different types of location. The first, or 'innovation' stage tends to occur in established industrial/metropolitan regions, with the new product being introduced to other areas through exports. A 'growth stage' follows, during which demand expands to a point where it becomes feasible to invest in production facilities in these other areas. Finally, as manufacture of the product becomes routine, there begins a phase of 'standardized production' in which firms seek out low-cost locations for manufacturing plant while closing their manufacturing operations in more expensive lo-

cations (Erikson and Leinbach 1979; Malecki 1986; Norton and Rees 1979). Meanwhile, urban–rural decentralization has been given further impetus by the growth in rural population and per capita incomes associated with the rural turnaround' (Ch. 2; see also Brown and Beale 1981; Zuiches 1981). In this context, it is employment growth in retail trade and local services that has been most important, particularly in non-metropolitan areas which have attracted high levels of retired in-migrants or which have emerged as centres of recreational or governmental functions (Morrison and McCarthy 1979).

These factors have also helped to create a *regional* dimension to economic decentralization. In general, the southern and western parts of the country have gained at the expense of northern and eastern regions. In particular, it has been the Manufacturing Belt which has lost ground in terms of production jobs and jobs in producer services, while the 'Sunbelt' states of the South, Southwest and West have gained most, partly in terms of production jobs in labour-intensive manufacturing processes, and partly in terms of jobs in the high-growth industries in both manufacturing and services (Ballard and James 1983; Beyers 1979; Rees 1983a). It is a sign of the times that the two States with the highest proportions of their workforce in manufacturing are now North Carolina and South Carolina, with their low-wage furniture factories and textile mills and their high-tech branch plants. In general terms, it appears that Sunbelt States have been able to benefit from relative advantages not only in terms of labour unionization (Fig. 5.3) and energy costs (Table 5.4) but also in terms of business climate (Fig. 5.4), labour costs, local taxes, local government boosterism, land costs and federal expenditure patterns (Clark 1980; Peet 1983; Perry and Watkins 1977: Sawers and Tabb 1984). In addition, the metropolitan areas of the Sunbelt have proved attractive to industry because they had never acquired the now-inefficient infrastructure and fixed physical capital of earlier phases of economic development:

They could be constructed from scratch to fit the needs of a new period of accumulation in which factory plant and equipment were themselves increasingly predicated upon a decentralized model . . . There was consequently no identifiable downtown factory district; manufacturing was scattered throughout the city plane. There were no centralized working-class housing districts (for that was indeed what capitalists had learned to avoid); working-class housing was scattered all over the city around the factories. Automobiles and trucks provided the connecting links, threading together the separate pieces. The corporate city became . . . the Fragmented Metropolis. No centers anywhere. Diffuse economic activity everywhere (Gordon 1984: 45–6).

In a sense, then, Sunbelt growth can be seen as the combined product of urban-rural decentralization and metropolitan decentralization. Such an interpretation is supported by the types of employment growth which characterize the rise of the Sunbelt: (a) production jobs in branch plants in industries such as apparel,

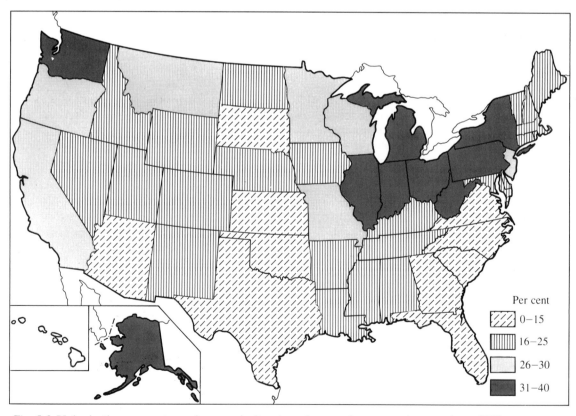

Fig. 5.3 Unionization: percentage of non-agricultural employees who were union members, 1980

Table 5.4: Variations in energy costs: cost of 1500 megawatt hours of electricity to industrial users, January 1983

Most expensive		Least expensive	
Utility company	*Bill ($)*	*Utility company*	*Bill ($)*
San Diego Gas and Electric Co	199 354	Gulf States Utilities Co	
Consolidated Edison Co of New York	191 446	(Louisiana and Texas)	16 498
South Norwalk Electric Works		City of Tacoma	26 730
(Connecticut)	140 446	The Washington Water Power Co	34 514
Jersey Central Power and Light Co	135 226	City of Eugene	36 269
United Illuminating Co		Montana Power Co	36 608
(Connecticut)	132 075	Sacramento Municipal Utility District	36 891
Hawaiian Electric Co	130 731	City of Seattle	37 700
Atlantic City Electric Co	122 893	Pacific Power and Light Co	39 559
Philadelphia Electric	121 295	City of Palo Alto	41 072
Long Island Lighting Co	121 092	Puget Sound Power and Light Co	42 242
Ohio Edison Co	120 151	City of Provo	44 000
Detroit Edison Co	118 244		

Source: Energy Information Administration, Department of Energy, *Typical Electric Bills*, 1983, Tables 32 and 33, p. 278

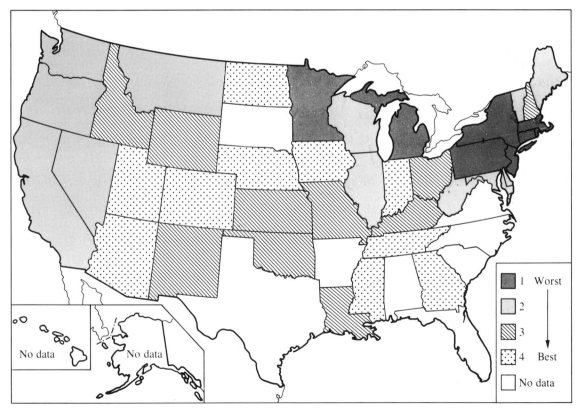

Fig. 5.4 Variations in local business climate
Source: Peet (1983), p. 128

textiles and electronics; (b) production jobs in both branch plants and in locally-based firms in high-growth industries – mainly computer hardware, scientific instruments, aerospace, and chemicals and plastics; and (c) service jobs catering both to these industries and to the increased population attracted to retirement and leisure communities.

The corollary of these gains in the Sunbelt has been the relative – and in some aspects, absolute – decline of economic activity in the old economic core of the Manufacturing Belt. For some communities, the consequences of plant shutdowns have been disastrous. In Youngstown, which has become the symbol of industrial decline, the closure of the Campbell Steel Works in 1977 eliminated over 10 000 jobs at a stroke (Buss and Redburn 1983; see also Gordus, Jarley and Freeman 1981). In Illinois, the closure of the Wisconsin Steel Works eliminated nearly 4000 jobs one Friday evening in 1980, with the workers receiving no notice and no severance pay. Wisconsin Steel had been owned until 1977 by the International Harvester Company. When the works began to make losses, as a result of poor management and stiff competition from Japan, it was sold to Envirodyne, a small California-based engineering firm, 'in a transaction that makes sense only when seen through the prism of US tax laws' (Fallows 1985: 49). As a result, International Harvester saved over $100 million in pension obligations, anti-pollution investments and operating losses. When the steel works closed in 1980, Envirodyne in turn escaped serious losses because it had set up a shell corporation to protect it from liability for some $62 million in unfunded pension obligations. The workers, of course, enjoyed no such escape. Indeed, the company's creditors acted so swiftly that even the workers' final pay cheques bounced.

In overall terms, it has been estimated that the Mid-Atlantic region (New Jersey, New York, Pennsylvania) lost over 175 000 jobs (net) during the period 1969–76 whereas the South Atlantic Region (Delaware, DC, Florida, Georgia, Maryland, North Carolina, South Carolina, Virginia, West Virginia) experienced a net gain of over 2 million jobs in the same period (Bluestone and Harrison 1982). This represents a job loss of 1.5 per cent in the Mid-

Atlantic region and a gain of 24.4 per cent in the South Atlantic region, compared with a net gain of some 15 per cent in the US as a whole (Table 5.5). Such contrasts have led many writers to characterize the economic geography of contemporary America in terms of a polarization of fortunes with the *Frostbelt* (a.k.a. 'Snowbelt' or 'Rustbelt') of northern and eastern States losing jobs to the *Sunbelt* of southern and western States (see, for example, Weinstein and Firestine 1978). During the 1970s, when the overall performance of the national economy began to show signs of falling away, this conception of regional change received a good deal of attention and, not surprisingly, widespread currency. But, although it is clearly not without foundation, it is a rather *simplistic* view. For one thing, the rate of job losses due to the closure or contraction of firms has been fairly uniform between regions, and the number of jobs relocated between regions has been relatively small: most of the regional variations in job generation can be accounted for by the birth and expansion of companies. Table 5.5 shows that in the US as a whole between 1969 and 1976, eighty jobs were lost for every 100 created; and that there were substantial job losses in *every* region. Even California, the archetypal Sunbelt State, has been seriously affected by shutdowns. In Los Angeles alone, almost 18 000 jobs were lost between 1978 and 1982, many of them the result of closures by large corporations like Uniroyal, Ford, US Steel, Pabst Brewing and Max Factor. In the State as a whole in the single year of 1980, more than 150 major plants closed down, displacing more than 37 000 workers (Bluestone and Harrison 1982). In short, the net gains of the Sunbelt States (and the net losses of the Frostbelt States) conceal a complex pattern of ebbs and flows.

This leads to a second major weakness in the idea of a simple shift of economic activity from Frostbelt to Sunbelt: the variation of experience within each. The western parts of the Manufacturing Belt, for example, experienced a healthy net gain in manufacturing employment during the 1960s and 1970s; while during the prolonged recession after 1973 the trend in manufacturing employment actually reversed from loss to gain in both Connecticut and Massachusetts (Rees 1983b). Similarly, there

Table 5.5: Jobs created and destroyed as a result of openings, closings, relocations, expansions and contractions of private business establishments in the US, 1969–76 (in thousands of jobs)

		Employment change 1969–76					
		Jobs created		*Jobs destroyed*		*New job change*	
Region	*Number of jobs in 1969*	*By openings & immigrations*	*Expansion*	*By closures & out-migrations*	*Contraction*	*Number*	*Per cent*
US as a whole	57 936.1	25 281.3	19 056.1	22 302.3	13 183.2	8 851.9	15.2
Frostbelt:	32 701.2	11 321.5	9 470.4	11 351.7	7 212.1	2 228.1	6.8
Northeast	15 824.6	4 940.4	4 347.5	5 881.5	3 589.0	-182.6	-1.2
New England	3 905.3	1 251.2	1 131.0	1 437.2	952.1	-7.1	-2.6
Mid-Atlantic	11 919.3	3 689.2	3 216.5	4 444.3	2 636.9	-175.5	-1.5
Midwest	16 876.6	6 381.1	5 123.0	5 470.2	3 623.2	2 410.7	14.3
East North Central	12 563.6	4 670.6	3 581.8	3 962.6	2 651.7	1 638.1	13.0
West North Central	4 313.0	1 710.6	1 541.2	1 507.6	971.5	772.7	17.9
Sunbelt	25 234.9	13 959.8	9 585.7	10 950.5	5 971.0	6 624.0	26.2
South	16 044.5	8 934.2	5 964.6	6 824.3	3 803.3	4 272.2	26.6
South Atlantic	8 204.1	5 651.2	1 913.0	3 547.9	2 014.2	2 002.1	24.4
East South Central	3 065.2	1 518.2	1 089.9	1 211.0	631.9	765.2	24.9
West South Central	4 775.2	1 764.8	2 962.7	2 065.4	1 157.2	1 504.9	31.4
West	9 190.4	5 025.6	3 621.1	4 126.2	2 167.8	2 352.7	25.6
Mountain	1 941.9	1 226.1	953.6	977.9	481.0	720.8	37.1
Pacific	7 248.5	3 799.6	2 667.6	3 148.3	1 686.8	1 632.1	22.5

Source: Based on Bluestone and Harrison (1982), Table 2.1, p. 30

are large and consistent differences within the Sunbelt in terms of economic well-being, to the extent that the conception of the Sunbelt as a coherent economic region has been described as 'sloppy regionalizing' (Browning and Gessler 1979). As Tabb (1984: 9) puts it: 'Take away Texas, Florida, North Carolina, Arizona and, in early postwar years, California, and the growth rates look very modest'. Furthermore, it is clear that steep disparities still exist even within 'prosperous' Sunbelt States. The peripheral regions of Texas and Florida, for example, contain many blighted, worn-out towns and cities; while high-growth centres such as Houston contain large numbers of low-income households and are beginning to face some of the consequences of excessively rapid growth: housing shortages, sewage disposal and water supply problems, subsidence, traffic congestion, land speculation and inadequate public services (Feagin 1984). Finally, the return of low oil prices in the mid-1980s meant that a significant element of the Sunbelt's comparative advantage came into question. By 1985, economic indicators had already begun to reflect signs of distress in the likes of Texas, while clearly indicating a new boom in parts of the Frostbelt (particularly in New England). Like the 'rural turnaround' (Chs 2 and 6), the rise of the Sunbelt may prove to be a distinctive but rather short-lived consequence of spatial adjustments (i.e. decentralization) associated with the economic and social imperatives of advanced capitalism.

Attention has already been drawn to the decentralization of employment associated with the *international* redeployment of capital by transnational corporations. It is difficult to establish in any detail the locational impact within the US of the consequent loss of economic activity. It is clear, however, that although the whole of the US has been affected it has been the Manufacturing Belt which has been hardest hit by the new international division of labour (Storper and Walker 1984; Trachte and Ross 1985). On the other hand, it has been the Manufacturing Belt which has benefited most from the striking increase since 1971 in investment in the US by West European- and Japanese-based transnational corporations; though recent foreign investment has extended to California, Texas and the eastern coastal States of the South. In general, this suggests a lagged response by foreign investors to the changing economic geography of the US (McConnell 1980).

Consolidation: headquarters offices and R and D activity

The structural and functional reorganization of US business which helped to precipitate the spatial decentralization of the economy has also made for a certain amount of centralization which has helped to consolidate the economic position of the northeastern metropolitan core. In particular, the restructuring of activity by large corporations in their attempts to adjust to changing national and international conditions has resulted in a marked conservatism in the location of two key functions: headquarters offices and R and D establishments.

The most striking feature of the geography of *corporate headquarters* has always been the dominance of the Manufacturing Belt in general and of New York and Chicago in particular (Borchert 1978; Stephens and Holly 1980). In 1975, 62 per cent of the 500 largest industrial corporations had their headquarters in the Manufacturing Belt, as did 66 per cent of the 300 largest corporations in retailing, banking, insurance, transport and utilities. The New York metropolitan area alone accounted for 27 per cent and 25 per cent respectively of these headquarters locations, while the Chicago metropolitan area accounted for a further 9 per cent of the industrial corporate headquarters and 9 per cent of the headquarters in other sectors. Elsewhere, both in the Manufacturing Belt and beyond, concentrations of headquarters offices tend to reflect the geography of urbanization, so that the more important 'control centres', in terms of corporate business, are the major entrepots and central places which developed under earlier phases of economic development as points of optimal accessibility to regional economies.

During the phase of advanced capitalism, the relative importance of the control centres of the Manufacturing Belt has decreased somewhat, with cities in the Midwest, the South and the West increasing their share of major company headquarters offices (Armstrong 1979). Atlanta, Denver, Houston, Minneapolis and Seattle have been the major beneficiaries of this shift, though no new control centres have emerged to counter the dominance of New York, Chicago and the other major cities of the Northeast. One interpretation of this shift is that it is simply a reflection of changes in the urban system: high-order urban areas tend to be higher-order business control centres because of their reserves of entrepreneurial talent, the array of support services that they can offer, and their accessibility in both a regional and a national context (Wheeler 1986). The shift away from the Northeast is also related to regional variations in economic specialization. Recent growth in headquarters office employment has been most rapid in trade and service industries rather than manufacturing, and it has been the growing cities of the South and West – Atlanta, Dallas, Los Angeles and San Francisco, in particular – which have been most successful in attracting headquarters offices in these sectors. In contrast, Manufacturing Belt cities such as Detroit, Cincinnati, Philadelphia and Pittsburgh have missed out almost entirely in attracting new jobs in the headquarters of service- and trade-based corporations (US Department of Housing and Urban Development 1980). It should be noted that the dynamics of these changes in headquarters locations stem from (a) mergers and acquisitions and (b) the differential growth of metropolitan areas drawing on specialized regional economic bases: actual relocations of headquarters offices have been relatively unimportant. In contrast, there has been a significant amount of relocation *within* metropolitan areas. Thus, for example, of the forty actual departures of large headquarters office complexes from New York City between 1968 and 1974, only six went to Sunbelt cities, one moved to St Louis and one to Denver; the rest moved to suburban Connecticut, New Jersey or New York (Stephens and Holly 1980).

In overall terms, however, 'there has been a process of cumulative and mutual reinforcement between relatively accessible locations and relatively effective entrepreneurship' (Borchert 1978: 230). This has made for a high degree of inertia in the geography of economic control centres and this, in turn, has consolidated the economic position of the metropolitan areas of the Northeast through the multiplier effects of concentrations of corporate headquarters. Pred (1974) points out that these multiplier effects operate in two ways: a general process of 'cumulative causation' related to the increased activity in ancillary services, infrastructural provision, and so on; and a more specific effect whereby the vitality of the corporate administrative sector contributes to the growth and circulation of specialized information concerning business activity, thus generating further employment in a relatively well-paid sector and sustaining the area's attractiveness for headquarters offices. The other side of this inertia, given the increasing integration of US business through mergers and acquisitions, is that an increasing proportion of jobs in America are 'externally controlled' by headquarters in the major control centres. The implications of this are several. It has been suggested, for example, that the local absence of higher-order corporate functions limits the profile of local employment opportunities, leading to a 'deskilling' process, the suppression of entrepreneurial drive and enthusiasm, and the retardation of technological innovation. A very high degree of external control will also make for a very 'open' regional economy, so that international economic fluctuations are transmitted into such regions (e.g. the South) relatively quickly. The corollary of this is that the branch plants of large corporations tend to be poorly integrated with their local economy, thus attenuating any potential multiplier effects.

Another important feature of the reorganization of economic activity under advanced capitalism has been the proliferation of *research and development* (R and D) facilities. Large companies' need to maintain a diversified range of products in order to avoid the risk of market saturation has been the main reason for this proliferation, though companies of all sizes have come to recognize the need for R and D laboratories in order to develop new products, improve existing products and make use of ideas acquired from other companies. Malecki, who has examined the geography of R and D activity in the US in detail (Malecki 1979a, 1979b, 1980), suggests that the overall pattern can be interpreted in terms of (i) the availability of highly qualified labour and (ii) corporate organization. In relation to the former, he suggests that amenity-rich locations (cities with a wide range of cultural facilities, well-established universities and pleasant environments) which are attractive to highly-qualified personnel tend to be favoured as locations for R and D activity. Malecki also notes that existing concentrations of R and D activity tend to be attractive because of the potential for 'raiding' other firms' personnel. In relation to corporate organization, Malecki observes that corporate-level or long-range R and D is best performed in or near headquarters complexes in a central laboratory where intra-organizational interaction can be fostered. In firms with independent divisions producing quite different product lines, however, R and D activity tends to be located in separate divisional laboratories. Such a pattern is particularly common for conglomerates which have acquired firms with active R and D programmes in existing laboratories. Finally, some industries, whatever the organizational structure of the firms involved, require R and D laboratories to have close links with production facilities, resulting in a relatively dispersed locational pattern corresponding to the pattern of plant location.

The net result of these locational forces is in fact a marked agglomeration of R and D laboratories in major control centres and manufacturing regions. It is the metropolitan areas of the Manufacturing Belt which dominate the geography of corporate R and D activity. As Malecki (1980) points out, most of these are either major control centres with concentrations of headquarters offices or major manufacturing centres with a significant element of headquarters office activity. Elsewhere, R and D tends to be concentrated in 'innovation centres' – university cities with diversified economies, some high-technology activity and a strong federal scientific presence (e.g. Austin, Huntsville, Lincoln). In terms of locational trends, Malecki has shown that:

Although industrial R and D appears to be evolving away from a dependence on some large city regions, especially New York, it remains, at the same time, a very markedly large-city activity . . . The comparative advantage of city size, particularly in centers of corporate headquarters location, manufacturing activity and university and

government research, shows little sign of reversing . . . (Malecki 1979a:321).

Indeed, It appears that the number of R and D laboratories in Cincinnati, Cleveland, Columbus, Detroit, Hartford–Springfield, Indianapolis, Providence, Rochester and St Louis has grown faster than average, despite their northeastern location. It has been New York and Chicago, together with Albany, Baltimore, Buffalo, Pittsburgh and Philadelphia, where the expansion of R and D activity has most clearly failed to keep up with the national rate. Outside the Northeast, the most striking gains in R and D activity have been associated with San Diego, Las Vegas, Tucson, Kansas City, Memphis, Huntsville and Knoxville. Thus, like headquarters offices, R and D laboratories exhibit a strong tendency for inertia overlain by a certain amount of decentralization from Frostbelt to Sunbelt. Moreover, these patterns also have important implications for regional economic development, for the urban areas in which concentrations of R and D activity exist will tend to consolidate their comparative advantage over other areas in the generation of new products and new businesses (Clark 1972); and they will also benefit from the short-term multiplier effects of employment generation in a particularly well-paid sector. Conversely, cities and regions with little R and D activity are likely to be at a disadvantage in keeping up with the new economic context of advanced capitalism.

'High-tech' industries: a new economic geography?

Advanced capitalism has not only seen the evolution and realignment of the 'old', industrial economy; it has also seen the emergence of new industries based on entirely new technologies: semiconductors and computer software, for example; and, more recently, biotechnology, photovoltaics and robotics. Because they are so new, relatively little is known about their spatial implications, though they are widely believed to consist of highly competitive, innovative firms whose activities collectively will not only create substantial numbers of new jobs but also serve a 'seedbed' function for the economy as a whole (Markusen

1983). The possibility thus emerges of an entirely new dimension to the economic geography of the US, with concentrations of high-tech, 'sunrise' industries initiating new patterns of regional growth through new multipliers of cumulative causation (Castells 1985). The available evidence, however, suggests that although these high-tech industries do represent an important new source of employment and income, they are more likely to reinforce existing trends than to precipitate major changes in the economic landscape (Armington 1986).

Studies of high-tech industries undertaken on behalf of the California Commission on Industrial Innovation confirm that job growth has been significant and is likely to continue expanding rapidly (Feldman 1983; Hall *et al.* 1983; Markusen 1983). Employment in the computer software industry, for example, doubled to 250 000 in the 1980s and was expected to grow to 450 000 by 1990, while employment in robotics was expected to rise from around 10 000 in 1980 to around 100 000 in 1990 (though a much greater number of jobs in other sectors will of course be displaced by the application of robotics). Altogether, it was anticipated that four of the high-tech industries – computer software, photovoltaics, biogenetics and robotics – would generate about 3 million jobs, directly and indirectly, by 1990. Such estimates were brought into question in 1985, however, by a sudden and unexpected sales slump in some high-tech industries – semiconductors, personal computers and computer software, in particular – partly in response to misjudgements about demand, partly as a consequence of Japanese trade barriers, and partly as a result of the strength of the US dollar, which boosted the consumption of imported high-tech manufactures.

The Californian research suggests that the structure and location of high-tech employment is a microcosm of the broader trends which have dominated advanced capitalism. Thus 'the studies suggest that the occupational, ethnic and gender composition of new jobs in high-tech sectors will tend to worsen the current trend toward the "disappearing middle", that is toward a labor force bifurcated between high-paid professionals and low-paid service workers'

(Markusen 1983:19). In regard to corporate structure, high-tech industry is distinctive for its tendency towards the proliferation of small breakaway companies set up by key employees; but at the same time, the larger and more established firms have soon been drawn into the process of mergers and acquisitions, either as the dominant element (in horizontal and vertical integration) or as a subsidiary element (in diagonal integration).

In relation to spatial patterns, high-tech employment is characterized by localized agglomerations which are already beginning to respond to the imperatives of decentralization which have affected the rest of the economy (Glasmeier 1985). The archetypal agglomeration of high-tech industry is the concentration of semiconductor firms in the so-called Silicon Valley at the southern tip of San Francisco Bay between Palo Alto (the location of Stanford University) and Santa Clara (Saxenian 1983a). Here, the original concentration of semiconductor research and production in the 1950s has generated significant external economies – including a specialized workforce, a specialized array of producer services and a unique social, cultural and educational environment – which have not only sustained the continued agglomeration of new semiconductor firms but also attracted other electronics enterprises and high-tech industries. Nearly a third of all employment in biotechnology, for example, is located in California, and of this over 90 per cent is located in the San Francisco Bay area (Feldman 1983). Software employment also tends to be localized, mainly in California (Los Angeles and the San Francisco Bay area), and in Massachusetts (outside Boston, clustered along Route 128), Robotics employment, closely associated with the traditional machining industry, tends to be split between older manufacturing centres like Detroit and new high-tech centres in Massachussetts, Texas, Colorado and California.

Within these subregions, high-tech employment is very much a suburban phenomenon: 'Both Silicon Valley and Route 128 around Boston are newly-developed, auto-based, suburban areas whose jobs and tax base do not overlay the inner city poor nor the central city jurisdiction' (Markusen 1983:26). But because high-tech firms have tended to be very self-conscious about their 'address', these sub-regions have become crowded and expensive. In the Palo Alto/Santa Clara area, housing costs are at least 50 per cent more than in other West Coast housing markets and close to 100 per cent more than the US average, while journeys to work have recently become longer and more fraught (Saxenian 1983b). As a result, it has proved increasingly difficult for firms to attract and retain sufficient numbers of qualified personnel without providing very high salaries and a wide range of fringe benefits. The outcome has been the familiar combination of corporate functional and spatial *reorganization*. More routine production tasks and downstream marketing and service functions are beginning to be dispersed, while managerial and developmental activities are retained in order to maximize the external economies of the right 'address'. Thus, for example, Intel Inc. has recently established branch plants in Aloha (Oregon), Chandler (Ariz.) and Albuquerque; National Semiconductor Inc. has established branch plants in Tucson and Salt Lake City; and American Microsystems Inc. has switched its manufacturing capacity to Pocatello (Idaho) (Saxenian 1983b). Furthermore, some of the larger corporations in the computing and semiconductor fields have begun to redeploy at the international scale, partly in order to acquire foreign technology and expertise and partly in search of cheaper labour (Harrington 1986).

The role of government in urban and regional development

As we saw in Chapter 4, the role of the state is intimately related to the mode of production. Under advanced capitalism, federal expenditure has grown to nearly 25 per cent of GNP and the composition of these outlays has changed radically. In 1950, more than half of all federal outlays were devoted to national defence while less than a quarter were channelled towards health, education, income security, employment and training, and other 'human resource' programmes; by 1980, the

priorities were reversed (Break 1980; Reischauer 1981). Meanwhile, a good deal of federal activity has come to be involved in supporting businesses; both directly, by providing subsidies for ailing companies and incentives for new ones, and indirectly, by guaranteeing prices, building freeways and, in particular, acting as a major customer for everything from military hardware to paper clips. As a result, 'there is virtually no area of production and distribution of goods and services in which government is not integrated with private business' (Katznelson and Kesselman 1975: 123). What is important in the present context is that all this activity has a geographical expression. In the following section, we examine the spatial implications of patterns of federal spending and briefly outline the geography of federal spatial economic policies.

The impact of federal spending

Four major categories of federal expenditure can be recognized:

1. The salaries of government employees, including clerks, bureaucrats and workers in the armed services, schools, public health, the FBI and the courts. Much of this expenditure is of course localized in Washington, DC (where around a third of all earnings come from federal employment), and in neighbouring Maryland and northern Virginia. Elsewhere, federal employment is most prominent in small- and medium-sized cities with large defence installations.

2. Transfer payments to particular population groups (e.g. armed forces veterans, the unemployed, families with dependent children, the elderly) and particular industries (e.g. agricultural subsidies). These expenditures involve complex flows of monies and are geographically localized only in as much as the 'target' populations and industries are localized (though as we have seen (p. 108) the *effectiveness* of these payments may vary considerably from one area to another).

3. Purchasing and subcontracting from businesses in the private sector. This includes a wide range of items – buildings, roads, dams, power stations, military equipment,

Table 5.6: Characteristics of major federal grant-in-aid programmes

Form of aid and name of programme	Eligible recipients	Eligible activities	Degree of targeting to distressed communities
Revenue-sharing programmes:			
General Revenue Sharing	State and local governments	Very broad – excludes only education	Slight – all governments eligible
Anti-Recession Fiscal Assistance	State and local governments	Very broad	Some – primarily to areas of high unemployment
Block grant programmes:			
Comprehensive Employment and Training Act	State and local governments	Fairly broad – with focus on social services	Some – primarily to areas of high unemployment
Social Services (Title XX)	States	Fairly broad – with focus on social services	None – sub-allocations made by States
Community Development Block Grants	Local governments	Fairly broad – with focus on physical development	Some – primarily to large urban communities
Categorical grant programmes:			
Urban Development Action Grants	Local governments	Narrow – to support local development initiatives	High – eligibility criteria based on community distress indicators
Local Public Works Grants	Local governments	Fairly broad – to support local public facilities programmes	Some – primarily areas of high unemployment

Source: US Department of Housing and Urban Development (1980), *The President's National Urban Policy Report 1980*, Table 11–2, p. 11–5

office equipment and publications, for example – which make for highly localized impacts in terms of employment and/or economic multiplier effects.

4. Direct grants, most of which are intended to influence the behaviour of recipients (notably state and local governments) in order to achieve some national purpose. These include (i) revenue-sharing funds, designed to even out geographical disparities in state and local government fiscal resources, (ii) block grant programmes relating to broad functional areas and allowing considerable local discretion as to how funds are used, and (iii) categorical grant programmes, more closely focused and with tighter federal control (see Table 5.6)

Against these expenditure patterns we have to set the geography of federal taxation. Around 40 per cent of all federal revenues is derived from personal income taxes, with another 25 per cent coming from taxes on

pension trusts and a further 15 per cent from taxes on corporate profits. To a large extent, therefore, the geography of federal revenues reflects the geography of income and economic health in the US. In addition, the detailed *structure* of the tax system can have important geographical implications. Indeed, the *President's National Urban Policy Report* for 1980 concluded that 'the tax system is perhaps the most pervasive federal influence on patterns of economic development. Taxes influence the relative cost to businesses of new capital versus existing machinery, of low-wage or lower-skilled workers versus others, and of land in growing areas which is rising in value as opposed to land whose value may be falling' (US Department of Housing and Urban Development 1980: 3–18). The tax breaks offered under the Investment Tax Credits scheme (which are geared to encourage business investment in new equipment and machinery), for example, tend to benefit growth industries in growth areas; as do the more generous rates of depreciation allowed for new industrial and commercial plants. On the other hand, it should be acknowledged that studies of industrial location have established fairly clearly that tax differences between States are not a significant factor in inducing industrial *relocation* (Rees 1983b; Waslyenko 1981).

Although it is not possible to quantify the local effect of these structural characteristics of the tax system, it is possible to specify the magnitude of the net flows of monies between the federal government and individual States and, as we have seen (Fig. 4.9), these are substantial. The marked disadvantage of States in the Manufacturing Belt and the Northeast has been interpreted by some as a component of Frostbelt–Sunbelt economic decentralization, precipitating accusations of the South, in particular, obtaining preferential treatment from the federal government (Fainstein and Fainstein 1978; Rees 1983b). This 'conspiracy theory' in turn led to the idea of a 'Second War Between the States' being propagated by national current affairs journals. Central to this idea was the manipulation of the political 'pork barrel' (see Ch. 4).

But it is difficult to assemble evidence for consistent relationships between federal outlays, social needs and political representation, and the idea of 'conspiracy' or an economic 'war' is certainly overdrawn (Dilger 1982; Jusenius and Ledebur 1976). It is California, for example which has received the most valuable defence contracts by a good margin; and although defence funds have tended increasingly to flow to other parts of the Sunbelt, a large proportion of all such funds find their way back to the Manufacturing Belt as businesses subcontract parts of the work. Similarly, while R and D contracts awarded by the National Aeronautics and Space Administration (NASA) have been allocated disproportionately to the Los Angeles area, subcontracting has diffused the impact, with Manufacturing Belt cities receiving a substantial share of the work (Malecki 1981).

What *is* important about patterns of federal expenditure in the present context is that the *marginal impact* of these expenditures seems to have been much greater in the South and West. By improving the infrastructure of communications, transportation, sewage facilities and energy, the federal government helped to establish the preconditions for the development of new industries in the Sunbelt. By direct and indirect investment in electronics research, semiconductors, computers, aeronautics and scientific instruments in the South and West, the federal government enabled the Sunbelt to capture some of the most dynamic activities of advanced capitalism. 'At the same time', observe Watkins and Perry (1977:50), 'federal spending, irrespective of its absolute magnitude, has been relatively less successful in improving the industrial vitality of the Northeastern central cities'.

Federal economic policies for distressed regions

It must be recognized at the outset that the US 'has really never had a sustained, comprehensive, integrated or effective regional or area-based set of policies' (House 1983: 34). In a society which has for a long time viewed 'least government' as the 'best government', policy-making has been reactive rather than anticipatory, and the funds devoted to regional economic policies have been limited. Moreover, in order to muster the necessary coalitions in Congress, spatial policies have had to be very loosely defined – to the extent that their effectiveness has been greatly reduced. Emphasis has been on self-help, with eligible areas entitled, under their own initiative, to participate in federal programmes. And, in order to avoid the charge of unduly influencing the balance of market forces, the federal government has always steered clear of combining direct grants to industry in distressed areas with negative restraints on industry in more prosperous areas: a strategy which has been particularly successful in other capitalist economies.

The roots of regional economic policies

The strains and dislocations of the Great Depression of the 1930s not only mobilized concern over uneven regional development but also led to the first real experiments in regional planning under Roosevelt's New Deal. In 1933 the National Planning Board was created in order to coordinate all public-works projects affecting natural resources. Following a request by Congress, the Board's remit was extended to include the preparation of a comprehensive national plan based on river-basin development, and in the process it was renamed (in 1935) the National Resources Committee. By 1937, it had fostered widespread recognition of the desirability of State and city planning boards and won acceptance for the idea of federal funding for State planning (Graham 1976). Meanwhile, the Resettlement Administration had been set up (in 1935) from an amalgam of New Deal programmes which had been scattered throughout different governmental agencies. Its major concern was with technical assistance to poor farmers and with resettling rural families in new, more productive settings (which led it to flirt wlth the idea of cooperative villages). It also became involved in the construction of Greenbelt New Towns, though it built only three: Greenhills (Ohio). Greenbelt (Maryland) and Greendale (Wisconsin); a legal controversy over a fourth township outside New Brunswick resulted in the entire Greenbelt programme being declared unconstitutional by the US District Court of Appeals.

The most famous of the New Deal regional planning experiments is the Tennessee Valley Authority (TVA), which was established in 1933 on the legacy of a large dam which had been constructed at Muscle Shoals, Alabama, to supply electricity for two munitions factories during World War I. Given a broad remit, including the 'economic and social well-being of the people', the TVA applied itself during its first 5 years to a variety of projects. In addition to building dams, selling electricity and producing fertilizer, it greatly improved navigation and flood control on the Tennessee River, developed a 'grass-roots' agricultural programme and collectivist afforestation programme, and initiated several New Towns. From 1938, however, the TVA began to focus on electricity production and flood control, deliberately neglecting its regional planning function in response to internal feuding and external political pressure. Indeed, the whole set of New Deal experiments had to be soft-pedalled after the presidential election of 1936 in response to widespread fears of 'New Deal Sovietism'. By concentrating on energy and flood control, the TVA was able to survive; and by charging lower rates to bulk users of electricity than to domestic consumers, it began to attract a number of large-scale industries. Between 1930 and 1950, the Tennessee Valley gained 160 000 factory jobs, an increase of more than 80 per cent (Friedmann and Weaver 1979. In 1950, the President's Water Resources Policy Commission attempted to re-emphasize some of the broader aspects of comprehensive river-basin planning but by then the idea of regional development had lost its attraction: national economic growth was the focus of attention, and the TVA was left as a kind of hybrid industrial development corporation, searching for outlets for its ever-increasing hydro-electric output.

Nevertheless, the TVA remains a vast enterprise, employing some 45 000 people, spending $2200 million annually (1982), and supplying electricity to over 6 million people.

Regional economic assistance since 1950

Following World War II, the first real interest in regional development at the federal level did not come until the early 1960s, when President Kennedy responded to the 'rediscovery' of problem regions in America by creating the Area Redevelopment Administration (1962). Its objective was to stimulate employment by making loans to small businesses and by making loans or grants for infrastructural improvements in prescribed areas (mainly centres of high unemployment in the urbanized Northeast and areas of low income in the rural South) in accordance with Overall Economic Development Programs which had to be agreed by the relevant local governments (Estall 1977). In the same year, the idea of river-basin planning was revived, with the Water Resources Planning Act creating the first of several River Basin Commissions. These, however, like the Delaware (1961) and Susquehanna (1970) Basin Federal Inter-State Compact Commissions – but unlike the TVA – were restricted to water resource planning and had no powers to fund economic development projects.

These initiatives were followed up by President Johnson in his Great Society programme. In 1965, the Area Redevelopment Administration was reorganized as the Economic Development Administration (EDA) and given a much larger budget. The basic strategy was again to provide funds for infrastructural improvements and grants to businesses, and the criteria for assistance were extended to include high unemployment, population loss, low median income, a sudden rise in unemployment, or economic distress in an Indian reservation. In order to coordinate development in problem regions which straddled State boundaries, four Regional Planning Commissions were set up: for the Ozarks, the Coastal Plains, New England and the Four Corners (of Utah, Colorado, New Mexico and Arizona). Separate legislation established a fifth Regional Planning Commission, the Appalachian Regional Commission (ARC), with a relatively generous level of funding and a relatively autonomous role (Bradshaw 1985; Estall 1982). It has been the ARC which has been the showpiece of American regional planning, embracing every level of government in thirteen States. Of the $5212 million in funds which it disbursed between 1965 and 1985, around 60 per cent has been spent on highway construction, with a further 12 per cent on vocational educational programmes and 10 per cent on health-care projects. The legislation did not allow any funds to be used for the relocation of firms or facilities. Like the EDA, the ARC adopted a growth-centre strategy: the experience of their predecessor, the Area Redevelopment Administration, had already shown that a 'worst-first' strategy meant channelling funds towards areas with the least potential for growth.

In the event, though, neither the EDA nor the ARC were able to concentrate their efforts in a small enough number of sufficiently large growth centres. In Appalachia over 260 growth centres had been designated by 1975. Some of these 'centres' actually consisted of two or more communities up to 50 miles apart, while others were merely greenfield sites identified as suitable for industrial development. As a result, most growth centres have failed to generate any significant 'spread' effects in their hinterland (Levitan and Zickler 1976). The EDA, with its more modest level of funding, had abandoned the idea of growth centres by the early 1970s. Nevertheless, its efforts have also been diffused

as more local political interests have laid claim to a share of the regional development pork barrel. By 1980, three new Regional Commissions had been established, covering the Southwest Border, Old West and Pacific Northwest regions. Meanwhile, the Ozarks, Coastal Plains and Four Corners regions had been extended, and three more Regional Commissions (Mid-America, Mid-Atlantic and Mid-South) had been proposed by President Carter, providing almost 'wall-to-wall' coverage of the conterminous US (Estall 1982).

Overall evaluations of these policies have been critical, although it is generally acknowledged that there have been some notable local achievements and that the ARC has been particularly successful in fostering intergovernmental cooperation, establishing an efficient highway system and instigating a dramatic improvement in vocational education and health services. The ARC itself also points, with some justification, at the turnaround in net migration flows, the increase in manufacturing employment, and the reduction in poverty within the region (Table 5.7). It remains open to considerable debate, however, as to how much these achievements may be directly ascribed to the ARC and how much to the natural operation of market forces and/or the infusion of federal funds through increased transfer payments such as health and unemployment benefits and Aid to Families with Dependent Children (Batteau 1983; see also Martin 1979). It has been the conservatism of the EDA and the ARC which have attracted most criticism, however. In particular, their emphasis on infrastructural improvements at the expense of direct incentives to industry has been compared very unfavourably with the more radical regional development policies of other countries (Zysman 1980). In this context it is important to understand that the rationale for infrastructural investment has been rooted not in economic theory but in political pragmatism. As Rees (1983b) points out, it is much safer to opt for an emphasis on infrastructural investment because failure is difficult to define: if the investment stimulates economic development, all is well; if it does not, then local residents at least have the benefits of improved amenities. On the other hand, if investment

Table 5.7: Socio-economic change in Appalachia

| | Per capita money income | | | | Persons below poverty level | | | | Per cent population change |
| | Total | | Per cent of US | | Number (1 000) | | Per cent | | |
	1969	1979	1969	1979	1969	1979	1969	1979	1970–80
Appalachian region	$2 505	6 221	80.3	84.9	3 228	2 771	18.1	14.0	11.1
Appalachian portion of:									
Alabama	2 430	6 147	77.9	83.9	463	395	22.1	16.6	13.7
Georgia	2 419	6 301	77.6	86.0	136	134	17.0	12.3	35.6
Kentucky	1 732	4 856	55.5	66.2	334	275	38.8	26.0	22.9
Maryland	2 599	6 327	83.3	86.3	30	25	14.7	11.9	5.2
Mississippi	1 861	4 956	59.7	67.6	139	105	33.8	22.1	15.3
New York	2 845	6 135	91.2	83.7	117	124	11.5	12.0	2.5
North Carolina	2 437	6 095	78.1	83.2	190	164	18.7	13.8	17.2
Ohio	2 443	6 073	78.3	82.9	176	159	16.0	12.9	11.7
Pennsylvania	2 790	6 770	89.5	92.4	664	587	11.4	10.0	1.1
South Carolina	2 571	6 473	82.4	88.3	104	97	16.2	12.6	20.6
Tennessee	2 340	5 983	75.0	81.6	381	337	22.4	16.6	19.6
Virginia	2 050	5 614	65.7	76.6	113	83	24.4	15.2	16.9
West Virginia	2 333	6 179	74.8	84.3	380	287	22.2	15.0	11.8
United States	3 119	7 730	100.0	100.0	27 125	27 383	13.7	12.4	11.4

were to be made in industrial development and the venture were to collapse, failure would be outright and very conspicuous.

A more fundamental problem has been that the whole idea of regional economic development rested, in the first instance, on a fragile political alliance between the interests of declining industrial areas and those of backward rural areas. Once the resulting benefits began to be tapped by a broader constituency of local political interests, the alliance lost much of its impetus. And, as national economic growth began to falter, regional economic development came to be perceived as a zero sum game, with the gains of one region being seen as the losses of others. Moreover, the emerging crisis of larger urban areas from the early 1970s onwards, coupled with the emergence of the Sunbelt as the apparent locus of 'natural' employment growth, meant that *metropolitan* economic problems provided a much sharper focus for federal policy. The 1960s had already seen the introduction of federal aid to inner-city neighbourhoods in the form of the Community Action Program and the Model Cities Program (see Ch. 7).

In the 1970s, several federal policy initiatives were introduced which were more broadly targeted on metropolitan areas. These include a variety of transportation programmes, together with a massive commitment to job training and work experience in areas of high unemployment under the Comprehensive Employment and Training Act (CETA). Most important in the present context, however, was the Urban Development Action Grant (UDAG) programme, initiated in 1978 to stimulate private sector employment and to improve the fiscal health of severely distressed cities (Jacobs and Roistacher 1980). With a relatively substantial budget compared to other federal programmes, the UDAG programme had by 1980 all but eclipsed the EDA programme and had come to represent the principal dimension of spatially targeted federal economic aid. By the last days of the Carter administration, however, the logic of such aid had come into question. A report issued by the President's Commission for a National Agenda for the Eighties (1980) argued that it was naïve and unrealistic to attempt to fly in the face of economic transformation and spatial change. In

particular, it was suggested, the central cities of the Manufacturing Belt could not expect to be restored to the prosperity and influence that they had enjoyed throughout the industrial era. As a result, the report concluded that the government should stop trying to ward off the inevitable by subsidizing specific cities. Rather, it suggested, the government should set about removing barriers to mobility that prevent people from migrating to places of economic opportunity. As the *New York Daily News* headline put it: 'FEDS TO NORTHEAST: DROP DEAD'. With the accession of the Reagan administration later in 1980, the idea of any kind of federal intervention in local economic development came into question, along with most other forms of federal aid (see p. 207). Thus, while severely curtailing expenditure on health, public employment, social services, food stamps, and so on, the federal government began to transfer responsibility for many programmes to State governments under the banner of 'New Federalism' (US Department of Housing and Urban Development 1982). More than ever, therefore, the most notable feature of American spatial economic aid is its insignificance in relation to overall patterns of economic development.

Overall perspectives: urban and regional outcomes

In this section we attempt to draw together the implications of the various trends described in previous sections of this chapter in terms of the overall economic organization of US space. To this end, we shall look in turn at urban and regional patterns with reference to (a) functional economic specialization and (b) the more general perspective of local economic prosperity.

The urban system under advanced capitalism

Although the basic framework of the American urban system had been established by 1920, its components have displayed a high degree of volatility as new dimensions of economic organization have worked their way through the system (Morrill, Sinclair and Dimartino 1984: South and Poston 1982). Borchert (1983) has charted the changes which have occurred in rates of metropolitan growth since 1920, showing how this volatility takes on a coherent pattern when set against oscillations in national and regional business cycles, the rise and fall of particular industries, the emergence of new relationships between resources and technology, and the associated flows of migrants within and between regions. The outcome has been a marked redistribution of population within the urban system, with the cities of the South and West gaining rapidly in relation to those of the Manufacturing Belt, the Northeast and the Midwest (Fig. 7.4). At the same time, of course, there have been important changes in the functional organization of the urban system (Dunn 1980, 1983). Whereas the urban system from the turn of the century until the immediate postwar era was characterized by the dominance of large manufacturing centres (mostly, but not exclusively, from the Manufacturing Belt), the urban system under advanced capitalism is characterized by the key role of metropolitan areas specializing in service industries, particularly producer services:

In this new urban system, dominance is defined increasingly by the capacity of these service centers to organize and expand production on a systemwide basis – more and more international in dimension – and increasingly less by their ability to get the goods out locally, as was the case in the past (Noyelle 1983: 126).

What is remarkable about this transformation is that many of these new service-oriented centres are large manufacturing centres of the previous epoch which have been fundamentally transformed in terms of economic structure; while only a limited number of Sunbelt cities seem to be reaching a dominant status. This conclusion is based on the results of an analysis of the employment structure and functional characteristics of the 140 largest US cities in the mid-1970s (Noyelle and Stanback 1981). The analysis suggests the emergence of a three-tiered urban hierarchy, consisting of (1) diversified producer-service centres or 'nodal centres', (2) specialized producer-service centres, and (3) dependent centres (Fig. 5.5).

First-tier cities are characterized by large concentrations of national and regional head-quarters of large corporations, well-developed banking facilities, dense networks of producer-service firms (insurance, accounting, advertising, legal counsel, public relations, R and D, etc.), and concentrations of important educational, medical and public-sector institutions; and they also tend to be important centres for the wholesale distribution of manufactured goods. They include the 'national nodal centres' of New York, Los Angeles, Chicago and San Francisco, together with 'regional nodal centres' (e.g. Atlanta, Dallas, New Orleans, Philadelphia and St Louis), and 'subregional nodal centres' (e.g. Charlotte, Mobile, Oklahoma City and Richmond).

By comparison, the service specialization of *second-tier* cities tends to be more narrowly defined. Most are specialized in management and technical production for well-defined industries (e.g. steel in Pittsburgh, office equipment in Rochester, semiconductors in San Jose) and are therefore characterized by concentrations of the headquarters offices, R and D facilities and technically-oriented production establishments of large firms in those industries. Figure 5.5 shows that these 'functional nodal centres' are heavily concentrated within the old Manufacturing Belt. Noyelle and Stanback also recognize 'government/education centres' as a distinctive subgroup of second-tier cities. In addition to Washington, DC, these include Albany, Austin, Madison and Raleigh-Durham. In general, companies headquartered in second-tier cities must obtain high-order producer-services such as banking and advertising from firms based in first-tier cities.

Most of the *third-tier* cities are smaller size, though there are several important exceptions (including San Diego, Buffalo, Albuquerque and Tampa). Four sub-categories are recognized:

1. 'resort/retirement/residential centres', such as Albuquerque, Fort Lauderdale, Las Vegas and Orlando; most of them in the South and West;
2. 'manufacturing centres', such as Buffalo, Chattanooga, Erie and Rockford; nearly all of them located in the old Manufacturing Belt;
3. 'industrial/military centres' such as Hunts-

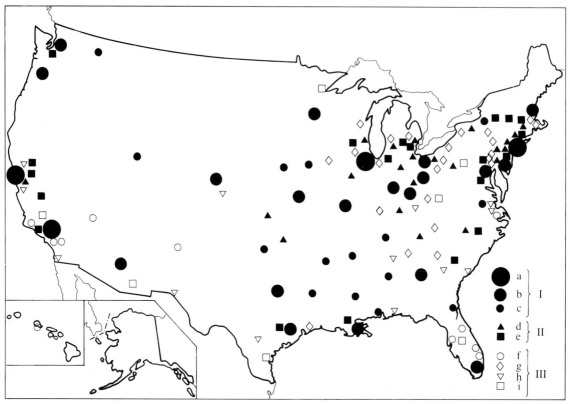

Fig. 5.5 The urban system under advanced capitalism. a = national nodal centres, b = regional nodal centres, c = subregional nodal centres, d = functional nodal centres, e = government/education centres, f = resort/retirement/residential centres, g = manufacturing centres, h = industrial/military centres, i = mining/industrial centres
Based on data in Noyelle and Stanback (1981)

ville, Newport News and San Diego; most of them in the South and West; and

4. 'mining/industrial centres' such as Duluth and Charleston (W.Va.).

What these sub-categories have in common is that they are largely subordinate to the decisions taken in upper-tier cities, with their industrial base biased heavily towards direct production and assembly work and their service base containing a disproportionate number of 'secondary' jobs. Further analysis (Stanback and Noyelle 1982) suggests that the basic structure of this new urban system is likely to develop in directions that will intensify these differences. Thus, key services are likely to continue to grow almost exclusively in cities of the first two tiers, while the 'dependent' centres of the third tier are likely to remain highly

specialized (and therefore more vulnerable to the fluctuations of business cycles) either in production activities or consumer services.

Distressed cities

This brings us to the question of economic well-being and patterns of prosperity within the urban system. Here we can draw on the index of economic distress prepared by the Department of Housing and Urban Development in relation to the UDAG programme. This index is based on a series of minimum standards relating to the rate of growth of population, incomes, and manufacturing and retail employment and maxima in relation to the incidence of poverty, pre-1940 housing, and unemployment. Cities score one point for each criterion

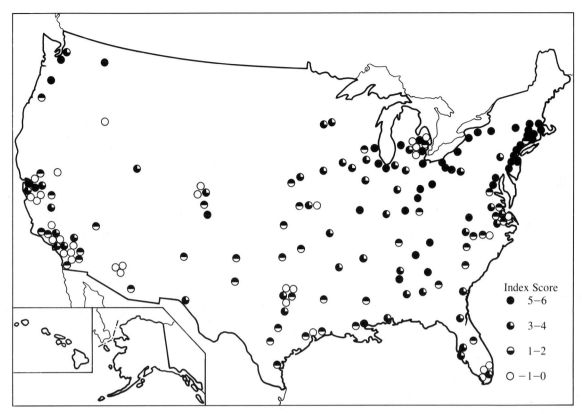

Fig. 5.6 Prosperity and distress in the urban system, 1982
Source of data: Data Systems Division, US Department of Housing and Urban Development

not met, but lose a point if the incidence of poverty is less than half the national norm. The index thus ranges from −1 (for the most prosperous cities) to 6 (for the most distressed); cities with an index score of 3 or more are eligible for aid under the UDAG programme. Figure 5.6 shows the overall pattern of prosperity for cities with a population of 100 000 or more, using HUD data for the fiscal year 1982. This map clearly illustrates the urban distress that has come to be associated with the Manufacturing Belt, though it is equally clear that urban distress is by no means the prerogative of the Snowbelt. High levels of distress are also found in the South (including Atlanta, Birmingham, Chattanooga, Knoxville, New Orleans and Roanoke) and the West (including Oakland, Portland, Spokane and Tacoma). On the other hand, a few of the most prosperous cities are to be found within the Manufacturing Belt, where the likes of Livonia, Sterling

Heights and Warren (all outside Detroit) reflect the decentralization of prosperity at the metropolitan scale.

The regional system under advanced capitalism

To a large extent, of course, the pattern of regional economic specialization under advanced capitalism reflects the metropolitan specializations described above. Yet small-town and rural America still account for a considerable proportion of the overall economy. Figure 5.7 illustrates the dominant economic specialization in 1970 of the 171 Economic Areas recognized by the Bureau of Economic Analysis, together with the second-order specializations of regions not overwhelmingly dominated by a single sector of activity (for details of the analysis, see Dunn 1980). It should be noted that agriculture

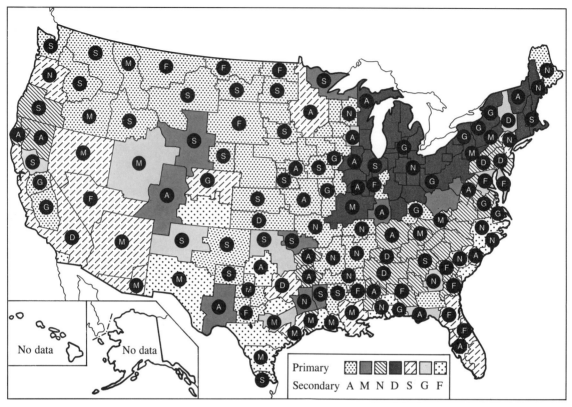

Fig. 5.7 Regional industrial specialization under advanced capitalism. A = agriculture; M = manufacturing; N = non-durable manufacturing; D = durable manufacturing; S = transportation, trade and services; G = professional and government; F = armed forces
Source: Dunn (1980), Map 13, p. 103

is the most extensive regional specialism, accounting for 53 of the 171 subregions; though Dunn (1980) points out that there has been a marked decline in agricultural dominance since 1940, when there were 97 agricultural sub-regions. In particular, agricultural dominance has disappeared from the Southeast, one of its traditional strongholds. It has largely retreated to the Northern Plains and Northern Mountain regions: two fingers of agricultural specializ-ation – one running along the course of the Mississippi and another extending into the West Texas Plains – are all that remain of agricul-ture's southern dominance.

Mining continues to dominate the sub-regional economies associated with Appalachian and southern Illinois coal, southwestern oil, western Mountain minerals, and Superior Iron ore; though mining, like agriculture, is gener-

ally in retreat. In contrast, non-durable manu-facturing (food processing, textiles, apparel, printing, etc.) has shown considerable territo-rial gains since 1940. Figure 5.7 shows that in 1970 it dominated an area stretching from Phil-adelphia and Harrisburg through the Southeast as far as Fort Smith and Texarkana. In the Northeast and Upper Midwest, meanwhile, the Manufacturing Belt continued to be dominated by durable manufacturing (furniture, machinery, motor vehicles, etc.). The broad mixture of activities covered by trade, transportation and services provided a second-order specialization for many regions throughout the country, reflecting the overall shift within the economy as a whole towards services. They were the dominant economic activity in New York, reflecting its role as an international business and commercial capital. The Los Angeles,

Minneapolis, Portland, Omaha and New Orleans subregions were also dominated by these activities because of their importance as broad regional servicing centres. In the Florida peninsula and the Reno, Las Vegas, Phoenix and Tucson subregions, on the other hand, it has been the retirement/recreation syndrome which has resulted in the dominance of these activities.

The expansion of professional services (medical, educational, legal and business) and government civilian employment is reflected by the fact that whereas only one subregion – Washington, DC – was dominant in these activities in 1940, twelve more specialist subregions had been added by 1970. These include the regions around Albany, Austin, Baltimore, Madison, Oklahoma City, Sacramento, Salt Lake City, Santa Fe, Springfield (Illinois) and Tallahassee. For most of these subregions, this new specialization owes a good deal to the combination of the presence of State government administrative headquarters and major universities. Finally, the expanding influence of federal defence spending has been reflected by a marked extension of the number of subregions dominated by armed forces employment. In 1940, Norfolk, Pensacola and San Diego were the only specialist military subregions. By 1970 the Wilmington (SC), Columbia and Charleston (SC) subregions had joined Norfolk as armed forces specialists in the Southeast. Mobile, Lake Charles and Corpus Christi joined Pensacola on the Gulf Coast. San Antonio, Waco, Wichita Falls, El Paso and Pueblo emerged in the Southwest, and Seattle joined San Diego as a West Coast specialist military subregion.

Patterns and trends of regional prosperity and distress

The decentralization of economic activity which lies behind this new spatial division of labour in the US has also made for a striking convergence in regional prosperity. As Fig. 5.8 shows, the most dramatic convergence in regional per capita income in fact took place between 1930 and 1950, though the overall trend has continued throughout most of the postwar period. It should be noted, however, that the onset of national economic recession during the 1970s checked the rate of convergence appreciably, and there has recently been some indication of a slight widening of regional per capita income differentials (ACIR 1980). Moreover, the broad picture described by Fig. 5.8

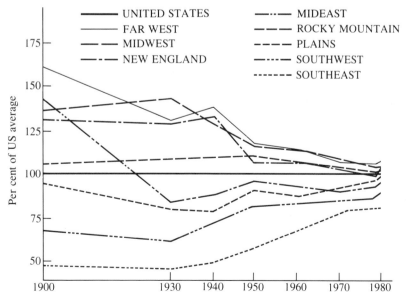

Fig. 5.8 Regional change in per capita incomes, 1900–80

obscures some important subregional trends. Keinath (1982) has investigated these trends for the 1970s at the level of the Economic Areas used by Dunn (1980). In this research, Keinath used a four-fold typology of subregions based on per capita income levels and rates of change in per capita incomes (Table 5.8). According to this typology, 'prosperous' subregions are characteristic of the Pacific Northwest, California, much of Texas, the Denver–Cheyenne area, the Middle West and northwestern fringe of the Manufacturing Belt, and Washington, DC (Fig. 5.9). 'Declining prosperity' dominates the metropolitan seaboard of the Northeast, from Philadelphia to Boston; but otherwise it is restricted to a few isolated subregions: Chicago-Gary, Cincinnati, Rochester and

Table 5.8: Typology of Economic Areas

Rate of increase in per capita incomes compared to the national average	Per capita income level compared to the national average	
	HIGH	LOW
HIGH	Prosperity Area	Developing Distressed (Area)
LOW	Potential Distressed Area (or Declining Prosperity Area)	Distressed (Area)

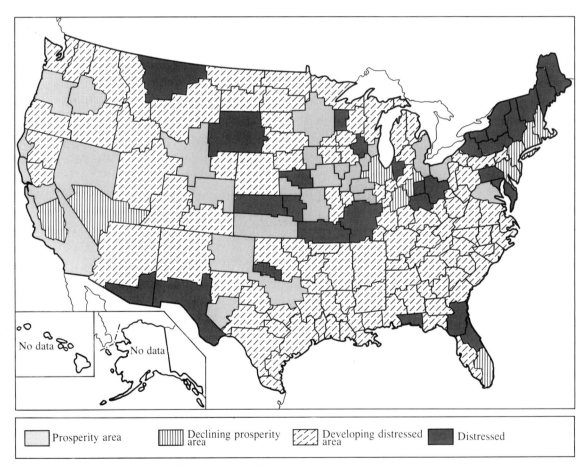

| | Prosperity area | Declining prosperity area | Developing distressed area | Distressed |

Fig. 5.9 Regional prosperity and distress, 1971–78
Source: Keinath (1982), Fig. 1, p. 345

southeastern Florida. 'Distressed' subregions are particularly concentrated in upstate New England and New York but they are also found in the Sunbelt (e.g. northern Florida, the southern parts of Arizona and New Mexico, southwestern Oklahoma), the Middle West (e.g. west-central Kansas and western South Dakota). The rest of the country is characterized by subregions that are catching up in terms of the average national per capita income, emphasizing once again the economic decentralization of the US. In conclusion, however, it must be acknowledged that even these subregional data provide only a crude picture of spatial variations in economic prosperity. In subsequent chapters we shall examine more closely the striking contrasts which exist in the economic organization and social well-being of communities and subgroups in specific spatial settings.

Chapter 6

RURAL AMERICA

Despite its contracting importance in terms of population and employment, the rural dimension of the US remains essential to the character of regional landscapes, cultures, politics and settlement patterns. Moreover, although the minds and muscle of America lie in the city, its heart and soul still seems to rest in the country. Most Americans would prefer to live in the country or in small towns rather than the city, and believe that urban living has changed the American way of life for the worse. 'Thank God I'm a Country Boy' sings John Denver. In fact, as in all countries which have undergone industrialization, there has developed a symbiotic, if not symmetrical, relationship between the rural and the urban dimensions of American life. Positive 'wave' effects and negative 'backwash' effects stemming from the growth of urban America have created interdependencies that bind together urban and rural America (Berry 1972; Lamb 1975). In this chapter, we outline both the image and the reality of contemporary rural America. The land policies, population movements and agricultural systems that have shaped rural America are described, and vignettes of some of America's major rural heartlands are presented. Finally, we analyse some of the processes which are currently reshaping rural America: the industrialization of agriculture, the evolution of public policy, the penetration of manufacturing industry, and the arrival of incomers.

Rural America: ideal and reality

What is valued as 'American' is often tied to an image of rural America that is grounded in myths and misconceptions as well as historic facts. Although the US has been predominantly urban for over 50 years, rural America remains for many the standard for what is good, valuable and central to the American way of life (Fischer 1976). The American rural ideology

Top left: Haynes farm, N. Charlestown, New Hampshire *Credit*: USDA Soil Conservation Service *Top right*: Abandoned farm house, North Dakota *Credit*: USDA Soil Conservation Service *2nd left*: Texas plains *Credit*: Paul Knox *2nd right*: Wheat harvesting in Oklahoma *Credit*: USDA *3rd left*: Rural poverty: Mexican Americans in San Diego, Texas *Credit*: USDA *3rd right*: Miller Farm, Cedar Falls, Iowa *Credit*: USDA *Bottom left*: Trailer home in Appalachia *Credit*: Paul Knox *Bottom right*: St Charles, Virginia *Credit*: Paul Knox

manifests itself in a multitude of ways. In art and literature, for example, the clash between technology and a rural pastoral environment is a common theme which can be traced to a romanaticization of the countryside that occurred in reaction to the industrialization and urbanization of nineteenth-century America (Marx 1964). The aggrandizement of rural life has profoundly affected American politics and economic policies. Beginning with Jefferson's call for an agrarian society based on yeoman farmers and continuing into contemporary political life, rural America has played a role well beyond its importance as measured by economics and population. Before the Supreme Court's redistricting decisions of 1962 and 1964 which mandated 'one person/one vote' for legislative redistricting, the influence of rural America on the body politic was both ideological and structural. With more equitable redistricting of State legislatures, suburban interests began to dominate State governments, but the ideological influence of rural America on State and federal policies is still strong (see Ch. 4).

One of the many paradoxes of rural America is that the image does not necessarily conform to historical fact or contemporary conditions. The individualism promoted by the frontier experience was counterbalanced by collective actions common to many frontier communities (e.g. barn raisings and rural cooperatives); small family farms have always existed juxtaposed to large plantations or, more recently, to corporate farms; and rural America's indelible imprint on American politics was often the result of self-centred, prejudicial motives designed to promote the interests of a small minority (Morgan 1969). Given these paradoxes, what then is the structure and character of contemporary rural America? To answer this question, we must recognize first that rural America is complex and diverse. Moreover it has been in constant flux as the nation's economy and population composition have changed. Rural America today differs markedly from what it was under industrial capitalism. Waves of foreign immigrants have had their impact on the composition of rural population and on rural culture. Economic transformations and international demographic movements combined to change the work and social environments of rural America and in doing so

have increased the gap between the myth and the reality.

Understanding the realities of rural America requires a definition of its limits and its structure. Yet defining rural America either geographically or socially is fraught with problems. Lewis (1983), for example, argues that rural areas consist of those in which 'extensive', as opposed to 'intensive', land uses predominate. Such an approach has little utility in marking the geographic limits of rural America because land-use data are not readily available, and in many areas extensive uses dominate the landscape but most residents work in metropolitan centres. The gentle rolling horse pastures of northern Virginia fail to convey the reality that most of the residents in this pastoral setting work in Washington, DC, or its suburbs.

As we have seen (Ch. 2), 'rural' to the US Census Bureau is a 'type of residency' concept rather than an area to be outlined on a map. As such, one can accurately count the number of *rural* residents (59.5 million or 26.3 per cent of the total population in 1980), but not set clear geographic limits to rural America. *Non-metropolitan* counties have an areal expression and thus can be mapped to define the geographic extent of counties that lie outside metropolitan America. The geographic extent of non-metropolitan counties conveys the impression that the US is primarily rural, which it is in terms of area. But this impression is at odds with the realities of population proportions (only 24 per cent of population is in non-metropolitan counties). Moreover, reliance on non-metropolitan to define rural counties does not provide a reasonably accurate representation of the geographic limits of rural America because of ambiguities in the concept. Non-metropolitan counties, as we know, may include cities of less than 50 000 within their boundaries. In 1980, for example, 38 per cent of the persons living in non-metropolitan counties were urban residents. On the other hand, metropolitan counties include persons (14 per cent of the metro population in 1980) engaged in what are considered rural occupations, e.g. farming, or who do not live in an urban setting. Thus the use of non-metropolitan counties rather than defining strictly rural areas only permits us to identify those counties which lie outside the immediate hinterland of large urban centres, and thus by implication are more 'rural like' that those counties within SMSAs.

Defining what is distinctive about rural society is as difficult as defining its geographic limits. From the earliest stages of industrialization and urbanization, scholars have argued that important rural/urban distinctions exist in social institutions, values, norms and behaviour (see, for example, Tonnies 1887; Wirth 1938; and the review of these ideas by Fischer 1976). Contrary to this view is the argument that social differences between urban and rural are inconsequential in comparison to those associated with gender roles, race and class, and that, moreover, a convergence between urban and rural lifestyles and values is occurring because of the homogenizing effects of a highly integrated industrial economy.

Though similarities exist in the social characteristics and behaviour of urban and rural residents, one must take care in not overstating the extent of the convergence. Differences between metropolitan and non-metropolitan counties are still present on a number of social indicators (Table 6.1). Residents in non-metropolitan America generally have lower socio-economic status, have more people below the poverty level, have poorer health status, a different family status and have higher scores on an index of alienation (see Ross, Bluestone, and Hines 1979 for further information on the construction of the indicators). Moreover, on behavioural and attitudinal measures, such as religious values and participation, political attitudes and social participation, differences between rural and urban populations still exist (Fischer 1975b).

These and other differences are, to some extent, the result of the distinctive cultural and economic histories of urban and rural America. Most immigrants to urban America during the industrial period came mainly from eastern and southern Europe. Rural America, in contrast, was settled by persons with different cultural backgrounds. Germans and Scandinavians constituted a major component among early settlers to the upper Middle West; French culture was pre-eminent in large sections of southern Louisiana; Hispanic culture left a strong imprint on the rural Southwest; black culture in America began in rural America; and American Indians have left their imprint on the

Table 6.1: Social indicators for metropolitan and non-metropolitan counties – 1970[1]

	Metropolitan	*Nonmetropolitan*
Socio-economic status	115.7	96.1
Health status	106.1	98.5
Family status	99.3	100.2
Alienation	99.2	100.2

[1] Social indicators are from Ross, Bluestone and Hines (1979). Socio-economic status was defined by four variables: median family income, families with male heads not in poverty, school attainment, and dwellings with complete plumbing – higher values indicate higher socio-economic status. Health status was defined by three variables: mortality from all causes, infant mortality and mortality from influenza and pneumonia – higher scores indicate poorer health status. Family status was defined by the variables: proportion of children living with both parents, difference in per cent of males and females in the labour forces, and per cent of families with female heads – higher scores indicate a more traditional family structure. Alienation was defined by the variables: mortality from suicides and from cirrhosis of the liver – higher scores indicate greater alienation.

rural West. The migration of rural minorities to urban America eventually blurred many of the early distinctions between rural and urban, but migration was only one of the manifestations of the nation's economic realignment which transformed rural America. The 'invisible hand' of the market ignores and exploits cultural distinctions as it seeks to rationalize social organizations. As market forces led to common structural changes in the rural economy and the technology and products of urban America diffused throughout the countryside, rural–urban convergence quickened. More recently, technological developments in communications and the centralization of control of the popular media have accelerated the pace of convergence by transmitting urban culture across vast stretches of rural America. Beginning with rural electrification, through the arrival of 'full watt' radio stations which enabled teenagers in South Dakota to listen to the same programmes as their counterparts in the south Bronx, to television with its national networks, cable TV and 'satellite dishes' which have proliferated across the rural landscape giving even the most isolated rural resident access to world culture, the popular media have had a strong homogenizing influence on rural preferences, values and attitudes. Today's rural resident is exposed to culture, sports, world events and entertainment previously known only to the city resident. Visual evidence of this urban/rural convergence is evident throughout rural America. Prefabricated 'New England' cottages have spread across the plains of Kansas, designer jeans adorn the country folk of rural Appalachia, and small rural towns sport the flashing neon signs that signal the newest line in fast-foods franchises.

What is particularly striking about rural America, however, is that despite the strong forces for convergence, its distinctiveness still shows through in many parts of the country. Imprints of earlier settlements, agricultural systems and cultures are still evident on the rural landscape, and are reflected in regional differences in domestic architecture (Kniffen 1965), farm buildings (Noble and Seymour 1982; Sloan 1966), religion (Zelinsky 1961; Jordan 1980), landform terminology (Miller 1969), and language and dialects (Allen 1973). Cynics charge that these landscape artifacts are only of archeological interest, but such residuals are indicative of the resilience and strength of rural culture and the values and attitudes inherent in it. The cultural heritage of rural America has been an anchor to the past, a counterbalance against the great homogenizing forces of the nation's political economy. Thus to interpret the structure of contemporary rural America, both past and current cultural and economic forces must be examined and their interdependences understood.

Shaping rural America: land, people and work

Synthesizing the historic development of rural America is difficult because the settling of the country was influenced by a host of internal and external factors. Three, however, merit special attention:

- Land policy/land acquisition
- Migration/adaptation
- Agricultural assemblages and linkages

A discussion of each follows. We then show how these and other factors shaped the rural landscape in different areas of the country, using vignettes of three regions – the Southwest, the South and the Midwest. Finally, the major forces for contemporary change in rural America are discussed.

Land policies

The US rural settlement pattern evolved in response to many different factors, but land policies and attitudes about private property were particularly important in shaping the morphology of rural settlement and in conditioning the economic and social institutions of rural America.

The initial and enduring value placed on private ownership of property has had a major impact on the organization of both rural and urban America (Warner 1972). Rights of the individual property owner over those of public or collective ownership were quickly established in colonial America. In the earliest colonial settlements, such as the Chesapeake Bay colonies, land ownership was the key to achieving status. Access to land was restricted by the large *land grants* allocated to trading or other Crown companies and, therefore, the status differential between the landowners and the non-owners expanded (Mitchell 1983). The presence of vast quantities of land on the edge of settlement that could be obtained simply by establishing residence and avoiding the eyes of the colonial government made ownership possible for many otherwise landless colonials. Still, many settlers were never able to purchase land because they lacked capital or because, as with blacks, legal rights to property were denied. The creation of small, individual farmsteads on the edge of settlement was beneficial to the larger settlements on the coast because frontier settlement acted as a buffer against Indians and later against French expansionist forces emanating from the interior. Also the yeoman farmer was an efficient producer and ready consumer of goods, a combination ideally suited to the mercantile economic system of the period.

Despite the advantage of a frontier buffer, for geopolitical reasons the British colonial government alternately encouraged or discouraged the expansion of the colonies' western frontiers – at that time the Appalachian highlands region. Even when official policy prohibited further frontier settlement, illegal squatting proceeded unabated in the sparsely inhabited areas within and to the west of the Appalachian highlands. Early settlers were protected from official retributions by their isolation, for they went unnoticed if the settlements were not large. Isolation and dispersion offered the early frontier family protection against its three chief rivals for land: the colonial government, land speculators and large landowners. Protection against the latter did not last long, however, because as the density of settlement increased, large portions of land came under the ownership of a small group of owners. In 1746 in the Shenandoah Valley of Virginia, for example, 40 per cent of the land in local communities was owned by only 10 per cent of the landowners (Mitchell 1977). Inequities in land ownership created civil disturbances in the frontier agricultural areas and challenged the colonial government's rights to control land distribution.

After the Revolutionary War the new US government had to confront the same question faced by the British – what to do with the vast amounts of publicly-owned land. Since that time, the federal government has continued to wrestle with issues concerning the sale and use of *public lands*. The most important of these have been:

- How much land should the national government acquire?
- Of the land acquired, how much should be retained and how much should be sold to private or other governmental levels?
- What should be the terms of disposal – price, tenure, and restrictions?
- Should private use of federal land be permitted and, if so, under what conditions?
- How much effort and resources should be spent on federal lands to preserve them?
- What forms of inter-governmental management arrangements should be made for land acquired by the federal government?
- What type of land-use planning should be used with public lands and what groups should participate in that planning? (Clawson 1983: 2–3).

How the government chose to deal with these issues influenced the speed, density and pattern of settlement in the nation's new territories and the types of agricultural systems found there.

Long-term federal ownership of land was an anathema to the nation's early leaders because of their distrust of a highly centralized, powerful federal government and because of their fundamental belief that private property was the foundation of personal freedom. But after the War of Independence, individual States had claimed vast tracts of land west of the Appalachians for themselves, and armed hostilities between States over conflicting claims were a definite possibility. These claims threatened the power of the national government and endangered the newly formed union, so to defuse the tension the national government assumed control of all lands beyond existing State boundaries and granted to itself the sole right to own and to manage new lands added through territorial expansion. Because leaders like Jefferson believed that yeoman farmers were the backbone of the new republic, they advocated the speedy and cheap disposal of land to help the formation of a large farming class. The *Northwest Ordinance* of 1785 was the policy instrument designed to carry out that goal.

The Ordinance was drafted by a committee headed by Jefferson so it reflected many of his ideas about an agrarian democracy and the importance of a class of yeoman farmers in building a national identity. The influence of the Ordinance on settlement patterns was far-reaching, for it established a rectilinear survey system based on prime meridians and baselines for subdividing land in the newly acquired territories, and it established land alienation policies which encouraged dispersed farmsteads. The rectilinear system was only one of several survey systems in use at the time (Fig. 6.1), but after 1785 it became the official system for all land purchased and owned by the federal government. Its popularity as a policy was because it provided a quick and accurate way of establishing property boundaries, thus

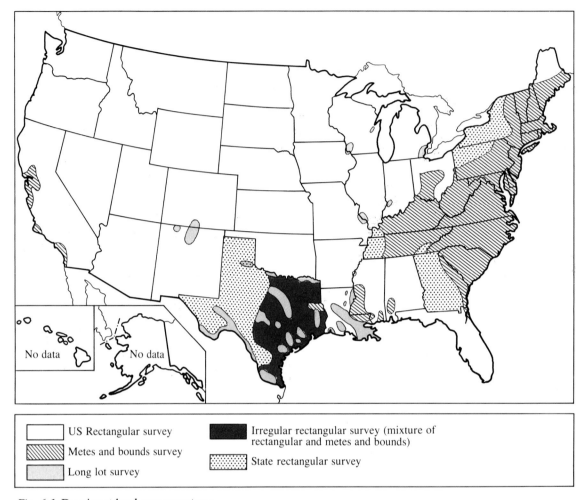

US Rectangular survey

Metes and bounds survey

Long lot survey

Irregular rectangular survey (mixture of rectangular and metes and bounds)

State rectangular survey

Fig. 6.1 Dominant land survey systems

helping the rapid disposal of land (Johnson 1974). In the rectilinear system, land was surveyed into square mile sections (640 acres or 259 hectares) with thirty-six sections being defined as a township, a basic administrative unit. Sections could be subdivided when necessary into half sections, quarter sections, and so forth, as long as the original, geometry of the survey was preserved. An early criticism of the system was that, unlike the metes and bounds system, the farmer could not select land on the basis of environmental quality to obtain the range of local physical environments necessary for a successful farm. This criticism proved to be unfounded for, although the geometric requirement of the survey made it

difficult. many farmers were able to combine 40 acre units in ways that did maximize local environmental conditions (Johnson 1974). The geometry of the system did, however, influence the structure of the rural road network, the organization of fields and farmsteads, and the structure of rural administrative units (Thrower 1961); and, along with regulations about the minimum size of land to be sold, it encouraged a pattern of rural settlement that became widespread throughout much of the nation. As Hudson writes:

Anyone who has traveled across the prairies and plains gathers an impression of the region's settlement fabric. A grain elevator rises predictably against the horizon, followed by a church steeple or school poking up above a canopy of cottonwoods. Up close, a small cluster of false-front store buildings lines Main Street, with perpendicular rows of white frame houses on one side of the highway and a railroad depot on the other. These perceptions mark one's passage through yet another of the villages that look so much alike to the outsider. The geometry is more regular when viewed from the air: individual structures are lost, but the regular spacing of towns along a railroad line that cuts across the rectangular grid of farms and fields is all the more remarkable. It is the dominant settlement pattern in a broad region beginning with the Grand Prairie of Illinois on the east, stretching northwest to the Canadian prairies, south through Texas, and west to the Rocky Mountain front (Hudson 1985: 5)

The federal policies that set minimum parcel sizes for land sales have always sparked controversy, for they establish financial barriers to landownership. The larger the parcel size and the higher the cost to the settler, the more difficult it was for those without large amounts of capital to purchase land. The large parcel size initially established by the Ordinance encouraged land speculation companies to purchase large blocks of land and sell them later to individual settlers as smaller parcels at a handsome profit. Pressure from frontier politicians, farmers and special interest groups continually lobbied for a reduction in the acreage purchase requirement, so that by 1832 the minimum parcel size had been reduced to 40 acres from the initial 640. Even with reductions in the size of the cadastral unit, the cost of establishing a new farm in the Middle West in the mid-1800s was estimated to be more than $1000 (Anki 1974; Danhof 1941). High frontier interest rates (ranging from 30 to 120 per cent) and the expense of land improvement costs made ownership of even inexpensive land beyond the capabilities of most potential homesteaders. To buy land, many resorted to land mortgages, loans in which the land to be purchased is used as collateral for the sale. Land mortgages enabled settlers to become landowners, but the system led to a long-standing feeling of distrust of financial institutions by farmers because foreclosures on land mortgages became common. This attitude of distrust became embodied in the agrarian political movements of the late nineteenth century.

Instead of land mortgages, others seeking farm ownership began as tenants or as cash wage hands on existing farms, hoping to accumulate enough capital to buy their own farm (Bogue 1963). In 1880, for example, nearly 25 per cent of all farmers were tenants, and the proportion of tenant farmers increased steadily in subsequent decades even in areas outside the South, a region where tenancy had been institutionalized after the Civil War. The increasing rates of tenancy contradicted the popular view that it was a step upward on the '*agricultural ladder*' – the ladder whose rungs were (1) cash wage, (2) tenancy and (3) ownership (Ely 1917). The 'ladder' became the model for land ownership promoted by politicians and academics at the turn of the century, but in reality the dominant method of securing ownership was by inheritance. As Ostergren observed:

> Landed wealth was the symbol of the family's independence, past achievement, and future security. It was established at the cost of hard work and deprivation. Strategies for preserving it and passing it on to future generations were natural and important concerns (Ostergren 1981: 406).

The success of the agricultural ladder in achieving ownership was more mythical than real. It was promoted to stifle the social unrest which had been mounting among farmers. By the late 1800s the Populist movement, the Granger movement and the Farmer's Alliance arose to represent the special interests of agriculturalists. They articulated the belief among many farmers that urban financial and political institutions dominated American politics. The fact that many farmers supported the socialist movement in the early twentieth century attests to the degree to which they felt themselves alienated from the nation's wealth and from access to land. Into this breach came the agricultural ladder concept.

Mounting tenancy in the aftermath of the Homestead Act of 1862 and continuing on into the twentieth century belied the universally accepted ideology of broad access to and retention of real property. The agricultural ladder emerged in response to this contradiction. On the one hand, it made Jeffersonian agrarian idealism plausible, particularly with respect to land acquisition. It reinforced the legitimacy of private property in

Table 6.2: Summary of statistics on origin, disposal and present status of federal lands (millions of acres)

Origin	No. of acres	Disposal	No. of acres	Present federal land ownership, by agency	Public domain (no. of acres)	Acquired (no. of acres)	Total (no. of acres)
Never public domain	475	Disposal to States	328	Forest Service	160	28	188
Original States	305	Schools of all kinds	94	Bureau of Land Management	395	2	398
Texas	170	Swamp reclamation	65	National Park Service	62	7	68
Public domain	1 838	Other	169	Fish & Wildlife Service	39	4	43
State cessions	237	Granted or sold to		Other Department of			
Louisiana Purchase	530	homesteaders	288	Interior agencies	4	3	7
Red River Basin	30	Granted to veterans		All other	17	16	34
Cession from Spain	46	as military bounties	61		—	—	—
Oregon Compromise	184	Granted to railroad					
Mexican cession	339	corporations	94				
Purchase from Texas	79	All other	374				
Gadsden Purchase	19						
Alaska Purchase	375						
Total US	2 313	Total	1 114	Total federal land ownership	678	60	738

Source: Clawson (1983), Table 2.2, p. 26

land and deflected academic thought from an objective assessment of endemic tenancy. In the face of persistent landlessness and even recidivism among those aspiring to landownership, the model reaffirmed faith in upward tenure mobility. In doing so it contributed materially to the containment of rural unrest gathering momentum before and during the 1930s (Kloppenburg and Geisler 1985: 69).

Settlers also tried to overcome the lack of capital by simply ignoring the legalities of land purchase and squatting on the land, claiming ownership simply by their presence. The number of squatters became a major political issue in the nineteenth century, and political alliances were drawn along economic lines. The pro-squatter coalition included small farmers and the labour unions who wanted cheap land available to keep the supply of labour down and wages up. Opposing squatting were industrial capitalists who wanted to retain a surplus of labour in the emerging industrial cities of the East and large landowners in the West who believed that squatting reduced their access to and use of public lands. Squatting was eventually granted legitimacy with the passage of the Homestead Act of 1862. Under the Act any citizen could file a claim of up to 65 hectares (160 acres) of public land if they agreed to settle and farm the land for at least 5 years. Provisions of the Act, which called for single ownership and living on the land, created a policy context in which small family farms and dispersed settlement were inevitable.

Land disposal activities of the federal government and policies like the Homestead Act are reflected in the historic statistics on federal lands (Table 6.2). Approximately 80 per cent of the nation's current territory was part of the public domain at one time in its history. Sixty per cent of that acquired land was sold or given to the private sector or to State and local governments. Of the land sold or granted to the private sector, the largest single allocation was to homesteaders.

Controversies still rage over federal land ownership, management and disposal policies particularly in western States which still have vast tracts of federal lands within their borders (Fig. 6.2). Although some public land is used for national parks (9 per cent), the vast proportion (79 per cent) is in forest or range land and is administered by the Forest Service or the Bureau of Land Management. The continued ownership of these lands by the federal government has pitted the federal government against western State governments. Known as the 'Sagebrush Rebellion', the conflict is over whether ownership and management of public lands should be transferred to State governments, and with that transfer those subsidies which the lands provide. Advocates of continued federal ownership fear that transfer of control would result in the disposal of land by States to private interests and the eventual misuse of the land, for most of it is susceptible to erosion if overgrazed or heavily farmed. State ownership proponents, including President Reagan (who as a western governor was one of the early members of the 'sagebrush gang'), see federal management practices as too restrictive, prohibiting States and the private sector from fully developing the resources on these public lands. Thus the controversy over federal, State and private ownership of land continues, influencing land utilization within rural America and colouring the politics of the nation.

Migration/adaptation

As we saw in Chapter 2, US residents have long been geographically restless. In a country in the early transitional stage of modernization, as was the US during most of the nineteenth century, the movement of rural folk to the frontiers of colonization played an important role in shaping rural culture and economy (Zelinsky 1971). 'Rural folk', with their cultural baggage, aspirations and ability to adapt to the circumstances of a new environment, played a major role in shaping the character of rural America.

Pierson (1972) argues that migration, 'the M-factor', was more responsible for shaping the character of America than was the frontier because migration inevitably precipitated change. Change was inevitable, he argues, because institutions do not move easily, because long-distance migration is a selective process, and because migrants are exposed to new circumstances which require adaptation (Pierson 1972). The debate as to whether adaptation to new circumstances led to completely new values

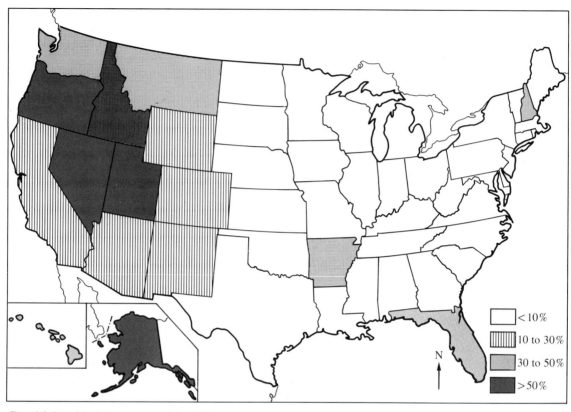

Fig. 6.2 Land in federal ownership, 1983

and behaviour in rural America has occupied historians, geographers and anthropologists since Turner (1920) proposed the frontier environment as 'the line of most rapid and effective Americanization'. The fallacies in Turner's grand theory have been demonstrated (see Berkhofer 1964 and Luebke 1980), and the importance of ethnic origins and cultural heritage recognized (Raltz 1979). However, to swing the pendulum completely to the other extreme and assign pre-eminence to cultural origins is also a misinterpretation of the history of rural America. A more realistic representation is offered by the Hudson who, in describing the frontier of the Dakota territory, emphasized that it 'was neither a melting pot nor a mosaic of rural ethnic enclaves', but rather the social and economic institutions in that frontier area were unique to a particular time and place (Hudson 1976: 65).

Migration to the nation's new agricultural land was a highly structured, selective and diverse process. The decision to relocate to a distant land or even to adjacent virgin land was usually a cautious and well-planned one. Three distinctive spatial *types of movement* were normally evident. One consisted of the relocation of migrants from nearby lands which only recently had been on the edge of settlement. A second type included movers from more distant, eastern agricultural areas and, less frequently, from the urban centres in the nation's core. Migrants to the Great Plains in the 1870s from New York and Pennsylvania who 'leap-frogged' the densely settled areas in the Midwest in order to relocate at or near the leading edge of agricultural development typify such moves. Finally, there were foreign immigrants who preferred the opportunities of rural rather than urban America. In all three cases, clearly definable paths or migration streams were formed because well-established information networks structured the origin–destination linkages. Friends and relatives who had moved in earlier periods gave accounts of the new lands, prompting migration by the less adventuresome or the less able who had initially remained at home. Informal networks functioned concurrently with the informational efforts of railroad and land speculation companies. Pamphlets, newspaper advertisements, salesmen and other promotional devices were used extensively to stimulate the sale of land. After 1860, railroad companies, in particular, moved aggressively to sell lands granted them by the federal government to finance the construction of railroads (Table 6.2). New farms and towns (see Hudson 1985) were needed if railroads were to return a profit on their new lines, many of which were of a highly speculative nature, so recruiters were sent to eastern cities and overseas to encourage people to purchase land and move West.

Migration to the new lands was highly selective. Selection was based on demographic attributes, such as age and sex, and on socio-economic attributes, such as income, occupation and family structure (Vedder and Gallaway 1971). To move long distances required both capital and a personality which would enable one to cope and to adjust to unforeseen circumstances. The new frontier agricultural areas did not transform the early settlers as much as it self-selected its residents, and the composition of the frontier population – socially, economically and psychologically – was different from that of the areas left behind. It was this compositional effect more than the environ-

mental influences of the frontier which helped shape the character of rural America.

An important compositional element in many portions of rural America was *ethnicity*. We have seen that during the period of industrialization the cities in the East and Midwest became homes to millions of immigrants (Ch. 2). Often obscured by the sheer volume of this urban flow is the fact that many agricultural counties also had large immigrant populations. In the Great Plains, a region thought by many to be devoid of diversity, the foreign-born proportion of the population in several States was high as late as 1900 (Table 6.3), and the cultural impact of these ethnic groups on rural areas in these States has been shown to be considerable (see Luebke 1980; Hudson 1973; Baltensberger 1983; and Ostergren 1980). Foreign immigrants constituted between 40 and 50 per cent of all new settlers in old Northwest Territory States like Illinois, Michigan and Wisconsin (Vedder and Gallaway 1975). Foreign immigration in these States continued well after the initial phase of settlement had passed, with foreign-born in-migrants replacing native out-migrants by a ratio of over 2 to 1 (Vedder and Gallaway 1975).

As national market forces gained strength in the agricultural economy, new forces of change emerged to further challenge existing rural institutions and values. Despite these new forces, the diverse ethnic composition of rural migrants left an indelible imprint that can still be seen in many rural areas today. Ostergren's

Table 6.3: Distribution of foreign-born persons in Great Plains State and territories by number and percentage of total population, 1860–1900

State or territory	1860 N	1860 %	1870 N	1870 %	1880 N	1880 %	1890 N	1890 %	1900 N	1900 %
North Dakota	1 774	36.7	4 815	34.0	51 795	38.3	81 461	42.7	113 091	35.4
South Dakota							91 055	26.1	88 508	22.0
Nebraska	6 351	22.0	30 748	25.0	97 414	21.5	202 542	19.1	177 347	16.6
Kansas	12 691	11.8	48 392	13.3	110 086	11.1	147 838	10.4	126 685	8.6
Oklahoma Territory	—	—	—	—	—	—	2 740	3.5	15 680	3.9
Indian Territory	—	—	—	—	—	—	13	.0	4 858	1.2
Texas	43 422	7.2	62 411	7.6	114.616	7.2	152 956	6.8	179 357	5.9
Montana	—	—	7 979	38.7	11.521	29.4	43 096	30.2	67 067	27.6
Wyoming	—	—	3 513	38.5	5 850	28.1	14 913	23.8	17 415	18.8
Colorado	2 666	7.8	6 599	16.6	39 790	20.5	83 990	20.3	91 155	16.9
New Mexico	6 723	7.2	5 620	6.1	8 051	6.7	11 259	7.0	13 625	7.0

Source: Luebcke (1980) Table 1, p. xvii

generalization about Scandinavian settlement in the Dakotas is appropriate to much of rural America. 'While migration and settlement in a new social and material environment altered the experience of the immigrant it did not erase his past' (Ostergren 1981: 411).

Agricultural assemblages and linkages

Agricultural systems consist of the assemblages of, and the linkages between, labour (quantity, skill and knowledge). capital (land and production technology), and market that occur in the production of consumable farm goods.

The structure of an agricultural system can be understood by considering the different assemblages of labour, capital and market and the relationships linking them together at any point in time and in a particular region. Assemblages and linkages in a system respond to the composition of the farm population, the availability of capital and its distribution within the population, the ability of farmers to accommodate past practices within the constraints of their existing environment, governmental policies and practices pertaining to agriculture, and the transportation technology which ties a region to national markets and centres of innovation. Throughout much of the history of US agriculture, regional systems have responded differently to these factors; but, with the industrial restructuring of the economy, transportation technology became more and more important as it changed fundamentally the linkages between market, labour and capital. Urban growth increased demand, but without expanded rail networks, improvements in rural secondary roads, and new, specialized hauling vehicles like refrigerator trucks, the increased demand would have to have been met locally. With the transportation improvements, the farmer found it possible – indeed necessary – to respond to a national market. Responding required an increase in productivity which could only be achieved by investing large amounts of capital in the production system. As more and more capital was required in the production system, farming became controlled by larger and more diversified management arrangements, and a new system arose, 'agribusiness', a term coined by Davis and Goldberg

in 1957 to describe the new character of farm management structure.

In the geographic literature, Von Thünen's early formulation of agricultural locational theory has served as the basis for understanding the linkages between the market and the other elements in agricultural assemblages (see Harvey (1966) for a review of other approaches). According to Von Thünen, the economic rent for a parcel of farm land is not a function of the surplus generated by differentials in land quality (the Ricardian interpretation) but rather it is a function of the profit differentials in agricultural products when sold at the market. Differentials are derivatives of two factors: the market demand for commodities and the cost of transporting them to the market. If we assume that production costs are uniform across an area and that transport costs are a linear function of distance then, according to Von Thünen, economic rent becomes a function of transportation costs which are determined by distance and per unit costs. The latter costs are influenced by the weight, bulk or perishability of the commodity. In this model, agricultural production systems become arranged geographically on the basis of distance from the market (Chisholm 1979). Commodities with a high market value and high transport costs are located nearest the market, while commodities which can be shipped cheaply (such as cattle because they can be driven to market) are produced in the areas more remote from the market. Since land adjacent to the market will return the highest profit (assuming no differences in soil or production methods among farmers), economic rents are highest there. The value of the land forces farmers to alter their production systems in order to maintain ownership. Over time, concentric zones of agricultural commodities develop. Within the zones, a gradation in production intensity occurs in which intensity peaks near the market and reaches zero at the fringe where farming is not profitable.

Von Thünen's theory has been used in the American context to explain the pattern of agricultural intensity at both micro and macro scales. The shift from micro to macro scale requires a translation from a single market to multi-market context, but this is accomplished by substituting an urban core, Megalopolis in the US, as the single market, and by considering the secondary effects of larger, dispersed individual markets, such as Chicago for example. Both modifications can be easily incorporated into the original Von Thünen model. If Megalopolis is assumed to be the market, agricultural intensity in the country conforms generally to the Von Thünen model, according to Muller (1973) and Jones (1976). The intensity of the production systems begins to decline as one moves away from the market, starting with the truck farming areas along the eastern coast, through the mixed farming regions of the Middle West, continuing through the cash grain farms in the eastern Great Plains, and eventually to the extensive farm and ranch operations in the West.

While the Von Thünen model is a useful framework for considering the broad influence of the urban system on agriculture, an historical perspective is required to understand how the current system evolved in response to market and other economic forces. From 1870 to 1920 when the nation was industrializing, five forces caused agriculture to be *restructured*:

- completion of the frontier settlement (the Census Bureau declared the frontier to be 'officially' closed in 1890);
- invention and widespread adoption of improved farming implements;
- growth of and improvements in transportation;
- promotion of scientific knowledge;
- expansion of domestic and foreign markets with increased urbanization (Schafer 1936).

The combined effects of these forces resulted in increased agricultural productivity, the formation of a national agricultural marketing system, the development of highly specialized, capital-intensive production systems, and new management structures in which labour and management became distinct entities: in sum, the industrialization of agriculture.

These structural transformations reorganized the geography of agriculture in the country. In its earliest stages, American agriculture consisted of a collection of semi-autonomous, isolated agricultural systems. Linkages to national or international markets through a hierarchy of service centres and gateway cities were important for some cash crops (cotton and tobacco, for example), but in most areas trade

was local and subsistence farming prevalent. At the same time, a high proportion of labour and capital inputs originated from within the local region. Diffusion of agricultural technology moved slowly because of poor communications and because of the resistance of many farmers to new methods of production.

Technological developments in transportation improved farmers' access to markets and to one another. Expanding markets for agricultural commodities increased competition between domestic agricultural areas. Those regions near the urban core, such as the Midwest, were the first to respond to new demands, but eventually the demand for increased productivity was felt in even the most isolated regions. Eventually, physical capital replaced the need for wage hands or tenants, and a labour surplus precipitated out-migration from rural counties and kept wages low in rural, non-farming economic enterprises.

As agricultural production systems became integrated into a national system and scientific production technology became more widespread, regional agricultural specialization increased. Spatially distinct, specialized agricultural systems emerged as the dominant geographic pattern in American agriculture. Regional concentration and specialization began early in the twentieth century, but the trend proceeded most rapidly after World War II in response to the tremendous demand for food in the postwar economy (Winsberry 1980). With specialization and increased productivity, less land was devoted to agriculture and the geographic extent of farming declined precipitately. In 1950, for example, 'agricultural; counties' – counties with at least 20 per cent of labourers' and proprietors' income coming from farming – were distributed widely across the country. By 1970 the number of agricultural counties by this definition had declined significantly (Fig. 6.3).

The path to agricultural industrialization did not occur uniformly, however. Environmental factors, such as soils and climate, were emphasized initially by geographers in explaining this variability. Baker, for example, in his seminal article on agricultural regions of the 1920s, stressed the role of climate – 'the control of physical conditions over agricultural development, instead of being mitigated by the process

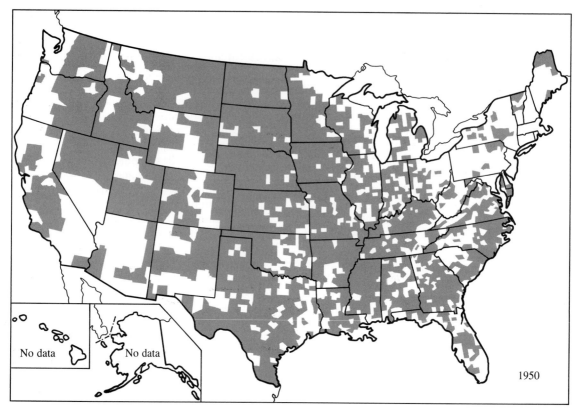

1950

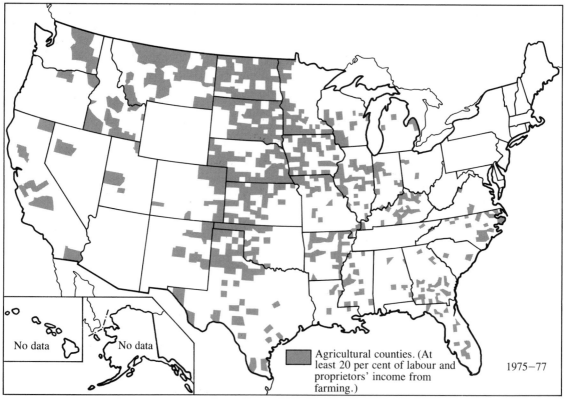

Agricultural counties. (At least 20 per cent of labour and proprietors' income from farming.)

1975–77

Fig. 6.3 Agricultural counties, 1950 and 1975–77
Source: Bergman (1981), Fig. 3, p. 36 and Fig. 4, p. 37

of science and invention, has been intensified and enforced' (Baker 1926: 465). Climate, soils, hydrology and topography have certainly influenced farming patterns in the US, but assemblages have also been affected by tradition and the cultural heritage of farmers. Rural America was settled by populations with very diverse cultural backgrounds, and examples of regional, ethnic farming practices have been plentiful. Studies of American agricultural regions provide numerous examples of how the early settlers adapted their farming practices to the new environment, maintaining what could be used from the old and modifying other practices to suit new conditions. Space does not permit a comprehensive review of all contributions of culture, market and environment in all regions. Instead, three regional vignettes are presented to show their importance to particular agricultural systems and to the rural social geography of particular regions of the country.

Regional vignettes

Earlier we examined some of the different regional schemes used to describe the broad cultural hues that colour the geography of the US (Ch. 3). Three of these regions – South, Midwest and Southwest – have been selected as case studies. The three have very different physical environments, have been settled at different times in the country's history, and have had distinctive agricultural systems. Moreover, each has had at least one important ethnic or racial group shape their social geography, each has had a strong regional self-identity, and eventually each region's rural economies have been integrated into the nation's economic structure. Thus each vignette illustrates how national and regional cultural, economic and social factors have interacted to shape the rural social geography of America.

The South

Southern agricultural systems offer a good example of how cultural, economic and environmental factors influence the structure of agricultural assemblages and linkages, and how these impart a particular character and set of values to a rural society. For much of its history, cotton was 'King' in the South. The association in time and place of cotton, plantations and slavery was an assemblage that forged the character of southern society and influenced the political history of the entire country. The history of the South until the twentieth century was linked to the rise and fall of cotton production, but since then cotton production has diminished, and the association of the 'New South' with cotton is now more through its textile and clothing manufacturing plants.

Plantations as farm types first appeared with tobacco production in Virginia. Initially, indentured servants provided the labour, but blacks from Africa eventually came to dominate the workforce, and slavery as a southern institution began. The cotton plantation had its origins not in Virginia, but in the coastal regions of South Carolina. Cash crops like rice, indigo and cotton were plantation crops grown on the chain of Sea Islands situated along the coast of South Carolina and Georgia. Market and environmental factors quickly caused rice and indigo to vanish as cash crops, but when settlement moved inland, cotton was found to be well suited to the climate and soils, and it quickly became *the* plantation cash crop. The invention of the cotton gin in 1793 by Eli Whitney helped diffuse cotton and plantations more rapidly, but the increased demand for cotton in national and international markets brought about by the growth of the US and British textile industries was perhaps more important in causing the expansion of cotton production in the South (Aiken 1971).

Before the Civil War, cotton production expanded spatially in concert with plantations. As an agricultural system, the antebellum plantation had several distinguishing characteristics.

- a size large enough to distinguish it from the family farm (lower limit of 260 acres);
- a division of labour and management functions;
- specialized agricultural production (although other crops were grown, plantations were mono crop in production);
- a settlement pattern which reflected a high

degree of control of the cultivating power (not coincidentally it also provided total social control over blacks);
- a large input of cultivating power per unit of area (Prunty 1955).

The plantation was ecologically destructive because mono cropping was dominant and because owners re-invested little capital into the land. Soil depletion was a serious problem in most plantation areas, a condition which led to continual pressure to push cotton production, the plantation and slavery further and further west. By 1860, cotton production was concentrated in seven areas:

- Central Piedmont from Virginia to Georgia;
- Inner Coastal Plains;
- Alabama Blackbelt;
- Middle Tennessee Valley and northern Alabama;
- Mississippi Alluvial Plain;
- Arkansas River Valley; and
- Black Prairie of Texas.

In all seven areas, sizeable concentrations of blacks and plantations could be found. These seven regions persisted as major cotton-producing areas along with two new ones which developed shortly after the Civil War – the southern High Plains of west Texas and the Red River Valley in Texas and Oklahoma – until the 1920s.

The western expansion of southern culture was possible because cheap land existed at the edge of the frontier, but the westward momentum was eventually blunted by the political conflicts that arose over southerners' insistence that slavery be exported along with cotton. Those conflicts eventually erupted into the Civil War. The assemblages associated with cotton production changed radically after the Civil War and the emancipation of the black population. The antebellum plantation disappeared, but cotton persisted as the principal cash crop of the region until the Great Depression. After the Civil War a sharecrop/tenant system replaced the plantation in the cotton assemblage. In the new system, land was controlled by a single owner, usually the old plantation family, but management of the labour force became fragmented as farm labourers, usually blacks, were allocated a unit

of land to farm. In exchange for use of the land and some farming capital, the tenant was obligated to the owner either for a share or a fixed amount of the cash crop. In the sharecrop/tenant system, tenants, many of them black, were dispersed across the rural landscape, and the economic and social controls afforded the whites under the old system were replaced by new forms of control. Economic control was maintained by creating a class of landless tenants, by keeping 'shares' at a marginal subsistence level, by encouraging indebtedness through company stores or personal loans, and by restricting ownership of land through strict enforcement of discriminatory finance practices. Social control took the form of *de jure* segregation, threats and violence against blacks, and a paternalistic attitude among southern landowners toward their tenants.

The Civil War did not destroy cotton production, but in the first three decades of the twentieth century six factors acted in concert to bring the downfall of King Cotton:

- a labour shortage caused by the migration of blacks to northern industrial cities (Ch. 2);
- the economic depression of the 1930s;
- the boll weevil infestation in the South;
- competition from new cotton-producing areas in California, Texas and other southwestern States;
- the emergence of alternative, more profitable agricultural enterprises for southern farmers;
- the federal cotton allotment programme which restricted cotton acreage as a way of controlling prices (Prunty 1951; Hart 1977).

These factors led to a reorganization of the economy of the rural South and of the spatial pattern of cotton production. By the 1920s only four areas in the old cotton-producing States were still centres of cotton production: (1) the Mississippi Alluvial Valley; (2) a small region in northern Alabama; (3) two areas in east Texas; and (4) southern and western Texas (Hart 1977). Of the four, only the Mississippi Alluvial Valley and west Texas areas remain as major cotton-producing areas in today's South. Agriculture is still important to the economy of the rural South, but it is much more diversified than in the past. Cattle, poultry, soybeans, tobacco, peanuts, fruits and vegetables, and cash grains are now produced where previously only cotton was found.

As we have seen (Ch. 5), industry has been moving into southern, rural counties to take advantage of cheaper labour, lack of unions and lower energy costs. A diversified employment market now exists where previously agriculture was the only employment opportunity available. A variety of industrial products are produced in the region's rural factories including textiles, clothing, chemicals and food products. But one industrial group which has grown especially rapidly and which has had a major influence on the appearance of the southern landscape is the forest products industry. Furniture manufacturing developed into a major industry in the Piedmont areas of Virginia and the Carolinas in the early twentieth century, originally in response to the availability of quality hardwood forests, but now cheap labour and access to eastern markets keep the industry in the region. Growth in the forest-products industry has been greatest, however, not in furniture but in the pulp/paper sector. When the southern long needle pine proved to be an excellent raw material for pulp, thousands of acres previously devoted to agriculture were converted to timber. Large diversified forest-product corporations, such as Georgia Pacific, moved aggressively to purchase land in the region to ensure an adequate, long-term timber resource base (Hart 1980). As a consequence, where cultivated fields once dominated the landscape, the traveller through the region is now struck by the monotony of woodlands.

Southerners take pride in the history of their region, but most recognize that economic and social change are essential if it is to compete in today's world markets. The decentralization of industry has laid the foundation for economic change. The Civil Rights movement of the 1960s led to progress in race relationships in the region, although continued resistance to ending all vestiges of racial segregation suggests that more must be done. Nevertheless, further change is inevitable as blacks exert their political power through the ballot box. The radical restructuring of the region's economic and social systems in the last two decades rivals the revolutionary changes brought on by the Civil War. The King is dead and in its place has emerged a more healthy and diversified economy and social system.

The Middle West

Historically, Midwestern agriculture has stood in sharp contrast to the plantation economy of the South. For many Americans, their image of the 'typical' farm is based on the Midwestern stereotype although, as Shortridge has noted, agreement over where the Midwest stereotype is located varies through time and space (Shortridge 1984, 1985). Family operations, high productivity, diversified production systems, and neat, orderly farmsteads have been common dimensions of the stereotype, but these are becoming less common because industrialization has changed the traditional character of farming in the region.

One reason why farming in the region developed into one of the world's richest, most productive, and most highly industrialized is because the region is favoured physically. The climate is ideally suited to growing a variety of grains and producing excellent pastureland for livestock. Portions of the region are covered with glacial till which is not particularly productive, but large sections have rich prairie soils or are blessed with lacustrine soils from old glacial lakes. Prairie soils were initially avoided by settlers who chose to locate in the mixed woodlands/grassland openings between the forest and the prairie (Jordan 1964). In fact, the settlement of the Midwest can be considered as two different stages: the settling of the woodland openings before 1850; and the movement out on to the prairies after 1850. The thesis that prairies were perceived as infertile and unproductive by Europeans who were more familiar with the woodland environment has been presented to explain the early avoidance of Prairie land (see Ch. 3); but it seems equally likely that the prairies were initially left vacant for pragmatic reasons. The tightly-packed sod made breaking the soil difficult until the introduction of steel-plated ploughs. Settlement was also delayed because the prairie soils were poorly drained, and sustained productive use of the land required the construction of costly drainage systems. This added cost deterred many from venturing out into the prairies during the initial stages of settlement (Hart 1972).

Early immigrants to the Midwest came from three sources. One stream of settlers, the Scots/Irish, came from upstate New York and New England, migrated into the area via the Erie Canal and the Great Lakes routeway and settled in the northern and central sections of the region. A second stream, coming from Kentucky, were descendants of earlier pioneers who had settled in the Appalachian plateaus and valleys. The third group came from southern Pennsylvania, followed the Ohio River Valley into southeastern Ohio, and eventually moved across the entire region. This group is noteworthy because they are acknowledged to be the originators of the Midwestern crop complex, i.e. a three-field rotation scheme of corn/small grains/hay, that came to dominate Midwestern agriculture (Higbee 1958). Farmers from Germany and Switzerland had originally settled in southeastern Pennsylvania and developed there a rich agricultural economy based on central European farming practices. Descendants of these settlers formed the major component of the migration stream entering southern Ohio. By the mid-nineteenth century immigrants coming directly from Germany, Switzerland or Scandinavian countries complemented the second and third generations of earlier immigrants from these countries. These immigrant groups continued to be a major element of the region's growth and population composition until the 1920s.

While southern Pennsylvania was the agricultural heart for much of Midwestern agriculture, important aspects of the system originated in other areas or evolved within the region as farmers adapted to environmental and market conditions. By 1860, eastern States in the region were already well integrated into the urban markets of the Northeast:

By 1860, then, the North was like a long animal whose head rested in the eastern urban region; its body, including factories, shops and commercial farms stretched from fifty to one hundred miles inland and a little like the Cheshire cat, faded back into the woods, hills and flatlands of the (Mid) West, half dissolved and uncertain in outline . . . the seaboard's food needs, including hay for workstock, were mainly supplied from a vast

farming area which had begun organizing itself for two decades into cropping regions on a continental scale (Parker 1975: 6).

Market effects on cropping patterns were quick to appear and followed the settling of the region from east to west. Wheat, for example, the principal cash crop in early stages of settlement because it could be shipped more cheaply to market from isolated locations, was replaced by corn (maize) which became the key crop within the region's mixed farming complex. The pre-eminence of corn has been attributed to climatic factors, but its flexibility, used either as a cash crop or as silage for livestock, made it much more suitable to a mixed farming system which had to respond quickly to yearly changes in market conditions. The combination of corn/grain/hay has remained intact to the present day as the basic crop assemblage in States like Ohio, Indiana and Illinois. Only the widespread adoption of soybeans as a cash crop in these States has threatened the dominance of this particular crop complex. But wheat was not totally displaced by corn as a cash crop in the region. As the frontier pushed westward, wheat was continually being replaced by the corn assemblage until settlement reached the prairies on the western edge of the region. There it became permanently established as the principal cash crop in States like Kansas and Nebraska.

If corn is the dominant crop in the agricultural system of the region, the system could not function profitably without hogs, for they are the key ingredient to the success of the mixed agriculture complex. Initially, cattle were the principal livestock component of the assemblage, having been brought to the region by Scots/Irish pioneers. Cattle are still evident in large numbers throughout the western and northern sections of the area, but hogs dominate because they are more efficient converters of silage into meat, are easier to manage on smaller, family farm operations, and are prolific breeders that mature into marketable products quicker. The latter characteristic is particularly important because it gives farmers flexibility in adjusting to market conditions. When corn prices are high, the grain can be sold for cash and hog production kept to a minimum.

However, when pork prices are high, farmers can quickly convert corn into pork to take advantage of the market price.

The emergence of the Middle West as part of the industrial core of the US had a significant impact on the region's agricultural systems. Reductions in the rural labour force caused by rural to urban migration, the increased demand for products resulting from urban population growth, and the loss of good agricultural land to suburban growth created pressures on Midwestern farmers to become more productive. Manufacturing firms within the region quickly responded to the demands for increased productivity. Farm machinery and other farm technology produced within the region enabled farmers to shift quickly to capital-intensive production methods. Land grant colleges (colleges which were required to have a curriculum in agriculture) established under the Morrill Act assisted in the diffusion of new technology. The success of Midwestern land grant universities such as Ohio State, Michigan State, Wisconsin, Minnesota and Illinois attests to the importance of this legislation to the region. Extension programmes at the land grant colleges enabled farmers to keep abreast of the latest farming technology, management practices and market conditions. Serving as the link between agricultural research and the farmer, the extension agent played a major role in making Midwestern agriculture more scientific and technologically oriented. The agents' role as technology brokers was made easier by Midwestern farmers' traditional faith in science and technology, particularly when it could often be shown to improve their profit margins (Hart 1972). That faith in technology has led many Midwestern farmers to invest heavily in expensive machinery and new technology even to the point of incurring heavy indebtedness. The indebtedness created few problems if farm prices rose, farmland appreciated, and the government was willing to help farmers through

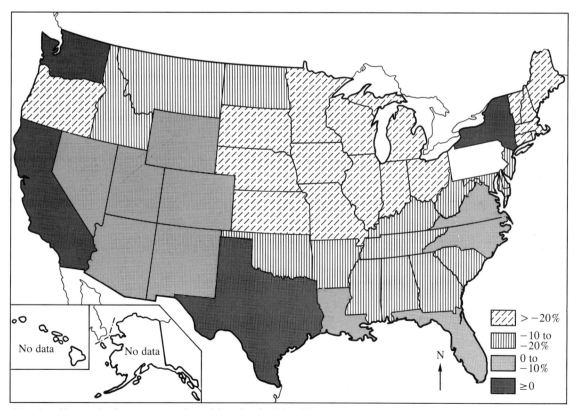

Fig. 6.4 Change in the acreage value of farmland, 1981–85

difficult seasons with price support programmes because creditors saw farming as a safe, profitable long-term investment. However, sharp declines in farm prices in the 1980s, significant depreciation in the value of farmland (Fig. 6.4), and a movement in the federal government to cut back or curtail federal support programmes for agriculture has changed the investment picture in agriculture. Farm foreclosures have increased sharply in the 1980s and many young rural residents have been forced to leave agriculture or have been unable to secure sufficient capital to expand their small, marginal operations. The financial crisis in agriculture has fallen most heavily on the medium-sized, family farm operation. the backbone of Midwestern agriculture. If these trends continue, the economic and social foundations of Midwestern rural communities will be challenged and major structural changes will be forthcoming in farming and in other dimensions of Midwestern rural society.

The Southwest

The social geography of the American Southwest results from the interplay of three separate populations which have lived in the region – American Indians, Spanish/Mexicans (Mexicans as a national group are the result of intermarriages between the original Spanish settlers of Mexico and the indigenous Indian population of that country), and Anglos (Meinig 1971). All three have contributed to the region's distinctive history and social geography. Indians, the original inhabitants of the region, practised a variety of economic systems ranging from irrigated farming by Pueblo tribes to nomadic hunting by Apaches. Through successive waves of Spanish, Mexican and Anglo settlement, the Indians were killed, assimilated or relocated to reserves where they have maintained a semi-autonomous political existence within the region. Though small in population, Indian reservations occupy extensive territory in the American Southwest today (over 9 million acres (3.6 million hectares) in Arizona), and evidence of Indian culture is still very prominent in States such as Arizona, New Mexico and Oklahoma.

The introduction of Spanish influence in the region began in the 1600s with the colonization of the upper Rio Grand Valley near the present sites of Santa Fe, Taos and Albuquerque, New Mexico, by Spanish colonists from Mexico. Spanish and eventually Mexican culture (Mexico gained its independence from Spain in 1821) expanded its influence in the area by establishing transportation connections between colonies and the core of Spanish settlement in northern Mexico and by encouraging further colonization in the northern frontier. During the early phase of colonization, many of the indigenous Indian cultures were forced on to marginal lands within the area, assimilated into Spanish culture, eliminated through warfare, or migrated to new areas yet untouched by Spanish influence. In the 1700s, Spanish settlements in southern Arizona near the present site of Tuscon, in southern Texas, and in southern California were established and became secondary core areas for the further expansion of Hispanic culture in the region (Nostrand 1970).

Anglo influence in the region began in the early 1800s as traders and trappers from the East contacted settlers who were pushing outward from the New Mexico area. Contact and exchange increased with the establishment of a series of trade routes, such as the Santa Fe Trail, connecting gateway cities on the edge of the American frontier, such as St Louis, with the towns in the Spanish core. The number of Anglos settling in the region was small and consisted mainly of traders and merchants who vied with their Mexican counterparts for the resources of the region. The number of Americans was small, but the economic competition was fierce and far-reaching. The trade became a rivalry between New York or New Orleans and Vera Cruz as ports of entry for this remote interior of North America. Thus New Mexico itself became not just a distant terminus but, for the first time, a link in a wider network. Despite the interpenetration of these two commercial systems, the balance was strongly in favor of the Anglo-Americans and their aggressive commercial tactics were a portentous display of the general power of their expansionist tendencies (Meinig 1971: 19).

Conflicts stemming from trade were escalated by the movement of ranchers out of Texas into land claimed by Mexico. Mexico blamed the

US for encouraging expansion of territorial claims, although for much of this time Texas was an independent republic bent on its own territorial imperative. Trade conflicts and territorial rivalries along with the geopolitical realities of Manifest Destiny eventually led to the Mexican War in 1846, and the later secession of most of the territory consisting of the American Southwest by Mexico to the US in 1848. Even with the acquisition of the territory, however, American influence in the core of the region was subordinate to Mexican cultural dominance until the end of the Civil War.

After the Civil War, ranchers from Texas moved westward into New Mexico, Arizona and Colorado, bringing with them a ranch complex which soon became identified with the region. The development of the Southwestern ranch system is an interesting example of multiple origins of an agricultural assemblage. The ranch assemblage was thought originally to be of Spanish origin. Some of the herding practices and terminology used by ranchers in nineteenth-century Texas were undoubtedly taken from early Spanish ranchers in the region. The pre-eminence of longhorn cattle, the use of horses in herding cattle, ranch terms such as lariat, rodeo, dogie and corral to mention a few, point to a strong Spanish influence (Myres 1969). Origins of the assemblage were not, however, exclusively Spanish, for a strong Anglo influence can be identified. Cattle herding was a common frontier activity in the American South. Starting originally in South Carolina, an Anglo ranch complex was pushed westward across the South in front of the plantation economy. With the rapid spread of the southern plantation agricultural system, ranching in the South was only an itinerant agricultural practice until it reached portions of Texas where it found a permanent niche in the economy of the area (Jordan 1972, 1977). The Anglo version had many traits which later became associated with the ranching as practised in the American Southwest, including roundups, branding of cattle for ownership identification, trail drives and open grazing. It was a hybrid agricultural assemblage, involving both Spanish and Anglo traits, which then found its way into the old Spanish core area of the Southwest.

With the adoption of ranching throughout the region, regular routes were established for marketing cattle, and 'cattle drives' became a common practice for a brief period. Trail drives west to California, north to Kansas and Colorado, and east to East Texas crisscrossed the region, providing modern-day novelists and screen writers with endless opportunities for romanticizing the Western cowboy, his loyal horse and his trusty 'six shooter'. Unfortunately for lovers of the West as portrayed by Western writers like Zane Grey and Louis L'Amour, technological advances show no deference to inefficient agricultural institutions no matter how romantic they may seem (actually the life of the cowboy differed greatly from the accounts of the western novelists; being a cowboy was a hard, dirty, dangerous occupation that many willingly abdicated when given the opportunity), and by the 1880s railroads had replaced cattle drives as a means of moving cattle to market.

Ranching was not the only agricultural system established in the region. In the eastern edges of the region where aridity was less severe, cash crops of cotton or grains and mixed farming/livestock operations were plentiful. Initially the assemblages resembled those in the upper or lower South (Jordan 1967). As farming moved on to the marginal semi-arid areas in western Texas and Oklahoma, a move made possible by the new dry-farming practices originating from Plains States to the north and by the increased access to urban markets resulting from an expansion of the region's railroad network, the size and scale of farming increased. The crash of agricultural markets in the 1920s and the drought of the 1930s wrought havoc on the rural Southwest. Farm foreclosures, widespread evictions of tenants, and the migration of 'dustbowl' residents from Oklahoma and Texas to California and intervening States were tragic indicators of the cyclical nature of agricultural markets and the region's climate.

The economic collapse and human tragedy of the Great Depression led to a restructuring of the region's agricultural systems. Ranching and farming remained important to the region's economy, but new technologies and market conditions prompted new assemblages and linkages. Irrigation, made possible by large dam projects on the region's major rivers or by deep wells, became an essential part of farming. Irrigated farms in the Gila River Valley of Arizona, the Imperial Valley in California, and the Rio Grande Valley in Texas and New Mexico are now some of the most productive commercial farm operations in the entire country. Extensive use of irrigation, however, requires large capital investments and large farms in order to obtain favourable profit margins. The economies of scale of irrigated farming led to consolidation of smaller farms into larger operating units and adoption of new, corporate management structures. Extensive use of irrigation has also created severe environmental problems in some areas in the region. Depletion of water in underground aquifers is now a reality in western Texas and Oklahoma, while in other areas soil salinity has caused the abandonment of acreage previously irrigated and used for farming.

Since the Great Depression the economy of the region has been cushioned from cycles in its agricultural economy by its mineral wealth. In many southwestern States the most prominent rural structures in the past 40 years have been oil derricks and pumping stations. As the nation's dependency on energy expanded, oil-producing States experienced economic bonanzas. Four States in the region – Texas, California, Oklahoma, and New Mexico – accounted for approximately 50 per cent of all petroleum production in the country in 1980. Texas alone produced 31 per cent of the total in that year. It is its energy resources not its agricultural systems which have attracted new capital and spurred economic growth in the region in the past two decades. However, recent reductions in energy prices suggest 'boom and bust' cycles that are all too reminiscent of those earlier cycles associated with agriculture.

Through all the changes in the area's economy, the cultural diversity in the American Southwest has continued. Hispanic influence not only persists but has increased with the continued immigration of Mexican Americans into the region (Ch. 2). Despite attempts to assimilate them, the Indian population remains an important component of the social composition of the region. Now, however, a new immigrant group has entered the region, bringing with it the potential for change. The new immigrant group – the Frostbelt refugees and their advance guard of 'Snowbirds' – have flocked to non-metropolitan counties in the region. The region's ability to integrate these new immigrants within the persistent cultures of the area will determine what new social and economic structures will prevail in the American Southwest in the future.

Reshaping rural America: contemporary forces for change

The current dynamics of rural America can be traced to recent structural changes in the nation's economy, for they have altered the type and level of integration between urban and rural America. The consequences for rural America of this restructuring have been far-reaching, including increases in manufacturing employment in non-metropolitan counties, industrialization of agriculture, greater political involvement in the farm economy, and redistribution of the population to rural areas. Despite these changes, agrarianism still persists as an American ideal even though farming and its associated lifestyle have become less significant to the economy and social organization of rural America. Americans still cling to an image of life forged in the crucible of rural living, not realizing that the forge has become a part of corporate America.

Rural industrialization

Manufacturing enterprises have always been present in rural America, usually in response to local resources. Early firms were never a major component of the industrial economy of the country, nor did they use a sizeable proportion of the rural labour force. Movement of manufacturing into rural America began in earnest in the late 1960s. Rural industrialization has involved the location of firms in non-metropolitan counties on the edge of the urban fringe and in counties well beyond metropolitan limits. Since the 1970s a regional redistribution of industry from the North to the South and to the West has been incorporated within the

Table 6.4: Per cent changes in non-farm wage and salary employment in the US, 1962–78

Area and industry	US (% change)	Northeast (% change)	Census region Northcentral (% change)	South (% change)	West (% change)
Metro	50.2	20.8	42.0	82.2	77.0
Goods producing	14.4	–12.2	12.1	51.8	34.8
Service performing	77.0	47.6	69.7	102.0	102.5
Non-metro	64.8	48.2	56.1	68.2	99.2
Goods producing	46.6	4.5	44.3	55.9	73.7
Service performing	81.5	81.1	68.0	81.1	117.2

Source: Haren and Halling (1979), p. 29

decentralization process (Ch. 5). The consequences of the redistribution and decentralization of industry are evident in the figures for non-farm employment in non-metropolitan counties (Table 6.4). Industrial employment gains for non-metropolitan counties exceeded those for metro counties in all parts of the country, but those in the rural South and West surpassed the gains in the Northeast and North Central States in all categories of employment.

It is not clear whether the increased activity in non-metropolitan industrialization has had a positive effect on rural well-being. Real income has increased in some rural communities experiencing industrial growth (Summers *et al.* 1976), but in others no significant increase in household income has occurred (Seyler and Lansdale 1979). Also, it is not clear whether inequalities in rural income have decreased with the new wave of economic development. Rural areas near metropolitan centres have experienced some improvements in income inequalities, but more remote areas have not (McGranahan 1980). Finally, it is not clear whether the increase in industrial activity has increased the likelihood of employment for the resident population. Sometimes new firms have simply used the existing labour surplus and minimal in-migration has occurred. Elsewhere, additional employment opportunities in the industrial sector have fostered in-migration and jobs have gone mainly to new migrants. The two conditions. income gains and indigenous

employment gains, appear causally related, for in-migration typically responds to the wage level of the new firms. High wage industries stimulate in-migration, whereas firms with low wage levels provide less of a stimulus for population growth (Heaton and Fuguitt 1979).

Industrialization of agriculture

The connotations implicit in the terms 'agribusiness' and 'farm' epitomize the magnitude of the changes that have occurred in agriculture in the last 40 years. Forces that began the transformation of agriculture in the early twentieth century – increased demand, improvement in transportation technology, reduced rural labour force, shrinking land availability, and greater reliance on science and machine capital – accelerated after World War II, and led to the industrialization of agriculture.

Two important structural changes occurring with agricultural industrialization have been an *increase in the size of farms* and an overall *reduction in the number of farms* (Fig. 6.5). The result is greater concentration of farm acreage in the fewer, larger operations. Caution in evaluating trends in US farm data is necessary because definitional changes in what constitutes a farm make comparison difficult. However, these definitional problems do not mask an obvious increase in farm size (average in 1978 was 440 acres/178 hectares) or a decline

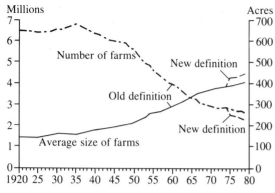

Fig. 6.5 Trends in the number and average size of farms
Source: US Department of Agriculture (1981)

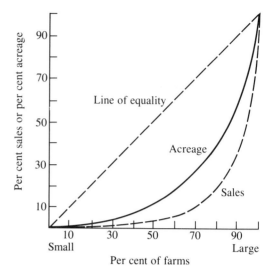

Fig. 6.6 Degree of concentration of agricultural units in the US, 1980

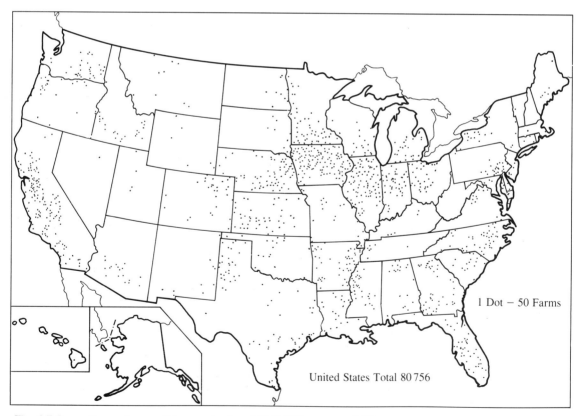

Fig. 6.7 Large farms: farms with annual sales of $200 000 or more, 1978
Source: US Bureau of the Census 1978, Fig. 78–M45, p. 27

in the number of farms (2.2 million in 1984 versus 6.8 million in 1935). Trends for both farm size and number clearly correspond with the periods of rapid industrialization of agriculture. The number of farms remained stable in the 1920s, increased slightly with the migration to the rural areas during the Great Depression, and declined swiftly and steadily after World War II. Increases in farm size exhibited a similar pattern of change. If we consider farm sales rather than size, concentration of farm production is even more evident (Fig. 6.6). In 1980, farms with agricultural sales of over $100 000 constituted only 12 per cent of all farms of the US, but their sales accounted for over 68 per cent of the market value of all agriculture commodities. Conversely, 37 per cent of all farms averaged less than $5000 in sales, and these amounted to only 3.1 per cent of all sales of farm products.

Large and small farms differ on several other important attributes (Table 6.5). Larger farms have a greater proportion of their production under contract, rely less on off-farm income, receive more money from the federal government for support of agricultural commodities, and have higher debt levels. Larger farms also are more capital-intensive, are more bureaucratic in their organization, rely more heavily on cash-wage labour, have higher fixed costs, are major beneficiaries of special tax loopholes, and are initiators of agricultural research (Vogeler 1981). Large farms, as measured by sales, are also very concentrated in their geography (Fig. 6.7) The major regional concentration begins in the Middle West and extends to the Great Plains, stretching from the Canadian border to the High Plains of west Texas. Most of the high-sales farms within this region are engaged in either cash-grain or livestock production. Smaller concentrations of the high-sales farms are evident throughout the eastern coastal plains from Florida to New England; the alluvial valley of the Mississippi River; and the irrigated basins and valleys of the Southwest. Here a variety of commodities are produced, including poultry, tobacco, citrus, peanuts, sugar and dairy products.

Scholars of American agriculture caution that size or sales are not necessarily the best indicators of the degree to which farming has become industrialized. According to Gregor (1982), the level of capital investment in the production system is a better indicator. Using capital and labour investments in agriculture, Gregor developed two indices of agricultural industrialization, *scale* (size of the operation) and *intensity* (measures of input, e.g. labour, capital and energy) and regionalized the country accordingly. Counties which had high scores on the *intensity* factors (Fig. 6.8A) were concentrated in the eastern section of the nation, giving support to Von Thünen's theory that agricultural intensity is a function of distance to market. The largest contiguous block of counties with high intensity was in the cash-grain, mixed farming and dairy areas of the Middle West. Along the eastern coast, counties with high intensity were associated primarily with dairying and truck farming. In the South, the production of citrus in Florida, tobacco and peanuts in the coastal plains of the Carolinas and Georgia, and poultry in the Piedmont sections of these States account for the most of the counties with high-intensity rating. In the West, counties with higher intensity scores were mostly located in the irrigated agricultural areas of southern and interior California, of southwestern Arizona, and of the Pacific Northwest.

The *scale* dimension of industrialization has a very different geography (Fig. 6.8B). Counties which rank high on this dimension are widely spread in the West. In the eastern half of the country, only the Mississippi Alluvial Valley, the Middle West and southern Florida have a sizeable number of contiguous counties with high scores on the scale dimension.

By combining the scale and intensity indices, Gregor (1982) constructed a typology of agricultural industrialization and analysed its geography (Fig. 6.9 and Table 6.6). It is clear from his analyis that agricultural industrialization has achieved its highest level in the Middle West. Other areas where highly industrialized farm counties are concentrated include the northeastern metropolitan core, southern Florida, the valleys in the Pacific Northwest, the southern portion of the alluvial Mississippi Valley, two linear regions in the mid-South (a northern area which was primarily engaged in poultry production and a southern one which was based on tobacco and other specialty crops), the west Texas High Plains, and the

Table 6.5: Farm attributes by sales categories, 1978

Sales category ($1 000)	Per cent of all farms	Per cent total acreage	Per cent total value	Per cent of sales under contract	Per cent of all govt payments	Per cent of all capital purchases	Per cent of farms in debt	Per cent of total farm debt	Ratio of farm/non-farm income
500 or more	1.0	11.8	30.9	58.2	7.1	11.6	87.3	16.7	0.79
200–499	3.3	14.9	18.7	21.9	14.6	16.4	86.3	17.4	0.49
100–199	7.4	19.3	19.2	14.3	22.7	21.3	83.9	19.5	0.30
40–99	15.9	23.9	19.1	5.1	33.6	24.9	73.5	21.7	0.26
20–39	10.9	10.5	6.0	0.4	10.3	8.5	63.1	7.8	0.11
10–19	11.5	7.2	3.1	0.05	4.3	6.1	54.0	5.0	0.08
5–9	12.8	4.8	1.7	0.04	3.8	4.4	42.6	4.2	0.06
2.5–4	13.8	3.6	0.9	0.01	2.0	2.8	39.4	3.1	0.03
Less than 2500	23.3	3.9	0.5	0.01	1.5	3.8	35.0	4.6	0.02

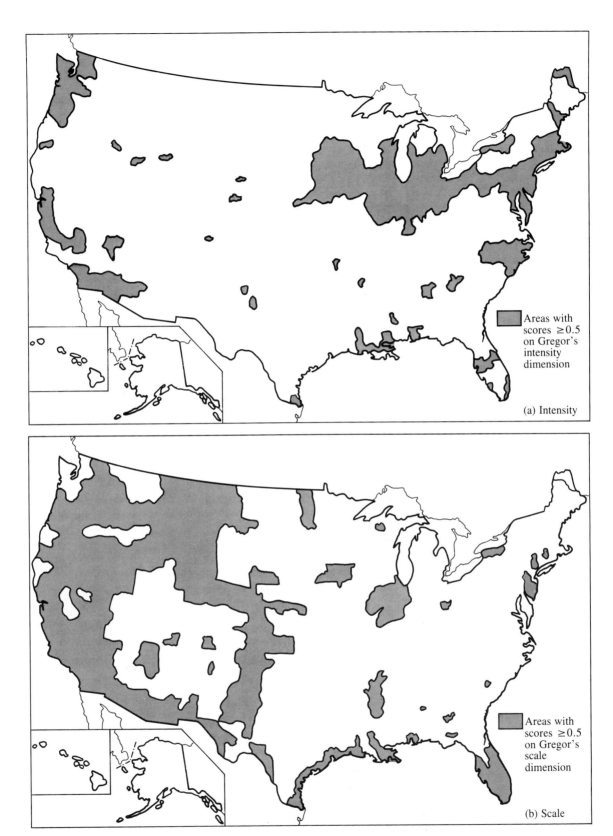

Fig. 6.8 The industrialization of agriculture: (A) intensity, (B) scale
Generalized from Gregor (1982), Figs 4.1 (p. 163) and 4.4 (p. 178)

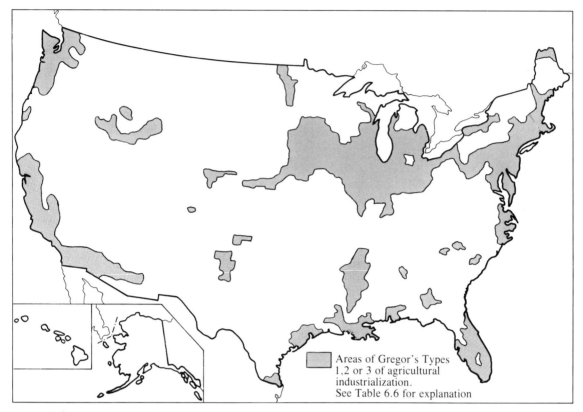

Areas of Gregor's Types 1,2 or 3 of agricultural industrialization. See Table 6.6 for explanation

Fig. 6.9 Regions dominated by industrialized agriculture
Generalized from Gregor (1982), Fig. 5.1, p. 190

Snake River farming area of Idaho. Apart from these areas, the vast majority of rural counties have agricultural systems that were not industrialized according to these two indices. In short, while industrialization dominates American agricultural production and sales, its distribution is highly concentrated.

Major changes in the management structure of farming have come with agricultural industrialization. *Vertical and horizontal integration*, corporate strategies common to the secondary sector of the economy, have made their appearance in farming. In agriculture, as in manufacturing, vertical integration involves incorporating all phases of the production system under one owner, usually a single corporation or holding company. Typically, vertical integration in agriculture means controlling production from the initial inputs into the agricultural system, e.g. seeds, fertilizer or machinery, to the distri-

bution of the final product. This arrangement enables corporations to distribute production costs across all phases of the operation, allowing them to undercut competitors in any sector if necessary. Vertical integration is particularly desirable in agriculture because profit margins in certain phases of the system, e.g. wholesaling, are much higher than in actual farming operations.

Horizontal integration occurs when a firm expands and takes over firms engaged in similar practices to increase market share and to exert some control over prices. Although horizontal integration is evident in farming, it is much more common with firms that produce input resources for farmers and with firms that process or market agricultural commodities. For example, fifteen firms provide over 60 per cent of all farm inputs, forty firms account for almost 70 per cent of all food processing, and

Table 6.6: Typology of industrialized agriculture by Gregor

| Types | Dimension Scores | |
	Intensity[1]	Scale[2]
1	high	high
2	high	moderate
3	moderate	high
4	high	low
5	low	high
6	low	low

[1] The intensity dimension consists of a factor dimension in which the following variables had high factor scores: machine hire, custom work and fuel expenditures/farm acre; labour expenditures/farm acre; machinery and equipment investments/farm acre; crop expenditures/farm acre; land and building investments/farm acre; crop investments/farm acre; livestock–poultry expenditures/farm acre; and livestock–poultry investments/farm acre.

[2] The scale dimension consists of a factor dimension in which the following variables had high factor scores: machine hire, custom work and fuel expenditures/farm; machinery and equipment investments/farm; labour expenditure/farm; land and building investments/farm; crop investments/farm; livestock–poultry expenditure/farm; and livestock-poultry investments/farm.

Source: Gregor 1982

forty-five companies account for over 75 per cent of all wholesale and retail food revenues (Vogeler 1981).

Horizontal and vertical integration commonly occur jointly, creating a system where input resources, production and marketing are spatially and administratively integrated under single ownership to maximize profit. These operations typically are owned either by corporations or large family partnerships. Management functions are completely separated from the actual production unit, creating the so-called 'suitcase and sidewalk farmers' (Kollmorgen and Jenks 1958a, 1958b). In the larger operations, management is located in the city, and members of the board of an agricultural corporation may come from the industrial sector, creating complex overlapping corporate board memberships (Smith 1980).

Complex management schemes are growing in number and size, and are engaged in most types of agriculture, although certain crop and livestock operations are more frequently integrated (Table 6.7). In some cases, agricultural products are the principal commodity of the firm, while in others agricultural sales represent only a small fraction of total corporate profits. Perdue Farms, Inc. is an example of the

Table 6.7: Production contracts and vertical integration of crop and livestock products, 1970

Item	Production/ marketing Contracts	Vertical integration
	Per cent	Per cent
Feed grains	0.1	0.5
Hay and forage	0.3	—
Food grains	2.0	0.5
Vegetables for fresh market	21.0	30.0
Vegetables for processing	85.0	10.0
Dry beans and peas	1.0	0.0
Potatoes	45.0	25.0
Citrus fruits	55.0	30.0
Other fruits and nuts	20.0	20.0
Sugar beets	93.0	2.0
Sugarcane	40.0	60.0
Other sugar crops	5.0	2.0
Cotton	11.0	1.0
Tobacco	2.0	2.0
Oil-bearing crops	1.0	0.4
Seed crops	80.0	0.5
Miscellaneous crops	5.0	1.0
Total crops	9.5	4.8
Feed cattle	18.0	4.0
Sheep and lambs	7.0	3.0
Hogs	1.0	1.0
Fluid grade milk	95.0	3.0
Manufacturing grade milk	25.0	1.0
Eggs	20.0	20.0
Broilers	90.0	7.0
Turkeys	42.0	12.0
Miscellaneous	3.0	1.0
Total livestock products	31.4	4.8

Source: Mighell and Hoffnagle (1970)

former. It began as a small operation producing poultry and eggs for the New York City market. It eventually expanded its operation to include facilities for producing and storing feed grain for the poultry and for processing and packaging the broilers. By 1978 the company had sales of over $200 million a year and represented one of the larger agribusinesses in the country (Smith 1980). Boeing Aircraft, Dow Chemical, Beatrice, and Tenneco are examples of industrial firms which have expanded into agriculture. Tenneco, one of the country's largest conglomerates, has undertaken one of the biggest investments in agriculture. It manages large farms and owns a major farm-machinery company and a food container operation, is a major wholesaler of fresh fruits, and operates a large retail chain. Tenneco as an agribusiness controls farming from the seed to the consumer's plate.

The extent of corporate control of farm production is difficult to verify because reporting of ownership arrangements is hidden in the different types. The Department of Agriculture provides data on farm incorporation, but these can be misleading because many family operators incorporate for tax and inheritance reasons. On the other hand, many of the largest agribusinesses are family partnerships which are not incorporated. Also, the amount of corporate influence over farming is even greater than is suggested by the number of integrated agribusiness operations. Many independent farmers produce commodities under contract to processors or distributors. Under the contract system, individual farmers sign an agreement with a specific company to deliver a specified quantity and quality of a commodity at a contracted price. Contracts enable farmers to reduce the risk of losing money when market prices are low at the time of harvest, but it also means private operators cannot take advantage of higher market prices when they occur. Under the contract system the farmer remains an independent operator but loses marketing autonomy. In effect, he becomes a cash-wage employee of the contracting firm. 'Contracts give the agribusiness the advantage of treating farmers as employees without the responsibility of paying them as employees' (Vogeler 1981: 138).

Contractual arrangements can be found with most types of farming, but are more prevalent in larger farms and with certain types of commodities. Contracted crops are usually those whose market value can fluctuate dramatically within a short period and that cannot tolerate long-term storage in order to wait for more advantageous market conditions. Fluid milk products, vegetable production and the citrus fruits are examples of commodities commonly grown under contract within the US (Table 6.7).

With industrialization and its accompanying structural changes have come increases in productivity (Table 6.8), not just overall

Table 6.8: US farm output, input and productivity indices (base year 1967 = 100)

Year	Output	Input	Productivity
1920	51	98	52
1925	51	99	51
1930	52	101	51
1935	52	91	57
1940	60	100	60
1945	70	103	68
1950	74	104	71
1955	82	105	78
1960	91	101	90
1965	98	98	100
1966	95	98	97
1967	100	100	100
1968	102	100	102
1969	102	99	103
1970	101	100	102
1971	110	100	110
1972	110	100	110
1973	112	101	111
1974	106	100	105
1975	114	100	115
1976	117	103	115
1977	119	105	114
1978	122	105	116
1979	129	108	119
Increase			
1920–29	2	4	0
1930–39	6	–3	8
1940–49	14	5	11
1950–59	14	–2	16
1960–69	11	–2	13
1970–79	28	8	17

Source: Heady (1982), p. 39

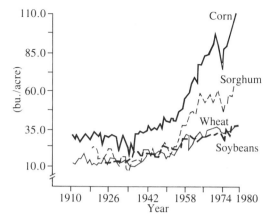

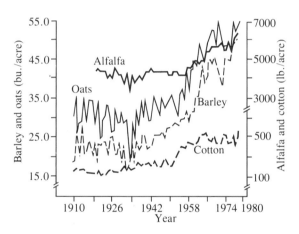

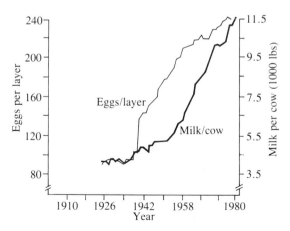

Fig. 6.10 Changes in the productivity of agriculture, by commodity, 1900–80
Source: Heady (1982), pp. 35–6

productivity but in almost every crop and live-stock types (Fig. 6.10). The increases in productivity not only permitted the agricultural sector to keep pace with domestic demand despite a smaller percentage of the population engaged in farming (3.3 per cent in 1980), but they have also enabled the US to become a major producer of foodstuffs for countries throughout the world. However, there have been costs associated with the rise in productivity. Scale economies have forced many of the smaller family farms out of exist-ence; farm *indebtedness* has reached astronomi-cal limits, more than $100 000 million by 1980; soil erosion and other forms of environmental degradation resulting from the new, intensive forms of farming have reached serious pro-portions; and farm surpluses threaten the stability of farm prices and the entire farm economy. All of these have converged in the 1980s to create a major crisis in agriculture. As Campbell summarizes:

In the 1980s, a combination of high interest rates, excess production of many farm commodities, a weak demand for farm products, and bad weather produced the worst economic conditions for farmers since the 1930s (Campbell 1985).

These conditions threaten the very foundations of the system, the medium-sized farm oper-ation, according to former Secretary of Agri-culture, Robert Bergman (Bergman, 1981). Many of the problems and structural changes that confront farmers are beyond their control, some are the result of errors in judgement by the American farmer, and still others are the result of government agricultural policies.

Government agricultural policies

A major characteristic of modern agriculture in the US is the active role taken by the federal government. This role is not new for, as we have seen with the Northwest Ordinance, it has always had a vested interest in the development of agriculture. With urbanization and indus-trialization, the government's interest shifted from dispersing land to improving productivity. An example is the Hatch Act which established research funds for agricultural colleges formed under the Morrill Act. Later, as productivity increases came to threaten the economic and social structure of rural America, maintenance of a stable farm economy became the central concern, and the national government's role became more extensive and complex (the ideological role in the agricultural ladder concept, for example). After the Great Depression, the federal government took upon itself the role of salvaging an agricultural system that was bankrupt. Since then the US government has continued to be an active, though not always welcome, partner with the farmer in the agricultural economy. The involvement has taken many directions, but three policy roles have been particularly important in influencing the geography and structure of agriculture: (1) foreign trade agricultural policies; (2) federal subsidies to agriculture; and (3) tax expenditures for agriculture.

A large share of agricultural production in the US is now destined for *foreign markets*. In the 1950s, approximately 10 per cent of all agricultural production was exported to foreign markets. By the end of the 1970s that figure had risen to over 30 per cent, and with some commodities like wheat between 50 and 60 per cent of all production was destined for foreign markets. The increased share of agricultural production being exported to foreign markets has meant that the farmer is influenced by a new set of political and economic factors, all of which lie beyond his control. As a result, unexpected short-term fluctuations in farm prices have occurred which have had serious financial consequences for the farmer. For example, President Carter's decision to stop wheat sales to the USSR after the Afghanistan invasion dealt grain farmers a serious blow. When the embargo was lifted in the 1980s, the USSR had established new trade agreements with other wheat-exporting countries, and the US was unable to re-establish its previous export levels. More recently, the increased strength of the US dollar in foreign exchange made US agricultural commodities less competitive in world trade, creating more domestic surpluses and lower farm prices. Because of the price vagaries of international trade and the links between international trade and international diplomacy, the US government has increasingly become more involved in international trade policies. This involvement includes modifying monetary policy to make US commodities more competitive in foreign markets, introducing programmes to curb domestic surpluses by instituting cooperative trade agreements with foreign governments, setting up foreign assistance programmes which are linked to the sale of agricultural commodities, and creating embargoes on exports to selected foreign countries.

The export of food in connection with government aid programmes has increased the demand for US agricultural products in foreign markets and helped absorb some of the domestic surplus. There are, however, costs associated with having a larger share of production exported. It has created unstable price conditions in the domestic market at times. When a large share of production is exported, domestic supplies are reduced, prices are raised at home, and the US consumer must pay the extra cost. Domestic prices are most affected when production falls below expected output because of climatic or other environmental conditions because foreign sales are usually contracted before harvest, and a large share of the production is already committed to foreign exchange regardless of the total output of foodstuffs for the year. To help stabilize prices in foreign exchange, the US government indirectly subsidizes foreign purchases. In 1972, for example, it has been estimated that the US government indirectly subsidized the Soviet grain purchase of that year to the amount of $160 million (Hopkins 1979). Greater reliance on foreign markets has also encouraged the concentration of production into larger farms, which can be more easily integrated into the foreign trade market because of the volume of output they can guarantee.

Growth of the export market for agricultural goods has politicized the world food situation and encouraged the use of food as an article for negotiation in foreign policy. With the arrival of OPEC and its control over world oil prices, considerable pressure arose in the US to use its vast agricultural resources in a similar fashion. Earl Butz, Secretary of Agriculture under President Nixon, openly acknowledged that 'food is a weapon, it is now one of the principal negotiating tools in our kit' (Butz 1976).

Increased reliance on US grain by the Soviet Union was thought to be a major factor in the state of detente which occurred during the 1970s (Maddox 1977), and President Carter's use of grain embargoes and Reagan's repeal of them are recent examples of the geopolitical realities of international agricultural trade. But in spite of the potential for using food as a diplomatic weapon, its actual use has in fact been limited and, according to Paarlberg (1979), it has little potential for future use.

The federal government has always played an indirect role in encouraging domestic production, but it was not until the collapse of farm prices in the late 1920s and the depression years of the 1930s that it began to intervene directly in *price supports* for agricultural commodities. Intervention was deemed necessary to save the agricultural system from almost total collapse; it has endured since then, however, for political rather than economic considerations. Price support programmes are insurance for the farmer against unfavourable market conditions. Under various support systems, the federal government either agrees to ensure farmers a parity price for their commodities or to pay them not to plant specific crops, that is, acreage control. The parity price ensures that the current price for a commodity will give the farmer the same purchasing power as he/she had in 1910–14. Thus, if a bushel of wheat would buy one pair of shoes in 1910–14, at parity it would be able to purchase a pair of shoes in the current market. Under a price support programme the government agrees to pay the farmer some proportion of the difference between the market price and the parity price.

Formulas for price supports for agricultural products have changed since their inception, but 'official' goals of the programmes remain the same: (1) to ensure the continued existence of the family farm, (2) to maintain a reasonable level of income for farmers, and (3) to ensure the availability of an adequate food supply at reasonable prices (Bergman 1981). While official justification for many of these programmes has been to 'protect the family farm', the net effect has been the reverse. Because subsidies are linked to the size of the production unit, much of the money goes to larger farms (see Table 6.5). Since subsidies are paid to the landowner rather than the farm worker, they keep land prices artificially high, making it more difficult for the smaller operator to expand. The small operator must either continue to farm a small, uneconomical production unit, or go into debt to expand his landholding.

The cost of parity programmes to taxpayers has been estimated to exceed $10 billion (US) a year. (Vogeler 1981). In the dairy industry alone, price supports cost the federal government approximately $2.4 billion (US) to keep dairy products off the market. This comes to about $10 000 for every dairy farmer in the country, and it represents close to twice the budget allocated to the National Science Foundation or to the Agency for International Development's programmes for Third World development projects (Donahue 1983). Besides increasing the cost of food to consumers, price supports tend to maintain the status quo of production systems and of the geography of agricultural production. If price supports on a commodity remain high for an extended period, small producers and marginal areas can remain actively engaged in unproductive agricultural endeavours. Areas which lack a comparative advantage for particular forms of farming can continue to compete with the support of the government. A good example is tobacco farming in southeastern States like North Carolina and Virginia. Without federal price supports, tobacco farmers in the region would be unable to compete with foreign suppliers. Consumers complain that parity prices keep food costs high, but the dependency relationship between the government and the farmer is difficult to break, since congressmen from farming districts are loath to eliminate price supports for fear of the political repercussions. Special interest farm groups, such as the dairy lobby, invest heavily in political campaigns to ensure the continued support of the government. Even conservative congressmen who profess great faith in the fairness of the free market in allocating costs and benefits, such as Senator Helms of North Carolina, routinely support price support programmes for farm constituents in their district.

Parity prices enable the government to protect farmers from short-term fluctuations in market prices, but *acreage control* programmes are policies which attempt to control market prices by controlling the supply of agricultural commodities. In acreage control programmes, farmers are encouraged either by direct cash payments or by commodity payments to remove land from production and in doing so reduce the production of a crop and keep its prices at a profitable level. With policies such as the Soil Bank programme, crop land removed from production had to be converted to other uses, e.g. timber or pasture. In other acreage control or 'set-back' policies, conversion was not required. Where conversion was required, acreage control programmes have led to new agricultural land use practices and patterns. For example, the conversion requirement of the Soil Bank programme caused many southern farmers to convert marginal cotton land into timber and in doing so meet the needs of a growing southern pulp/paper industry. Often the acreage control programmes have been self-defeating. Reducing the acreage planted to a crop without regulating total output simply encourages farmers to increase productivity on existing land. Acreage controls have not been effective in reducing surpluses, because they encourage farmers to increase their capital investment on existing land and so surpluses have actually increased.

The federal government also supports agriculture through its *tax expenditure policies*. Tax laws have benefited both the large farmer and the non-farm person who wishes to dabble in agriculture to obtain tax advantages. They have encouraged absentee ownership, have led to overproduction of certain commodities because these are good tax shelters, and have encouraged sizeable capital investments in unnecessary equipment in order to take advantage of depreciation allowances. Attempts to close tax loopholes and price supports meet with strong opposition from the large agribusinesses who benefit from the financial windfalls they bring.

Since the government first became an activist in agricultural policy in the 1930s, important farm legislation has been plentiful. Most of this legislation has been enacted to protect the farmer from market eccentricities. It is somewhat ironic that many farmers, the group thought to be the backbone of individual initiative and enterprise, have been carefully protected from the invisible hand of the market.

Non-metropolitan migration and social change

Population growth in non-metropolitan America in the 1970s was widespread regionally, occurred for a multitude of reasons, and represented a radical 'turn-around' in the history of rural areas of the country (Ch. 2). Growth in the decade occurred in all sizes of places in non-metropolitan counties – cities from 10 000 to 50 000; small towns from 2500 to 10 000; small villages of less than 2500; and outside any form of town or village (Bogue 1985). The resurgence of growth in the smaller places raises questions about the impact of the new residents on the social institutions in these communities. In one sense, small towns have a curious dilemma. To preserve a traditional mode of small town living that was revered and thought to be worth maintaining, growth should be slow and manageable, but on the other hand, 'small towns fear stability for there is little in the national experience to prepare a community to accept slow growth or, perhaps, no growth at all: nothing which prepares it to grow old gracefully' (Lewis 1972: 349).

Growth can have many consequences for rural/small town America. Most fundamental are changes in social relationships, community social structures, local political/power relationships and community values. In a more pragmatic sense, growth can lead to higher land values, increases in living costs, greater expenditures for public infrastructures and services, and environmental deterioration. All are possible outcomes given the recent upsurge in non-metropolitan growth, though assessments of the actual impacts of growth have differed. Some accounts report that conflict between old and new residents have developed over funding of education, health care and other public services (Price and Clay 1980). Statements like:

Newcomers want more entertainment;
Newcomers are used to having more public services;
Newcomers want snow removal and trash service and other services a small town can't provide
(Johansen and Fuguitt 1984: 188)

from public officials in small towns suggest that increased demands for services are a potential basis for divisions based on old and new residents. Yet despite the potential for divisiveness, the bulk of the research suggests that serious social/political conflicts have not emerged on a widespread basis. Differences in demographic and social characteristics exist (de Jong and Humphrey 1976), but these have not led to a radical transformation of the social structure of rural America (Johansen and Fuguitt 1984).

The absence of major social conflicts given the size and composition of non-metropolitan in-migration is somewhat surprising. Yet it leads to an important conclusion. Rural and urban America have been converging in their social and economic characteristics, social behaviour and values for some time, and the recent growth is simply the latest phase of the longer process. The relocation of urban/suburban residents to rural areas and small towns did not cause a mixing of oil and water, for a new and different emulsion had long been fermenting. As Sokolow concludes:

. . . the newcomer–oldtimer dichotomy may not be the central cleavage in growing rural communities that it was once thought to be. Instead of length of residence, the political divisions today seem to be based on class, education, age, and how one views the world – all characteristics of politics in more urban places (Sokolow 1981: 180).

Class has always been an important element of the social structure of rural America. As we have seen in this chapter, it was originally determined by land ownership. Today, the class structure in rural areas is influenced by several factors, including race, occupation and education; but wealth or income has become the principal determinant. Rural incomes historically have been lower than those in urban centres. As an illustration, in 1983 farm family income was approximately $5000 lower than that for non-farm families ($18 756 versus $23 585) (Banks and Mills 1984), and in 1982 non-metropolitan incomes were lower than metropolitan incomes by approximately $6000 ($20 867 to $26 743) (US Bureau of the Census 1984). Besides lower incomes, inequalities in wealth within rural areas are greater. These inequalities are not only a result of locational and social/demographic factors (McGranahan 1980), but they also reflect a recurring relationship evident in places of all sizes in the US: places with lower incomes have greater inequities in income distribution (Betz 1972; Chiswick 1974; and Gunter and Ellis 1977).

The lower incomes in rural America have led to high incidences of *poverty*. As Table 6.9 illustrates, in the last three decades the proportion of the population below the federal poverty level has always been higher in non-metropolitan versus metropolitan counties and in farm versus non-farm populations regardless of race or whether the measure is family or personal income. Rural poverty is concentrated geographically. As a region, the South has the highest percentage of its non-metropolitan population below the poverty line and, as Fig. 6.11 shows, the location of high poverty non-metro counties in 1980 (high poverty counties were defined as those in the lowest quintile ranked on median family income and in the highest quintile ranked on the percentage of persons below the poverty level) large pockets of poverty are present within the South. In fact,

Table 6.9: Poverty rate for families and individuals: 1982, 1975, 1959

	Per cent below poverty level					
	Families			Individuals		
	1982	*1975*	*1959*	*1982*	*1975*	*1959*
Farm	18.6	13.7	42.8	22.1	16.4	NA
Non-farm	12.1	9.5	15.7	14.8	12.1	NA
Non-metropolitan	14.5	12.1	28.2	15.1	15.4	33.2
Metropolitan	11.1	8.5	11.7	10.4	10.8	15.3

Source: Bogue (1985), Table 16–4, p. 608

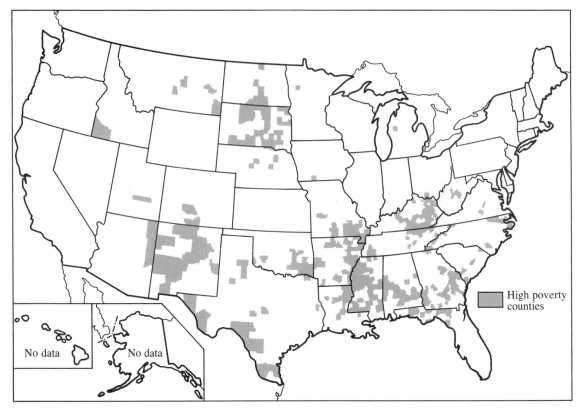

Fig. 6.11 The distribution of non-metropolitan poverty, 1980

the only sizeable concentration of high poverty counties outside the South is in the Dakotas. Many of the high poverty counties in 1980 have a long history of poverty, and are among those defined as having persistent poverty by the federal government in 1969 (Fig. 6.12; Davis 1979). As defined by the Department of Agriculture, persistent low-income counties have a common profile. They have a higher percentage of their earners from agriculture, poorer health status, lower family status and socio-economic status, and a higher score on a measure of alienation (Davis 1979).

At the macro scale, explanations for the lower economic status of rural America and the persistence of poverty there emphasize the forces which lead to uneven development in advanced capitalist economies (Ch. 5). But we must also recognize the existence of a number of local-scale factors that work to keep poor rural families in a perpetual state of poverty (Fitchen 1981):

- *The continued impact of history*: 'The antecedents of today's rural poverty and marginality are the historical forces of earlier times' (p. 186).
- *The crippling economic situation*: 'Difficult and painful as these day-in, day-out money situations may be, however, chronic poverty is even more serious in its long-run effects' (p. 187).
- *Inadequacies of the social structure*: . . . there are neither viable local-level social groupings nor satisfactory structural bridges linking people with the larger community. (p. 188).
- *Barriers to upward mobility*: '. . . upward mobility appears impossible for some people. Their limited economic resources are barely adequate to maintain their present low position, and far too meager to propel them upward' (p. 189).
- *Corrosive stereotypes*: 'Those who are blanketed by these stereotypes despair of ever

Fig. 6.12 Persistent low-income rural counties, 1969
Source: Davis (1979), Fig. 5, p. 5

being able to convince the outside world what they do not deserve the negative judgment' (p. 191).

- *Constant pressure of too many problems at the same time*: 'With so many potential sources of trouble, there is no way to predict when or where a new and acute problem will arise' (p. 191).

- *Difficulty of balancing aspirations and achievements*: 'An inescapable fact of everyday reality in the poverty-stricken areas is the disparity between aspirations and achievements. People are constantly faced with this disparity, and they are aware of its power to erode emotional strength' (p. 193).

- *Failure syndrome*: 'Repeated experiences of failure, almost unavoidable for many people, lead to low self-esteem and lack of confidence' (p. 196).

- *Psychosocial deficits from early childhood*: 'Whatever psychosocial difficulties the child

experienced in his earliest years are often reinforced and worsened by his experiences in the outside world, primarily in school' (p. 199).

- *The closing of horizons*: 'This closing-in of horizons is both a curse and a salvation to young adults. . . . Thus, horizons close, and limits may come to feel welcome, rather than constraining' (p. 200).

Urban poverty in the US is more visible and more prevalent because larger numbers of Americans live in cities. But the continued persistence of rural poverty even in light of the decentralization of population and production has evoked a sense of desperation and frustration: desperation among those who must live with the realities of poverty, and frustration for public officials – planners and politicians – who have been unable to remove the persistently poor rural counties from their marginal status.

Chapter 7

METROPOLITAN DEVELOPMENT

Although in 1980 over 70 per cent of the population of the US was 'urban' (i.e. living in places of over 5000 population), cities are a relatively recent phenomenon in North America and few have more than three centuries of history. As we saw in Chapter 5, it was the rapid growth of commerce and industry in the nineteenth century that really fostered the development of the urban system. Indeed, it was not until after 1920 that the population of the US was more urban than rural, a ratio that was reached in England by 1850. Despite the recency of urban development in the US, American society today is highly urban: perhaps more so, in terms of lifestyle, than British society. This points to an interesting contradiction. There has been, on the one hand, a strong and pervasive theme of anti-urbanism in American history, yet today urban products and services pervade virtually every facet of American culture. Capital and technology developed in urban places have inte-

grated all but the most remote parts of the country into the national markets. Americans traditionally distrust cities and associate the positive values of freedom and democracy with an agrarian, rural society. Cities, at least in the minds of many influential writers, are places of vice, strife and dereliction of the human spirit. A recently published dictionary of quotations about cities contains many such anti-urban sentiments. Thomas Wolfe, for example, wrote that city people 'endure their miserable existence because they don't know any better. City people are an ignorant and conceited lot. They have no manners, no courtesy, no considerations for the rights of others, and no humanity . . . It is a selfish, treacherous, lonely, self seeking life' (quoted in Clapp 1984: 262). Rene Dubos wrote that 'Man can be adapted to anything – to the dirt and noise of New York City – and that is what is tragic . . . Life in the modern city has become a symbol of the fact that man can become adapted to starless skies,

Top left: Suburban housing *Credit*: US Department of Housing and Urban Development   *Top right*: Urban renewal: Detroit's Renaissance Center *Credit*: US Department of Housing and Urban Development   *Middle left*: Manhattan, New York *Credit*: Paul Knox   *Middle Centre*: Upper Manhattan, New York *Credit*: Paul Knox   *Middle right*: South Boston: inner suburbs *Credit*: Paul Knox   *Bottom left*: Baltimore Harbour *Credit*: US Department of Housing and Urban Development   *Bottom right*: Metropolitan decentralization *Credit*: US Department of Housing and Urban Development

treeless avenues, shapeless buildings, tasteless bread, joyless celebrations, (quoted in Clapp 1984: 72).

While the existence of cities may be a necessary evil, many Americans would prefer not to live there themselves and still hold as the ideal habitat the small town or rural place – even as they compromise by living in suburbia! However, there are today few parts of the continental US, even the most remote canyons of the West, whose inhabitants do not have access, via mail-order catalogues, telephone and satellite cup TV antennae (which sprout like inverted mushrooms throughout rural America), to the projects, opinions and value system of the dominant urban society. The diet, clothes, leisure time activities (or inactivities) and mores of Graham, Texas (population 1258) are not dissimilar from those of Dallas, Texas, or Baltimore, Maryland. The home of 'Country and Western' music is Nashville (population 455 651 in 1980) and even the quintessential frontier character has been urbanized in the movie 'Urban Cowboy'.

Just as American society is imbued by values and ideas which originated in cities, so American cities in turn reflect the dominant themes in American culture. Partly because American cities are young, and partly because until very recently Americans had a tendency to look at the future and value the new over the old, relatively few cities have a landscape which contains significant remnants of over a century ago. The bicentennial celebrations of 1976 spurred interest in historic preservation, but many 'historic' American places are replications rather than preserved or renovated. American cities reflect the high value which Americans place on individual freedom, including freedom from governmental regulation and control. While most cities (Houston until recently being a notable exception) have long had some form of governmental control of land use through zoning ordinances, exceptions to such regulations are usually easily obtained, and there is little State or federal control over urban land use. Consequently, the American urban landscape reflects the working of a market economy more faithfully than do Western European cities. The development and demise of residential, commercial and industrial

areas reflects the changing profitability of different locations as relative accessibility, social use value and investments change. Contemporary American cities reflect these changes, especially those which have occurred since World War II.

The emphasis in American society on individualism rather than communalism, and on competition rather than cooperation, is evident in the landscape at both the scale of the individual housing unit and at the scale of the Central Business District. It is apparent flying into Dallas airport and observing, from several thousand feet, the numerous individually maintained backyard swimming pools, or viewing the skyline of Manhattan where the competition between corporate developers is reflected in the struggle to construct ever taller skyscrapers. At ground level, US cities reflect a combination of private affluence and public squalor in which the so-called 'tragedy of the commons' (the more people who share responsibility, the less responsible any single individual feels) is apparent. While private homes and corporate office buildings and their plazas are clean and well maintained, American cities are more littered than their European counterparts, and maintenance of public spaces (even vital infrastructure) is often inadequate.

This chapter begins with a description of the structure of the typical American city and the various theories which have been advanced to explain that structure. Particular attention is paid to the dramatic suburbanization which has occurred in the post-World War II period. The causes of both suburbanization and the more recent migration of people and businesses from northern cities to the South are discussed, and the reasons for the more recent revitalization of parts of older cities are explored. Finally, selected issues in current metropolitan development are considered.

Internal structure of American cities

While every city has unique features which give it distinctiveness and individuality, US cities also have many characteristics in common so that one can conceive of a 'typical' American city. Some of the features of the quintessential American cityscape are architectural in scale. Thus virtually every US city has skyscrapers (albeit some have only modest multi-storey office blocks), ranch-style suburban homes and commercial strips with the omni-present Golden Arches of McDonalds. But there are also similarities in urban structure, in the arrangement of land uses, from city to city.

Urban land use is the outcome of economic, social and political forces as well as the physical properties of land (e.g. its terrain and drainage). While the relative strength and directions of these forces varies between cities, some regularities are obvious. For example, in most cities the tallest buildings are downtown and there are deteriorating mixed-use neighbourhoods on the perimeter of the central business district. In general, the density of residential development and the value of individual housing units increases with distance from the city's centre. However, most cities also have some elite residential neighbourhoods closer in, often occupying sites with scenic views and other amenities. Boston's Beacon Hill is a famous example. Industrial development is typically located on transportation routes, whether water, rail or highway.

Clearly, these regularities are not merely coincidental. Most of the classic theories to explain them are based on models of accessibility and 'land rent' similar to those developed by Von Thünen (see p. 162). In cities, some activities require a central location with access to pedestrian traffic and to 'face-to-face' contacts with other businesses. Thus specialized retail and service establishments locate downtown and pay high land prices or rent. Other establishments less dependent on 'walk-in' business, and those with high space requirements, find a less central location with lower land rent to be more economical. Similarly, if the assumption is made that the city centre is also the centre of employment, and that residents seek to minimize commuting costs, then demand for residential neighbourhoods close to the centre would, *ceteris paribus*, be higher, land more expensive and residential density higher. Empirical observations have shown that this theoretical model is generally appropriate in American cities (Knos 1962; Yeates 1965),

but there are factors other than simple accessibility to the centre which must be taken into account if the spatial structure of most cities is to be understood. There are, for example, often several centres and more numerous subcentres of employment within a city. Accessibility is not merely a function of distance from the centre, but also depends on such factors as proximity to highways. Congestion at the centre may reduce accessibility by increasing time spent travelling. The accessibility model assumes 'perfect knowledge' and economic rationality. Yet in reality some residents will trade off accessibility for increased residential space, while others will pay more for scenic or historic locations. A wide range of other factors ranging from racial discrimination or transportation modes, to technological change in communications or energy costs, influence the patterns of land use in a city.

Despite these caveats, the accessibility model is the basis of several theories of urban land use. The earliest and simplest model was advanced by Burgess in the 1920s (Park *et al* 1925). At the centre of the city is the major business district with stores, offices and government buildings, theatres and the like (Fig. 7.1A). Surrounding the central business district (CBD) is a zone of factories, wholesale warehouses and transportation depots. Next is a zone of transition which in former years housed the wealthy, but now is occupied by low-income residences intermixed with business and light manufacturing. Beyond the zone of transition are three residential zones which increase in affluence with distance from the centre. Although this model was advanced over 60 years ago, it is still helpful in explaining in gross terms the spatial structure of US cities. It could be thought of as anomalous, for example, that the affluence of residential neighbourhoods tends to increase with distance from the centre. This is not, of course, true in other parts of the world. In South America, for example, the elite more usually live near the centre, while in North America the poor typically live on the most expensive land. This apparent contradiction is partially explained by the fact that the poor have less money to spend on transportation, so must live near the centre of employment. Consequently, they live at higher

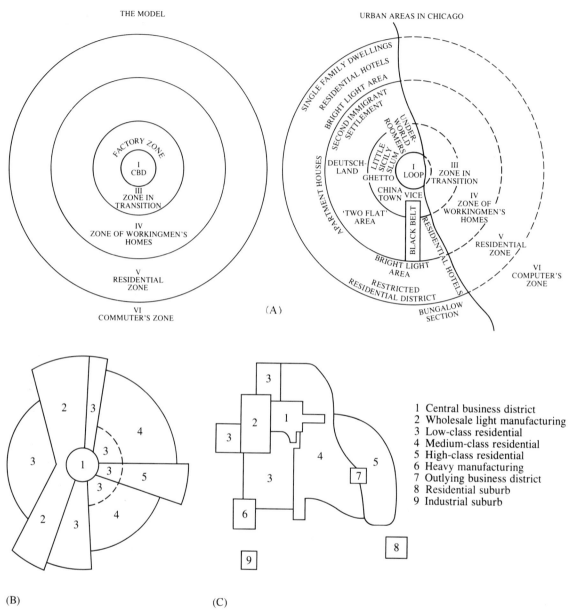

Fig. 7.1 Classic models of the structure of US cities. (A) The Burgess concentric zone model, (B) Hoyt's sectoral model, (C) Harris and Ullman's multiple nucleii model.
Source: (A) Park *et al.* (1925), Charts I and II, p. 53; (B) and (C) Harris and Ullman (1945), Fig. 5

densities, occupying less space, although the rent per acre is high. More affluent people who can afford automobiles and petrol can purchase more space for their housing dollar in the outer suburbs.

The simple concentric zone model was modi-fied by later research. Hoyt's sector theory (1939), based on empirical data from 142 cities, superimposed sectors on the basic concentric pattern (Fig. 7.1B). Hoyt found, for example, that the high rent residential areas do not typically form an unbroken ring, but rather

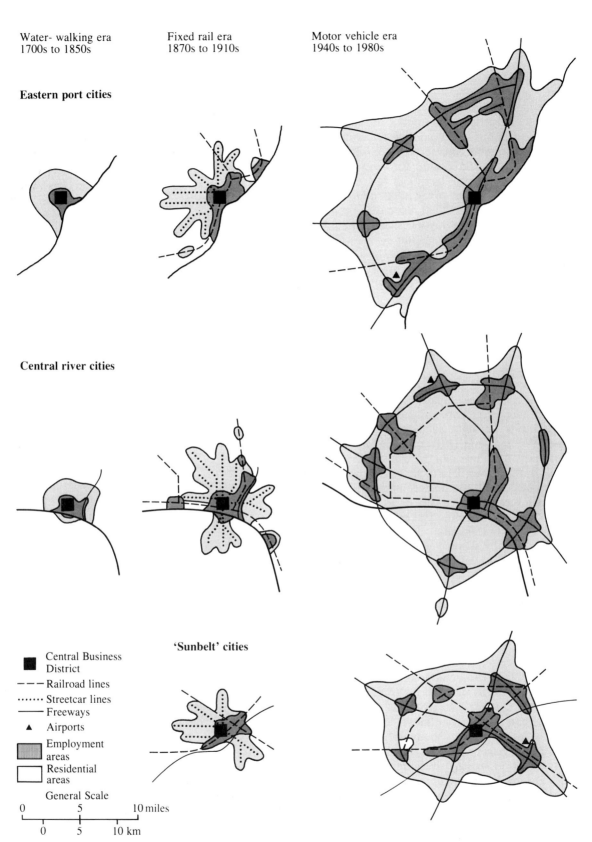

Water- walking era
1700s to 1850s

Fixed rail era
1870s to 1910s

Motor vehicle era
1940s to 1980s

Eastern port cities

Central river cities

'Sunbelt' cities

■ Central Business District

--- Railroad lines

······ Streetcar lines

— Freeways

▲ Airports

▨ Employment areas

□ Residential areas

General Scale

0   5   10 miles

0   5   10 km

Fig. 7.2 The evolution of the internal structure of North American metropolitan areas
Source: Baerwald (1984), Fig. 2, p. 16

concentrate in several peripheral neighbour-hoods and sometimes extend in towards the centre as a wedge.

The concentric zone model predated the intensive use of the automobile for commuting to work, shopping and services. While in 1920 there was one automobile for every thirteen persons in the US, by 1950 the equivalent figure was one car for every 3.8 persons. By the mid-1970s, Americans had more cars than chil-dren per household (Hayden 1984). In contrast to such forms of transportation as the streetcar, bus or rapid transit, the automobile is free from fixed routes so the rapid growth of auto ownership had a tendency to 'homogenize' space and reduce the relative differences in accessibility between parts of the city. It is important to emphasize, however, that the differential timing and interaction between urban growth and successive transport technol-ogies resulted in some significant regional differences (Fig. 7.2). Meanwhile, other factors, such as zoning to separate noxious industry from residential neighbourhoods, or the symbolic associations between such functions as retail business and tourism, became increasingly important in influencing land use. At the end of World War II, Harris and Ullman (1945) described a 'multiple nuclei' model (Fig. 7.1C) in which they proposed that cities could be seen as a number of commercial and industrial foci around which residential districts develop and differentiate by income. More recently, it has been possible to develop models of urban struc-ture based on the synthesis of masses of socio-economic data by statistical techniques such as factor analysis (Knox 1987). As a result, it is now recognized that the classic American city of the postwar era has a structure which is dominated by *sectoral* differentiation in terms of socio-economic status, *zonal* differentiation in terms of socio-demographic patterns, and *clustered* patterns of ethnicity (Fig. 7.3).

Elements of each of these hypothetical models can be found in most American cities, but no single model adequately explains the unique patterns of land use of individual cities, nor are they particularly helpful in explaining such recent developments in American cities as gentrified inner-city residential neighbourhoods or outer suburban industrial parks.

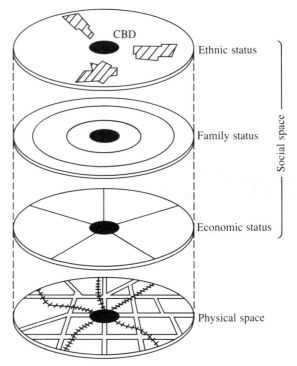

Fig. 7.3 Idealized model of the ecological structure of US cities
Source: Murdie (1969), p. 8

Landscape in a typical city

Anycity, USA, is laid out on a grid street pattern. At its centre are new glass and steel corporate towers designed by Philip Johnson or I. M. Pei. One of its main retail streets has been converted to a brick-surfaced pedestrian mall. It is lined by a mixture of large depart-ment stores, older establishments catering to lower income consumers, and a scattering of new boutiques, record stores, health clubs and bookstores with racks of greetings cards. Larger cities often have a new downtown covered mall, perhaps converted by Rouse from a former warehouse or public building. Within the city centre is an imposing town hall, county head-quarters or domed State capitol building surrounded by green lawns and sporting the appropriate flags. Adjacent to downtown are several old industrial districts located near rail lines or canalized rivers. There are still a few active mills, factories and warehouses, but others are boarded up awaiting 'adaptive reuse' or demolition. Some signs of redevelopment appear in warehouses converted to residential condominium apartments or artists' lofts. Nearby is skid row where homeless people (including an increasing number of women) drink from bottles in paper bags and varieties of 'adult' entertainment are purveyed. Not far from the city centre is an historic district of renovated Victorian homes with shady trees, olive green doors, brass fittings and wrought iron lamp standards. But most of the inner-city housing is in apartment blocks and terraced or semi-detached houses in various stages of deterioration and renovation.

Perhaps the most quintessentially American part of Anycity is its postwar suburbs. Sprawling in most directions for several miles are single family ranch-style or split-level homes on lots of an eighth of an acre. Most have garages, with the second family car (or boat or pick-up truck) parked in the driveway. The gridiron street pattern is replaced by a curvilinear one in more affluent neighbourhoods. There are few fences or hedges nor, compared to the equivalent European neighbourhoods, many flower beds. There are green lawns with sprinklers in the summer, and driveways cleared by snowblowers in winter.

Anycity's suburbs have local shopping centres with convenience stores and fast-food outlets, often close by some apartment complexes or a 'planned unit development' of condominium townhouses. The suburban fringe is also the location of large 'regional' shopping centres, anchored by one or more flagship stores and surrounded by an ocean of parking lots. Increasingly, industrial parks, seeking cheaper land and lower taxes, locate in suburban tracts – especially those adjacent to interstate highways. The parks are both the site of manufacturing industries and of corporate office buildings. As the outer suburbs or the rural–urban fringe is reached, the lots are larger and land once farmed lies unworked, awaiting the best offer from a developer.

In Anycity the contrasting processes first of continued expansion, decentralization and suburban growth and, secondly, of inner-city redevelopment are occurring simultaneously in response to some of the same economic factors. Since the process of large-scale suburbanization predated the significant redevelopment of the centre, the processes stimulating that expansion and its consequences are discussed next.

Suburbanization, inter-regional shifts, and central city decline

Although cities in all parts of the world have outlying residential areas or suburbs, nowhere have suburbs expanded faster and on as spectacular a scale as in the US. Suburbs are not merely a twentieth-century phenomenon: the earliest American suburbs date back to small rail suburbs in the first half of the nineteenth century. However, the mid-twentieth century has witnessed, as we saw in Chapter 5, a combination of factors which stimulated the decentralization of residents and capital from the central cities, especially those in the North and East, and to suburban areas and, later, to non-metropolitan areas and to cities in the Sunbelt. This movement of people and capital from central cities, stimulated by governmental policies, led to the steady deterioration of central cities. This section summarizes the major causes of these shifts.

Causes of central city decline

During the Great Depression and World War II, housing construction in the US, as elsewhere, was slow. After the war, the housing deficit was exacerbated by the baby boom and the consequent demand for more and larger houses. The provision of mortgage insurance by the Federal Housing Administration (FHA), starting in 1934, and the Veterans Administration (VA) after World War II, brought suburban single family homes within the financial reach of millions of households and fuelled the construction of rapidly built tract homes. These government programmes encouraged the construction of new housing rather than the rehabilitation of the older urban housing stock. The eligibility criteria for mortgage insurance, by stipulating neighbourhood stability as a requirement, encouraged the formation of ethnically homogeneous suburbs and militated against the suburbanization of racial minorities.

The Interstate Highway system, intended at its origin during the Cold War primarily as a defence strategy to enable men and material to be moved rapidly during emergencies, also enabled commuters speedily to reach the outer suburbs from the CBD. The construction of these multi-lane highways simultaneously took swaths of land from residential and other uses in the inner cities and stimulated the sprawl of peripheral suburbs. It also presaged the complete dominance of the private automobile over public transportation in cities. 'From 1945 to 1950 alone, annual transit ridership fell by 30 per cent (23 to 17 billion trips), and by the later 1970s the yearly passenger volume was less than 6 billion' (Muller 1981: 53). The ubiquity of the private automobile in American cities has very significant ramifications for urban form, mobility, environmental quality and even architecture.

The socio-cultural imperatives for residential migration to suburbia were probably strong, but more difficult to document. As the white middle class left central cities, a larger proportion of the resident population was low income, belonging to a minority ethnic group, and was either young or old. In the 1960s, civil disturbances in a number of distressed cities exacerbated the fears of middle-class residents. Increasing crime, deteriorating public services and environmental quality were push factors. So also were the high property taxes. Since American cities are typically separated jurisdictionally from their suburbs, there is a multiplicity of local taxes in any one metropolitan area. Central cities provide such services as police and fire protection to residents and to commuting employees from suburbs. The cost of such services, and the higher service needs of the low-income resident population, results in higher tax rates in central cities than in newer peripheral suburbs. Hence, purchasers of both residential and business properties can often lessen their local tax burden by locating in newer suburban locations. This was perhaps particularly true of businesses and industries whose space needs increased with changing production technology. The change in factory architecture from multi-storied mills to horizontal production lines housed in sprawling one-storey buildings required large parcels of land which were both less obtainable in cities and for which the tax bill was greater.

At the same time as the Interstate Highway system encouraged residential suburbanization, so too the improvements in road transportation tended to 'homogenize' space and to reduce the locational advantages of port and railroad centres. Containerization (the transport of material in large boxes which can be transferred, with their cargoes, from trucks, to trains to ships) also reduced such traditional transshipment activities as partial processing and repackaging. The homogenization of space accompanying transportation technology change has been even more marked in the advances in communications technology. Telecommunications and computerized information processing has enabled the transmission of data, letters and even video film over any distance at great speed (Kellerman 1984). Thus an insurance company, for example, which once benefited from close proximity to Wall Street and other financial centres, now can locate its main offices in a remote suburb while maintaining direct electronic links with sources of vital information. The new headquarters of the Longlines division of AT & T in Bedminster, New Jersey, epitomizes this trend. The offices of this huge multinational corporation are located in the rolling hills of an affluent outer suburb.

Meanwhile, as discussed in Chapter 5, postwar factory automation reduced the demand for labour in industrial cities and resulted in higher levels of unemployment, while labour-intensive industries sought cheaper labour in new locations where labour unions were less strong. Subsequently, the rapid conversion from an economy dominated by manufacturing goods to one in which the provision of services is the largest employment category resulted in the further decline of some older manufacturing cities. Increasing 'agglomeration diseconomies', or negative consequences of high density, such as traffic congestion and pollution, have also decreased the attractiveness of large cities to both residents and businesses. Ironically, federal governmental regulation of pollution in the 1970s encouraged the movement of industrial firms from older cities by setting ambient air quality standards. Such regulations determine how much pollution may be added by industrial growth on the basis of the current air quality. If a place already has high levels of pollution, new or growing industries must install expensive pollution control equipment to reduce their emissions. If, however, those plants are built in a relatively clean place, then higher emissions are permitted and less investment in equipment is required. Consequently, such polluting industries as petroleum refining and chemicals may choose to reduce costs by seeking locations away from large industrial centres where ambient air quality is already poor.

More nebulous than the foregoing reasons, but perhaps of considerable significance in central city decline, is the dissatisfaction with what can be perceived as a too complex and over-regulated urban society. The relative simplicity and autonomy offered by life in a single family home in suburbia or the small town in Texas can be attractive to individuals and the freedom from regulation attractive to business. Technology and affluence brought air-conditioned homes and cars within the financial reach of many who were thus able to create habitable microclimates in the hot, humid southern summers. During the energy 'crisis' accompanying the oil embargoes of the mid-1970s there was relative dependability of energy supplies in the South, while in the Northeast there was rationing and long queues at petrol stations, and some industries had to close production lines during part of the day due to interrupted electrical supplies.

The relative strength of each of these factors stimulating out-migration of businesses, industries and especially middle-income residents from central cities is impossible to ascertain and, indeed, there is undoubtedly a synergistic effect between them (Berry 1981). The result was that central cities lost populations: the total populations of all central cities declined by 4.6 per cent between 1970 and 1977 (Sternleib and Hughes 1979). While most metropolitan areas, including suburbs, continued to grow in population overall, those in the North and East did so at much slower rates, as is evident from Fig. 7.4. In the first 7 years of the 1970s the white population of central cities declined by 8.1 per cent while the black population increased by 4.2 per cent. Average family size

decreased dramatically from 3.47 to 3.30 persons, as more and more people lived by themselves (reflected in a 30.7 per cent increase in 'primary individual households'), and the divorce rate continued to rise, contributing to a 27.5 per cent increase in female-headed households. The number of people in poverty increased and employment declined.

The exodus of taxpaying residents and businesses, combined with the increased service needs of the resident population, led to fiscal stress in a number of cities. Deteriorated housing, abandoned properties and vacant stores abounded. Various federal governmental programmes to remedy urban distress failed to alter the fundamental direction of urban decline. The Urban Renewal programme, on which close to $10 000 million was spent in a 25-year period up to 1974, the programmes of the War on Poverty of the 1960s, and the Model Cities programme (on which $2500 million was expended) each had some local positive results, but also had some negative consequences and relatively small enduring effects. Today, the main legacy of this era in the urban landscape is the tracts of still vacant land in many cities. Created by 'slum clearance' schemes with the goal of attracting new investment by making land available for development near central business districts (CBDs), the hoped-for developments frequently failed to materialize. Meanwhile, since government spending on programmes such as defence, farm subsidies and water projects was many times greater than spending on urban programmes, federal dollars flowed to the South and West where such industries and projects were concentrated. In 1975, for each dollar a State sent to Washington in federal taxes, the South got back $1.14, the West $1.18, while the Northeast region received only 86 cents and the North Central 76 cents. In the late 1970s, while there was criticism of federal 'bail outs' of fiscally distressed cities in the North (such as New York and Cleveland), considerably greater sums of federal money were being spent on military bases, installations and contracts in southern and western States. As indicated in Chapter 5, defence spending has been seen by some as having played a major role in shaping patterns of urban and regional change (Sternleib and Hughes 1979).

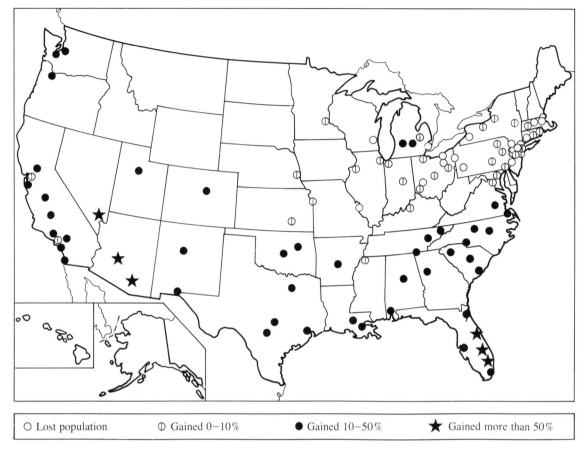

| ○ Lost population | ① Gained 0–10% | ● Gained 10–50% | ★ Gained more than 50% |

Fig. 7.4 Population change in the largest 100 SMSAs, 1970–80
Source: Holcomb and Beauregard (1981), Fig. 1, p. 13

Urban revitalization

In the latter half of the 1970s there were signs that the fortunes of American cities would finally begin to improve. Despite the continued distress of many major cities, small sections of many cities experienced a new wave of investment land redevelopment. Impressive new office buildings, hotels, convention centres and retail malls were opened with great media fanfare in such cities as Boston, Baltimore and Los Angeles. Numerous accounts appeared of 'gentrification', by young, affluent professionals who were buying and renovating architecturally interesting housing in formerly poor neighbourhoods of Philadelphia, Washington and New Orleans, and the press heralded the advent of the renaissance of America's cities.

There were, indeed, changing conditions which encouraged, if not a 'back to the city movement', then a 'stay in the city' by people and businesses who would have found it more advantageous to suburbanize a decade earlier. The energy crisis of the mid-1970s led to a rapid escalation of energy costs as well as the reduction in the reliability of supplies referred to earlier. The costs of heating, cooling and maintaining sprawling single family suburban homes doubled in a short time period. Commuting costs in large 'gas guzzlers' further strained family budgets. A rapid escalation of the cost of mortgages in 1980 placed ownership of the newly built homes beyond the financial reach of 80 per cent of US households. Since new units are most commonly built in suburbia, this depressed the suburban housing market. High interest rates also reduced the demand for large, less affordable suburban housing units. First-time home buyers increasingly looked for smaller, less costly housing units, finding them both in new suburban 'townhouse' developments and in the older urban neighbourhoods (Edmonston and Guterbock 1984).

As noted in Chapter 2, the decade of the 1970s witnessed significant demographic changes in American society, particularly in cities. The average size of a household fell as more people chose to live alone, as the divorce rate rose (typically creating two households from one) and as the birth rate fell. Women increasingly postponed marriage and childbirth, resulting in the birth of fewer children. On the other hand, women entered the work force in greater numbers and attained positions in professional and managerial occupations in increasing proportions (Sternleib, Hughes and Hughes 1982). There were, then, in the later 1970s and into the 1980s growing numbers of young, affluent people, both married and single but mostly childless, for whom living in close proximity to the city centres had considerable appeal.

The cultural, entertainment and retail variety and specialization of the downtown area provides interesting leisure opportunities, consumer choice and services (such as restaurants and dry cleaners) which save time. The housing stock, whether rental apartments, condominium or cooperative apartments and townhouses, or (less commonly) the single family or terraced house, consists of smaller units with a higher proportion of one and two-bedroom units, rather than the suburban three- or four-bedroom average. On the other hand, there are usually opportunities for home ownership with its considerable tax and investment advantages, and also opportunities to invest sweat equity by renovating a rundown house (Palen and London 1984). Whether the housing unit is renovated by the purchaser or a contractor, the opportunity to redesign one's living space and to include those amenities and aesthetics one desires may be thought preferable to the alternative of purchasing a relatively well-maintained but mundane suburban house. With few or no children, the poor reputation of many urban public schools is not a deterrent to urban residence since affluent parents can

afford private schools. For two-career couples with jobs in the city, a central location reduces both the time and financial cost of commuting.

At the same time, city centres offered increasingly attractive residential possibilities, the suburbs, particularly the older, inner ring of suburbs, began to acquire some of the disamenities previously associated with cities (Allman 1978; Masotti and Hadden 1973). Among these were increasing crime and pollution levels. On the other hand, those suburbs which used large lot zoning (requiring, for example, quarter-acre residential building plots) to protect watersheds and other aspects of environmental quality, also effectively zoned out moderate and even middle-cost housing, making them less attractive to first-time home buyers.

Trends in the national economy also encouraged urban revitalization. During the late 1970s, high inflation rates and slow economic growth encouraged the conservation of existing central city investments rather than expansion in new locations. Cities already have expensive infrastructure (streets, sewers, water supply) in place, while a firm expanding in suburbia may be required to provide such services or to pay for part of the cost of constructing them. During the 1980s, inflation slowed, but interest rates rose attracting significant investment to American cities especially from abroad. Canadian investments have been particularly prominent in such cities as New York and Denver.

Although, as noted earlier, many federal programmes directed to the problems of urban distress have not been unadulterated successes, the infusion of public capital and concentrated governmental attention in such programmes as Community Development Block Grants (CDBG) and Urban Development Action Grants (UDAG) did have some significant local impacts. The UDAG programme, begun in 1978 and continuing, though with lower funding, in the Reagan administration, provided grants through a competitive process to cities for redevelopment projects. Though the criteria for eligibility and selection include distress measures (Ch. 5), an important determinant as to which projects will be funded is the amount of private sector investment which will be 'leveraged' by the public subsidy and the probability that the project will be financially successful. Hence there has been a tendency for UDAG funds not only to be distributed to many cities (to garner wide congressional support), but to be allocated disproportionately to cities which are not among the *most* distressed, and thus most risky for investment (Holcomb and Beauregard 1981). Notwithstanding such tendencies, it is certain that the regeneration of portions of many cities has been stimulated and facilitated by government intervention (De Giovanni 1984).

Some argue that urban redevelopment is a process necessary to capitalism (Smith 1979). The earlier investment in expensive central land and property, which generated large debts, must be protected and the land, if necessary, redeveloped with new properties to increase its market value. If capital deserts central cities, it abandons significant previous investment. Since the built environment of an earlier historic stage, such as industrial capitalism, may be inappropriate to the generation of profits in the present period of advanced capitalism, redeveloping areas once devoted to factories and warehouses into offices and shops is necessary. As the economy is increasingly dominated by the production of services rather than goods, the creation of environments in which to produce and consume those services is vital (Gottman 1983). The redevelopment of some cities is virtually completely devoted to service provision, as in the case of Atlantic City, New Jersey. There, legalized casino gambling has resulted in the recent investment of well over a thousand million dollars in casino hotels which constitute over half of the assessed property in the city (Sternlieb and Hughes 1983). While this investment has done little to alleviate the severe problems of unemployment and housing for the poor of that city, it has resulted in large profits for casino investors. On a smaller, more individual scale, the process of gentrification enables 'urban pioneers' and speculators to realize large profits by the rapid escalation in value of renovated homes in gentrifying neighbourhoods.

There are, then, numerous concurrent and sometimes contradictory processes operating in American cities. The contemporary city is no static phenomenon but rather an ephemeral stage in the evolution of urban forms. Much of the American city today bears witness to processes which operated in earlier decades of the century, but there are also new patterns of land use, new landscapes and new social relations emerging from the particular combination of factors influencing metropolitan development in the 1980s. Some of these changes are as yet small in scale and one can but speculate as to whether they represent long-term trends or minor perturbations. In the next section we will explore some of these newer aspects of the geography of American cities, and end the chapter with a consideration of some of the related ethical and political issues which have geographical significance.

The American city of the 1980s

As an overall result of the opposing forces of urban decline and urban regeneration, it can be said that most large American cities are continuing to decentralize, decline and become increasingly distressed, at least at the macro or metropolitan scale. At the same time, however, most cities are experiencing intense but very localized regeneration on a microscale. In 1980, forty of America's seventy-five largest cities had lost population in the preceding decade, and this loss continued into the 1980s. As Table 7.1 indicates, each of the ten most distressed cities in the US, as listed in a 1984 Congressional report, declined in population, losing, on the average, 17 per cent of their residents. In contrast, most of the least needy cities gained population, several growing by over a third during the decade of the 1970s. As can be seen further from Table 7.1, all but one of the most distressed cities are in the Northeast or Midwest (see also Fig. 5.7, which shows the overall pattern), while the least distressed cities are larger: five are among the ten largest cities in the US, while of the least distressed cities only Houston is rated among the ten most populous cities. Distressed cities also have a larger number and proportion of minority people, particularly black residents. In 1980, a majority of the residents in half of the ten most needy cities were either black or of 'Spanish origin' (predominantly Mexican or Central

Table 7.1: Population characteristics for big cities with the highest and lowest levels of resident need, 1980

	Population size rank	Per cent change population 1970–80	Per cent black	Per cent Spanish	Per cent total minority
	10 highest need				
Newark	46	−13.8	58	19	77
Detroit	6	−20.5	63	2	65
Atlanta	29	−14.1	67	1	68
Cleveland	18	−23.6	44	3	47
Baltimore	10	−13.1	55	1	56
Buffalo	39	−22.7	27	2	29
Philadelphia	4	−13.4	38	4	42
New York	1	−10.4	25	20	45
Chicago	2	−10.8	40	14	54
St Louis	26	−27.2	46	1	47
	10 lowest need				
Tulsa	38	+9.3	12	2	14
San Jose	17	+36.9	5	22	27
Wichita	51	+1.0	11	3	14
Houston	5	+29.3	28	18	46
Virginia Beach	56	+52.4	10	2	12
Seattle	23	−7	9	3	12
Honolulu	36	+12.4	1	5	6
Austin	42	+36.3	12	19	31
Charlotte	47	+30.3	31	1	32
Denver	24	−4.3	12	19	31

Source of data: National Urban Policy Advisory Committee (1984)

American in western cities, and Puerto Rican, Cuban and other Caribbean countries in eastern cities).

This loss of population, both absolute and relative, reflects the continued economic decline of cities as investments are dispersed to suburbia and to the Sunbelt. As industries expand outside of northern cities, labour migrates to places which offer (or are perceived to offer) better employment opportunities and lower living costs. But not all the population is mobile. Left behind in declining cities are the elderly and those close to retirement, recent immigrants relying on support of ethnic communities, low-income people who are not in the labour force (e.g. single mothers of pre-school children), who have few job skills or are 'structurally unemployed' due to changes in the local economy and, of course, millions of people who have lived in the city much of their lives and have deep familial and social attachments to it.

Urban fiscal stress

The need for public services, both 'hard' and 'soft', is high. The hard services, e.g. police, fire, infrastructure and transportation, typically serve not only the resident population but millions of suburban commuters who work in the city but may pay no taxes to support those services. High densities, tall buildings and an older housing stock increase the costs of fire protection. Poverty and social inequality are correlated with high crime rates and concomitantly expensive police protection. Much of the infrastructure of America's cities is ageing and in need of renovation and replacement – another very costly process, but one which, if deferred, increases current maintenance costs (*Urban Resources* 1983). While much of the cost of major transportation improvements in cities (highways, subways, etc.) is borne by the federal government, States and cities often provide some matching funds and are responsible for maintenance. Soft services, or human services such as welfare, nutrition, education and programmes for the elderly, are also partially funded by federal and State governments. However, the greater concentration of people needing such services in the city is a heavy burden on many city governments. In the US, public education is a major financial cost of local government. Efforts to racially desegregate schools and to equalize per capita spending on children's education have only been partially successful, and wide disparities still exist between the quality of education and levels of achievement in central city, compared to suburban, schools. Central city children have, on the average, greater need for compensatory education which further adds to the cost of public education in cities (Judd 1985).

Concurrent with rising demand and costs of governmental services has been a relative fall of public revenues due to a declining tax base. When industries and businesses move out of the city leaving vacant buildings, and middle-class out-migrants are replaced by lower income residents, both the value of the property and its ability to generate taxes decreases. The median value of central city, owner-occupied housing is some 15 per cent lower than in suburban areas, while about 80 per cent of local tax yields come from property taxes. Revenue from sales taxes is lost when retail stores move to suburban malls. Increasing the city's tax rates can be counterproductive by driving business out and deterring new businesses and residents from moving in (Judd 1979).

As a consequence of these trends, some cities have experienced severe 'fiscal crises' which have resulted in reduced services, the lay-off of public employees, and a further decline in the quality of life for city residents (Alcaly and Mermelstein 1977; Gorham and Glazer 1976). During the first half of the 1980s the abrupt reduction or elimination of various federal programmes which served urban populations (e.g. food stamps, the Comprehensive Employment and Training Act which funded job training for low-income people, several programmes of the Economic Development Administration including small business loans and grants, and various housing subsidies for low-income people) added to cities' difficulties. During the 1980s there has been a tendency for increasing inequality both between cities and within cities. Old industrial cities of the Northeast and Midwest have become increasingly distressed, while some cities in the South and West have experienced rapid growth as energy and high-technology industries (such as computers, electronics, aerospace and telecommunications) expanded (Perry and Watkins 1977; Sawers and Tabb 1984). While rapid urban growth is not without its problems, they are more amenable to solution than those of decline. Sunbelt urban problems of overbuilding and high vacancy rates (experiences in cities such as Houston and Denver in the mid-1980s), or the urgent need for new infrastructure, are more tractable than those of Snowbelt cities facing uncertain futures. Within cities, particularly the largest cities, the flight of the middle class left behind the poor, but redevelopment and gentrification has resulted in a small but significant increase in affluent residents. At a time (1984) when a quarter of New York City's population was below the federal poverty level, when there were more homeless and hungry people in the city than at any time since the Depression, and the unemployment rate was 10 per cent, still many businesses were thriving, the number of jobs in the city was the highest in ten years and the number of tourists was the second highest in history (Goodwin 1984). The central city in the 1980s is home to both the richest and poorest Americans.

Housing markets and residential patterns in the 1980s

As noted earlier, the postwar period has been one of massive expansion of single family home building in suburbia, aided significantly by federally insured mortgages and by major tax deductions on mortgage interest payments. Residential patterns in American cities are typically segregated by income and frequently by ethnicity. Various mechanisms operate to maintain this segregation. The mortgage market favours financially secure borrowers who are buying homes in stable neighbourhoods. Homogeneity of housing value and of social characteristics of residents insures the neighbourhood against changes which could threaten the value of the house, and thus protects the investment. On the other hand, investment of mortgage capital in neighbourhoods which are racially and economically mixed, and which contain a diversity of building and tenure types, is more risky and mortgages are more difficult to obtain. At the extreme, some neighbourhoods are considered by mortgage-lending institutions to be too risky, in some cases regardless of the condition of the particular structure for which a mortgage is sought or the credit worthiness of the loan applicant. In such cases, banks may unofficially (and illegally) 'redline' a neighbourhood and reject loan applications for properties within it. Such actions lead to a self-fulfilling prophecy, since without investments the neighbourhood does indeed deteriorate and property values decline. Segregation by race and ethnicity is partly a consequence of free choice (people choosing to live in a particular ethnic community) but is also the product of discrimination in the housing market. While such practices as 'steering' (showing, for example, only homes in black neighbourhoods to black home buyers) and 'blockbusting' (creating a wave of panic selling by white home owners who fear a decline in property values if black families buy on the block) are unethical and illegal, they also persist (Knox 1987).

The typical residential pattern in American cities has been, then, one of higher-density, multifamily rental units near the centre of the city, ringed with older neighbourhoods of apartment buildings, two and three family houses and smaller single family homes occupied by both owners and tenants. Beyond that are inner and outer suburbs containing homes of increasing size, decreasing age and increasing value with distance from the centre.

However, the last decade has witnessed the emergence of new housing patterns. The rapid increase in the price of houses and the escalation of interest rates after 1980 has priced most American households out of the single family new house market. The average price of a new home (including all new housing in units in single and multifamily structures) rose to over \$100 000 in 1984 at a time when interest rates on mortgages were around 15 per cent. This priced a new home beyond the financial reach of 80 per cent of American households. These facts, combined with the demographic trends towards smaller households, have led to a rapid increase in the demand for condominium apartments and small townhouses. Of the estimated 85.4 million households in the US as of March 1984, nearly 20 million consisted of a single person. The average household size had fallen to 2.71 persons (Wald 1984). In the centres of many cities, new luxury condominium tower blocks are rising and older apartment buildings are being converted to condominium or cooperative ownership. Such conversions bring the benefits of home ownership to their purchasers, but frequently displace former tenants who cannot afford the downpayment and mortgage costs on their apartment. Condominium and co-op homes still account for only a small percentage of all homes, but the number of such units tripled between 1972 and 1981. In some cities, such as New York, apartment buildings primarily occupied by low-income residents have also been converted to cooperative ownership after their landlords defaulted on property taxes. In cases of default, ownership of the building commonly reverts to the city, which then organizes and may subsidize the conversion.

In the suburbs, clusters of townhouses, often arranged as a 'planned unit development' with communal ground and recreation facilities maintained by a company, are increasingly common. Some are occupied predominantly by young singles and families, others are restricted 'retirement communities' from which young adults and children are excluded. The professional landscaping and maintenance of these suburban developments and the regulatory control of such things as the colour of paint used on homes and the size and style of additions such as fences or patios creates an ordered and homogeneous landscape which contrasts with the eclecticism of older urban neighbourhoods.

Another relatively recent housing pattern is the gentrified neighbourhood in a revitalizing city. Commonly close to the central business district, a neighbourhood with older, but structurally sound, houses, often with architectural interest such as brownstone or Victorian 'gingerbread', and with some amenity such as a scenic vista or a cultural facility, may undergo intensive rehabilitation. In the early stages, young pioneers carry out much of the renovation themselves. As the neighbourhood is discovered and becomes increasingly upgraded, house prices rise rapidly and renovation is more professional. Ultimately the neighbourhood may, as in the case, for example, of Society Hill in Philadelphia, become an exclusive enclave of affluence with carefully maintained historic streetscaping and exquisitely renovated houses (Cybriwsky, Ley and Western 1986). Gentrified neighbourhoods still constitute a very small portion of the city's fabric and some reports suggest that the pace of residential gentrification had slowed by the mid-1980s.

Metropolitan governmental fragmentation

As we saw in Chapter 4, American metropolitan areas are characterized by governmental fragmentation. Typically, suburbs are jurisdictionally separated from central cities and have independent taxing and regulatory powers. Metropolitan governments, where they exist, commonly have limited powers of coordination and planning. Consequently, urban decentralization can be seen as a product of lower suburban tax rates; but it also exacerbates the gap between the fiscal health of central cities and their suburbs. With more vigorous local economies, suburbs can improve the quality of their public facilities and services (such as schools, parks and street maintenance) attracting new residents and businesses. Equally significantly, governmental fragmentation has also enabled suburbs to exercise a certain amount of selectivity regarding types of new residents and businesses. A mechanism which has come to be called 'exclusionary zoning' has allowed municipalities to zone out low- and moderate-income residents by stipulating minimum lot sizes and providing little land zoned for multi-family (apartment) housing. Environmental regulations to preserve water tables or clean air can prevent the growth of polluting industries, and building codes can increase the cost of construction, effectively placing it out of the financial reach of the lower end of the market. Exclusionary zoning practices, while challenged legally in various States, have nevertheless contributed significantly to socio-economic and racial segregation in some American metropolitan areas (Palm 1981).

The gap between poor central cities and richer suburbs has widened since 1970. The President's 1984 National Policy Report noted that the median income of central cities fell from 99 per cent of the 1970 national median income to 93 per cent of the 1982 figure, while the median income of suburban families remained stable at about 115 per cent of the national median. Furthermore, the gap was widest in the largest metropolitan areas. While the nation's largest cities control a major share of all jobs, the proportion of all jobs located in the largest fifty-six fell from 41 per cent in 1970 to 37 per cent in 1981 (National Urban Policy Advisory Committee 1984). In central cities, the kinds of employment which have increased have often been both highly specialized professional and whitecollar jobs requiring high levels of education and training, and low-skilled jobs in such places as hotels and shops in which wages are low, personnel turnover is high, there are few benefits and little career mobility. The first category of jobs are often held by suburban commuters. In 1981, 40 per cent of all central city jobs in major metropolitan areas were held by suburban residents. While there are obvious benefits to central cities of having new and growing businesses requiring a specialized workforce in that tax revenues are enhanced, and such business generates other economic activity, suburban commuters typically spend most of their money in their home community and their purchasing power is only a minor contribution to the city's economy. On the other hand, the low skilled jobs are held by city residents many of whom could be said to belong to the 'secondary' labour force. They are employed intermittently, with no security, and are usually not unionized. The continuous upgrading in skill level necessary to keep up with such changes as the replacement of typewriters with word processors, or the higher 'social skills' required of a salesperson in a chic boutique or a waitress in an upscale restaurant leaves the undereducated, inarticulate, and those whose appearance does not conform to contemporary fashion at a considerable disadvantage.

New suburban landscapes

Meanwhile, the suburbs of America's cities reflect the country's generally robust economy as both production and consumption have decentralized. It was the latter, both residential and retail consumption, which led the way in the postwar period. Accompanying the sprawl of housing over the peripheral urban landscape has been the growth of giant-sized regional shopping centres (Baerwald 1978). A phenomenon which blossomed in the 1960s, by the 1980s the *suburban shopping mall* has replaced downtown as the retail centre for many Americans. The typical suburban shopping centre is a climate-controlled, enclosed mall, sometimes with two storeys of shops, surrounded by a sea of parking lots. It is located near the intersection of major highways and is often accessible only by car. The mall is 'anchored' by one or several major department stores, the prestige of the anchor store helping to determine the quality of the other retail outlets. The mall's management provides maintenance and security and also tries to ensure, by leasing agreements, that an appropriate retail mix is maintained. Malls are not only the commercial centres of suburbia, but are frequently social centres in their own right. Teenagers 'hang out' there not only to buy records and clothes but to be where the action is. Senior citizens arrange bus trips to the mall and there are even occasional live shows to replace the perrenial musak, and eclectic 'art' exhibitions which range from reproductions of Van Gogh's sunflowers or fluorescent matadors painted on velvet to high-quality, original and very expensive work by local artists. Historically, urban buildings, whether public or private, have often presented an impressive exterior architecturally, while their interiors may be more modest. Hence the ornate town hall, pseudo-gothic cathedral, opulent storefront with neon and display windows epitomize urban architecture. The architecture of the suburban mall in contrast is typically one of bland and anonymous ex-teriors, but luxurious and well-maintained interiors.

The success of suburban malls (Muller (1981) reports that the nation's 20 000-plus shopping centres now account for well over 50 per cent of the total US retail trade) has led cities to try to replicate mall settings in downtown locations. Some, such as Philadelphia's Gallery One, have similar retail mixes as suburban malls, but new versions, such as Rouse's marketplaces in Boston's Quincey Market, New York's South Street Seaport, St Louis Union Station and Baltimore's Harborplace, cater primarily to a luxury, tourist market and concentrate on specialty foods and goods rather than on typical consumer durables. The Northern New Jersey executive who commutes to a job on Wall Street in Manhattan may eat luncheon oysters on the half shell at the South Street Seaport, but buys his $300 suit at the mall in suburban Paramus. Some warn against the attempt to revive retail trade in central cities by developing malls of either variety. The conventional mall requires prohibitively large parking areas and access to a large middle-income market. 'A Ghiadelli Square or Faneuil Hall's success may be a tribute to unique settings or, for that matter, a reward, on a national level, for an original idea. Continuous emulation may prove disastrous. The "Ghiadelli Squaring of America", midwifed by federal funding in scores of downtown settings may yield highly costly platitudes, not economic revitalization' (Sternleib and Hughes 1981: 16).

As we have seen, the decentralization of *manufacturing industry* occurred for reasons of cheaper land and taxes, good freeway access and skilled labour supply. Muller (1981) argues that the image and prestige of certain suburban communities is a particular additional attraction: companies will expend considerable resources to locate in a fashionable place. An area adjacent to Route One in central New Jersey has experienced extremely rapid growth in the 1980s, attracting many high-prestige corporations. Part of the enticement is that a 100 square mile area around Princeton uses that town's address and zip code, even though the governmental jurisdiction of Princeton is only a few square miles. An address in California's Silicon Valley or Cambridge, Massachusetts (home of Harvard University) are similarly prestigious. It is common for a large firm to have its corporate headquarters or main office located at an impressive address, whether in a big city (Fifth Avenue, New York), or an 'upscale' suburb, but its production and back-office facilities (where much of the work of purchasing, billing, inventorying and the like occurs) are located more anonymously in cheaper locations (Stephens and Holly 1980).

A phenomenon which is expanding in both numbers and size is the *suburban industrial park*. Though not a new idea, the advantages of efficient and economical provision of such routine services as transportation and utilities, or specialized facilities for hazardous waste disposal or optic-fibre telecommunications are increasingly attractive. The old agglomeration of heavy industries like steel and ship building are mirrored today in concentrations of 'high-tech' electronics, engineering and light manu-facturing firms. Today's suburban industrial parks often feature attractive landscaping with manicured lawns and 'natural' woodlands, and may offer dining and recreational facilities. Industrial parks often resemble in appearance the corporate office parks which accommodate the burgeoning tertiary and quaternary sectors. The office industry was traditionally located in the CBD because of the advantages of accessi-bility to other businesses, for 'face-to-face' contact with other business people, and because a central location was accessible to a large labour pool. However, rapid change in communications technology has made spatial proximity to other businesses less necessary, and the skilled clerical workforce has subur-banized. The suburbs offer many other advan-tages such as cheaper land, better access to airports and sometimes greater prestige or better image than central cities. During the 1970s and 1980s, corporate headquarters, back-office functions and small office companies moved, with sometimes dramatic rapidity, from central to peripheral urban locations. Muller (1981) reports that by 1978, 170 of the Fortune 500 (the largest corporations in the country) were headquartered in suburbia, compared to only 56 in 1969. This trend of corporate subur-banization raised consternation among older corporate cities such as New York. However, in the mid-1980s there is a boom in office building both in the CBD (e.g. Manhattan) as well as in suburban localities.

The suburbanization of commerce, industry and offices has caused a convergence both in the functions, and to a lesser extent the appear-ance, of suburbs and cities (Erickson 1983). There are today few functions which are unique to the CBD. Even such specialized services as live theatre, gourmet restaurants or specialized hospitals abound in affluent suburbs. Indeed, functions and services which are still more exclusively urban rather than suburban are those which cater to the poor – shelters for the homeless, soup kitchens and free health clinics. Similarly, the average suburb lacks extensive tracts of deteriorated housing or abandoned factories which exist in most of America's distressed cities. The appearance of the environment built for commerce, industry and offices differs between central and suburban locations. As discussed earlier, although the suburban shopping mall is mirrored in the new in-town malls, the scale of the latter is usually smaller. Manufacturing plants and offices in the suburbs can be indistinguishable to the casual observer, being housed in anonymous, modern buildings surrounded by parking lots or lawns. The suburban skyscraper, while typically smaller in scale, is nevertheless not uncommon. Suburbs are no longer the 'bedrooms of cities': today they have been urbanized and are func-tionally, if not administratively, part of the city.

Urban policy and metropolitan development

As discussed earlier in this chapter, despite localized revitalization, many of America's large cities, especially those in the Northeast and Central regions, have continued to lose jobs and population since World War II, and are today home to many of America's poor. Ironically, despite federal programmes intended to improve the economy of cities and to address the issue of urban distress, there is some justi-fication for the argument that, overall, federal programmes have done more to exacerbate the decline of cities than to prevent it.

Historically, cities were considered the

responsibility of the State in which they were located, and it was not until the Great Depression and the New Deal that cities were seen also as national assets and problems. The federal programmes to address the economic crisis were aimed both at distressed people (social security and unemployment insurance) and at distressed places (the Works Progress Administration which provided employment through the construction of public works and various slum clearance and housing schemes). Nevertheless, such postwar programmes as FHA and VA mortgages, the large income tax deductions allowable on mortgage interest payments, and the construction of Interstate Freeways greatly facilitated the exodus of the middle class from cities, paving the way for their decline.

More recently, as we saw in Chapter 5, the underlying assumption that cities should be 'saved' by governmental intervention has been challenged. The controversial report on a National Agenda for the Eighties issued in the final year of the Carter administration suggested that urban policy should not 'inadvertently seek to preserve cities in their historic role' but should allow places to transform and adjust: 'Federal urban policy efforts should not necessarily be used to discourage the concentration and dispersal of industry and households from central urban locations' (President's Commission for a National Agenda for the Eighties 1980: 165, 167). The report argued that federal programmes had become too 'spatially sensitive' and that while it is politically rewarding to award grants to local governments, and concentrating funds can maximize economic multipliers, nevertheless it should be kept in mind that the underlying purpose is to aid *people*, even when this means helping their migration from depressed *places*. Indeed, subsidized relocation for unemployed job seekers was a major proposal of the Commission. Rather than trying to stimulate economic and job growth in old central cities, government should ameliorate the pain of adjusting to new economic patterns while encouraging the transition.

Since Carter lost the 1980 Presidential election to Reagan, none of the policies recommended by the Commission were implemented, although the Reagan years might be interpreted as an extreme version of the *laissez-faire* policy suggested in 1980. The underlying assumption of the Reagan urban policy has been that the future of America's cities depends upon the strength of the country's economy. The priorities of the administration are those of building a strong national defence and reducing the role of government in American life. Glickman (1984) argues convincingly that in the absence of a strong urban policy (indeed of *any* urban policy) the most important federal programmes affecting cities are those non-urban programmes such as tax policy and defence. In the early years of the first Reagan term, numerous social, small business and housing programmes which had formerly impacted mainly urban places were cut or eliminated. The new tax legislation cut federal income taxes for all, but did so more for those at the upper end of the income scale than those at the lower. Corporate taxes on profits and on new investments in capital equipment were reduced, as was the share of the total federal tax burden borne by business (as opposed to individuals). Spatially, these policies had negative impacts on older cities. Since many of the recipients of the eviscerated social programmes live in cities, and as the median income of suburbs is 30 per cent higher than that for cities, income tax cuts favouring the affluent were relatively disadvantageous to cities. Corporate tax cuts favoured profitable, capital-intensive firms which tend to be located in the South and West US rather than the less profitable, labour-intensive firms of the Northeast and Central regions. Increases in the already huge defence budget favours those regions (the West Coast and parts of New England) where aerospace and other military industries are concentrated. Taxation legislation which allowed more rapid depreciation on capital investment in equipment and plant also favoured growing over declining regions.

In summary, there has been no real federal urban policy in the 1980s. Distressed cities increasingly turned to the private sector for their salvation, forming 'public–private partnerships' for urban redevelopment (Fosler and Berger 1982). By enticing private sector investment (often with public sector subsidies) some city governments were quite successful in transforming at least small sections of the downtown area into new retail malls, office blocks and hotel/convention centres. In such cities as Pittsburgh, Portland (Oregon), Baltimore and New Orleans, such collaboration between local governments and business resulted in conspicuous landscape transformations and the generation of economic activity. It has been argued that these gains are not cost free and that the loss of public control over decisions about the city's future, the diversion of public monies from social services to hard services, and the conversion to an environment of consumption and profit making, are heavy prices to pay (Holcomb 1985). Many, however, would disagree and salute the initiatives of the profit sector in city life.

Chapter 8

GEOGRAPHIC ASPECTS OF SOCIAL PROBLEMS

It is important to delineate at the outset what constitutes a 'social problem'. In American English, the word 'problem' implies less a puzzle to which one seeks a solution, but rather more an undesirable condition to which remedies may be known but not necessarily implemented. A social problem then becomes an undesirable condition of society, rather than of an individual. Individual needs for security, love, fulfilment and recreation may or may not be satisfied, but only if and when individuals' problems become sufficiently widespread or severe as to have reverberations for a wider group does it become a social problem. Thus, spouse abuse, for example, was long tolerated as an albeit undesirable behaviour within the family. Only when it became apparent that domestic violence breeds violence outside the family and the sheltering of abused spouses and children became a financial cost to local governments did this 'personal' problem become a social problem.

There is, of course, no unanimity either about what constitutes social problems nor which of the many are more critical in American society today. In general, politically liberal Americans tend to emphasize such issues as poverty, discrimination and other forms of injustice, environmental pollution and the threat of nuclear war. More conservative people stress the prevalence of crime, of alcoholism and 'substance abuse', and the growing number of teenage mothers and abortions. Whether the economic inequality endemic in American society is an inevitable condition of its capitalistic structure or the result of inequality of opportunity or effort which can be addressed by government programmes in education or by economic growth to improve incentives for hard work, is widely debated. This chapter will consider how a spatial perspective can contribute to the understanding of both the causes and solutions of social problems, before going on to review some of these issues in detail. Various conditions in US society which are regarded as problematic are discussed, and the contributions which geographic analysis has made or could make are summarized.

Top: Metropolitan poverty: inner-city residential hotel used mainly by the elderly (ground floor space is taken up by a funeral home and a bar) *Credit*: Paul Knox   *Middle*: Small-town poverty: Haymond, Kentucky *Credit*: US Department of Agriculture   *Bottom*: Ethnic poverty: Harlem, New York *Credit*: Paul Knox

American social problems: geographic causes, consequences and solutions

Many social problems in the US have as their root cause the inequality in the social distribution of the goods of society. There is unequal access of individuals to money and to the things that money can buy (shelter, food, land and more money). Such material inequality both causes or amplifies inequalities in such factors as susceptibility to crime, to ill-health, to poor education and even to mental illness, drug abuse and prejudice. The US is among the wealthiest countries in the world and, compared to many other countries, enjoys both a decent standard of living for most of its people and a gap between rich and poor the size of which is tolerated by the majority. On the other hand, in a country where absolute poverty could be eliminated rapidly through redistribution, and where the government has been, at least in rhetoric, waging war on poverty for decades, the significant inequality which persists has both causes and consequences susceptible to geographic analysis. The work of David Harvey (1973), Richard Peet (1972), David Smith (1977, 1979), Neil Smith (1985) and others examines the spatial patterns of social inequality and, in positing reasons for the incidence of poverty and its associated conditions, also suggests solutions.

Just as the divergence in income between the most and least affluent segments of society is not as great in the US as, for example, in developing countries such as Brazil or India, so too the spatial contrasts of wealth and poverty are not so stark. Nevertheless, there are areas of the US where poverty can perhaps be considered endemic – such as in parts of Appalachia, many Indian reservations, parts of the rural South, and the racial ghettoes of most large cities. It is, of course, people, not places, who are poor, but the concentration of poverty in a place can exacerbate the negative consequences of poverty. A local government in whose jurisdiction much of the population is poor cannot raise sufficient revenue in taxes to provide strong social services or public education. The lack of investment from both the public and private sectors in housing produces a contagious effect such that a poorly maintained house in a deteriorated neighbourhood retains more of its value than an equivalent house in a wealthy neighbourhood. The child who attends a school in which most of her peers are from homes in which diet is inadequate, parental supervision weak and there are no role models to suggest that application in school work will bring rewards in life, has less incentive to compete in the conventional ways which American society expects. In brief, location or place can both influence a person's financial life chances and deeply affect the quality of their life.

In analysing the relationship of the discipline to social well-being, Harvey was among the earliest geographers in the US to show that economically efficient spatial distributions are not necessarily just, and that in a democratic society (including capitalist democracies) consideration must be given to justice in deciding where, for example, new investments should be located. As Harvey notes, quite apart from the ethical issue of the value of equality, if a group of people in a particular place is consistently deprived and bears social costs without compensating benefits, they are likely to become a source of economic inefficiency in the long run. They both cease to participate in the social process of production (being unemployed or underemployed) and various antisocial behaviours ranging from crime to drug addiction require the diversion of public resources to address them (Harvey 1973).

Harvey also drew attention to the issue of spatial externalities. The saying that no person is an island could be applied to places. Decisions taken, and events which occur, frequently have reverberations beyond the immediate local environment, ripples which can be both positive and negative in effect (Carey and Greenberg 1974). A chemical plant, for example, generates employment and tax revenues for the local area as well as profits for often distant shareholders and products for a widespread market. But it may also produce pollutants which affect those downstream or downwind, resulting in adverse health effects for people who may enjoy none of the aforementioned benefits. A 'half way house' (for prisoners nearing the end of their term of incarceration) which is located in a residential neighbourhood can benefit the prisoners by reintroducing them to open society gradually, but can negatively affect the property values in the adjacent neighbourhood if it is seen as a facility with undesirable residents. Every society has 'LULUs' (locally unwanted land uses) but the US has a strong claim both to more kinds of land uses which are considered undesirable but necessary (ranging from prisons and brothels to garbage incinerators and discount stores), and to a governmental structure which generates more discussion and controversy than most (Popper 1983, 1984). There are, of course, also desirable amenities which people seek to have located nearby – such facilities as parks and libraries, or the clean, high-technology research and development centres which bring in tax revenues and high wages and are often aesthetically attractive. The location of both public and private noxious and salutary facilities can exacerbate or ease social problems.

It should not be assumed that all social problems in the US have fundamentally geographic causes or solutions, any more than they are all traceable to poverty and injustice. Nevertheless, even such less obviously spatial problems as alcoholism, child abuse or suicide exhibit spatial patterns which may be useful to analyse both in exploring possible causal correlations and in planning strategies to alleviate or reduce them. The following portions of this chapter discuss problems of US society which have proven to be amenable to geographical analysis. The conclusion goes on to suggest other social problems which have so far been somewhat neglected but which might usefully be explored from a geographical perspective.

Geographic patterns of social inequality

While some would argue that the root cause of American social inequality is the economic inequality inherent in a capitalist economy, few would argue that poverty not only exists but is unequally distributed in society both spatially and between categories of people. Perhaps more geographic attention has been paid to the spatial correlates of poor people than to the possible underlying structural causes of

inequality, and to the inequalities and injustices which result from the inherent racism, agism and sexism of contemporary American life. Such 'isms' are, of course, by no means restricted to America, and one of the positive aspects of life in America is that such prejudices are more openly recognized and more officially addressed than in most other countries. Geographers have begun to contribute to this public analysis by documenting the conditions of racial ghettoes, exploring the restricted world of the elderly, or the spatial variation in the legal and economic rights of women versus men. Before turning to some of this work it is useful to summarize the geography of income inequality and poverty in the USA.

Income is the most convenient and most widely used surrogate for measuring the general economic status and control over the goods of society of a person or group. It should be remembered, however, that data on per capita or average incomes do not accurately reflect wealth. People who own great wealth (in land or stock holdings, for example) report as 'income' only the interest on their wealth. There were, for example, 248 000 millionaires (persons with assets over $1 000 000) in the US in 1976 (US Department of Commerce 1984). In the same year, the wealthiest 0.5 per cent of the population owned 13.8 per cent of the wealth in the US. While such wealthy people also usually have high incomes, the income figure alone does not accurately reflect the extent of their assets and power. It could also be argued that the income of poor people is not always an accurate surrogate for their level of living since it does not include such subsidies as rental assistance or food stamps (Fig. 8.1). Nevertheless, despite these and other cautions, per capita or family average incomes are the best single measure of access to the material benefits of society.

Tables 1.1 and 8.1 illustrate the extent of regional and inter-urban disparities in average income within the USA. These gradients are significant, but they are small in comparison with income disparities found within single States and cities. For example, whereas in the US in 1983 average per capita income was $11 675, ranging from $16 820 in Alaska (which also has a high cost of living – Connecticut is the most affluent mainland State with an

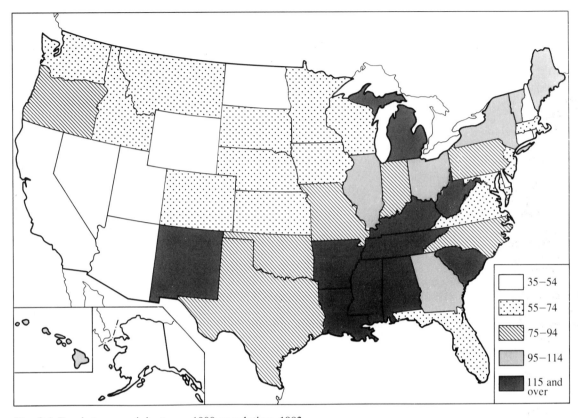

Fig. 8.1 Food stamp recipients per 1000 population, 1983

average of $14 826) to Mississippi at $8072, much greater contrasts can be found within a State such as Texas which has a strong average income (eighteenth in rank) but whose affluent ranchers and energy industrialists are balanced by over 2 million people living in poverty. Over a quarter of the State's black and Hispanic populations were in poverty in 1983, while fewer than 12 per cent of the white population were. Similarly, within a city like New York one can find millionaires residing on the Upper East Side of Manhattan less than a mile from thousands of people living beneath the official poverty line ($10 178 for a non-farm family of four in 1983).

The *poverty* rate, although fluctuating, remains high. In 1960 there were nearly 40 million (or 22.2 per cent) of Americans below the official poverty line. Twenty years later, in 1982, after the Great Society programmes and the War on Poverty, there were 34 million or 15 per cent of the population who were poor.

There are marked differences in poverty rates for various groups of the population. In 1982, one in every seven Americans over the age of 65 were poor (although that represents a significant improvement over the 1960 equivalent statistic of one in three). In 1983, nearly 13.8 million children lived in poverty and constituted 40 per cent of the total poor population of the US. The number of poor children increased by 3 million from 1968 to 1983, even though the total population of children decreased by 9 million (Congressional Budget Office 1985). Comparing poverty rates across race, the incidence of poverty among blacks and Hispanic Americans has consistently been over twice that for whites. In 1983, for example, the poverty rate for whites was 9.7 per cent of the population, compared to 32.4 per cent for blacks and 26.1 per cent for Hispanics: a differential which holds across different regions, spatial settings, and age and household characteristics (Table 8.2). Comparison of poverty rates by gender is

Table 8.1: Per capita money incomes for the fifty largest US cities, 1981

City		City	
New York, NY	$8 737	St Louis, MO	$7 054
Chicago, IL	8 333	Kansas City, MO	8 809
Los Angeles, CA	9 816	El Paso, TX	6 550
Philadelphia, PA	7 109	Atlanta, GA	7 809
Houston, TX	10 724	Pittsburgh, PA	8 277
Detroit, MI	7 090	Oklahoma City, OK	10 014
Dallas, TX	10 329	Cincinnati, OH	8 095
San Diego, CA	9 584	Ft Worth, TX	8 988
Phoenix, AZ	8 922	Minneapolis, MN	9 482
Baltimore, MD	7 076	Portland, OR	9 300
San Antonio, TX	6 936	Honolulu, HI	9 264
Indianapolis, IN	8 897	Long Beach, CA	9 978
San Francisco, CA	11 026	Tulsa, OK	11 059
		Buffalo, NY	7 140
Memphis, TN	7 542	Toledo, OH	8 246
Washington, DC	10 680	Miami, FL	7 244
Milwaukee, WI	8 285	Austin, TX	8 950
San Jose, CA	10 030	Oakland, CA	9 171
Cleveland, OH	6 799	Albuquerque, NM	8 817
Columbus, OH	7 925	Tucson, AZ	7 954
Boston, MA	7 783	Newark, NJ	5 292
New Orleans, LA	8 017	Charlotte, NC	9 287
Jacksonville, FL	8 217	Omaha, NE	9 194
Seattle, WA	11 006	Louisville, KY	7 542
Denver, CO	10 319	Birmingham, AL	6 896
Nashville-Davidson, TN	8 571		

Source: US Bureau of the Census, *Statistical Abstract of the US 1985*, Table 757, p. 454

Table 8.2: Poverty in America

	Per cent families below poverty level			
	All races	White	Black	Spanish origin
Total	12.3	9.7	32.4	26.1
Northeast	11.0	8.9	29.3	38.4
Midwest	12.1	9.8	38.0	24.8
South	13.7	9.8	33.1	23.3
West	11.6	10.2	23.8	23.1
In metropolitan areas	11.1	8.2	30.6	25.8
In central cities	16.3	10.8	34.2	29.5
Outside central cities	7.8	6.8	22.2	20.7
Outside metropolitan areas	14.8	12.5	38.3	28.1
Age of householder:				
15 to 24 years	29.5	23.3	66.4	46.6
25 to 44 years	14.2	11.3	34.0	28.0
45 to 54 years	8.8	6.8	24.9	18.5
55 to 64 years	8.6	6.9	23.8	17.0
65 years and over	8.7	6.8	27.2	19.1
Size of family:				
2 persons	10.1	8.1	28.7	21.8
3 persons	11.4	9.0	29.9	26.3
4 persons	11.7	9.3	31.1	24.0
5 persons	21.5	17.8	38.0	33.8
7 persons or more	36.3	25.8	60.0	40.6

Source: US Bureau of the Census, *Statistical Abstract of the US 1985*, Table 764, p. 458

a little more complex since most households contain an adult of both sexes. However, many data point to the greater incidence of poverty among women. In 1983, 40 per cent of the people living in households headed by women were poor and nearly half of all poor families were headed by women. In brief, poverty in the US is strongly linked to *age* (whether child or elderly), *gender* (female), *race and ethnicity* (especially black or Hispanic), and *household type* (especially single female-headed households).

Spatially, high incidences of poverty are generally positively associated with race, but less so with age or gender. For example, poverty rates are high in the South – the five States which, in 1980, had the highest such rates for families were all southern (Mississippi 18.7 per cent, Louisiana 15.1 per cent, Arkansas 14.9 per cent, Alabama 14.8 per cent, Kentucky 14.6 per cent, compared to a national average of 9.6 per cent) and have higher than

average proportions of blacks in their populations (Fig. 8.2). As noted in the previous chapter, the most distressed cities in America all have high ratios of minorities in their populations, and within cities black and Hispanic neighbourhoods are frequently those with the lowest average incomes. On the other hand, places with high concentrations of elderly are less likely to be poor. Florida and Arizona, for example, States which attract large numbers of retired people (at 17.4 per cent, Florida has the highest ratio of persons over 65 of any State), have poverty rates similar to the national average. The explanation for this lies in the fact that it is the more affluent elderly who can afford to retire to the sun, while those in poverty 'age in place' and live in age-integrated places. While the spatial distribution of women and children is not identical with that of men, it is much more similar (there is much less spatial segregation by gender than by age or race) thus except at the microscale there is little

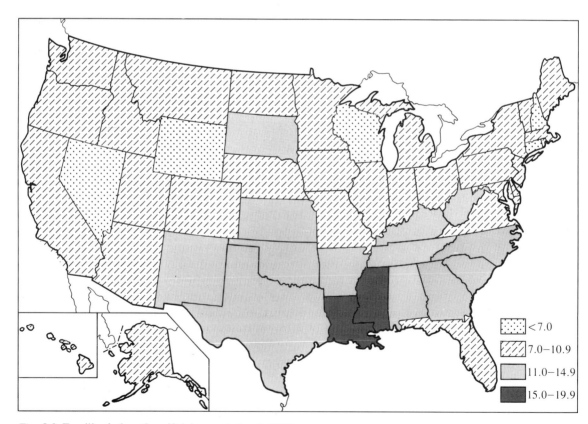

Fig. 8.2 Families below the official poverty level, 1980

spatial indication of the 'feminization of poverty'.

Landscapes of poverty, both urban and rural, are nevertheless quite recognizable in the US. While hunger and malnutrition, for example, are not very visible to visitors or to America's own middle classes, it does not take much of a detour from the beaten track to encounter food stores routinely accepting food stamps, soup kitchens for the homeless and hungry, and 'thrift bakery outlets' selling day-old bread. The size and quality of maintenance of the housing stock, the modal age of cars parked outside, the mix of services (whether storefront church or aerobic dance studio), the amount of greenery and landscaping in cities and, in rural areas, the presence of abandoned petrol stations, chicken farms and unscreened scrap yards are all key components of the landscapes of poverty.

The geography of prejudice and discrimination

The Declaration of Independence proposed that all men [*sic*] are created equal and are endowed with certain unalienable rights. In theory, American social organization is based on this premise, but in reality deep inequalities exist, originating from underlying prejudices and stereotypes. While discrimination based on ethnicity, age and gender often results in the economic inequalities discussed previously, there are other manifestations which are geographically significant, and sometimes spatial patterns of segregation serve to reinforce the feelings of prejudice. In this section we explore some issues related to the geography of prejudice against some groups in American society.

Gender problems and the feminization of poverty

There is growing recognition of the fact that while men and women live in the same communities and even the same homes, their experience of and behaviour in those spaces can be quite different. Even in childhood, females are socialized to stay closer to home, not to explore far, and to develop a 'healthy fear' of strange people and places. The smaller home range of the girl is mirrored in adult life by the greater concentration on local neighbourhood space and shorter journey to work of the typical female compared to her male counterpart. This restricted spatial experience is both a product of social expectations about women's roles and a contribution to those stereotypes. While women in most cultures are more 'place bound' than men, the relatively strong progress towards gender equality in the US has still not eliminated the difference. As a result, most women are more tied to the home both functionally (having greater domestic responsibilities than men) and perhaps emotionally than are men. While women in increasing numbers are employed outside the home (by 1980 slightly over half of working-age women in the US were in the labour force, although fewer than a quarter of them worked full-time, year-round), they are more likely than men to take a job closer to home or within reach of public transportation (Hanson and Johnson 1985). This spatial restriction (a function of child care, domestic responsibilities and lesser access to automobiles) contributes to the considerable occupational and income disparities between the sexes. In a society so reliant on the private automobile as is the US, the environment has come to be designed for car drivers, so that the lack of access to a car is a more severe handicap than in, say, Britain. While women are a majority of the population, they are only 41 per cent of the licensed drivers and studies indicate that not only do males own cars more often than females, but when ownership is shared, the man has more frequent use of the household vehicle (Fox 1983). Ironically, a group of women who *do* have access to car – the stereotypical suburban housewife with a station wagon – may find it a mixed blessing as the sprawl of suburban communities dictates a role as household chauffeur. Many a mother spends hours a week transporting family members.

Although women and men are theoretically equal in the eyes of the law, some US laws have different impacts on men and women, and there are spatial variations both in legal protections and their effects. Some States have legislation which bars discrimination on the basis of sex, but in others (conspicuously in the South), there are no such legal guarantees. The Equal Rights Amendment (ERA) to the US Constitution, originally introduced in 1923 and passed by Congress in 1972, failed to obtain ratification by the required two-thirds of the States by the 1982 deadline. The States which did not ratify the ERA are concentrated in the South, but also include Illinois, Arizona, Nevada and Utah. In the latter state, Mormon religious beliefs about women's appropriate roles is an explanatory factor. Political conservatism, especially in rural Illinois, has been suggested in the other cases (Mazey and Lee 1983). As a result of the failure of the passage of ERA, there are today differences between States in such laws affecting women as divorce, child support, access to credit and housing, and employment.

A recent and critically important social problem which has received much media attention is the 'feminization of poverty'. In the late 1970s and early 1980s there was a dramatic increase in the proportion of the poverty population which was female. Two-thirds of adults who are poor are women. Women head half of all poor families, but only 15 per cent of all families are female headed. Among blacks, in 1982, 47 per cent of all families were headed by women and nearly 60 per cent of these were in poverty, while the equivalent 1980 data for Hispanics was 23 per cent female heads, of whom 55 per cent were in poverty. The two fundamental explanations for this increase in poverty among women are the significantly lower occupational status and wages of working women and the rapid increase in divorce and teenage pregnancy.

In 1980 the median income of female household heads was $10 408. In the same year, a third of all women working full-time, year-round, earned less than $7000 while the median white male income was $17 000. Such women averaged 62 cents for every $1.00 their male counterparts were paid. Hence while poverty for men is often a function of unemployment, women form a large part of the working poor. Women are employed overwhelmingly in low-paid occupational categories. In the US, about 40 per cent of employed women are clerical workers. In manufacturing, women are over-represented in such low-paying industries as clothing and textiles rather than higher paying auto or energy plants. Most women in service industries are in direct delivery rather than management positions. Rather little analysis

has yet been made of the spatial aspects of women's employment, but there are indications that some industries, such as the 'back offices' of corporations, seek to locate in places with a good supply of cheap but docile female labour (Nelson 1984). Ironically, the same big cities which offer increasingly attractive employment and living opportunities to the upwardly mobile career woman are also the home to growing numbers of low-income women, many of whom are struggling to bring up children alone.

In addition to low status in the field of employment, the growing feminization of poverty results from the high and growing divorce rates and from out-of-wedlock births. Between 1960 and 1980 the divorce rate in the US grew by 141 per cent. If current rates continue, half of all marriages will end in divorce, and two-thirds of black marriages will do so (Thornton and Freedman 1983). Divorce is seen by some as a social problem in itself – an indication of a deteriorating and unstable family life and of social stress. An alternative view sees many divorces as appropriate adjustments to changing personal needs and views the greater social acceptance of divorce as beneficial. Some support for this view is provided in the greater reported satisfaction Americans have with their marriages than was the case 20 years ago. However, whichever view is taken, the economic disbenefits of divorce, which are usually borne disproportionately by women and children, are indisputable. In the US, only 7 per cent of divorced women received alimony regularly, and a Census Bureau study found that fewer than half of all children living with their mothers after a divorce were supported by payments from their fathers (Preston 1984). Divorce rates vary regionally and tend to be higher in the West and lowest in the Northeast which has a higher proportion of Catholics and Jews in the population (Fig. 8.3). Because divorce frequently produces a precipitous decline in the economic status of women, they are often unable financially to remain in the marital home and move to rental housing in more marginal neighbourhoods. Local regulations in some places, which limit the number of unrelated individuals sharing a household, reduce the potential for sharing residential space. Only about half the States (none of which are southern) have laws prohibiting sex

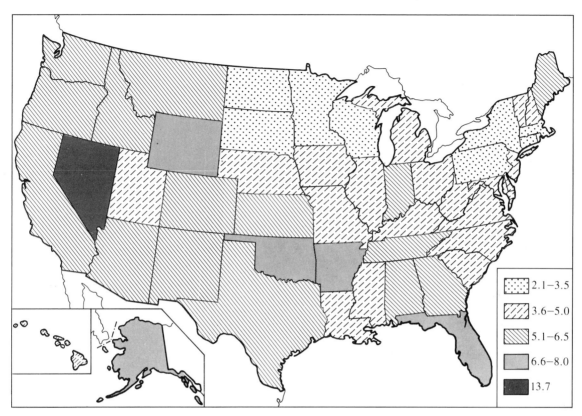

Fig. 8.3 Divorces per 1000 population, 1984

discrimination in real estate transactions and financing (Brown *et al.* 1977), and home ownership by women in the US is low. In 1980, only 18 per cent of owner-occupied houses were owned by women and almost half of these home owners were over 65 years old, often inheriting the house on the death of their spouse (Shalala and McGeorge 1981).

Interestingly, the redolently geographical title of 'displaced homemakers' has been applied to the increasingly large category of women who, because of the death of, or divorce from, a spouse, find that not only their economic means of support has gone, but their unpaid household labour has no market value. Typically lacking social security, unemployment insurance or welfare assistance (assuming no dependent children), such women are certainly displaced from their former niche in society, and often from their former home as well. The prevalence of displaced homemakers is presumably higher in older suburbs where middle-aged

women may have spent two decades raising children while their husbands had waged work. In more affluent suburbs, widows and divorcees are less likely to be destitute and in working-class inner-city neighbourhoods women more frequently seek some employment to contribute to the family's support.

The growing number of children living with only their maternal parent is only partly attributable to divorce. Unmarried motherhood is a growing phenomenon, especially among young women. Teenage pregnancy is seen by many as a serious social problem. 'National figures indicate that between the ages of thirteen and nineteen, 225 out of every 1000 white and Hispanic girls, and 515 out of every 1000 black girls, will give birth' (Campbell 1984: 34). Campbell reports that in New York City 30 000 teenagers become pregnant each year, about half obtaining abortions. In 1982, babies born to teenage mothers accounted for 17 per cent of all black and Hispanic births in New York.

While not all these teenagers are unmarried, the majority are, and it is estimated that 70 per cent of New York's teenagers giving birth will be on welfare within a year. As Goodman succinctly puts it, '. . . the absolute easiest way to be poor is to be born out of wedlock to a young woman . . . 92.8 per cent of all children in black, single female-headed families where the mother is under 30 and did not complete high school, are in poverty' (Goodman 1985: 88). The causes of the increase in teenage motherhood are controversial and beyond our scope here, but suffice it to note that rates of teenage maternity are highest in cities and among minority and low-income populations. Teenage motherhood is both associated with and results in high rates of hardship and deprivation. There are above-average incidences of low birth weights and high infant mortality among the offspring of teenage mothers.

While the feminization of poverty is a national trend, the problem is more severe in *locations* in which there is already a higher proportion of poverty and of minority populations. Single female heads of households are concentrated in central cities (Smith 1985). In some places, low-income women are highly segregated – many inner-city housing projects accommodate primarily female householders and their children. While it may be argued that the spatial concentration of such families facilitates the delivery of social services such as child and health care, the resultant ghettoization both stigmatizes and makes vulnerable those families. Children attending the local school have classmates from similarly disadvantaged homes and the probability of synergistic effects of multiple deprivations increases.

The *causes* of poverty among men and women differ. In a study which listed all the possible sources of poverty, about half (e.g. poor health, racism) can apply equally to both sexes, but the other half (divorce, sexism, pregnancy) apply to women only (Pearce and McAdoo 1981). And most of these causes show varying intensity over space, partly because, as we have seen, social attitudes and State legislation towards women's roles and rights are geographically varied within the US. Lee and Schultz (1982) found that, using indicators of income, education and occupation, overall women have better conditions or status in the Northeast and West US, but it is also in these regions that the disparity between male and female status is greatest. Men do best in places where the differences between the sexes are greatest, but then so, ironically, do women!

The foregoing discussion by no means exhausts the issues related to sex discrimination which are of geographical interest. Differences by State in legal access to funding for abortion, in health care and nutrition programmes for pregnant and new mothers, and to birth control education reflect differential patterns of well-being for women. Economic fluctuations and spatial patterns of disinvestment affect, of course, the well-being of both sexes, but women are not infrequently victims both of unemployment but of increased incidence of abuse from unemployed spouses. The underlying patriarchy of the built environment, public displays of pornography, and the psychological and material restrictions on women's mobility are also environmental manifestations of prejudice based on gender (Hayden 1984). The particular social problem of sex discrimination adversely affects at least half (and one might argue all) of American society.

Age

That America is a youth-oriented society is a well-known cliché. A country which is both historically young, and has a relatively young median age for an advanced industrialized country, has developed many values and mores based more on the promise of youth than the wisdom of age. It is a society which is conventionally child-oriented, and in which ageing is deferred as long as possible by whatever means are available. It is also, however, a society in which demographic and social changes are producing trends contrary to the conventional wisdom. While age discrimination is far from absent, it could be argued that though psychological and social prejudice is still directed against the old, economic discrimination is now more felt by children.

Senior citizens: the golden age?
Between 1960 and 1980 the number of people in the US over the age of 65 grew by 54 per cent. During the decade of the 1970s the elderly

US population grew at a higher rate than that of the total population of India (Preston 1984). On the other hand, the number of children under the age of 15 declined by 7 per cent from 1960 to 1982 due to falling birth rates (see Ch. 2). The growing numbers of elderly, who are, of course, enfranchised, has led to an increase in political power by this group and a rapid improvement in their economic situation. In 1960, 35.2 per cent of persons over 65 years old were in poverty. By 1982 that figure had been reduced to 14.6 per cent – just under the national rate for all persons. If non-cash transfer payments such as Medicare are taken into account, real poverty among the elderly declines even further to an estimated 4 per cent in 1982 (Preston 1984). Meanwhile, the proportion of all children under 14 years living in poverty rose from 16 per cent in 1970 to 23 per cent in 1982. Additionally, in the first half of the 1980s there was a rapid decline in transfer payments (such as Aid to Families with Dependent Children) to children. In 1983, 13.8 million children were living in poverty in the US and they constituted 40 per cent of the total poor population. A federal government study on 'Children in Poverty' reported that almost half of all black children and more than a third of Hispanic children were poor (Congressional Budget Office 1985). Much of the increase in poverty among children is, of course, related to the growth of female-headed households and the feminization of poverty discussed previously.

Although discrimination against the old is decreasing economically, it is still manifested in other ways which have geographical significance. The self-segregation of the elderly into retirement communities is partially a desire to be protected both from violent crime and from the more subtle violence of rejection from a society with youthful norms of beauty and behaviour. Consumer tastes as portrayed in advertising are very much those of youth, despite the growing economic power of the old. Thus the landscape of commercial advertising (a landscape element quite dominant in the American environment) still reflects a society in which the old should neither be seen nor heard (except on the subject of laxatives).

Florida, with 17.4 per cent of its population over 65 years in 1982, has the highest proportion of elderly, largely as a result of retirement migration. The northern Great Plains States have higher than the 11.6 per cent national average because while younger people have migrated from the rural areas such as the Dakotas, Nebraska and Kansas, the elderly have remained to constitute a growing segment of the population. A large elderly population can present challenges to society in straining the supply of health-care facilities, in constituting a voting block which can (though by no means always does) oppose school bonds, and which places particular demands (for housing, transportation, meals on wheels, etc.) on local governments (Biggar 1984). However, as the economic situation of the elderly improves, and as federal level programmes such as Social Security and Medicare assume an increasingly greater role in governmental redistribution, the social issues related to spatial concentration of the elderly are diminishing. There remain, nevertheless, the more personal problems of being elderly in a youth society. Geographers have written about the limited spatial worlds of the elderly, their greater dependence on place for both material and psychological well-being, and the costs of displacement and environmental change. Decreasing personal mobility with age due both to infirmity and lack of either a car or a driver's licence can reduce access to friends and services, and diminishes the quality of life (Golant 1979).

Childhood: new realities of a youth-oriented society

More attention has been paid by geographers and others to the problems of ageing than to those of childhood. Although geographers have contributed to such social issues as school desegregation and spatial inequalities of funding for education, the deeply serious problems experienced by many children in the US have been largely ignored by the discipline. 'Right to Lifers' (anti-abortionists) consider high *abortion* rates as one of the most critical problems facing society. Regarding abortion as a moral question for society rather than for the individual, anti-abortionists feel that children are being legally denied the potential for life. The abortion rate, as measured by the number of legal abortions per 1000 live births, averaged 426 for the US as a whole in 1982; however,

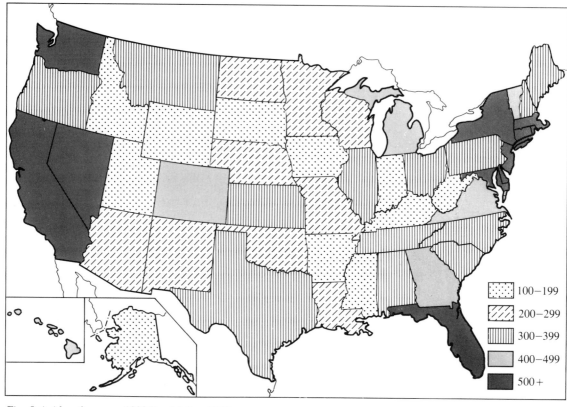

▦	100–199
▨	200–299
▥	300–399
▨	400–499
■	500+

Fig. 8.4 Abortions per 1000 live births, 1982

there were wide interstate variations (Fig. 8.4). Utah, with a strong Mormon influence, had the lowest rate at 100, while in New York State the rate was highest at 731. Pregnancies of residents in large cities are more likely to be terminated by abortion than is the case in suburban or rural areas. In Washington, DC, in 1982 there were 1517 legal abortions for every 1000 births. Those who support legal abortion nevertheless deplore high abortion rates as indicative frequently of a lack of birth control knowledge and the inability of the mother to support a child. Increasingly, females who are themselves still children become pregnant. In 1980, 40.9 per cent of births to unmarried women were to those under 20 years of age, and nearly 30 per cent of legal abortions that year were for women in that age group. Knowledge of the geographical incidence of births to unmarried women and of abortions is essential for the effective delivery of services such as birth control education, maternal and infant nutrition, day care, health and other supportive services.

Child abuse reached apparently epidemic proportions in the early 1980s and though it is thought to be prevalent in every socio-economic sector, the incidence of reported abuse rises during economic recessions as unemployment strains both the psyches and purses of parents. While child abuse is seen as a serious and complex problem, having ramifications far beyond the particular household in which it occurs, virtually no geographic attention has been given to either its distribution, possible contributory environmental factors or the provision of services to reduce its incidence. Homicide is the second, and suicide the third leading cause of death among males 15–24 years of age in 1980. Homicide rates are highest in the South, while suicide rates are highest in the Mountain States. Recent research showing a consistently high rate of teenage suicide in these States over time suggest that they may be attributable to higher rates of stress, relatively low membership in organized religions, and perhaps the greater availability of guns (the preferred tool of suicide among males) (Greenberg, Carey, Popper, 1987).

Another problem of major current concern in society is that of *missing children*. Each year thousands of children 'disappear' from their homes. Many are taken by a non-custodial spouse, others run away from homes, while some are abducted. The phenomenon, which results in immense suffering to the children and their families, has become the focus of intense publicity and campaigns to locate missing children are underway. Clearly this is a locational problem, and missing children, especially runaways, tend to congregate in particular localities. Geographers could assist in alleviating the problem both by identifying such environments which are perceived as offering potential to runaways and perhaps by analysing probable routes and destinations of abducting parents and others. Interestingly, one of the strategies of the National Child Safety Council has been to urge all children to 'Learn and Memorize: Your full address, including city, state, and zip code: Where your home, city, state and country are on a globe or map of the world' (From a 1985 advertisement on a grocery bag!) A protection against being missing is to know where you live (even if it would be difficult to locate one's home within a city on a globe!).

Race and ethnicity

As discussed in Chapter 2, the US is, both in rhetoric and reality, a nation of immigrants. Apart from the 'Native' Americans or American Indians (who in 1980 numbered 1.4 million of the total US population of 226 million), other inhabitants of the country have arrived since its historic (as opposed to pre-historic) 'discovery' by Europeans. In 1980, 14 million people, or 6 per cent of the population of the US, was foreign born. Until the 1960s, most immigrants were European and the largest non-European origin group were descendants of slaves from Africa. However, following the abandonment in 1965 of a quota system which favoured immigrants from Europe, the largest wave of immigration in this century ensued with

the majority originating in Asia or Latin America. In 1984, immigration to the US constituted two-thirds of *all* the immigration in the *world*.

Despite considerable success in melding a society made up of people with widely differing cultural experiences, the 'melting pot' has not been without pain. Many new immigrants have faced prejudice which faded only slowly as the group became assimilated into the mainstream of economic and social life. Ironically, a group with one of the longest histories of residence in the country, Afro-Americans or blacks, continues to experience the worst discrimination, while the largest current group of immigrants, Hispanics, is probably the second most discriminated against group.

Probably both because race and ethnicity show much greater variation in spatial distribution than do gender or age (that is, there is considerably more segregation by race than by sex or age), and because ethnicity is an important factor in landscape formation, geographers have devoted considerably more attention to the former than the latter and have helped to document the deleterious effects of discrimination and segregation upon particular racial and ethnic groups. Residential segregation, experienced especially by blacks, has strong effects on access to goods and services, to property appreciation and even to social networks.

Black America

Although black Americans are one of the oldest immigrant groups, they could also be thought of as one of the most recent in attaining full legal status in the country. As late as the 1960s there were laws at all governmental levels which discriminated against blacks, denying them equal access to homes, education and employment. In 1980 there were 26.6 million black Americans who formed 11.7 per cent of the population. Prior to the twentieth century, the vast majority of blacks lived in the South, but as described in Chapter 2, the first half of this century witnessed a major migration from the rural South both to cities in that region and, more significantly, to urban areas of the Northeast and North Central States. Figure 8.5 illustrates this migration of blacks between 1900 and 1970 showing both the

1900

Fig. 8.5 Black population distribution, by State, 1900 and 1970
Source: Hartshorn (1980), Fig. 13–1 (p. 263) and Fig. 13–5 (p. 267)

interregional migration from South to North and intraregional movement from rural to urban areas. Fuelled by the promise of improved economic conditions and a more tolerant social environment, blacks left the farms of the South, where mechanization was in any case reducing labour demand, and moved to the industrial cities of the North where factories offered jobs. The Civil Rights movement of the 1960s combined with governmental programmes to alleviate poverty produced a significant (though far from sufficient) improvement in the status and well-being of black Americans. More recently, however, some of these gains have been lost and in the mid-1980s, despite the presence of a vibrant black middle class, the lot of many other black Americans is no better than 20 years ago.

On virtually every measure of socio-economic well-being, blacks are significantly worse off than whites. In 1982, the median family income for blacks was $13 598 compared

1970

Per cent black
population urban

0–20

21.1–40

40.1–60

60.1–80

80.1–100

States are drawn proportional to
their per cent black population

Represents 10 per cent

to $24 603 for whites. The average black household owns about one-third the wealth (equity in a house, financial assets, etc.) of the average white family – $26 608 for blacks compared with $68 891 for whites (O'Hare 1983). One in every three blacks lives in poverty. The unemployment rate for blacks is consistently over twice that of whites. In 1960 the median income of black families was 55 per cent of the median of white families. It was the same in 1982.

The causes of the persistent lower status of blacks are controversial. Legal and illegal forms of discrimination, many forms of racism both subtle and blatant, and the legacy of generations of unequal and inferior treatment are doubtlessly major contributors. In a classic case of 'blaming the victim', some commentators now point to the prevalence of female family heads as reflecting a matriarchal culture in which men have not been encouraged to

assume familial economic responsibilities. The fact that the conditions imposed by slavery and its aftermath, as well as the contemporary welfare system (which in half of all States denies aid to dependent children where there is an able-bodied male in the household) requires mothers to support their children, is conveniently ignored!

While the major migration of blacks to northern cities was in part a response to the economic opportunities there, the subsequent decline of manufacturing industries, employment loss, fiscal distress and growing poverty populations during the 1960s and 1970s led to a small reverse migration of blacks back to the South during the 1970s. More conspicuously, the limited but steady movement of blacks to the suburbs mirrors the growing disparity of socio-economic status within the black population. About a quarter of all black families earned incomes of over $25 000 in 1982. Many of these families had two wage earners and lived in the suburbs. The data indicate that married working black families with both parents in the labour force have a median income 3.4 times that of black families headed by single women (Felder 1984). Black families who live in suburban areas of major cities have the highest incomes of any black group defined residentially, but constituted only 14 per cent of all black families. In contrast, 54 per cent of black families live in central cities and had a median income of only $13 362 in cities of over a million residents in 1982. Regionally, black incomes were highest in the West (median $16 508) and lowest in the North Central region ($12 374). On the other hand, the difference between black incomes and white incomes is much greater in the South (with the exception of Florida) than it is elsewhere. In a ranking of the forty-eight SMSAs with a black population of 100 000 or more in 1980, Nassau-Suffolk (NY) came out best, with median black household incomes at 77 per cent the level of median white household incomes. In bottom-ranked Memphis (TN), median black household incomes were less than half of those of white households. Among the top ten metropolitan areas according to this measure, seven were outside the South, and the other three were in Florida. The biggest *absolute difference* between black and white median household incomes, however, was in Newark (NJ) ($10 806, compared to the average absolute difference for all forty eight SMSAs of $7941; O'Hare 1986).

Harold Rose, among others, has speculated about the implications of this growing disparity: '. . . [W]ill the continued movement of blacks to the suburbs, as occurred during the seventies, drive a wedge between black have- and have-not communities (anchored in core cities)? Or, do the communities constitute single economic and social entities that are mutually dependent upon each other?' (Rose 1985: 73). While the future of low-income black Americans depends more upon the will of non-blacks to bring about equality through employment, education, fair housing, and so forth, the political power of blacks to influence that process depends partially on the cohesion and unity of the black community. Residential integration may reduce the power of blacks as a voting block, but it can also improve their access to numerous services and amenities which affect one's quality of life, and indirectly increase political, through economic, power. The suburbanization of the black population is not necessarily increasing integration at an equivalent rate because many blacks are moving to predominantly black suburbs (Lake 1981). Racism may well be the most tenacious social problem in America.

Hispanic America
Hispanics are among the fastest growing population groups in the US today. In 1950 there were fewer than 4 million, but estimates for 1985 approached 18 million. Mexican-Americans constitute the largest subgroup (nearly 9 million) while Puerto Ricans on the mainland are the second (Puerto Ricans are US citizens whether on the island or mainland). It is estimated that a quarter of Hispanics have immigrated to the US within the last 10 years (Church 1985). The Hispanic population is young (the median age is 23 in contrast to 30 for all Americans) and has higher than US average fertility rates. If present trends continue, Hispanics could be the largest American ethnic group (including those of English ancestry) by the year 2000.

Hispanics are a culturally varied population which includes affluent Cubans as well as poor migrant farm workers from Central America. The median income of Hispanics in 1983 was $16 960 compared to $25 760 for non-Hispanic whites. Hispanic immigrants are typically much more upwardly mobile than the resident black population, and discrimination against them is less intense, though by no means uncommon. Half of all Hispanics live in Texas or California, with New York State having the third highest total. Although many immigrants come from rural areas, within the US nearly 90 per cent live in metropolitan areas and 50 per cent in central cities (Davis, Haub and Willette 1983). Los Angeles, with 2 million Hispanics, is the Mexican-American 'capital', although San Antonio has a majority Hispanic population and the first big-city Hispanic mayor. Miami is the centre of Cuban life in the US, and New York that of Puerto Ricans.

Other than issues related to discrimination, the major problem involving the Hispanic community is that of illegal immigration, discussed in Chapter 2. The number of illegal immigrants is, of course, unknown and estimates vary widely. Recent Census Bureau figures are in the range of 2 to 4 million people, of whom a majority are from Mexico and other Latin American countries. In 1984, over a million aliens were arrested crossing the US–Mexico border. Some of these arrests were of the same persons several times, and estimating the undetected crossings is impossible. Illegal immigrants may find an improved standard of living in the US, but they also live in some of the worst conditions within the country. Working for less than the legal minimum wage, without employment benefits, and unable to take advantage of a range of government services, illegal immigrants also face resentment even from within their own ethnic group since they will work for less and thus may hold down wages for legal immigrants.

The causes and costs of crime

Crime is generally regarded as a major social problem in the US and at times opinion polls indicate it as being the most important concern to the public. Crime rates, as measured by reported statistics compiled by the US Department of Justice, have shown steady, if occasionally fluctuating, increases since 1960. Crime consists of acts (of commission or omission) which are unlawful. It has numerous costs, some of which are more readily measurable than others. The financial costs of lost material goods, productivity and law enforcement are in the billions of dollars each year (Harries 1974). The losses of life (of victims) and liberty (of perpetrators), the physical and psychological suffering of both, and the social instability resulting from crime are incalculable.

Crime rates in the US, compared to other industrialized, urbanized societies, are rather high, particularly for some categories of crime. Homicide rates, especially those perpetrated with a gun, are notoriously high compared to Britain. However, it might be kept in mind that the US, with a written constitution and extremely long and complex sets of statutory laws at each level of government, also has more

laws to be disobeyed than does, for example, the UK. Seven crimes which are regarded as among the most significant are labelled 'index crimes' and used in various analyses of crime rates. The index crimes are criminal homicide, forcible rape, robbery, aggravated assault, burglary, larceny of property over $50 value, and automobile theft. Figure 8.6 shows the regional variations in this crime index for 1983.

Much of the geographic work on crime has been concerned with such variations in its incidence. Presumably knowing *where* crime rates of various kinds are high can help in the explanation of the causes of crime, and thus its prevention. Thus a body of research documents such things as the higher homicide rates of the South (Fig. 8.7), the tendency for crime rates to increase with city population size (Table 8.3) and, within cities, for crime to generally be concentrated in central areas and to decrease with distance from the centre (Fig. 8.8). The same, and related work, shows that high crime rates are positively associated with the prevalence in the population of youthful males, minority groups, single parent households, poverty, unemployment, low educational levels and poor housing (e.g. Herbert 1982).

It is at this point, however, that opinions differ about causation and policies to reduce crime. Put simply, one school of thought – that dominant in America – sees law as an expression of consensus in a value-neutral state. The analysis of where crime occurs can assist in such decisions as where to allocate law enforcement resources, and how to reduce the environmental opportunity for crime by design and planning. The design of 'defensible spaces', of brighter street lighting, of more frequent patrols by security officers will, indeed, often reduce crime rates in a local area. Liberal interpreters of the same spatial data urge such measures as improved economic opportunity and education in high crime areas. Noting that not only the perpetrators, but the victims, of much crime are from the same social and ethnic groups, they argue the carrot of better opportunity rather than the stick of greater punishment. A more radical interpretation, however, is that much behaviour which is labelled crime is actually resistance to the social control necessary in a society in which the highly unequal distribution of economic and political

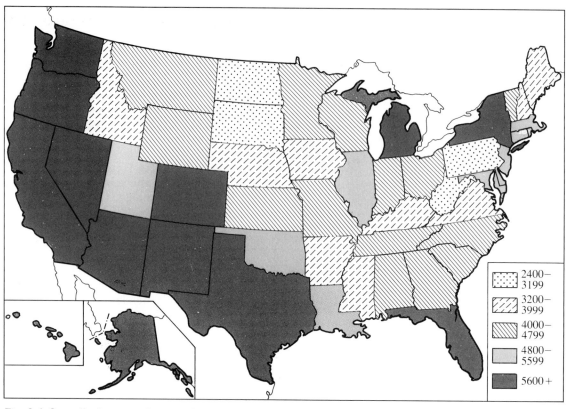

Fig. 8.6 Overall crime rate: known offences per 100 000 population, 1983

Legend:
2400–3199
3200–3999
4000–4799
4800–5599
5600+

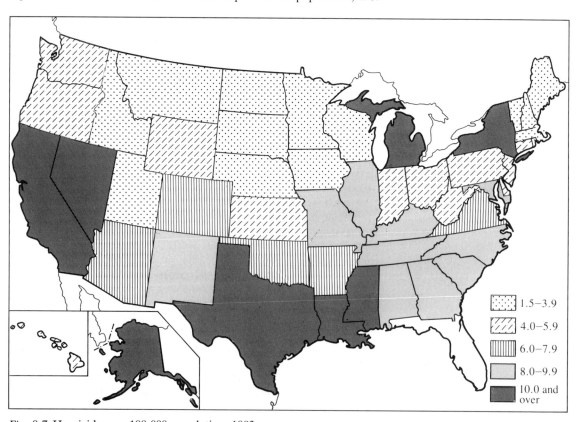

Fig. 8.7 Homicides per 100 000 population, 1983

Legend:
1.5–3.9
4.0–5.9
6.0–7.9
8.0–9.9
10.0 and over

Table 8.3: Urban crime rates: violent offences known to the police per 100 000 population

Cities with a population of:	1983	Average annual per cent change	
		1974–78	*1979–83*
250 000 or more	1 294	0.3	1.1
100 000–249 999	736	1.1	1.2
50 000–99 999	511	4.6	–0.7
25 000–49 999	403	2.4	–1.0
10 000–24 999	297	2.5	–1.5
Fewer than 10 000	260	3.0	–1.8
Selected cities:			
New York	1 868	1.2	0.1
Baltimore	2 003	–1.1	0.5
Washington	1 915	–3.1	4.5
Detroit	2 169	–4.5	6.8
San Francisco	1 403	8.9	–4.3
Los Angeles	1 692	5.4	2.8
Dallas	1 149	7.0	–3.0
Memphis	1 138	–0.8	7.6
Philadelphia	1 003	–6.8	4.9
Chicago	1 317	–8.5	No data
Phoenix	625	2.0	–6.2
San Diego	582	4.6	–3.0
Indianapolis	893	0.6	2.4
San Antonio	609	–9.3	5.4

Source: US Bureau of the Census, *Statistical Abstract of the US 1985*, Table 278, p. 168

power serves the dominant class at the expense of the poor (Peet 1975; Herbert 1982). Such theorists also point to the relative lack of social concern about 'white-collar' crimes such as tax evasion or embezzlement, which involve many times the money that, for example, character-izes car theft, from the uniform crime index. Furthermore, they interpret 'street' crime (as opposed to 'suite' crime) as an informal redis-tribution of wealth or as an expression of the frustration of powerlessness. The fact that many of the victims of crime are themselves poor, and that in 'civil disturbances' much of the rioting and damage is confined to depressed neighbourhoods (Wohlenberg 1982) tends to support this thesis of frustration. The solution to crime in this case lies in the reduction and elimination of society's inequalities.

Most existing geographical work on crime focuses largely on description of spatial patterns of certain crimes together with analyses which demonstrate spatial, and suggest causal, corre-lations. There is little doubt that working 'within the system', geographers can assist law enforcement by locating concentrations and environmental characteristics of crime, and can improve the services available to victims by helping locate such facilities as rape crisis centres or shelters for battered women. Some argue, however, that such work legitimates a repressive and discriminatory 'criminal justice' system in which, for example, one's chances of execution for murder are several times greater if one's skin is black, and to be sentenced to certain overcrowded jails is to be sentenced to almost certain rape.

Alcohol and 'substance' abuse

Smith and Hanham (1982, 1985) have reviewed the considerable regional variations within the US of alcohol consumption, alcoholism and attitudes towards this intoxicant. What follows is based on their work. Dependence on alcohol, drunkenness and the behavioural and physio-logical consequences of alcohol addiction do

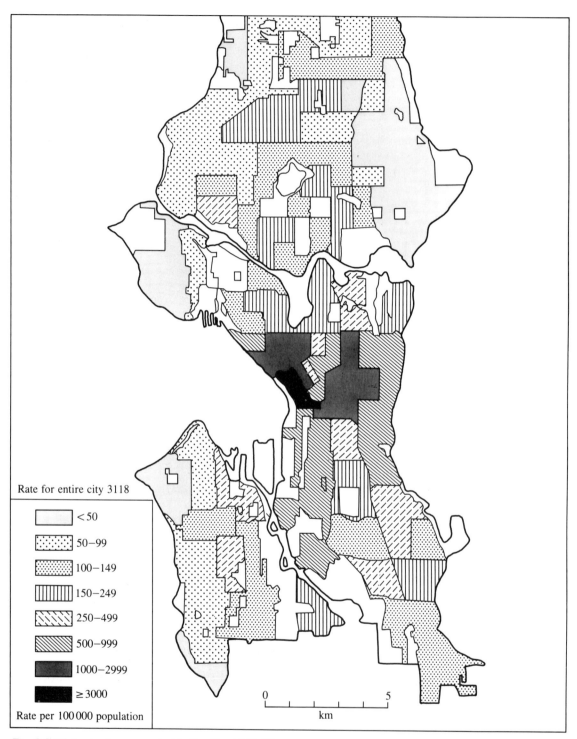

Fig. 8.8 Violent crimes reported in Seattle, 1960–70
Source: Harries (1974), Fig. 4.6, p. 76

not have merely individual costs. It is estimated that about 35 000 people die each year as a direct result of alcohol consumption (alcoholism, cirrhosis, etc.) and approximately 60 000 through accidents, homicides and suicides indirectly caused by alcohol. Alcohol abuse and alcoholism is conservatively estimated to have cost nearly $43 000 million in 1974, ignoring the hidden costs of domestic violence and the disruption of many lives. Conversely, alcohol is a major 'lubricant' of American society, being an element in such social interactions as weddings, business deals and block parties. It is used as a non-prescription drug to reduce stress, and is a large and profitable industry which employs thousands of people and generates considerable revenues for government.

Alcohol consumption patterns within the US (Fig. 8.9) show higher levels in the Northeast and West and lower in the Southeast and Midwest. Consumption patterns reflect atti-

tudes towards, availability of and preference for certain beverage categories of alcohol. The Temperance Movement and various regulations governing the sale of alcohol are strongest in the South where there is a preference for spirits, as opposed to wine or beer. Consumption is highest in the wine States of the Northeast and Pacific West. While alcoholism is not the only social problem caused by alcohol abuse (automobile accidents involving teenagers newly experiencing the drug are of great concern to many), its incidence is a surrogate measure of the problem. The incidence of alcoholics in the population (Fig. 8.10) shows strong (though far from perfect) correlation with consumption patterns and a better correlation with beverage preference variations. In general, States where beer is preferred over wine or spirits have lower alcoholism rates.

Analysis of geographical patterns can assist in seeking answers to questions which might

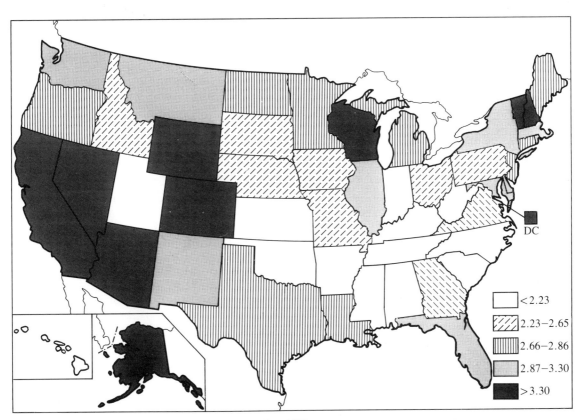

Fig. 8.9 Alcohol consumption, in gallons per capita, 1978
Source: Smith and Hanham (1982), Fig. 2, p. 23

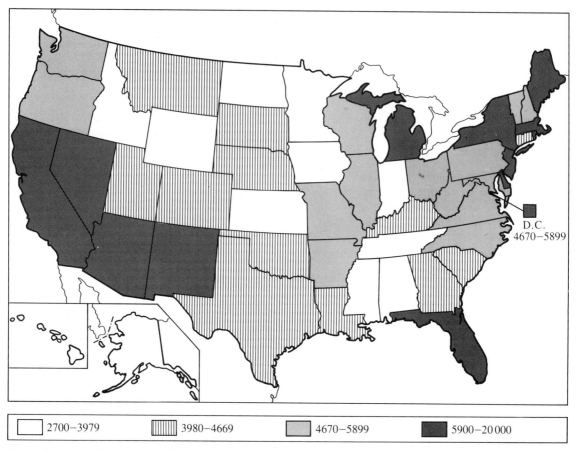

	2700–3979		3980–4669		4670–5899		5900–20 000

Fig. 8.10 Alcoholics per 100 000 adults, 1975
Source: Smith and Hanham (1982), Fig. 6, p. 41

reduce the problem of alcohol abuse. For example, do laws which restrict the availability of alcohol reduce consumption by alcoholics or merely change the type of beverage consumed? Do laws mandating later drinking ages (e.g. 21 years old as opposed to 18) reduce teenage drinking or merely increase the distance underage drinkers drive to obtain alcohol? What is the relationship between abstention rates in a locality and the prevalence of drinking? The answers to these and other questions can help in the very difficult task of formulating policy concerning alcohol in a society in which the substance plays so many, often contradictory, roles.

Perhaps because data on the sale and consumption of illegal drugs such as marijuana, cocaine, heroin and other narcotics are much more difficult to obtain and are less reliable, geographers have done little work on their spatial patterns of production and consumption. Despite the voluminous literature on the health effects, criminalization and political–economic issues involved in illegal drugs, geographers have to date contributed little to the study of this social problem. While knowledge of their production (e.g. the most abundant source of high-quality cannabis is probably Humboldt County, California) and consumption (e.g. the growing use of cocaine by young, upwardly mobile suburbanites) is widespread, and while law enforcement officials presumably have considerable information on supply routes and addiction patterns, geographers have yet to cultivate this fertile field of applied research. It might be argued also that substance abuse has greater problems for the individuals concerned than for society and that the 'externalities' of alcohol abuse for the wider society are greater than those of drug addiction. Nevertheless, both have heavy costs in deaths, illness, lost productivity, crime, and the need for addiction treatment and health care.

The nuclear arms race: the ultimate social problem?

While this chapter has been concerned with problems within American society, an under-lying threat to the survival of that society, and indeed to humankind, is that of nuclear war. Given its control over a large portion of the world's nuclear weapons, US participation in the arms race is of major concern both to Americans and to the rest of the world. While some might argue that the arms race is a political, rather than a social problem, or that it is a means to solving the problem of national defence and threats to peace, it indisputably has social costs. These include the psychological effects (especially on young persons) of living with the threat of nuclear war, the militariz-ation of the economy with the diversion of national resources from economically productive industries to defence, and divisive debates about optimum strategies for national security. Even if nuclear war is averted, the nuclear arms race is seen by many as a central problem in society.

Although geographers have not been at the forefront of scholarship in this issue, they have made contributions in several areas. They have helped document the probable effects of a nuclear attack on particular places and have criticized Federal Emergency Management Agency plans for 'crisis relocation' in the event of an attack (Bennett *et al*. 1984; Platt 1984). Scientific research, in which geographers are involved, concerning the intensity of a 'nuclear winter' which would follow nuclear war is also of value not merely in predicting effects but, more importantly, of raising public awareness of the 'unwinnability' of nuclear war, and thus its utter futility.

One measure of public concern about the nuclear arms race is the level of support for the nuclear freeze movement. The Freeze is a grass-roots political campaign initiated in 1979 in New England. In the early 1980s, support for the Freeze as expressed in local governing bodies' votes and in public referenda spread from New England to other parts of the country. By mid-decade the geographical pattern of support was strongest in the mid-Atlantic and New England regions, with additional concentrations in parts of the Midwest and Pacific States (Fig. 8.11). There was little support for the Freeze in the South or in the Mountain States of Idaho, Nevada, Wyoming and Utah. Explanations for this pattern seem to lie in both the propensity of a State to be politically innovative and in the political 'culture' of the area. Those States which display individualistic political cultures tend to show higher patterns of support (Cutter, Holcomb and Shatin 1986). It seems likely that geographical involvement in this area of research will expand and that the discipline can contribute more to reducing the threat that nuclear war poses to American, and indeed human, society.

Conclusions

The selection of social problems discussed in this chapter reflects both the interests and values of the author and the level of published geographical work on social issues. We have not dealt with some problems which could well be considered 'social' and to which geographers have contributed usefully, especially, for example, the reduction of environmental pol-lution, the conservation of natural resources, or coping with hazards and disasters whether 'natural' (earthquakes) or human-induced (toxic spills). The literature in these fields is large and beyond the scope of this chapter. There are similar issues which geographers and others are beginning to address. One, for example, concerns the ownership of American *land*. Despite the traditional value placed on open access to landownership in America (expressed, for example, in homesteading laws), actual landownership patterns are

Fig. 8.11 The nuclear arms race as a social issue: some spatial variations

concentrated in that there are very large tracts of land in the hands of relatively few people. As Popper (1982) has pointed out, large landowning monopolies can have negative effects for society, and in many cases their assumed efficiency is unproven. The sale of huge tracts of land on the edge of Tampa, Florida, led to explosive and unplanned urban growth. The coal company land monopolies in Appalachia concentrates economic and political power. Large-scale agribusiness forces the family farm out of production. Land speculation (holding tracts to sell at high profit at the appropriate moment) results in underutilized land and wasteful growth patterns. Access to landownership partially controls access to wealth, and so monopolies can inhibit equitable distribution of society's rewards. Popper points out, for example, that in 1940 black owner-operator farmers controlled a major part of the 46 million acres of American farmland under minority ownership. Today, due largely to the loss of many family farms, only 13.3 million acres are owned by blacks and other minority people.

There are also serious problems for which little geographical analysis yet exists, but which could be useful. *Hunger* and malnutrition continue to prevail in this rich country which produces abundant food and many of whose inhabitants overeat. Public concern about hunger resurfaces regularly in the media and in governmental and other reports. A Physicians Task Force report (1985) estimated that there were 20 million undernourished people in America (Lelyveld 1985) and that requests for emergency food more than doubled in many cities in the first part of the 1980s. At the same time, Americans waste more than 200 thousand million pounds of food (approximately 20 per cent of US food production) each year. While hunger is geographically concentrated in such places as the rural South and northern urban ghettoes, the causes of this distribution have little to do with local environmental conditions (such as droughts causing famine in Africa) or with food transportation systems. Hunger exists in close proximity to abundant food supplies which are inaccessible mainly on the basis of income, though occasionally on the basis of physical infirmity and immobility in old age. Nevertheless, knowledge about the spatial patterns of hunger in America can help alleviate the problem (through such programmes as soup kitchens, meals on wheels, nutrition education and food subsidies).

A similarly limited, in spatial extent, but nevertheless serious problem is that of *home-lessness*. Especially in big cities, thousands of people, including a growing number of women, live in the streets, in shelters or squat in empty buildings. The problem of homelessness grew in the mid-1980s as federal aid to build low-income housing virtually disappeared. In the winter of 1985–86, an estimated 9000 single adults and over 14 000 family members were homeless in New York City and relied on city shelters (McFadden 1985). The problem is obviously more acute in winter when lack of shelter may cause loss of life through hypo-thermia. Each winter a few people literary freeze to death on the streets of New York while others lead a nomadic existence carrying their worldly possessions in shopping bags from shelter to soup kitchen on a diurnal routine. While the homeless are mostly poor, many are also alcoholics or *mentally ill*. Recent move-ments to deinstitutionalize mental patients, while beneficial to some (in improving their chances of healthy reintregration into the community), have also 'dumped' people marginally capable of coping with life into complex environments with little support (Wolpert and Wolpert 1974). Identifying where both homeless people and sheltered mental

patients are can assist in appropriately locating shelters for the homeless and clinics and other support services for the mentally ill (Mair 1985; Wolpert and Wolpert 1976; Wolpert, Dear and Crawford 1975).

Mental illness may be seen both as a problem caused in part by society and one which has negative impacts on society. Rates of diagnosed mental illness are higher in urban than rural areas and higher in central cities than surrounding metropolitan areas. Whether these variations are the result of environmental conditions, of the migration of mentally ill people, or of better diagnosis in urban areas is debatable. A geographical study of psychologi-cal distress in Chicago found that it is more related to family status, residential mobility and income than to residential location (Daiches 1981).

In addition, it could be helpful to consider as social problems the *concerns of the affluent*. For many Americans, high on the ranks of their problems are obesity and ill-health resulting from the consumption of such luxuries as alcohol and tobacco. Conspicuous consumption of such items as cars, electronic equipment or houses may both cause, and reflect, social insecurity. Is contentment possible in a highly competitive society in which there is always somebody else who is much more successful?

Finally, we should note that, while far from utopian, the US is a society in which both individual and collective problems are faced, analysed, debated, and solutions sought. It is a society which experiments, and in which progress is sought and measured. It is one which is self-conscious about its weaknesses as well as confident in its strengths. While there is no unanimity about solutions to problems, neither is there any assumption of unanimity.

Chapter 9

LIVING IN AMERICA

Almost all of this book has presented discussions of what might be termed 'outsiders' views' of the US: descriptions and analyses of aggregate patterns of agriculture, population, industry and so on. But what is it like to live inside those patterns, to be in America? The general view of the US is that it is one of the countries with the highest material standards of living as measured by indicators of income and wealth, the possession of material goods, the consumption of energy, and so on. But can material standards of living be readily equated with more elusive concepts such as quality of life and welfare? And, more importantly for us, can we assume that, because Americans as a whole have such a high standard of living, that they all do, or are there substantial variations around the average, variations which have both geographical expression (people in some places are better off than others) and geographical causes?

In seeking answers to these questions, we are faced with a number of problems, most of which are concerned with the materials we use. The most important is the one already alluded to – how do we express such general concepts

as 'standard of living', 'quality of life' and 'welfare' in terms that allow us to map and analyse spatial differences? And then, given that we are able to make reasonable descriptions, which have geographical expressions, how do we know that these are in fact the result of geographical processes? For example, we know that Mississippi is one of the poorest States; just one-quarter of its residents were living in households with income above the designated poverty level in 1979. Does this mean that there is something about Mississippi that induces poverty – compared, say, to Maryland, where only 6 per cent were similarly classified? After all, Mississippi has a high percentage of blacks, and we know that centuries of discrimination have left blacks, on average, with much lower standards of living than whites. Fully 45 per cent of Mississippi's blacks were living at or below the poverty level in 1979, which seems to suggest that it is the State's racial composition that causes its poverty level. But only 20 per cent of Maryland's blacks were living in similar conditions, so there is still an apparent geographical difference to be accounted for.

Top left: Food stamp distribution in Washington DC *Credit*: United States Department of Agriculture   *Top right*: Education: computer graphics *Credit*: IBM Corporation   *Bottom left*: Suburban living *Credit*: Paul Knox   *Bottom right*: Urban living: apartment houses in New York City *Credit*: Paul Knox

Even when we have analysed spatial data on aspects of welfare (we will use this broad term for the rest of the chapter), we are still presenting the outsiders' views. What is it like to live in various places in the US? How do they differ, not in terms of separate variables but rather in terms of the quality of people's daily lives? The insiders' views are much harder to get than the outsiders', and all we can do here is hint at them.

The outsiders' views

The 1960s were a decade of great change in the US, in many ways. For us, the most important change was the growing interest in what we might term social welfare, as against economic welfare: the latter is concerned with jobs and incomes, with production and trade; the former is concerned with those things, too, but with many others as well, such as civil rights and disease, social discrimination and environmental quality. The two are linked, of course, in that prosperous people are usually healthy, but there is no necessary link between the overall prosperity of a population and the welfare of some of its members. Of course, people did not realize this for the first time in the 1960s. What did happen then was that social welfare was moved to a higher place on the political agenda, and politicians and bureaucrats in Washington and elsewhere began to pay much more attention to the quality of people's lives as well as their economic prospects.

The reasons for this switch are many, and untangling them is not our concern here. Suffice it to say that there was a growing realization that the US was a very divided society (J. K. Galbraith called it a division between 'private affluence and public squalor'), and that many Americans were not benefiting from the fruits of affluence. Michael Harrington, in *The Other America* (1962: 9), recorded, for example, that

In the Affluent Society of the United States, there are some fifty million poor Americans. Behind the High Street of prosperity lies 'the other America' – a shadowy district where between 40 000 000 and 50 000 000 people struggle to exist below the level of human dignity and decency.

Further, he showed that poor America is to most of its citizens an invisible land:

Poverty is often off the beaten track. It always has been. The ordinary tourist . . . does not go into the valleys of Pennsylvania where the farms look like movie sets of Wales in the thirties . . . And even if he were to pass through such a place by accident, the tourist would not meet the unemployed men in the bar or the women working at home for a runaway sweat shop . . .

Then, too, beauty and myths are not perennial masks of poverty. The traveller comes to the Appalachians in the lovely season. He sees the hills, the streams, the foliage – but not the poor . . . or perhaps he . . . decides that 'those people' are truly fortunate to be living the way they are and that they are lucky to be exempt from the strains and tensions of the middle class. The only problem is that 'those people', the quaint inhabitants of those hills, are undereducated, underprivileged, lack medical care, and are in the process of being forced from the land into a life in the cities where they are misfits (Harrington 1962: 11).

Was it any better in the cities? Clearly not, for as we have seen many of the nation's poor were – and still are – concentrated in the urban areas, again largely unseen. They are not hidden from view by hills and trees, but their affluent compatriots rarely see the living conditions in the ghettoes, for the freeways to suburbia provide only fleeting, voyeuristic glances at the physical fabric of those ghettoes – which is bad enough – and no contact at all with the human fabric. Poor, hungry, deprived and discontented America is spatially separated from rich, over-fed, over-endowed America.

Books such as Harrington's sensitized a small portion of the American population to the plight of those in the rural and urban ghettoes, and convinced some politicians that – for whatever motives – policies for change must be adopted. But policy cannot be built on rhetoric alone, however powerful. The politicians needed a factual base, against which they could cost the various proposals and formulate their legislation. And so their civil servants and concerned academics developed what became known as social indicators, assessments of social conditions against which social policies could be formulated.

The geography of social well-being

To geographers, with their deep appreciation of spatial variations in many aspects of the human condition – illustrated, for example, in a pioneering paper by Malcolm Lewis (1968) on 'Levels of living in the Northeastern United States' – this development of national social indicators was insufficient. What was needed was a set of *territorial social indicators*, which demonstrated not only variations and changes over time (which politicians could use to laud the success of their policies) but variations and changes over space. This case was made strongly in a pioneering book by David Smith (1973) on *The Geography of Social Well-Being in the United States*. Many have followed his lead (Cutter 1985), but by discussing his work we will get a clear insight into those spatial variations that geographers argue are so important to a full appreciation of welfare in the US.

A major problem that Smith faced, and it is still being faced by those working on these issues today, is the definition of welfare – clearly it is multi-faceted, with many separate components. Smith eventually decided on seven major components:

- Income, wealth and employment;
- The living environment – physical and built;
- Health;
- Education;
- Social order;
- Social belonging; and
- Recreation and leisure.

According to this scheme, high levels of welfare are enjoyed by people with well-paid jobs, living in pleasant environments, enjoying food, health and educational facilities, not experiencing crime and other social problems, fully participating in society and relatively satisfied with their membership, and with a range of cultural and recreational facilities available to them. Having decided on these components, Smith then had to get data to portray them. a

range of sources was explored, and data sets compiled for three separate analyses, at different scales. The data were not ideal – few are – but they gave a general impression of the spatial variability, which was his main goal.

The first analysis was conducted at the *State level*, employing data from six of the seven components (recreation and leisure was excluded). He produced a separate index for each of the six and also a composite index. The results are shown in Fig. 9.1.

Looking first at the individual components, five of the six maps show a clear north–south division, which not surprisingly comes out in the regional map too: this suggests that if the US as a whole is to be divided into two nations, then it is in the southeast that we have poor, hungry, deprived America. Indeed, it is only on the social disorganization component that the southeastern States do not rate in the bottom twelve – apart from Texas and Florida, which are somewhat anomalous relative to the regional norms. What the maps show is that although States such as Alabama and Georgia have on average the lowest incomes, the lowest welfare payments, the most dilapidated homes, the poorest diets, the highest infant mortality rates, the worst record of health care, the highest illiteracy levels, the lowest spending on education, the greatest racial segregation and the lowest electoral turnout, they do not also have the highest rates of alcoholism, venereal disease and suicide, of divorce, and of crimes. For the last group of pathologies, it is the States of the Southwest, plus Illinois, Maryland, Missouri and New York, which are the 'most disorganized'.

If the concentration of deprivation in one corner of the US is very clear from Fig. 9.1, there is no simple counterpart: a concentration of affluence and 'the good life'. A few States appear in the top twelve on several components (Michigan, for example, is absent only from the education map), but in general the geography is very variable. Thus the composite map has no block of top twelve, though in general the best areas appear to be the Pacific Northwest, the Upper Great Lakes, and much of New England, plus Colorado and Utah.

What this State level analysis tells us, therefore, is that within the US, levels of welfare,

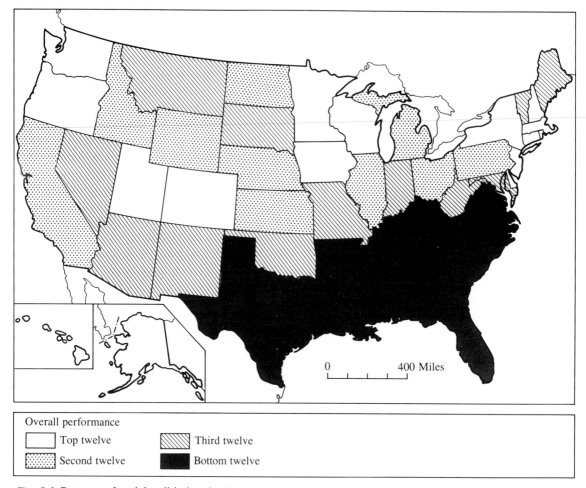

Fig. 9.1 Patterns of social well-being, by State
Source: Smith (1973) Fig. 7.1 (p. 88) and Fig. 7.2 (p. 89)

however defined, are in general lowest in the Southeast. People choosing where to live might either leave or not go there. But where should they go? In part, it seems, it depends on which aspects of welfare they rate highly. California offers prosperity, health and a good environment, for example; Montana offers a good education; and Maine has few problems of social disorder.

But is everywhere the same within those States? After all, for most people the State is rather an abstract concept, apart from its taxation and provision of certain governmental services. People live in places, not States. And so Smith repeated his analysis, this time at the level of the *metropolitan area*, using variables representing five components: material living standards; welfare; health; education; and social order. The resulting general pattern (Fig. 9.2) very largely replicates that for the State-level analysis; welfare is lowest in the metropolitan areas of the Southeast and highest in the Northeast. But there are substantial within-State variations. In Texas, for example, the quality of life is higher in Houston and New Orleans than in San Antonio, and higher still in Dallas and Fort Worth – but all are below the national average. Few States have some metropolitan areas above and some below that average: in California, however, coastal cities

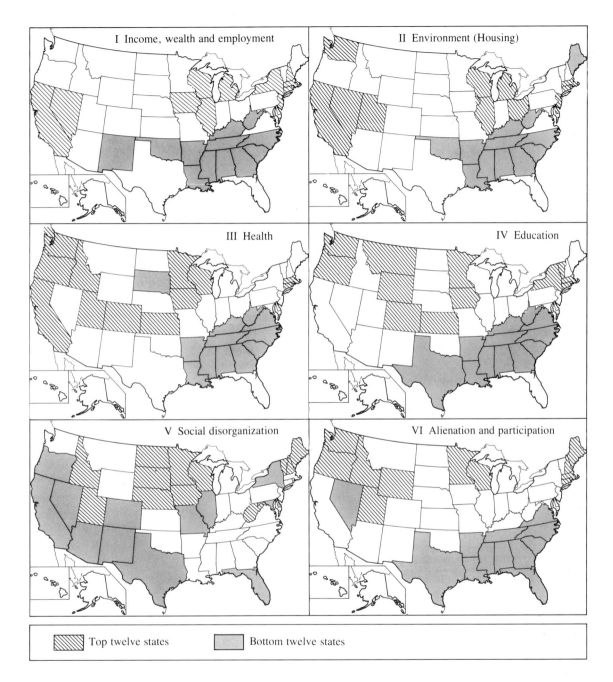

I Income, wealth and employment

II Environment (Housing)

III Health

IV Education

V Social disorganization

VI Alienation and participation

Top twelve states   Bottom twelve states

are generally better than inland ones; in Washington, Seattle is much better than Tacoma; and in Indiana, it seems people are better off in Indianapolis than Gary.

But have we yet got to the real scale, to the spatial level at which most people experience their daily lives? New York may rate very highly as a metropolitan area but, as any visitor will know, there are many New Yorks. Is an analysis that combines Harlem and Westchester County really telling us anything meaningful? And New York may be the largest metropolitan

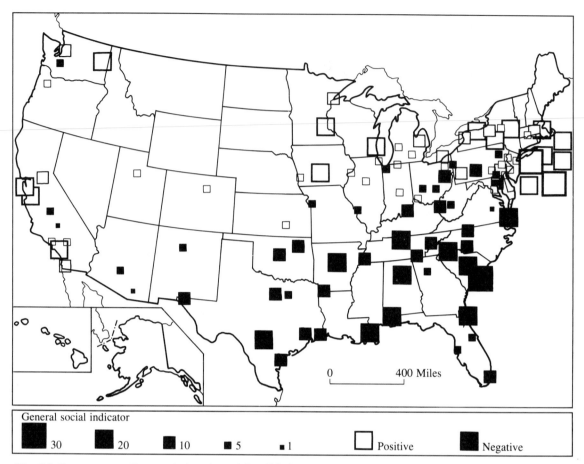

Fig. 9.2 Inter-metropolitan variations in social well-being
Source: Smith (1973), Fig. 8.2, p. 113

area but it is by no means untypical in this respect. Detroit is another metropolitan area that comes out as above average but, as Bunge's map of infant mortality rates makes graphically clear (Fig. 9.3), some parts are akin to countries of the Third World in certain aspects of welfare.

So we need to get inside the cities, to the spatial level of experience of daily life. Smith's third analysis, at the *census tract level*, did this, again using variables representing the first six components. The city that he studied was Tampa, Florida. This cannot in any way be claimed as representative of the country as a whole, but there is no reason to suggest that it is untypical. Certainly his maps (Fig. 9.4) are what we would expect. All six show the same

concentration of the lowest levels of welfare in the inner-city areas, which include the city's black ghetto.

Although to most people it is this last analysis that is closest to the reality of their daily lives, that does not mean that the other two scales are irrelevant. There are differences between States – in their welfare policies, for example – which have major impacts on individuals, and it is the metropolitan areas that provide the 'shell' within which people live: it is the city that is the labour market, for example, not the census tract.

Smith's was an academic study, which was the forerunner for many similar investigations of the welfare geography of the US. Some of these have sought an overview similar to that

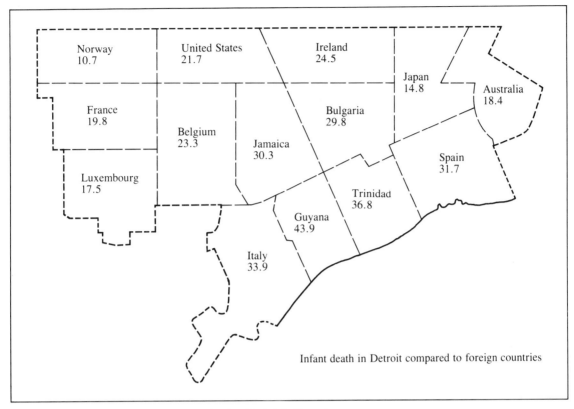

Infant death in Detroit compared to foreign countries

Fig 9.3 Infant mortality (deaths per 1000 live births) in Detroit
Source: Bunge (1975), Fig. 12.3E, p. 161

provided by Smith, and have used other, more recent data. (Smith himself – D. Smith 1985 – has studied changes in Atlanta over the period 1960–80, for example, and has concluded that the trends between 1970 and 1980 produced 'a racially as well as spatially more unequal city' – p. 27.) Others have focused on particular components of welfare (such as the geography of welfare payments discussed in Chapter 4). In Chicago, for example, a large study – the Chicago Regional Hospital Study – set out to investigate inequalities in health care. It concluded as follows:

What is it like to be sick and poor in the United States?
It depends on how sick, how poor and how old you are.
It depends or where you live.
It depends on the color of your skin.
It depends on your sex.

If you are either very poor, blind, disabled, over 65, male, white, or live in a middle- or upper-class neighborhood in a large urban center, you belong to a privileged class of health care recipients, and your chances of survival are good. But, if you are none of these, if you are only average poor, under 65, female, black, or live in a low income urban neighborhood, small town, or rural area, you are a disenfranchised citizen as far as health rights go, and your chances of survival are not good (de Vise 1973: 1).

For geographers, the particular interest is in unravelling the locational disadvantages, the health-care problems of people that result from where they live. It has been shown, for example, that there was a clear geography of disease, with the least healthy populations living in the areas of greatest overall social disadvantage. In Chicago, five disease clusters were identified:

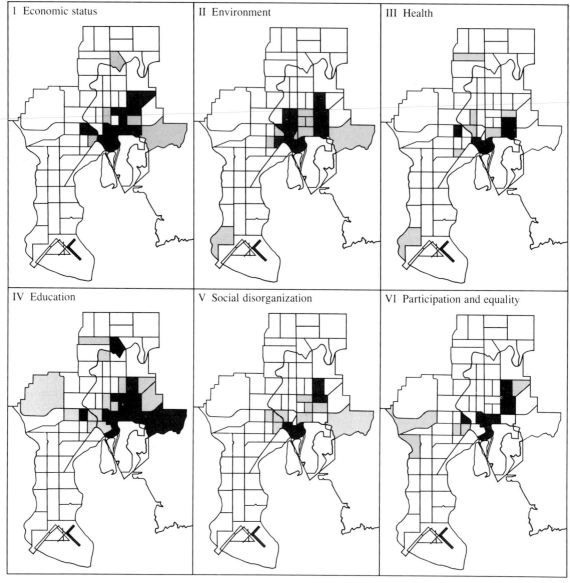

Fig. 9.4 Social well-being in Tampa, Florida
Source: Smith (1973), Fig. 9.2, p.125

- Gonorrhea, illegitimate births, diarrhoea, premature births, syphilis, measles, poisonings, tuberculosis and infant mortality – a group of diseases associated with poverty, and termed the Poverty Syndrome. Figure 9.5 shows the concentration of this cluster in certain parts of the city of Chicago, most of which are lived in by blacks.
- Mumps, whooping cough and chickenpox –

a group of contagious diseases termed the Density Syndrome, since they spread most rapidly in areas of high residential density.
- Rheumatic fever, scarlet fever and pneumonia – a group of diseases of the upper respiratory system (hence the Upper Respiratory Syndrome), which are frequently associated with poor, especially damp, living conditions.

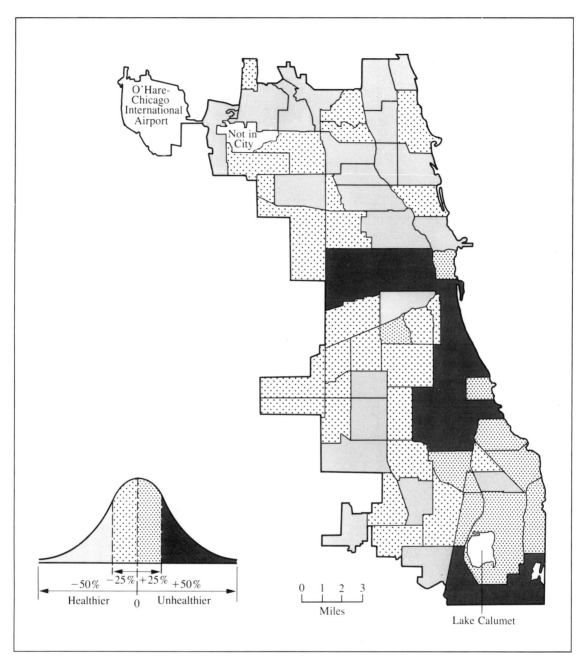

Fig. 9.5 Ill-health in Chicago: the 'Poverty Syndrome'
Source: De Vise (1973), Fig. 13, p. 34 (after Pyle 1968)

- Rubella and congenital malformations – the Rubella Syndrome.
- Infectious hepatitis – the Water Syndrome.

These disease clusters indicate a geography of demand for health care (though not the only geography, since they are concerned with diseases only and not with other conditions requiring treatment). The geography of health care supply did not match this demand,

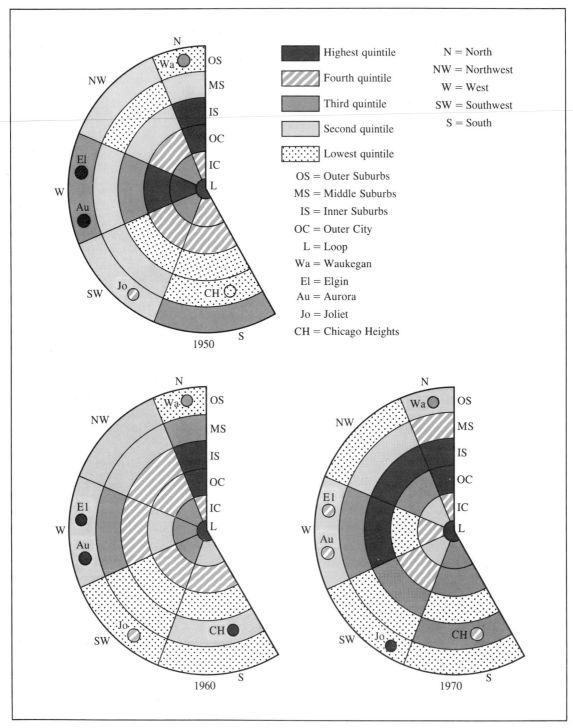

Fig. 9.6 Distribution of physicians per 1000 population in Chicago, 1950, 1960 and 1970
Source: De Vise (1973), Fig. 7, p. 17

however. Figure 9.6, for example, shows the changing geography of physicians' offices in the Chicago Metropolitan Area from 1950 to 1970. In general, the changes in that distribution are closely linked to the income and socio-economic status of the areas concerned. Overall, in 1970 Chicago had one physician to every 1000 people. The ten most affluent communities had 1.78 per 1000 in 1950, and 2.10 in 1970, whereas the ten poorest had 0.99 and 0.26 respectively; Chicago physicians were moving to serve the paying patients (and more were moving elsewhere, because Chicago as a whole was badly served).

Alongside these academic studies there has been a growth of popular interest recently in the spatial variations in welfare. Rand McNally, for example, now produce a *Places Rated Almanac* designed principally as a practical guide for people who are thinking of moving between different parts of the country (Boyer and Savageau 1985). This uses nine components to rank the 329 metropolitan areas studied:

- Climate and terrain;
- Housing;
- Health care and environment;
- Crime;
- Transportation;
- Education;
- Recreation;
- The Arts; and
- Economics.

Each metropolitan area is given a ranking for each component on the basis of points allocated for performance on a given set of criteria. The 'Economics' component, for example, is based on average household incomes (adjusted for taxes and living costs), rates of growth in personal incomes and rates of job expansion. The higher the ranking of a place (the closer to 1) the more desirable it is on that component.

Perhaps not surprisingly, all of the top ten places on the climate and terrain component are on the West Coast, whereas most of those in the lowest ranked places are in the Upper Great Lakes and the High Plains areas; such a geography is to be expected, assuming that the criteria are generally accepted. On housing, the highest ratings go to small places such as McAllen-Edinburg-Mission (TX), Joplin (MO)

and Danville (VA), and the lowest to the big cities plus some special cases – notably Anchorage and Honolulu. Big cities (and also Reno and Las Vegas!) rank low on the crime component too, but not surprisingly they perform well on the Arts. Putting all nine components together (Fig. 9.7), Pittsburgh comes out as the best-rated place in the US, followed by Boston, Raleigh-Durham (NC), Philadelphia, San Francisco, Nassau-Suffolk (NY) and Louisville (KY); at the bottom (working up from 329) are Yuba City (CA), Pine Bluff (AR), Modesto (CA), Dothan (AL) and Albany (GA). But of course it all depends on what you want from a place. Boston, Philadelphia, Raleigh-Durham and San Francisco, for example, all score very poorly on the housing and crime components, while Pittsburgh ranks 186 and 184 respectively on the housing and economics components. On the other hand, Boston, Philadelphia and Pittsburgh are ranked in the top twenty for health care and environment, education, and the Arts; and San Francisco is ranked top for climate and terrain, second for recreation, third for transportation, seventh for the Arts, tenth for health care and environment, and eighteenth for education. Meanwhile, Louisville ranks in the top fifty on only one category – health care and environment; it isn't that good for anything, but not very bad either (its lowest ranking is 163, for economics). If economics are all-important to you, then you should be in Midland (TX), Lafayett (LA), Portsmouth–Dover–Rochester (NH/ME), Enid (OK) or Oklahoma City (OK); but you may have to put up with other things – Midland, for example, ranks 238 on housing, 327 on health care and environment, 251 on crime, 300 on education, 208 on recreation, and 274 on the Arts, with an overall rank position of 258. Boyer and Savageau show that very few metropolitan areas are 'super-solid', with no rankings worse than 200; and only seventeen more are 'solid', with no more than one ranking worse than 200.

Preferences and constraints

A major difficulty associated with such studies, as just implied, is that they *assume consistent preferences across the whole population*. With

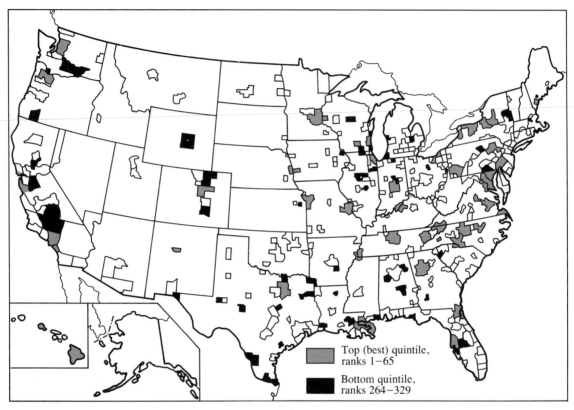

Fig. 9.7 Social well-being: overall ranking of 329 metropolitan areas
Source of data: Boyer and Savageau (1985)

some of the variables used, this is a reasonable assumption. Undoubtedly virtually everybody would appreciate a low cost of living, a crime-free and healthy local environment, a sunny climate and so on, although they may weight their relative importance to them differently (some will accept a higher cost of living if the sun always shines, for example). But on others there is a great amount of variation in people's attitudes. For example, some people are prepared to pay higher taxes (especially local property taxes) in order to finance the provision of good local services, such as education. But others (as shown in some of the 'Proposition 13 type' referenda held in several States in the late 1970s) are very much opposed to such taxation. In general, the poor are the most in favour, because they are net beneficiaries; the very rich, although net losers (they pay more in taxes than they receive in benefits), may be relatively unconcerned; but the middle-income

groups are most opposed to high levels of public spending, especially for policies from which they gain no benefits (e.g. education for households without children) and/or which they perceive as benefiting the poor (i.e. redistributing income downwards). The fragmented local government system in many States (see Ch. 4) allows them to express these preferences. Some live in what Miller (1981) calls 'minimal cities', where taxes are held as low as possible, service provision is as little as possible, and services are bought in on a 'user pays' basis, which avoids any subsidization of the poor by the rich. Similarly, some live in exclusive communities, very homogeneous in their income structure, thereby again avoiding any redistribution of income from rich to poor.

People, then, are able to express their preferences through choice of which municipality to live in; or so it seems. This was the basis of a classic paper by an economist, Charles Tiebout (1956), who argued that if there is a single government (metropolitan, State, or even federal) responsible for providing services it is unable to meet the diversity of demands within the population. But if you have a large number of governments, each offering a different package of taxes and services, people can choose that which best fits their preferences. In this way, a fragmented system of local government reflects the private sector, with a large number of suppliers seeking support from potential customers – in this case the communities – and any municipalities offering an undesirable package would have to alter their offerings in order to survive.

The problem with this argument (discussed in detail in Whiteman 1983) lies in the assumptions that it makes. One is that people are well informed and know about all the choices on offer. Another, much more important, is that *people are free to move to the municipality of their choice.* This is clearly not the case, however, for many municipalities have successfully excluded certain types of people – particularly the poor and blacks – by a variety of policies, such as exclusionary, low-density zoning, which influence the price of properties there, and in general neither federal legislation nor legal actions through the courts have been able to 'open up' such municipalities – almost invariably suburbs – to the poor (see Johnston 1984 for a full discussion of this). The relatively affluent are able to insulate themselves from the poor, to avoid contributing to the costs of services for them, and the poor are confined to areas in which they are the dominant category of residents and so any services that they want must be paid for by them and them alone (unless they can obtain subsidies from a higher-level government).

It is not only the relatively affluent who have escaped the cost of paying for local services for the poor. Industry and commerce are increasingly doing the same. They pay local property taxes too, and so contribute to the cost of service provision (for their employees and other local residents); because industrial and commercial land is more valuable than residential, their property taxes are relatively high. Thus to the extent that the relative poor live in municipalities/school districts with such non-

residential users, they are able to benefit from the latters' contributions to the local tax base. But, as we have seen, such users are increasingly deserting those municipalities – especially the old-established inner cities – and are shifting to the suburbs in large numbers. There they can either benefit from locations in municipalities almost exclusively zoned for non-residential users, where they pay very little in taxes since there is no demand for services from residents, or they are attracted to developments in middle-income suburbs, where good deals are offered to businesses in order to get some subsidization to residential users. (The competition for such developments is sometimes intense, as Herr (1982) demonstrates.)

At the metropolitan scale, therefore, choice of where to live is constrained not only by the operation of the business market but also by the use of the local government system to influence the characteristics of an area's residents and its tax bills. Thus, an individual metropolitan area may appear to rate highly as a place to live in, but for some elements of the quality of life the segmentation of the metropolitan area will be crucial: welfare will be much higher in some parts (usually the suburbs) than others (the inner city and some of the inner suburbs) and many of the poor elements in society will be deprived access to the former. Minneapolis–St Paul may appear to be a good place to live – relatively affluent and crime free – but does this apply to all parts of that metropolitan area? If not, then the characteristics tell us little about the experience of living in America today.

Indeed, one could argue that there are few real differences between metropolitan areas, and that the differences shown up in the sorts of analysis reported here are a reflection of the relative balance of rich and poor there; no more. Thus, wherever they are, the affluent live in attractive, exclusive, residential areas, whereas the poor are confined to low-quality districts where taxes are high (relative to income), facilities and services poor, and the streets unsafe. There are differences, of course; to most people, Miami has a better climate than Minneapolis–St Paul, as does Phoenix relative to Pittsburgh, and the flood of people to the Sunbelt in recent decades illustrates how people – or at least the relatively affluent – are responding to this. Once again. however, it is a question of 'who can choose?'

Another difference between places that affects all people relatively equally is in the *cost of living*. Some places are more expensive than others, according to the national consumer price index, which combines the costs of food, clothing, shelter, fuel, transport, medical and other necessities of day-to-day living. As well as a simple index, weighted according to the relative importance of the various categories of expenditure, separate indices are computed for different family types, with their own sets of weights. For a typical family of four (husband, aged 38, in employment; wife not in employment outside the home; and son and daughter aged 13 and 8, respectively), maintaining a moderate standard of living according to the Bureau of Labor Statistics' definitions, the index varied by 41 per cent in 1981: the four most expensive places were Honolulu ($31 893), Anchorage ($31 890), New York ($29 320) and Boston ($29 213), and the four cheapest were Dallas ($22 678), Atlanta ($23 273), Houston ($23 600) and St Louis ($24 498).

Why do such living cost differentials exist? Detailed analyses by Richard Cebula (1983) have identified four major influences on the average annual cost of living in 1966–79 for a four-person family living on an intermediate budget.

1. Population size – the larger the metropolitan area, the lower the cost, presumably because of the economies of scale associated with larger agglomerations;
2. Population density – the greater the density of population, the higher the cost, presumably because of the increased competition for space;
3. Income levels – the higher the per capita income the greater the cost, presumably because increased demand for goods and services pushes up prices; and
4. Right-to-work laws – States with right-to-work laws (i e. laws prohibiting compulsory trade union membership) have lower costs, presumably because organized labour has less leverage and therefore costs are being kept down.

In addition, Cebula showed, for a smaller sample of places, that: the greater the per unit cost of heating gas, the higher the average cost of living, and the higher the level of unionization the higher the average cost; he failed to find any relationship between property tax rates and living costs. Over time, he found that living costs increased more rapidly where: per capita income was growing rapidly; unionization was increasing rapidly; and State and local property tax rates were increasing rapidly.

The conclusion one might draw from Cebula's work is that the cheapest places to live are big, low-density cities, with cheap gas, a preponderance of poor people, right-to-work laws, low unionization and low property taxes. (Recall that he was studying comparable people, four-person families living on intermediate budgets, what he terms the 'budget for a moderate standard of living' – p. 55.) Of course, if everybody chose to move to such places, they could well become less attractive – density would increase, property taxes might rise, and so on. But to a large extent you only have a choice if you have a job.

This is the crux of any analysis; in a capitalist society, for the vast majority of the population *paid employment is necessary, though not sufficient, for achieving an adequate standard of living*. Thus, one's quality of life is intricately linked up with:

1. Job opportunities within commuting distance of one's home – for most people, the metropolitan area, if not some portion of it;
2. The number of competitors for those jobs; and
3. Ability to shift from one labour market to another (which could be: from one job to another in the same place; from one occupation to another in the same place; for one job to another, in another place; and from one occupation to another, in another place).

Individuals have virtually no control over the last two of these; jobs are moved from place to place according to the interests of their owners and managers, as shown in Chapter 5. and the locations of new opportunities are similarly a function of forces almost entirely outside the control of the individual workers. (Interestingly, to some extent workers may have a negative influence on their own job prospects. The pension funds of unions whose strength is in the Snowbelt States have been invested in the growth industries of the Sunbelt, for example, and the cheapest places to live in apparently include those where unions are weakest and, as a consequence, average wages low.) Nor, despite much popular rhetoric, do people have a similar opportunity to provide themselves with the educational qualifications to prepare for the labour market. Just as there are major inequalities in the provision of health-care facilities, so there are major inequalities in educational provision by the school districts which rely for much of their finance on the property taxes paid by their residents. An affluent district can afford to spend much more on providing educational resources, as a 1973 Supreme Court case relating to San Antonio, TX, showed: in Englewood, property was assessed at $5960 per student, and expenditure was $356 per student; in nearby Alamo Heights, the figures were $49 000 and $594 respectively, with the higher level of spending representing a much lower property tax rate. Despite the US being presented as a mobile country, both socially and geographically, many of its residents are raised in areas and in conditions out of which social escape is extremely unlikely, and geographical escape is probably only to similar conditions elsewhere.

All of these outsiders' views provide generalized descriptions of the average quality of life in various parts of the US, therefore, but they tell us nothing about the causes of those differences; to understand the 'welfare geography' of the country, we must first understand the economic geography, because in a capitalist nation economics are paramount. Nor do those descriptions tell us whether people have much control over their quality of life, beyond the control that they can exercise through the market place by the purchase or rental of a home at a particular location. At the local, intra-metropolitan, scale the combined operation of the housing market and the fragmented local government system means that the less affluent are effectively precluded from the 'nicest' places; the areas they are 'allowed' to live in are not only the less pleasant but also,

in many cases, the most expensive relative to income and the least well served by public facilities because of the weak property tax base. At the inter-metropolitan scale, moves can bring benefits, but if there are no jobs at the desired destinations, then the point of moving may be very slight. (There are other reasons for moves, of course, as the flood of retirees to Arizona and Florida in recent decades has shown. There is some evidence, too, of people moving from the less to the more generous States with regard to welfare eligibility and payment levels – see Fig. 4.10.) The spaces and places that people occupy are, in many respects, made by themselves but crucial aspects of the contexts – notably new employment prospects – are the activities of others, over which the vast bulk of the population has little or no control. Spaces and places are manipulated by the powerful in society, too, and the relatively powerless can only do their manipulation within the framework provided by that small community.

The insiders' views

But what are those local spaces and places like? We get some idea from the aggregate descriptions, but no more. State x seems to be more affluent than State y; metropolitan area a more crime-prone than metropolitan area b; suburb m better provided with school facilities than inner-city neighbourhood n; and so on. But what is it like to live in x or y or a or b or m or n?

The answers to such questions cannot be gained from the sorts of data collected by the census and other agencies; they must be sought from the people themselves. Two sources are generally used. The first is literature, which gives insights to the experience of space and place. The novels of John Steinbeck, for example, illustrate the problem of living through the Great Depression in some rural areas; William Faulkner's books tell us about rural society too, as represented in Yoknapatawpha County; Henry James tells us about life among Boston's elite in the nineteenth century; and the musical West Side Story about the experience of Puerto Ricans in New York.

These are not scientific studies in the sense we would normally apply, but they are nevertheless full of insights of what local, day-to-day life has been, and is, like in American places. We can do a lot worse in our attempts to appreciate the daily realities of life, as it is experienced, than to study American literature for its insights as well as its entertainment (Watson 1979).

The other course of action is to undertake detailed local case studies, in the field, of the sort usually associated with anthropology and ethnography. There is a substantial tradition of such work in American sociology, much of it associated with the world-renowned Chicago School of Sociology established there by Robert Park in the second decade of the present century. (There are many surveys of the work of this School: see, for example, Short 1981, Thomas 1983.) To geographers, the work of this School is generally associated with the model of the spatial organization of the city proposed by one of its leading members, Ernest Burgess (Fig. 7.1A). But those aggregate studies of the human ecology of the city were prepared to provide a framework for detailed field investigations of what Short terms 'the social fabric of the metropolis'. The outsiders' and insiders' views were to be combined for, as Burgess himself expressed it:

Statistical data and map-plotting tell us much, but they don't tell us all. They tell us very many things which require further investigation . . . Many of these questions, of course, can be further studied by statistical investigations; others, to be understood, require us to get below the surface of observable behavior (Burgess 1967: 8–9).

The result was a series of detailed case studies, most of them focused on the inner city since the ecological analyses found this to be the main area of social disorganization and it was with curing the ills of the city that Park, Burgess and their colleagues were particularly concerned. (For a brief review of the main studies, see Hannerz 1980.)

One problem associated with such studies is that they can readily become ends in themselves, detailed presentations of the results of a great amount of effort but with little attempt to draw general conclusions. Indeed, this is a criticism directed at the Chicago School, and

Hannerz (1980: 30) notes that 'two kinds of urban studies were created in Chicago; conceived in unity but drifting apart in terms of present-day markers of disciplinary implications'.

The ecological work became an important component of urban sociology and geography in the subsequent decades, and formed the foundations on which much of the literature on the outsiders' views discussed above has been based. But the ethnographies were not followed by a major research output, although some work continued and there has been a recent revival (as reviewed by Jackson 1985). By referring to that literature, however, we can get some insight into life in American cities, noting that the goal is that expressed by one of the Chicago ethnographers, reviewing his thesis on 'Street corner society' (Whyte 1967: 157):

The man who looks at slum districts through the glasses of middle-class morality is not . . . studying the slum district at all but only noting how it differs from a middle-class community. He seeks to discover what [the slum] . . . is *not*. My study was undertaken to discover what it was.

In presenting such a review, we can note that urban ethnographies suggest *three type areas* in terms of patterns of urban life: the inner city, a complex, high-density mosaic of overlapping communities; the suburbs, characterized by homogeneity; and the small towns.

One of the classic Chicago School monographs was Harvey Zorbaugh's (1929) study of *The Gold Coast and the Slum*, a few square miles to the north of the city centre which contained two social areas – the 'Gold Coast', an upper-income enclave on the lake shore; and the 'slum' – between which there was a rooming-house area. (The extent of these areas, and of their different characteristics, is shown in Fig. 9.8, taken from Zorbaugh's original.) The Gold Coast was characterized by a large number of contributors to the city's United Charities in 1920–21, whereas the slum contained a large number of welfare recipients; in between, the rooming-house area had concentrations of neither givers nor receivers. Regarding the Gold Coast, Zorbaugh (p. 6) wrote that

. . . the Lake Shore Drive is a street more of wealth than of aristocracy . . . an avenue of

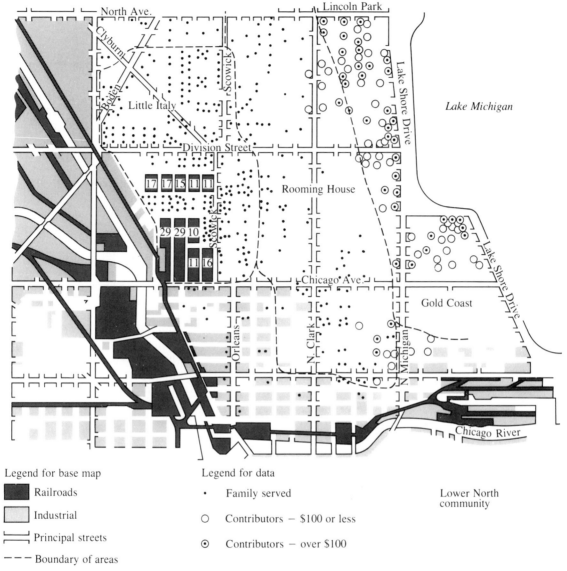

Legend for base map

- ■ Railroads
- ▨ Industrial
- ⌐⌐⌐ Principal streets
- - - - Boundary of areas

Legend for data

- · Family served
- ○ Contributors − $100 or less
- ⊙ Contributors − over $100

Lower North community

Fig. 9.8 Chicago's Gold Coast and slum in 1925. The dots and block totals indicate the number of families receiving welfare; open circles show contributions to United Charities
Source: Zorbaugh (1929), p. 175

fashionable hotels and restaurants, of small clubs and shops . . . On a warm spring Sunday 'Vanity Fair' glides along 'The Drive' and motor cars of expensive mark make colorful the bridle paths.

A few blocks inland is the rooming-house area, comprising

. . . houses with neatly lettered cards in the window: 'Furnished Rooms'. In these houses, from midnight to dawn, sleep some 25 000 people. But by day houses and streets are practically deserted . . . [for] It is a childless area, an area of young men and young women, most of whom are single, though some are married, and others are living together unmarried. It is a world of constant comings and goings, of dull routine and little romance, a world of unsatisfied longings (Zorbaugh 1929: 7).

Further inland, the slum takes over, where

Life . . . is strenuous and precarious . . .
Deteriorated stone buildings, cheap dance halls and
movies, cabarets and doubtful hotels, missions,
'flops', pawnshops and second-hand stores,
innumerable restaurants, soft drink parlors and
'fellowship' saloons, where men sit about and talk,
and which are hangouts for criminal gangs that live
back in the slum, fence at the pawnshops, and
consort with the transient prostitutes so
characteristic of the North Side . . . The slum
harbors many sorts of people: the criminal, the
radical, the bohemian, the migratory worker, the
immigrant, the unsuccessful, the queer and
unadjusted (Zorbaugh 1929: 9).

These three areas border each other and yet,
as Zorbaugh expresses it, they are many miles
from each other socially. Each is a separate
world, unvisited by residents of the others:

The isolation of the populations crowded together
within these few hundred blocks, the superficial
and externality of the contacts, the social distances
that separate them, their absorption in the affairs
of their own little worlds there, and not mere size
and numbers, constitute the social problems of the
inner city (Zorbaugh 1929: 15).

These pen-pictures of three adjacent social
areas, based on field experience rather than on
data collected by others which by their very
nature could not capture the nuances of life
portrayed by somebody who had been there,
not as a tourist (or academic voyeur) but as one
seeking to appreciate the texture of social life,
were drawn in 1929. But 50 years later, Hunter
reported that while much had changed, much
was still the same:

The Near North Side falls into that category of
local communities that has retained the same
functional niche and symbolic identification while
experiencing dynamic invasion and succession of
people and buildings throughout the last half
century. Metaphorically, it is new wine in old
bottles; the spatial and ecological *form* of the
community has remained, while the *content* has
changed over time. One may still find in the Near
North Side the clearly demarcated neighborhoods
of the Gold Coast lying along the lakefront to the
east, the Slum on the Chicago River to the West,
and in between the 'world of furnished rooms', the
'bohemia' of Towertown, and the 'Rialto of the
half world' along Rush Street, with its nightclubs
and bright lights (Hunter, 1983: 468).

The *physical* transformation, however, has
been substantial. The brownstone mansions
formerly occupied by the Gold Coast elite have
been replaced by 80–90-storey high-rise
condominiums; the slum housing has been
replaced by one of the largest public housing
projects in the country – but the residents are
still mainly of Italian descent and the project
is known as Cabrini Homes; and the rooming-
houses have been replaced by high-rise and
townhouse developments catering for young
professionals. The communities are similar,
within the context of national social change,
because they have been able to ensure that
despite the physical redevelopment the new
built environment catered for the groups
already resident there. Here, as elsewhere (see
Firey 1947 on Beacon Hill, Boston, for
example), local residents were successful in
their fights to maintain the known social fabric
of the metropolis within which their daily lives
were conducted.

These local communities are crucial to the
social life of the inner-city areas; they provide
a matrix within which social and cultural activities are structured and an environment within
which people feel relatively secure, as against
their usual feelings of insecurity when they face
the larger 'world outside' in all of its
complexity. The importance of this matrix was
one of the major generalizations to emerge
from the ethnographic studies. Of course, not
all areas have a strongly defined community
spirit, and not all residents participate in local
society, but to characterize the inner city as
containing a heterogeneous mass of unrelated
people lacking stable social relationships, as
some commentators (usually outsiders) have
done, is to ignore not only the reality of social
life there but also the informal social organizations through which social relationships are
sustained and reproduced. This was made clear
by Louis Wirth (author of a classic ethnography
on 'The ghetto') in his paper on 'Urbanism as
a way of life' (1938). He defined cities
according to their population size, density and
heterogeneity, and wrote that

the city is characterized by secondary rather than
primary contacts . . . face to face, but nevertheless
impersonal, superficial, transitory and segmental
(p. 12)

Our acquaintances tend to stand in a relationship of utility to us in the sense that the role which each one plays in our life is overwhelmingly regarded as a means for the achievement of our own ends. Whereas the individual gains, on the one hand, a certain degree of emancipation or freedom from the personal and behavioral controls of intimate groups, he loses, on the other hand, the spontaneous self-expression, the morale and the sense of participation that comes from being in an integrated society (pp. 12–13).

close living together and working together of individuals who have no sentimental and emotional ties foster a spirit of competition, aggrandisement, and mutual exploitation (p. 15).

But urban residents, especially inner-city residents, do not necessarily accept this impersonalized life-style based on economic contacts alone, and many act to create communities that counter these trends. Thus, according to Wirth,

. . . Being reduced to a state of virtual impotence as an individual, the urbanite is bound to exert himself by joining with others of similar interest into groups organized to obtain his ends. This results in the enormous multiplication of voluntary organizations directed towards a variety of objectives as there are human needs and interests. While, on the one hand, the traditional ties of human association are weakened, when existence involves a much greater degree of independence between man and man, and a more complicated, fragile, and volatile form of mutual interrelations (Wirth 1938: 22).

The associations that result are not 'communities' as the term is normally interpreted, associated with small towns where population turnover is low, but rather what another member of the Chicago School, Morris Janowitz, has termed 'communities of limited liability', which may or may not have spatial referents. People tend to become involved in the local area only under certain conditions – particular stages of the family and lifecycle, for example, or when the area is under threat from external sources. In the latter situation, as Gerald Suttles has shown in his 'The social order of the slum' (1968), 'defended neighborhoods' may be created to regulate social tensions, imposing well-known, if not clearly-defined on the ground, boundaries of local turfs that are transgressed only with potential danger. Such turfs seem, to Suttles, to reflect the reactions to tensions that are necessary in urban but not in rural areas:

with some exceptions, rural areas do not seem to have defended neighborhoods of the type present in the city. The delinquent gang, restrictive covenants, private guards, and doormen seem to be almost entirely urban phenomena (Suttles 1972: 29).

David Ley, in one of the small number of ethnographic studies conducted by urban geographers in the US, has illustrated this with a map of the gangs and their turfs in the Monroe district of Philadelphia (Fig. 9.9) which shows not only their spheres of influence but also the number of inter-gang incidents which he notes are 'often precipitated by the intrusion of one gang upon the territory of another' (Ley 1974: 130).

Within the inner city, the creation of communities with clearly defined territories is identified by many as a means not only of coping with outside intrusions but also of allowing groups to impose some form of order on the complex uncertainty of the urban environment and society (see Hunter 1978). Thus Ley's residence in Monroe for six months led him to describe the district as a 'frontier outpost', where the black residents had established an area of certainty for the conduct of daily life, within which their children learn a set of responses to the outside, white-dominated, world. They learn not only what types of behaviour are acceptable within the local community, but also what types of response are appropriate to other communities. Thus Hannerz (1969), in his book 'Soulside', an ethnographic study of part of the black ghetto of Washington, DC, discusses, among other things, the definition of sex roles within the community and the various institutions of ghetto social life (bootlegging, the numbers game etc.) plus interpretations of 'the world outside'; see also Whyte's (1967) discussion of the sexual roles of 'street wise society'.

In contrast to the social disorganization of the inner city perceived by many outsiders is the stability and organization of the small town in American society. The classic studies of these places – such as that of Muncie, Indiana, by Robert and Helen Lynd (1929) and of

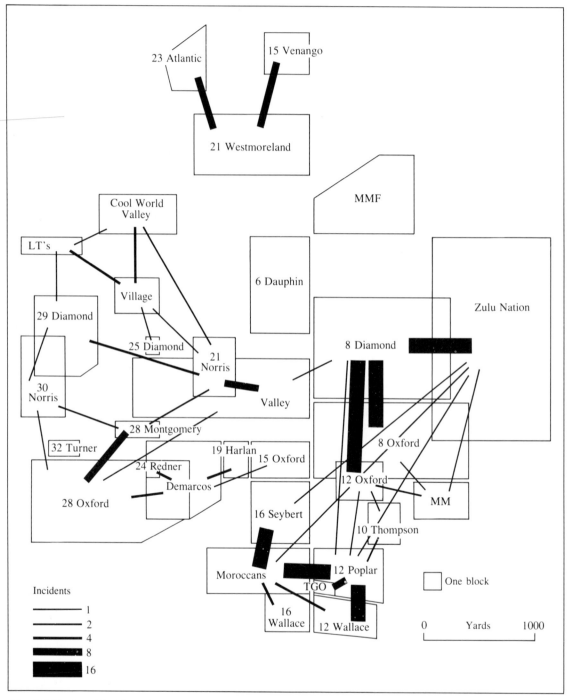

Fig. 9.9 Turf and incidents between thirty-two active North Philadelphia street gangs, 1966–70
Source: Ley (1974), Fig. 22, p. 131

Newburyport, Mass, by W. Lloyd Warner and his associates (see, for example, Warner and Lunt 1941) – are now somewhat dated, although their legacy continues to inform portrayals of such places today. Particular concerns of such studies were the issues of 'Who rules?' (of which the major study was that of New Haven, CT, by Dahl 1961). What the studies found was a very segmented society with relatively little social mobility; it was almost a caste system in which individuals 'knew their place' and accepted the role within society associated with it.

Between the small towns and the inner cities are the suburbs, the general view of which has been portrayed by Dobriner.

Social and personal differences are submerged beneath a great blanket of conformity. The chief delineating feature of suburbia is compulsive, frenetic, outgoing social life – togetherness, belongingness, Kaffeeklatsches, PTA, backfence gossip confabulations, cocktail parties, car pools, and the 'open door'. Suburbia is the melancholia of those whose individuality has succumbed to the inexorable pressures of The Organization, bureaucracy, mass culture, uniformity, conformity, monotony . . . Ideologically quiescent, escapist, frenetic, on the social level, suburbs lack both the liberalism and vitality of the city and the unsophisticated simplicity and strength of the rural village (Dobriner 1963: 6–7).

From the literature – much of it often designated as 'popular sociology', as with William H. Whyte's *The Organization Man* (1956), which described the suburb of Park Forest, – Dobriner identified ten images of suburbia: warrens of young executives on 'the way up'; middle-class; homogeneous; hot beds of participation; female-dominated and child-centred; transient; 'wellsprings of the outgoing life'; areas of adjustment; areas of religious revival; and 'political Jordans from which Democrats emerge Republicans'.

Such images present a very stereotyped view, and have been attacked in a variety of ways by studies which show the considerable variability within and between suburbs. (Particularly influential was Berger's (1960) study of *Working Class Suburb*.) Many of the extensive suburban tracts developed after World War II (see Checkoway 1980) did fit a lot of the stereotypes, however. Herbert Gans spent two years

in Levittown gaining material for his book, for example, and concluded that

most new suburbanites are pleased with the community that develops: they enjoy the house and outdoor living and take pleasure from the large supply of compatible people, without experiencing the boredom and malaise ascribed to suburban homogeneity . . . they do not develop new life styles or ambitions for themselves and their children. However, many of the changes that do take place were desired before the move. Because the suburb makes them possible, morale goes up, boredom and loneliness are reduced, family life becomes temporarily more cohesive, social and organizational activities multiply and spare-time pursuits now concentrate on the house and yard (Gans 1967: 409).

Indeed, so similar are many of the suburbs that Vance Packard, in *A Nation of Strangers* (1972), suggested that people were able to move from one to another, perhaps 2000 miles apart, and readily adapt – perhaps not even notice the difference. As Whyte put it in discussing the 'organization man':

More and more, the young couples who move do so only physically. With each transfer the decor, the architecture, the faces, and the names may change; the people, the conversation, and the values do not – and sometimes the decor and the architecture don't either. If there are no company people to help the newcomers break ice, there are almost bound to be some fellow transients nearby, and the chances are good that some of them will be couples that the most recent arrivals have run into somewhere else in this great new freemasonry of transients . . . But even if they know no one it will not make too much difference. Whatever their respective organizations they will share the same problems, the same kind of memories and aspirations. To use a favorite phrase, they talk the same language (Whyte 1956: 255).

The picture painted by all of these studies is of three polar or 'ideal types' of community in contemporary America. The first is the *stable small town*, with rigidly defined class and caste structures in which people are born into a particular place in society which they accept (assuming that they stay there) and social life is marked by long-term continuity. The second is the *inner-city mosaic of communities of limited liability*. This is where many new Americans congregate, along with the rootless from other parts of society. Some of the residents are alienated, experience shallow, superficial lives, and develop no close social relationships. (Some may be successful in the economic sectors; others may not – as on skid row.) But the inner city is not chaotic: much of it comprises dense, local communities of people with particular interests and backgrounds who have clustered together and formed communities to give some social stability in the complexity of urban life, marking out their territories and being prepared to defend them, and the ways of life that they contain, when threatened – whether by city planners or other communities. Finally, there are the *hyperactive, homogeneous suburbs* where family-centred social relationships characterize the lives of the middle class.

This typology is, of course, a simplification designed simply to illustrate the major features of living in America (see Fischer 1975b; and, for a more sophisticated typology, Suttles 1975). Where you can live, as shown in earlier chapters, depends very much on what you are – especially what your income is – and who you are – what your skin colour is. The type of area in which you find yourself will then provide a particular set of social resources, which you may or may not avail yourself of. Your life chances are a function of your position in society, something which you can influence (through educational and occupational success, for example) but rarely determine, because whether you can work depends on others. Your lifestyle is your own choice too, but this is strongly influenced by your employment, by the type of social environment you are raised in, the attitudes and values you absorb and learn from your parents and kin, your neighbours and schoolmates. Having been socialized to a particular way of life, you will probably want to maintain it, or at least some parts of it, choosing to live in a community that provides a similar environment for your children. Again, it is your choice, but it is constrained by circumstances that are outside your control.

In summary

Living in America for most people involves inhabiting a relatively secure, private and protected space – one's home – that is part of a larger conglomeration of such places. Beyond it is a complex economic, social and political environment, the nature of which varies greatly from place to place, sometimes over very short distances only. As outsiders, we can describe some of those variations and can give a general impression of what the places in which people live out their daily existence is like. But that general impression is frequently superficial and tells us very little about the quality of life, about what it is really like to live somewhere. For that, we need the insider's view – including our own – for daily lives are made up of social encounters and relationships, economic and political transactions, not data. Achieving such appreciation is difficult, for the methodology of understanding is much harder to apply than that of outside description. Without it, we will not really grasp what it is like not simply to be an American but to be an American living in a certain place.

What when we achieve that understanding? Will greater awareness improve society? It should, according to Richard Sennett in *The Uses of Disorder* (1970), because it will force us to accommodate to the variety that is America, especially urban America. We live, he claims, in a series of 'purified identities', separating ourselves in a variety of ways from segments of society. Not only do we fail to encounter much of society, however, but we also represent those non-encountered parts by a series of stereotypes. We have stereotypes of places – rural areas are presented frequently, and romantically, as idylls of placidity and stability, as 'good' places to live, whereas cities are vulgar, brash, dirty and altogether degrading: unfortunately, we have to work in cities, so we long to live in suburbs, the closest to the overall idyll that we can get. Much more importantly, we create stereotyped images of people according to characteristics – their sex, age, race and religion, and their income and 'class' – and treat them as members of a type rather than as individuals. Further, our representations of those types involve 'them–us' comparisons, and frequently 'they' are presented negatively (as with the common representation of blacks by many white Americans), based on second-hand, generalized knowledge rather than first-hand, deep experience. This acting on the basis of stereotypes is immature, according to

Sennett, and the cause of much tension in society, which can build up to produce inter-group conflict. as in the race riots of the late 1960s. We need to purge those purified ident-ities, he argues, and create a mature society in which people can accommodate to differences because they understand them. A better-informed and aware society is a more caring and harmonious society.

Awareness can promote accommodation. It can remove many of the stereotypes and foster the development of social cohesion. But it does not tackle the worst problems. As demon-strated here, the quality of life is inextricably linked to position in the capitalist system – *not who you are, but what you are and where you are*. While that basic source of inequality remains, we will always be looking at the vari-able welfare geography of the US, for the manipulation of space and place is part (a necessary part) of the creation and reproduc-tion of a capitalist society.

REFERENCES

Advisory Commission on Intergovernmental Relations (1980) *Regional Growth: Historical Perspectives*, A-74, Washington, DC.

Aiken, C. (1971) An examination of the role of the Eli Whitney cotton gin in the origin of the United States cotton regions, *Proceedings Association of American Geographers* **3**, 5–9.

Alcaly, R. E. and Mermelstein, D. (1977) *The Fiscal Crisis of American Cities*. Vintage Books, New York.

Allen, H. B. (1973) *The Linguistic Atlas of the Upper Midwest*. University of Minnesota Press, Minneapolis.

Allen, J. (1977) Changes in the American propensity to migrate, *Annals, American Association of Geographers* **67**, 577–87.

Allen, J. L. (1976) Lands of myth, waters of wonder: The place of imagination in the history of geographical exploration, in Lowenthal, D. and Bowden, M. J. (eds), *Geographies of the Mind: Essays in Historical Geography*. Oxford University Press, London, pp. 41–61.

Allman, T. D. (1978) The urban crisis leaves town and moves to the suburbs, *Harpers* **257**, 41–56.

Anki, R. (1974) Farm-making costs in the 1850s, in Whitaker, J. (ed.), *Farming in the Midwest 1840–1900*. Kimberly Press for the Agricultural History Society, pp. 186–211.

Anthony, C. (1976) The big house and the slave quarters, *Landscape* **20**, 8–19.

Archer, J. C. (1980) Congressional incumbent reelection success and federal outlays distribution: a test of the electoral-connection hypothesis, *Environment and Planning A* **12**, 263–77.

Archer, J. C. (1983) The geography of federal fiscal politics in the USA: An explanation, *Environment and Planning, C* **1**, 377–400.

Archer, J. C. (1985) Political geography of contemporary events VI: Some geographical aspects of the American presidential election of 1984, *Political Geography Quarterly*, **4**, 159–72.

Archer, J. C. *et al.* (1985) Counties, States, sections, and parties in the 1984 Presidential election, *The Professional Geographer* **35**, 279–87.

Archer, J. C. and Taylor, P. J. (1981) *Section and Party: A Political Geography of American Presidential Elections, from Andrew Jackson to Ronald Reagan*. John Wiley, Chichester.

Armington, C. (1986) The changing geography of high-tech businesses, in J. Rees (ed.), *Technology, Regions and Policy*. Rowman and Littlefield, Totowa, N J, pp. 75–93.

Armstrong, R. B. (1979) National trends in office construction, employment and headquarters location in US Metropolitan Areas, in P. W. Daniels (ed.), *Spatial Patterns of Office Growth and Location*. Wiley, London, pp. 61–94.

Babcock, C. M. (1965) *The American Frontier: A Social and Literary Record*. Holt, Rinehart and Winston, Inc., New York.

Baerwald, T. (1978) The emergence of a new 'downtown', *Geographical Review* **78**, 308–18.

Baerwald, T. (1983) Transportation and the decentralization of activity in North American metropolises, *Proceedings*, IGU Working Group on the Geography of Transport, Department of Geography, Athens, Georgia, pp. 1–20.

Baerwald, T. (1984) The geographic structure of modern North American metropolises. Paper presented to the 25th International Geographical Congress, Paris.

Baker, O. E. (1926) Agricultural regions of North America, *Economic Geography* **2**, 459–93.

Ballard, K. and Clark, G. (1981) The short-run dynamics of interstate migration: a space–time economic adjustment model, *Regional Studies* **15**, 213–28.

Ballard, S. C. and James, T. E. (eds) (1983) *The Future of the Sunbelt*. Praeger, New York.

Baltensberger, B. (1983) Agricultural change among Great Plains Russian Germans, *Annals, Association of American Geographers* **73**, 75–88.

Banks, U. and Mills, K. (1984) Farm population of the United States: 1983, *Current Population Reports, Series P-27, No. 57*. Bureau of the Census, Washington, DC.

Batteau, A. (ed.) (1983) *Appalachia and America: Autonomy and Regional Dependence*. University Press of Kentucky, Lexington.

Beale, C. (1975) *The Revival of Population Growth in Non-metropolitan America*, Center for Demography and Ecology, CDE Working Paper 75–22, Madison, Wisconsin.

Beale, C. (1977) The recent shift of United States population to non-metropolitan areas, 1970–75, *International Regional Science Review* **2**, 113–22.

Beale, C. and Fuguitt, G. (1981) Demographic perspectives on midwestern population redistribution, in Roseman, C. (ed.), *Population Redistribution in the Midwest*. North Central Regional Center for Rural Development, Ames, Iowa.

Beard, C. A. (1924) *Contemporary American History, 1877–1913*. Macmillan, New York.

Beck, M., Hager, M. *et al.* (1983) Battle over the wilderness, *Newsweek* (25 July), 22–31.

Beenstock, M. (1983) *The World Economy in Transition*. Allen and Unwin, London.

Bennett, J. O., Johnson, P. S. C., Key, J. R., Pattie, C. D. and Taylor, A. H. (1984) Foreseeable effects of nuclear detonations on a local environment: Boulder County, Colorado, *Environmental Conservation* **11**, 155–65.

Bennett, S. J. and Earle, C. V. (1983) Socialism in America: a geographical interpretation of its failure, *Political Geography Quarterly* **2**, 31–56.

Berger, B. (1960) *Working Class Suburb*. University of California Press, Berkeley.

Bergman, R. (1981) *A Time to Choose*. US Department of Agriculture, Washington, DC.

Berkhofer, R. F. (1964) Space, time, culture and the new frontier, *Agricultural History* **38**, 21–30.

Berry, B. J. L. (1972) Hierarchical diffusion: The basis of development and filtering and spread in a system of growth centers, in Hansen, N. (ed.) *Growth Centers in Regional Economic Development*. Free Press, NY, pp. 108–38.

Berry, B. J. L. (1981) Inner-city futures: an American dilemma revisited, in Stave, B. M. (ed.), *Modern Industrial Cities*. Sage, Beverly Hills, pp. 187–220.

Betz, M. (1972) The city as a system generating income inequality, *The Review of Regional Studies* **5**, 42–51.

Beyers, W. B. (1979) Contemporary trends in the regional economic development of the United States, *Professional Geographer* **31**, 34–44.

Biggar, J. (1984) *The Greying of the Sunbelt: A Look at the Impact of U.S. Elderly Migration*. Population Reference Bureau, Washington, DC.

Billington, R. A. (1960) *Westward Expansion.* Macmillan, New York.

Billington, R. A. (1981) *Land of Savagery/Land of Promise: The European Image of the Frontier in the Nineteenth Century.* W. W. Norton and Co., New York.

Blackburn, M. L. and Bloom, D. E. (1985) What is happening to the middle class?, *American Demographics* **7**, 19–25.

Blinder, A. S. (1982) The level and distribution of economic well-being, in Feldstein, M. (ed.), *The American Economy in Transition*, University of Chicago Press, Chicago, pp. 415–79.

Block, R. (1980) Frederick Jackson Turner and American geography, *Annals, Association of American Geographers* **70**, 459–93.

Bluestone, B. and Harrison, B. (1982) *The Deindustrialization of America.* Basic Books, New York.

Bohland, J., Rowles, G. and Hanham, R. (1985) The significance of elderly in-migration to changes in elderly net migration in the United States 1960–1980. Paper presented at the annual meeting of the Association of American Geographers, Detroit.

Bohland, J. Shumsky, L. and Knox, P. (1985) Location and professional conflict: Spatial patterns of allopaths and sectarian physicians in the period of industrial capitalism. Paper presented to the annual meeting of History of Medicine, Durham, NC.

Bohland, J. and Treps, L. (1981) County pattern of elderly migration in the United States, in Warnes, A. (ed.), *Geographical Perspective on the Elderly*, John Wiley, pp. 35–53.

Bogue, A. (1963) *From Prairie to Corn Belt.* University of Chicago Press, Chicago.

Bogue, D. (1969) *Principles of Demography.* Wiley, New York.

Bogue, D. (1985) *The Population of the U.S.: Historical Trends and Future Projections.* Free Press, New York.

Bogue, D., Shryock, H. S. and Hoermann, S. A. (1957) *Stream of Migration Between Subregions.* Scripps Foundation for Research in Population Problems, Miami University, Oxford, Ohio, p. 40.

Boorstin, D. J. (1958) *The Americans: The Colonial Experience.* Random House, New York.

Boorstin, D. J. (1965) *The Americans: National Experience.* Random House, New York.

Boorstin, D. J. (1973) *The Americans: The Democratic Experience.* Random House, New York.

Borchert, J. R. (1967) American metropolitan evolution, *Geographical Review* **57**, 301–32.

Borchert, J. R. (1978) Major control points in American economic geography, *Annals, Association of American Geographers* **68**, 214–32.

Borchert, J. R. (1983) Instability in American metropolitan growth, *Geographical Review*, **73**, 127–49.

Borchert, J. R. (1985) Geography and state–local public policy, *Annals, Association of American Geographers* **75**, 1:1–4.

Bouvier, L. and Agresta, J. (1985) The fastest growing minority, *American Demographics* **7**, 31–46.

Bowles, G., Beale, C. and Lee, E. (1977) *Net migration of the population, 1960–1970 by age, sex and color. Analytical Grouping of Countries*, Economic Research Division, US Department of Agriculture.

Boyer, R. and Savageau, D. (1985) *Places Rated Almanac.* Rand McNally, Chicago.

Bradshaw, M. J. (1985) Public policy in Appalachia, *Transactions, Institute of British Geographers* **10**, 385–400.

Break, G. (1980) The role of government: taxes, transfers and spending, in Feldstein, M. (ed.), *The American Economy in Transition.* University of Chicago Press, Chicago, pp. 617–56.

Brooks, V. W. (1936) *The Flowering of New England.* Houghton Mifflin Company, Boston, 1981.

Brown, B. *et al.* (1977) *Women's Rights and the Law: The Impact of the ERA on State laws.* Praeger, New York.

Brown, D. L. and Beale, C. L. (1981) Diversity in post-1970 population trends, in Hawley, A. H. and Mazie, S. M. (eds), *Nonmetropolitan America in Transition.* University of North Carolina Press, Chapel Hill, pp. 27–71.

Brown, R. H. (1948) *Historical Geography of the United States.* Harcourt, Brace and World, Inc., New York.

Brownell, J. W. (1960) The cultural midwest, *The Journal of Geography* **59**, 80–5.

Browning, C. E. and Gessler, W. (1979) The Sunbelt–Snowbelt: a case of sloppy regionalizing, *Professional Geographer* **31**, 66–74.

Bunge, W. (1975) Detroit humanly viewed: the American urban present, pp. 149–181 in Abler, R., Janelle, D., Philbrick, A. and Sommer, J. (eds), *Human Geography in a Shrinking World*. Dusburg, North Scituate, Mass.

Burgess, E. W. (1967) Research in urban society: a long view, in Burgess, F. W. and Bogue, D. J. (eds), *Urban Sociology*. Phoenix Books, Chicago, pp. 1–14.

Business Week (1979) The decline of US power, 12 March.

Buss, T. and Redburn, F. (1983) *Shutdown at Youngstown*. State University of New York Press, Albany.

Butz, E. (1976) *The Guardian*, 4 January.

Campbell, A. (1984) *The Girls in the Gang: A Report from New York City*. Basil Blackwell, Oxford.

Campbell, R. (1985) Crisis on the farm, *American Demographics* **7**, 30–2.

Campbell, R., Johnson, D. and Stangler, G. (1974) Return migration of black people to the South, *Rural Sociology* **39**, 514–28.

Carey, G. and Greenberg, M. (1974) Toward a geographical theory of hypocritical decision-making, *Human Ecology* **2**, 243–57.

Carney, G. O. (1980) Country music and the South: a cultural geography perspective, *Journal of Cultural Geography* **1**, 16–33.

Cash, W. J. (1941) *The Mind of the South*. Knopf, New York.

Castells, M. (1980) *The Economic Crisis and American Society*. Blackwell, Oxford.

Castells, M. (1985) High technology, economic restructing, and the urban-regional process in the United States, in Castells, M. (ed.), *High Technology, Space and Society*. Sage, Beverly Hills, pp. 11–40.

Cebula, R. J. (1983) *Geographic Living Cost Differentials*. Lexington Books, Lexington, MA.

Checkoway, B. (1980) Large builders, federal housing programmes and postwar suburbanization. *International Journal of Urban and Regional Research* **4**, 21–45.

Chisholm, M. (1979) *Rural Settlement and Land Use*. Hutchinson, London.

Chiswick, B. R. (1974) *Income Inequality: Regional Analysis Within a Human Capital Framework*. Columbia University Press, New York.

Church, G. (1985) A melding of cultures, *Time* **126** (8 July), 36–9.

Clapp, J. A. (1984) *The City, A Dictionary of Quotable Thought on Cities and Urban Life*. Center for Urban Policy Research, New Brunswick.

Clark, G. L. (1981) Law, the state and the spatial integration of the United States, *Environment and Planning A* **13**, 1197–1227.

Clark, G. L. (1982a) Volatility in the geographical structure of short-run U.S. interstate migration, *Environment and Planning* **14**, 145–67.

Clark, G. L. (1982b) Dynamics of interstate labor migration, *Annals, Association of American Geographers* **72**, 297–313.

Clark, G. L. (1985) *Judges and the Cities*. University of Chicago Press, Chicago.

Clark, G. L. and Ballard, K. (1980) Modeling out-migration from depressed regions: the significance of origin and destination characteristics, *Environment and Planning* **12**, 799–812.

Clark, G. L. and Ballard, K. (1981) The demand and supply of labor and interstate relative wages: an empirical analysis, *Economic Geography* **57**, 95–112.

Clark, G. L. and Dear, M. J. (1984) *State Apparatus: Structures and Language of Legitimacy*. George Allen and Unwin, London.

Clark, N. G. (1972) Science, technology and regional economic development, *Research Policy* **1**, 296–319.

Clark, T. A. (1980) Regional and structural shifts in the American economy since 1960, in Brunn, S. D. and Wheeler, J. O. (eds), *The American Metropolitan System*. Arnold, London.

Clawson, M. (1983) *The Federal Lands Revisited*. Resources for the Future, Washington, DC.

Cohen, J. M. (ed.) (1969) *The Four Voyages of Christopher Columbus*. Penguin Books, Baltimore.

Congressional Budget Office (1985) *Children in Poverty*. US Government Printing Office, Washington, DC.

Conzen, M. P. (1977) The maturing urban system in the United States, 1840–1910, *Annals, Association of American Geographers* **67**, 88–108.

Conzen, M. P. (1981) The American urban system in the nineteenth century, in Herbert, D. and Johnston, R. J. (eds), *Geography and the Urban Environment*, Vol 4, pp. 295–347.

Cooper, J. F. (1826) *The Prairie*. Pantheon Books, New York, 1954.

Copeland, G. W. and Meier, K.J. (1984) Pass the biscuits, pappy: Congressional decision-making and federal grants, *American Politics Quarterly* **12**, 3–21.

Cowart, A. T. (1969) Anti-poverty expenditures in the American States: a comparative analysis, *Midwest Journal of Political Science* **13**, 219–36.

Crevecoeur, H. de (1782) *Letters from an American Farmer*. E. P. Dutton & Co., New York, 1962.

Cribier, F. (1982) Aspects of retired migration from Paris: An essay in social and cultural geography, in Warnes, A. M. (ed.), *Geographical Perspectives on the Elderly*, John Wiley, New York, pp. 111–37.

Cronon, W. (1983) *Changes in the Land: Indians, Colonists, and the Ecology of New England*. Hill and Wang, New York.

Cutter, S. (1985) *Rating Places: A Geographer's View on Quality of Life*. Association of American Geographers, Washington, DC.

Cutter, S., Holcomb, H. B. and Shatin, D. (1986) Spatial patterns of support for a nuclear weapons freeze, *Professional Geographer* **38**, 42–52.

Cybriwsky, R. A., Ley, D. and Western, J. (1986) The political and social construction of revitalization in Society Hill, Philadelphia, and False Creek, Vancouver, in Smith, N. and Williams, P. (eds), *Gentrification, Housing and the Restructuring of Urban Space*. Allen and Unwin, Boston, pp. 92–120.

Dahl, R. A. (1961) *Who Governs?* Yale University Press, New Haven.

Daiches, S. (1981) *People in Distress: A Geographical Perspective of Psychological Well-Being*. University of Chicago Department of Geography Research Paper #197, Chicago.

Danhof, C. (1941) Farm-making costs and the safety valve, *Journal of Political Economy* **49**, 317–59.

Davis, C., Haub, C. and Willette, J. (1983) *U.S. Hispanics: Changing the face of America*. Population Reference Bureau, Washington, DC.

Davis, G. A. and Donaldson, O. F. (1975) *Blacks in the United States: A Geographic Perspective*. Houghton Mifflin, Boston.

Davis, J. and Goldberg, R. A. (1957) *A Concept of Agribusiness*. Alpine Press, Boston.

Davis, T. (1979) *Persistent Low Income Counties in Nonmetro America*. Economic Development Division; Economics, Statistics, and Cooperative Services; US Department of Agriculture, Washington, DC.

de Geer, S. (1927) The American Manufacturing Belt, *Geografiska Annaler* **9**, 233–359.

De Giovanni, F. F. (1984) An examination of selected consequences of revitalization in six US cities, *Urban Studies* **21**, 245–60.

de Jong, C. and Humphrey, C. (1976) Selected characteristics of metropolitan to nonmetropolitan area migrants: a study of population redistribution in Pennsylvania, *Rural Sociology* **41**, 527–38.

Denison, E. F. (1979) Explanations of declining productivity, *Survey of Current Business* **59**, 1–24.

Dickens, C. (1890) *American Notes for General Circulation and Hunted Down*. Estes and Lauriat, Boston.

Dickson, R. E. (1983) *Traveling exhibit on national parks*. US National Park Service, Washington DC.

Dilger, R. J. (1982) *The Sunbelt/Snowbelt Controversy: the war over federal funds*. New York University Press, New York.

Dillman, D. (1979) Residential preferences, quality of life, and the population turnaround, *American Journal of Agricultural Economics* **61**, 960–6.

Dobriner, W. (1963) *Class in Suburbia.* Prentice-Hall, Englewood Cliffs.

Donahue, J. (1983) The political economy of milk, *The Atlantic* **252**, 58–68.

Dubos, R. (1968) *Man, Medicine and Environment.* Praeger, New York.

Dunn, E. S. Jr (1980) *The Development of the US Urban System,* Vol. 1, *Concepts, Structures, Regional Shifts.* Johns Hopkins University Press, Baltimore.

Dunn, E. S. Jr. (1983) *The Development of the US Urban System,* Vol. 2, *Industrial Shifts, Implications.* Johns Hopkins University Press, Baltimore.

Dunning, J. H. and Pearce, R. D. (1985) *The World's Largest Industrial Enterprises 1962–1983.* St Martin's, New York.

Dye, T. R. (1984) Party and policy in the States, *The Journal of Politics* **46**, 1097–1116.

Easterlin, R. (1980) American population since 1940, in Feldstein, M. *The American Economy in Transition.* University of Chicago Press, Chicago, pp. 275–321.

Edmonston, B. and Guterbock, T. M. (1984) Is suburbanization slowing down? Recent trends in population deconcentration in US metropolitan areas, *Social Forces* **62**, 905–25.

Edwards, R. C., Reich, M. and Gordon, D. (eds) (1975) *Labor Market Segmentation.* Lexington Books, Lexington, Mass.

Egerton, J. (1974) *The Americanization of Dixie: The Southernization of America.* New York Harpers Magazine Press, New York.

Elazar, D. J. (1966) *American Federalism: The View from the States.* Thomas Y. Crowell, New York.

Ely, R. T. (1917) Landed property as an economic concept and as a field of research, *American Economic Review* **7**, 18–35.

Emerson, R. W. (1844) *Journals of Ralph Waldo Emerson,* 6, Emerson, E. W. (ed.). Forbes, New York, 1910.

Emerson, R. W. (1856) English traits, *The Selected Writings of Ralph Waldo Emerson.* Modern Library, New York, 14, pp. 523–690.

Energy Information Administration (1983) *Typical Electric Bills,* Department of Energy, Washington, DC.

Engels, R. and Forstall, R. (1985) Metropolitan areas are growing again, *American Demographics* **7**, 23–5.

Erickson, R. A. (1983). The evolution of the suburban space-economy, *Urban Geography* **4**, 95–121.

Erickson, R. A. and Leinbach, T. R. (1979) Characteristics of branch plants attracted to nonmetropolitan areas, in Lonsdale, R. E. and Seyler, H. L. (eds), *Nonmetropolitan Industrialization.* Wiley, New York, 57–68.

Estall, R. (1977) Regional planning in the United States: an evaluation of experience under the 1965 Economic Development Act, *Town Planning Review* **48**, 341–64.

Estall, R. (1982) Planning in Appalachia: an examination of the Appalachian regional development programme and its implications for the future of the American Regional Planning Commissions, *Transactions, Institute of British Geographers* **7**, 35–58.

Estall, R. (1983) The decentralization of manufacturing industry: Recent American experience in perspective, *Geoforum* **14**, 133–48.

Fainstein, N. and Fainstein, S (1978) Federal policy and spatial inequality in Sternlieb, G. and Hughes, J. W. (eds), *Revitalizing the Northeast.* Center for Urban Policy Research, Rutgers University, New Brunswick.

Fallows, J. (1982) Immigration, *Atlantic* **252**, 45–106.

Fallows, J. (1985) America's changing economic landscape, *Atlantic* **287**, 47–68.

Faulkner, W. (1942) The bear, in *The Portable Faulkner,* Viking Press, New York, 1946.

Feagin, J. R. (1984) Sunbelt metropolis and development capital: Houston in the era of late capitalism, in Sawers, L. and Tabb, W. K. (eds), *Sunbelt/Snowbelt.* Oxford University Press, New York, pp. 99–127.

Fein, A. (ed.) (1968) *Landscape into Cityscape.* Cornell University Press, Ithaca, NY.

Fein, A. (1972) *Frederick Law Olmstead and the American Environmental Tradition.* George Braziller, New York.

Felder, H. E. (1984) *The Changing Patterns of Black Family Income, 1960–1982.* Joint Center for Political Studies, Washington, DC.

Feldman, M. A. (1983) Biotechnology and local economic growth: the American pattern, *Built Environment* **9**, 40–50.

Ferejohn, J. A. (1974) *Pork Barrel Politics: River and Harbors Legislation, 1947–1968*. Stanford University Press, Stanford, CA.

Firey, W. (1947) *Land Use in Central Boston*. Harvard University Press, Cambridge.

Fischer, C. (1975a) The effects of urban life on traditional values, *Social Forces* **53**, 420–32.

Fischer, C. (1975b) The metropolitan experience, in Hawley, A. H. and Rock, V. (eds), *Metropolitan America in Contemporary Perspective*. Halsted Press, New York, pp. 201–34.

Fischer, C. (1976) *The Urban Experience*. Harcourt, Brace Jovanovich, New York.

Fischer, J. S. (1981) Structural adjustments in the Southern manufacturing sector, *Professional Geographer* **33**, 466–74.

Fishlow, A. (1965) *American Railroads and the Transformation of the Antebellum Economy*. Harvard University Press, Cambridge, Mass.

Fitchen, J. M. (1981) *Poverty in Rural America: A Case Study*. Westview Press, Boulder, Colorado.

Florin, J. (1971) *Death in New England*. University of North Carolina, Dept. of Geography, Chapel Hill.

Fogel, R. W. (1964) *Railroads and American Economic Growth*. Johns Hopkins Press, Baltimore.

Ford, L. (1971) Geographical factors in the origin, evolution and diffusion of rock and roll music, *Journal of Geography* **70**, 455–64.

Fosler, R. S. and Berger, R. A. (eds) (1982) *Public–Private Partnership in American Cities: Seven Case Studies*. Lexington Books, Lexington, MA.

Fox, M. (1983) Working women and travel: The access of women to work and community facilities, *Journal of the American Planning Association* **49**, 156–70.

Freeman, R. B. (1980) The evolution of the American labor market, 1948–80 in Feldstein, M. (ed.), *The American Economy in Transition*. University of Chicago Press, Chicago, pp. 349–96.

Friedmann, J. and Weaver, C. (1979) *Territory and Function*. University of California Press, Berkeley.

Fuchs, V. (1980) Continuity and change in American life, in Feldstein, M. (ed.), *The American Economy in Transition*. University of Chicago Press, Chicago, pp. 322–34.

Galbraith, J. K. (1958) *The Affluent Society*. Houghton Mifflin, Boston.

Gans, H. J. (1967) *The Levittowners*. Allen Lane, London.

Garreau, J. (1981) *The Nine Nations of North America*. Houghton Mifflin, Boston.

Gastil, R. D. (1975) *Cultural Regions of the United States*. University of Washington Press, Seattle.

Giedion, S. (1969) *Mechanization Takes Command: A Contribution to Anonymous History*. W. W. Norton and Co., New York, 1st edn 1948.

Glasmeier, A. K. (1985) Innovative manufacturing industries: spatial incidence in the United States, in Castells, M. (ed.), *High Technology, Space and Society*, Sage, Beverly Hills, pp. 55–80.

Glasser, W. (1978) *The Brain Drain: Emigration and Return*. Pergamon Press, New York.

Glassie, H. (1968) *Pattern in the Material Folk Culture of the Eastern United States*. University of Pennsylvania Press, Philadelphia.

Gleave, D. and Cordey-Hayes, M. (1977) Migration dynamics and labor market turnover, in Diamond, D. and McLoughlin, J. (eds), *Progress in Planning 8*, Oxford, Part 1.

Glickman, N. J. (1983) International trade, capital mobility and economic growth: some implications for American cities and regions in the 1980s, in Hicks, D. A. and Glickman, N. J. (eds), *Transition to the 21st Century*. JAI Press, Greenwich, Connecticut, pp. 205–40.

Glickman, N. J. (1984) Economic policy and the cities: In search of Reagan's real urban policy, *Journal of the American Planning Association* **50**, 471–8.

Golant, S. (1979) *Location and Environment of Elderly Population*. V. H. Winston and Sons, Washington, DC.

Gold, H. (1981) *A Walk on the West Side: California on the Brink*. Arbor House, New York.

Goldstein, S. (1976) Facets of redistribution: Research challenges and opportunities, *Demography* **13**, 423–34.

Goodman, E. (1985) Unwed motherhood isn't glamorous, *Home News* (28 May), 88.

Goodwin, M. (1984) Recovery making New York City of haves and have-nots, *New York Times* (28 July), 1, 27.

Gordon, D. M. (1979) *The Working Poor: Towards a State Agenda.* The Council of State Planning Agencies, Washington, DC.

Gordon, D. M. (1984) Capitalist development and the history of American cities, in Tabb, W. K. and Sawers, L. (eds), *Marxism and the Metropolis* (2nd edn). Oxford University Press, New York, pp. 21–53.

Gordus, J. P., Jarley, P. and Freeman, L. (1981) *Plant closings and economic dislocation.* W. E. Upjohn Institute, Kalamazoo.

Gorham, W. and Glazer, N. (eds) (1976) *The Urban Predicament.* The Urban Institute, Washington, DC.

Gottman, J. (1983) *The Coming of the Transactional City.* Institute for Urban Studies, College Park, MD.

Graff, T. and Wiseman, R. (1978) Changing concentrations of older Americans, *Geographical Review* **68**, 379–93.

Graham, O. L. (1976) *Towards a planned society: from Roosevelt to Nixon.* Oxford University Press, New York.

Greenberg, E. S. (1983) *The American Political System: A Radical Approach* (3rd edn). Little, Brown, Boston.

Greenberg, M. (1981) The changing geography of cancer mortality within metropolitan regions of the U.S., *Demography* **18**, 411–20.

Greenberg, M., Carey, G. and Popper, F. (1987) External causes of death among young adult white Americans, *New England Journal of Medicine*, 27 December.

Greenberg, M., Carey, G. and Popper, F. (1987) Violent death, violent states, and American youth, *The Public Interest*, **87**, 38–46.

Greenwood, M. J. (1975) Research on internal migration in the United States, *Journal of Economic Literature* **13**, 397–433.

Greenwood, M. J. (1981) *Migration and Economic Growth in the United States.* Academic Press, New York.

Gregor, H. (1982) *Industrialization of US Agriculture: An Interpretive Atlas.* Westview Press, Boulder, CO.

Grofman, B. *et al.* (1982) *Representation and Redistricting Issues.* D. C. Heath, Lexington, MA.

Gunter, W. P. and Ellis, C. M. (1977) Income inequality in a depressed area: A principal component analysis, *The Review of Regional Studies* **5**, 42–51.

Hale, R. (1984) Commentary: Vernacular regions of America, *Journal of Cultural Geography* **5**, 131–40.

Hall, P. and Markusen, A. (eds) (1985) *Silicon Landscapes.* Allen and Unwin, Winchester, MA.

Hall, P., Markusen, A., Osborn, R. and Wachsman, B. (1983) The American computer software industry: economic development prospects, *Built Environment* **9**, 29–39.

Hamilton, F. E. I. (1978) Multinational enterprise and the European Economic Community, in Hamilton, F. E. I. (ed.), *Industrial Change: International Experience and Public Policy.* Longman, London, pp. 24–41.

Hannerz, U. (1969) *Soulside.* Columbia University Press, New York.

Hannerz, U. (1980) *Exploring the City.* Columbia University Press, New York.

Hanson, S. and Johnson, I. (1985) Gender differences in work-trip lengths: Explanations and implications, *Urban Geography*, **6**, 198–219.

Haren, C. C. and Halling, R. W. (1979) Industrial development in non-metropolitan America: a locational perspective, in Lonsdale, R. E. and Seyler, H. L. (eds) *Nonmetropolitan Industrialization.* Wiley, New York.

Hareven, T. and Vinovskis, M. A. (eds) (1978) *Family and Population in Nineteenth-Century America.* Princeton University Press, Princeton, NJ.

Harries, K. D. (1974) *The Geography of Crime and Justice.* McGraw Hill, New York.

Harrington, J. W. Jr. (1986) Learning and locational change in the American semiconductor industry, in Rees, J. (ed.),

Technology, Regions and Policy, Rowman and Littlefield, Totowa, NJ, pp. 120–37.

Harrington, M. (1962) *The Other America.* Penguin Books, London.

Harris, C. D. and Ullman, E. L. (1945) The nature of cities, *Annals of the American Academy of Political Science* **242**, 7–17.

Hart, J. F. (1967) *The Southwestern United States.* Van Nostrand Reinhold, New York.

Hart, J. F. (1968) Field patterns in Indiana, *The Geographical Review* **58**, 450–71.

Hart, J. F. (ed.) (1972) *Regions of the United States.* Harper and Row, New York.

Hart, J. F. (1972) The middle west, *Annals, Association of American Geographers* **62**, 256–82.

Hart, J. F. (1975) *The Look of the Land.* Prentice Hall, Englewood Cliffs, NJ.

Hart, J. F. (1977) The demise of king cotton, *Annals, Association of American Geographers* **67**, 307–22.

Hart, J. F. (1980) Land use change in a piedmont county, *Annals, Association of American Geographers* **70**, 492–527.

Hart, J. F. (1984) Population change in the upper lake states, *Annals, Association of American Geographers* **74**, 221–43.

Hart, J. F. and Mather, E. C. (1957) The American fence, *Landscape* **6**, 3: 4–9.

Hartshorn, T. (1980) *Interpreting the City*, Wiley, New York.

Harvey, D. (1966) Theoretical concepts and the analysis of agricultural land use patterns in geography, *Annals, Association of American Geographers* **56**, 361–74.

Harvey, D. (1973) *Social Justice and the City.* John Hopkins Press, Baltimore.

Harvey, D. (1982) *The Limits to Capital.* Basil Blackwell, Oxford.

Hawthorne, N. (1835) Young Goodman Brown, in *Mosses from an Old Manse.* Ohio State University Press, Ohio, 1974.

Hayden, D. (1976) *Seven American Utopias.* MIT Press, Cambridge, MA.

Hayden, D. (1984) *Redesigning the American Dream: The Future of Housing, Work, and Family Life.* W. W. Norton, New York.

Heady, E. (1982) The adequacy of agricultural land: a demand–supply perspective, in Crosson, R. (ed.), *The Cropland Crisis.* Johns Hopkins Press, Baltimore.

Heaton, A. and Fuguitt, G. (1979) Nonmetropolitan industrial growth and net migration, pp. 19–35 in Longdale, R. and Seyler, H., *Nonmetropolitan Industrialization.* V. H. Winston and Sons, Washington, DC, pp. 19–35.

Heer, D. M. (1979) What is the annual net flow of undocumented Mexican immigration to the United States?, *Demography* **16**, 417–23.

Herbert, D. (1982) *The Geography of Urban Crime.* Longman, New York.

Herr, J. P. (1982) Metropolitan political fragmentation and conflict in the location of commercial facilities, in Cox, K. R. and Johnston, R. J. (eds), *Conflict, Politics and the Urban Scene.* Longman, London, pp. 28–44.

Higbee, E. (1958) *American Agriculture: Geography Resources, Conservation.* John Wiley, New York.

Hillard, S. B. (1982) Headrights grants and surveying in Northeastern Georgia, *The Georgraphical Review* **72**, 416–29.

Holcomb, B. (1985) The risks and rewards of urban revitalization by public–private partnership, *Rutgers Graduate Program in Geography Discussion Paper Series*, New Brunswick.

Holcomb, B. and Beauregard, R. A. (1981) *Revitalizing Cities.* Association of American Geographers, Washington, DC.

Hollon, W. E. (1966) *The Great American Desert.* Oxford University Press, London.

Hopkins, R. F. (1979) Lessons of fond diplomacy, in Fraenkel, R., Hadwiger, D. and Browne, W. (eds), *The Role of U.S. Agriculture in Foreign Policy.* Praeger, New York, pp. 137–52.

House, J. W. (1983) Regional and area development, in House, J. W. (ed.), *United States Public Policy.* Oxford University Press, London, pp. 34–79.

Hoyt, H. (1939) *The Structure and Growth of Residential Neighborhoods in American Cities.* Federal Housing Administration, Washington, DC.

Hudson, J. C. (1973) Two Dakota homestead frontiers, *Annals, Association of American Geographers* **63**, 442–62.

Hudson, J. C. (1976) Migration to an American frontier, *Annals, Association of American Geographers* **66**, 242–65.

Hudson, J. C. (1979) *The Plains Country Town,*

in Blouet, B. W. and Luebke, F. C. (eds), *The Great Plains: Environment and Culture*. University of Nebraska Press, Lincoln, pp. 99–118.

Hudson, J. C. (1985) *Plains Country Towns*. University of Minnesota Press, Minneapolis.

Hunter, A. (1978) Persistence of local sentiments in mass society, in Street, D. and associates, *Handbook of Contemporary Urban Life*. Jossey-Bass, San Francisco, pp. 133–62.

Hunter, A. (1983) The Gold Coast and the Slum revisited, *Urban Life* **11**, 461–76.

Immigration and Naturalization Service (1978) *1977 Annual Report: Immigration and Naturalization Services*. US Department of Justice, Washington, DC.

Jackson, G., Massnick, A., Bolton, R., Bartlett, S. and Pitkin, J. (1981) *Regional Diversity and Growth in the United States, 1960–1990*. Auburn House Publishing Co., Boston.

Jackson, J. B. (1970) Jefferson, Thoreau, and after, in Zube, E. H. (ed.), *Selected Writings of J. B. Jackson*. The University of Massachusetts Press, Boston, pp. 1–9.

Jackson, J. B. (1972) *American Space: The Centennial Years: 1865–1876*. W. W. Norton and Co., New York.

Jackson, P. (1985) Urban ethnography, *Progress in Human Geography* **9**, 157–76.

Jacobs, S. S. and Roistacher, E. A. (1980) The urban impacts of HUD's Urban Development Action Grant Program, in Glickman, N. (ed.), *The Urban Impact of Federal Policies*. Johns Hopkins University Press, Baltimore, pp. 335–62.

Jefferson, T. (1787) *Notes on the State of Virginia*, In Peden, W. (ed.). University of North Carolina Press, Chapel Hill, 1955.

Johansen, H. and Fuguitt, G. (1984) *The Changing Rural Village in America*. Ballinger, Cambridge, Mass.

Johnson, H. B. (1974) A historical perspective on form and function in upper midwest rural settlement, in Whitaker, J. (ed.), *Farm in the Midwest: 1840–1900*. Kimberley Press for the Agricultural History Society, pp. 38–52.

Johnston, R. J. (1979a) *Political, Electoral and Spatial Systems*. Oxford University Press, Oxford.

Johnston, R. J. (1979b) Congressional committees and department spending: the political influence on the geography of Federal expenditure in the United States, *Transactions, Institute of British Geographers* **4**, 373–84.

Johnston, R. J. (1980) *The geography of federal spending in the United States of America*. Research Studies Press, Chichester.

Johnston, R. J. (1982a) *Geography and the State*. Macmillan, London.

Johnston, R. J. (1982b) *The American Urban System*. St Martin's, New York.

Johnston, R. J. (1983) Politics and the geography of social well-being, in Busteed, M. A. (ed.), *Developments in Political Geography*. Academic Press, London, pp. 189–250.

Johnston, R. J. (1984) *Residential Segregation, The State and Constitutional Conflict in American Urban Areas*. Academic Press, London.

Johnston, R. J. (1986) The general good of the community: some perspectives on town planning and residential segregation – a Mount Laurel case study, *Planning Perspectives* **1**, 131–45.

Jones, R. (1976) Testing macro-Thunen models by linear programming, *Professional Geographer* **28**, 353–61.

Jones, R. (1982) Undocumented migration from Mexico: some geographic questions, *Annals, American Association of Geographers* **72**, 77–87.

Jones, R. (1984) Macro-patterns of undocumented migration between Mexico and the U. S., in Jones, R. (ed.), *Patterns of Undocumented Migration*. Rowan and Allenheld, Totowa, NJ.

Jordan, T. G. (1964) Between the forest and the prairie, *Agricultural History* **38**, 205–16.

Jordan T. G. (1967) The imprint of the upper and lower south on mid-nineteenth-century Texas, *Annals, Association of American Geographers* **57**, 667–90.

Jordan, T. G. (1972) The origin and distribution of open-range ranching, *Social Science Quarterly* **53**, 105–21.

Jordan, T. G. (1977) Early northeast Texas and the evolution of western ranching, *Annals,*

Association of American Geographers **67**, 66–87.

Jordan, T. G. (1978) Perceptual regions in Texas, *The Geographical Review* **68**, 293–307.

Jordan, T. G. (1980) A religious geography of the hill country Germans of Texas, in Luebke, F. (ed.), *Ethnicity on the Great Plains*. University of Nebraska Press, Lincoln, Nebraska.

Judd, D. G. (1979) *The Politics of American Cities: Private Power and Public Policy*. Little, Brown and Company, Boston.

Judd, D. G. (1985) Public schools and urban development, *Journal of the American Planning Association* **51**, 74–83.

Jusenius, C. L. and Ledebur, L. C. (1976) *A myth in the making: the southern economic challenge and northern economic decline*. Office of Economic Resources, Economic Development Administration, Washington, DC.

Kahn, H. (1967) *The Year 2000*. Macmillan, New York.

Kale, S. R. and Lonsdale, R. E. (1979) Factors encouraging and discouraging plant location in nonmetropolitan areas, in R. E. Lonsdale, R. E. and Seyler, M. R. (eds), *Nonmetropolitan Industrialization*. Wiley, New York, pp. 47–56.

Kasarda, J., Irwin, M. and Hughes, H. (1986) The South is still rising, *American Demographics* **8** (**6**), 32–9, 70.

Katznelson, I. and Kesselman, M. (1975) *The Politics of Power: A Critical Introduction to American Government*. Harcourt, Brace, Jovanovich, New York.

Keinath, W. F. Jr. (1982) The decentralization of American life: an income evaluation, *Economic Geography* **58**, 343–57.

Kellerman, A. (1984) Telecommunications and the geography of metropolitan areas, *Progress in Human Geography* **8**, 222–46.

Kerouac, J. (1957) *On the Road*. Viking Press, New York.

Key, V. O. Jr. (1949) *Southern politics in state and nation*. Knopf, New York.

Kloppenburg, J. and Geisler, C. (1985) The agricultural ladder: Agrarian ideology and the changing structure of U.S. agriculture,

Journal of Rural Studies **1**, 59–72.

Kniffen, F. (1965) Folk housing: Key to diffusion, *Annals of the Association of American Geographers* **55**, 549–77.

Knos, D. (1962) *Distribution of Land Values in Topeka, Kansas*. University of Kansas, Center for Research in Business.

Knox, P. L. (1987) *Urban Social Geography: An Introduction* (2nd edn). Longman, London.

Kollmorgen, W. and Jenks, G, (1958a) Suitcase farming in Sully County, South Dakota, *Annals, Association of American Geographers* **48**, 27–40.

Kollmorgen, W. and Jenks, G. (1958b) Sidewalk farming in Toole County, Montana and Traill County, North Dakota, *Annals, Association of American Geographers* **48**, 209–31.

Kuznets, S. (1964) Introduction: Population redistribution, migration, and economic growth, in Eldridge, H. T. and Thomas, D. (eds), *Demographic Analysis and Interrelations. Vol III. Population Redistribution and Economic Growth: United States, 1870–1950*. The American Philosophical Association, Philadelphia.

Lake, R. (1981) *The New Suburbanites: Race and Housing in the Suburbs*. Center for Urban Policy Research, New Brunswick, N J.

Lamb, R. (1975) *Metropolitan Impacts on Rural America*. University of Chicago, Department of Geography, Research Paper No. 162, Chicago.

Lansing, J. and Muller, E. (1967) *The Geographic Mobility of Labor*. Institute for Social Research, Ann Arbor, Michigan.

Lee, A. (1980) Aged migration: Impact on service delivery, *Research on Aging* **2**, 243–54.

Lee, D. and Schultz, R. (1982) Regional patterns of female status in the United States, *Professional Geographer* **34**, 32–41.

Lelyveld, J. (1985) Hunger in America, *New York Times Magazine* (16 June), 20 ff.

Levitan, S. and Zickler, J. (1976) *Too little but not too late: Federal aid to lagging areas*. D.C. Heath, Lexington, Mass.

Lewis, G. J. (1983) Rural communities, in

Pacione, M. (ed.), *Progress in Rural Geography*. Croom Helm, London, pp. 149–72.

Lewis, G. M. (1968) Levels of living in the Northeastern United States: a new approach to regional geography. *Transactions of the Institute of British Geographers* **45**, 11–37.

Lewis, P. F. (1972) Small town in Pennsylvania, *Annals, Association of American Geographers* **62**, 323–73.

Lewis, P. F. (1976) *New Orleans: The Making of an Urban Landscape*. Ballinger, Cambridge, Mass.

Lewis, W. A. (1978) *The Evolution of the International Economic Order*. Princeton University Press, Princeton.

Ley, D. (1974) *The Black Inner City as Frontier Outpost*. Rand McNally, Chicago.

Lindstrom, D. (1978) *Economic Development in the Philadelphia Region, 1810–1850*. Columbia University Press, N Y.

Little, C. E. (1984) What's happening in the countryside, *Country Journal* (May), 82–9.

Long, L. H. (1980) Back to the countryside and back to the city in the same decade, in Laska, S. and Spain, D. (eds), *Back to the City: Issues in Neighborhood Renovation*. Pergamon, Elmsford, N Y, pp. 61–76.

Long, L. H. and de Are, D. (1980) *Migration to Nonmetropolitan Areas: Appraising the Trend and Reasons for Moving*. US Bureau of the Census, Special Demographic Analysis CD 5-82, Washington, DC.

Long, L. H. and de Are, D. (1981) The suburbanization of blacks, *American Demographics* **3**, 17–21.

Long, L. and Frey, W. (1982) *Migration and Settlement: United States*. International Institute for Applied Systems Analysis, Laxenburg, Austria.

Long, L. and Hansen, K. (1975) Trends in Return Migration to the South. *Demography*, 12, 601–14.

Longino, C. and Biggar, J. (1982) The impact of population redistribution upon urban service delivery, *The Gerontologist* **22**, 153–9.

Lowenthal, D. (1968) The American scene, *The Geographical Review* **58**, 61–88.

Lowenthal, D. (1975) Past time, present place: Landscape and memory, *The Geographical Review* **65**, 1–36.

Lowenthal, D. (1976) The place of the past in the American landscape, in Lowenthal, D. and Bowden, M. J. (eds), *Geographies of the Mind: Essays in Historical Geography*. Oxford University Press, London, pp. 89–117.

Luebke, F. (ed.) (1980) *Ethnicity on the Great Plains*. University of Nebraska Press, Lincoln, Nebraska.

Lynd, R. and Lynd, H. (1929) *Middletown*. Harcourt, Brace, Jovanovich, New York.

McCarthy, H. (1861) The bonnie blue flag, in Commager, H. S. (ed.), *The Blue and the Gray*. The New American Library, New York, 1973, p. 555.

McCarty, K. and Morrison, P. (1977) The changing demographic and economic structure of non-metropolitan areas in the United States, *International Regional Science Review* **2**, 123–42.

McConnell, J. E. (1980) Foreign direct investment in the US, *Annals, Association of American Geographers* **70**, 259–70.

Macdonald, M. C. D. (1984) *America's Cities: A Report on the Myth of Urban Renaissance*. Simon and Schuster, New York.

McFadden, R. (1985) City called unprepared for surge in homeless, *New York Times* (6 October), 42.

McGranahan, D. (1980) The spatial structure of income distribution in rural regions, *American Sociological Review* **45**, 313–24.

McKelvey, B. (1973) *American Urbanization: A Comparative History*. Scott, Foresman, Glenview, IL.

McPhee, J. (1976) *Coming into the Country*. Bantam Books, New York.

Maddock, R. T. (1970) The economic and political characteristics of food as a diplomatic weapon, *Journal of Agricultural Economics* **929**, 31–42.

Madison, A. (1982) *Phases of Capitalist Development*. Oxford University Press, New York.

Magdoff, H. and Sweezy, P. M. (1981) *The Deepening Crisis of U.S. Capitalism*. Monthly Review Press, New York.

Mair, A. (1985) The homeless and the post-industrial city. Paper presented at Annual Meetings of the Association of American Geographers, Detroit.

Malecki, E. J. (1979a) Locational trends in R and D by large US corporations, 1965–1977, *Economic Geography* **55**, 309–23.

Malecki, E. J. (1979b) Agglomeration and intra-firm linkage in R and D location in the United States, *Tijdschrift voor Economische en Sociale Geografie* **70**, 322–32.

Malecki, E. J. (1980) Corporate organization of R and D and the location of technological activities, *Regional Studies* **14**, 219–34.

Malecki, E. J. (1981) Government-funded R and D: Some regional implications, *Professional Geographer* **33**, 72–82.

Malecki, E. J. (1986) Technological imperatives and modern corporate strategy, in Scott, A. J. and Storper, M. (eds), *Production, Work and Territory*. Allen and Unwin, Boston, pp. 67–79.

Mann, M. (1984) The autonomous power of the state: its origins, mechanisms and results, *European Journal of Sociology* **25**, 185–213.

Mansfield, E. (1982) Technology and productivity in the United States, in Feldstein, M. (ed.), *The American Economy in Transition*. University of Chicago Press, Chicago, pp. 563–96.

Markusen, A. (1983) High-tech jobs, markets and economic development prospects: evidence from California, *Built Environment* **9**, 18–28.

Markusen, A. (1985) *Profit Cycles, Oligopoly and Regional Development*. MIT Press, Cambridge, Mass.

Marsh, G. P. (1864) *Man and Nature*, in Lowenthal, D. (ed.). The Belknap Press of the Harvard University Press, Cambridge, MA, 1967.

Martin, R. C. (1979) Federal regional development programs and US problem areas, *Journal of Regional Science* **19**, 157–70.

Marx, L. (1964) *The Machine in the Garden: Technology and the Pastoral Ideal in America*. Oxford University Press, London.

Masotti, L. H. and Hadden, J. K. (eds) (1973) *The Urbanization of the Suburbs*. Sage Publications, Beverly Hills.

Mazey, M. E. and Lee, D. (1983) *Her Space, Her Place: A Geography of Women*. Association of American Geographers, Washington, DC.

Meeker, E. (1972) The improving health of U.S., 1850–1915, *Exploration in Economic History* **9**, 353–74.

Meinig, D. W. (1965) The Mormon culture region: Strategies and patterns in the geography of the American west, 1874–1964, *Annals of the Association of American Geographers* **55**, 191–20.

Meinig, D. W. (1971) *Southwest: Three Peoples in Geographical Change, 1600–1970*. Oxford Press, New York.

Meinig, D. W. (1972) American Wests: preface to a geographical interpretation, *Annals, Association of American Geographers* **62**, 159–84.

Mencken, H. L. (1936) *The American Language: An Inquiry into the Development of English in the United States*. Alfred A. Knopf, Inc., New York.

Mensch, G. (1983) *Stalemate in Technology: Innovations Overcome the Depression*. Ballinger, Cambridge, MA.

Meyer, D. R. (1983) Emergence of the American Manufacturing Belt: An interpretation, *Journal of Historical Geography* **9**, 145–74.

Michalos, A. (1980a) *North American Social Report: Vol. 1, Foundations, Population and Health*. Reidel, Dordrecht.

Michalos, A. (1980b) *North American Social Report: Vol. 2, Crime, Justice and Politics*. Reidel, Dordrecht.

Michalos, A. (1981a) *North American Social Report: Vol. 3, Science, Education and Recreation*. Reidel, Dordrecht.

Michalos, A. (1981b) *North American Social Report: Vol. 4, Environment, Transportation and Housing*. Reidel, Dordrecht.

Michalos, A. (1982) *North American Social Report: Vol. 5, Economics, Religion and Morality*. Reidel, Dordrecht.

Mighell, R. L, and Hoffnagle, W. S. (1970) *Contract Production and Vertical Integration in Farming, 1960 and 1970*. US Department of Agriculture Economic Research Service Report #479, US Government Printing Office, Washington, DC.

Miller, G. J. (1981) *Cities by Contract*. MIT Press, Cambridge.

Miller, J. L. (1969) The naming of the land in the Arkansas Ozarks: A study in culture processes, *Annals, Association of American Geographers* **59**, 240–51.

Mills, E. S. (1970) Urban Density Functions, *Urban Studies*, **7**, 5–20.

Mincer, J. (1978) Family migration decisions, *Journal of Political Economy* **86**, 749–73.

Mitchell, R. (1977) *Commercialism and Frontier: Perspectives on the Early Shenandoah Valley*. University Press of Virginia, Charlottesville.

Mitchell, R. (1983) American origins and regional institutions: The seventeenth-century Chesapeake, *Annals, Association of American Geographers* **73**, 404–20.

Moffet, B. (1985) Plethora of changes await 21st-century workers, *Home News* (21 January), A6.

Monahan, D. and Green, V. (1982) The impact of seasonal population fluctuations upon service delivery, *The Gerontologist* **22**, 160–3.

Moon, W. L. H. (1982) *Blue Highways: A Journey into America*. Fawcett Crest, New York.

Morgan, H. W. (1969) *From Hays to McKinley*. Syracuse University Press, Syracuse.

Morrill, R. L. and Donaldson, O. F. (1972) Geographical perspectives on the history of black America, *Economic Geography* **48**, 1–23.

Morrill, R. L., Sinclair, R. and Dimartino, D. R. (1984) The settlement system of the United States, in Bourne, L. S. and Sinclair, R. (eds), *Urbanization and Settlement Systems*. Oxford University Press, Oxford, pp. 23–48.

Morrison, P. A. and Abrahams, A. (1982) *Is Population Decentralization Lengthening Commuting Distances?* Rand Corporation, Santa Monica, CA.

Morrison, P. A. and McCarthy, K. F. (1979) *The changing demographic and economic structure of nonmetropolitan areas in the United States*. Rand Corporation, Santa Monica, CA.

Muller, E. K. (1977) Regional urbanization and the selective growth of towns in North American Regions, *Journal of Historical Geography* **3**, 21–39.

Muller, P. (1973) Trend surface of American agricultural patterns: A macro-Thunian analysis, *Economic Geography* **49**, 228–42.

Muller, P. (1981) *Contemporary Suburban America*. Prentice-Hall, Englewood Cliffs.

Murdie, R. A. (1969) *Factorial ecology of metropolitan Toronto, 1951–1961*. Research Paper #116, Department of Geography, University of Chicago.

Murphy, T. P. (1971) *Science, Geopolitics and Federal Spending*. D.C. Heath, Lexington, MA.

Myres, S. (1969) The ranching frontier: Spanish institutional backgrounds of the plains cattle industry, *Essay on the American West*. Walter Prescott Webb Memorial Lectures III, 19–39.

Naisbitt, J. (1984) *Megatrends*. Warner Books, New York.

Nash, R. (1967) *Wilderness and the American Mind*. Yale University Press, New Haven.

National Center for Health Statistics (1983) Birth of Hispanic parentage, 1980, *Monthly Vital Statistics Report*, Washington, DC.

National Urban Policy Advisory Committee to the Subcommittee on Investment, Jobs and Prices of the Joint Economic Committee of the Congress (1984) *Urban America: A Report Card*. US Congress, Washington, DC.

Nelson, K. (1984) Back offices and female labor markets: Office suburbanization in the San Francisco bay area. Unpublished PhD dissertation, Department of Geography, University of California, Berkeley.

Niemi, A. W. (1974) *State and Regional Patterns in American Manufacturing, 1860–1900*. Greenwood Press, Westport, Conn.

Noble, A. G. and Seymour, G. A. (1982) Distribution of barn types in Northeastern United States, *The Geographical Review* **72**, 155–70.

North, D. C. (1961) *The economic growth of the United States, 1790–1860*. Prentice-Hall, Englewood Cliffs.

North, D. C. (1966) *Growth and welfare in the American past*. Prentice-Hall, Englewood Cliffs.

Norton, R. D. and Rees, J. (1979) The product cycle and the spatial decentralization of American manufacturing, *Regional Studies* **13**, 141–51.

Nostrand, R. (1970) The Hispanic – American borderland: delimitation of an American cultural region, *Annals, Association of American Geographers* **60**, 638–61.

Nostrand, R. (1980) The Hispano homeland in 1900, *Annals, Association of American Geographers* **70**, 382–96.

Noyelle, T. J. (1983) The implications of industry restructuring for spatial organization in the United States, in Moulaert, F. and Salinas, P. W. (eds), *Regional Analysis and the New International Division of Labor*. Kluwer Nijhoff, The Hague, pp. 113–34.

Noyelle, T. J. and Stanback, T. M. Jr. (1981) *The economic transformation of American cities*. Conservation of Human Resources, New York.

O'Connell, M. (1981) Regional fertility patterns in the US: convergence or divergence, *International Regional Science Review* **6**, 1–14.

Odum, H. W. (1936) *Southern Regions of the United States*. University of North Carolina Press, Chapel Hill.

Odum, H. W. and Moore, H. E. (1938) *American Regionalism: A Cultural–Historical Approach to National Integration*. Henry Holt, New York.

O'Hare, W. (1983) *Wealth and Economic Status: A Perspective on Racial Inequity*. Joint Center for Political Studies, Washington, DC.

O'Hare, W. (1986) The best metros for blacks, *American Demographics* **8 (7)**, 26–33.

Olmsted, F. L. (1860) *Journey in the Back Country*. Schocken, New York, 1970.

Oppehheimer, V. K. (1970) *The Female Labor Force in the United States*. Greenwood Press, Westport, Conn.

O'Riordan, T. (1976) The role of environmental issues in Canadian–American policy making and administration, in Watson, J. W. and O'Riordan, T. (eds), *The American Environment: Policies and Perceptions*. Wiley, London, pp. 277–327.

Ostergren, R. (1980) Prairie bound: Migration patterns to a Swedish settlement on the Dakota frontier, in Luebke, F. (ed.), *Ethnicity on the Great Plains*. University of Nebraska Press, Lincoln, Nebraska, pp. 73–91.

Ostergren, R. (1981) Land and family in rural immigrant communities, *Annals, Association of American Geographers* **71**, 400–11.

Paarlberg, R. L. (1979) The failure of food power, in Fraenkel, R., Hadwiger, D. and Browne, W. (eds), *The Role of U.S. Agriculture in Foreign Policy*. Praeger, New York, pp. 38–55.

Packard, V. (1972) *A Nation of Strangers*. McKay, New York.

Palen, J. and Johnson, D. (1983) Urbanization and health status in Greer, A. and Greer, S. (eds), *Cities and Sickness. Health Care in Urban America*, Vol. 25, Urban Affairs Annual Reviews. Sage, Beverly Hills, Ch. 2.

Palen, J. and London, B. (1984) *Gentrification, Displacement and Neighborhood Revitalization*. State University of New York Press, Albany.

Palm, R. (1981) *The Geography of American Cities*. Oxford University Press, New York.

Park, R. E., Burgess, R. W. and Mckenzie, R. D. (1925) *The City*. University of Chicago Press, Chicago.

Parker, W. (1975) From Northwest to Midwest. Social bases of a regional history, in Klingaman, D and Vedder, R. (eds), *Essays in Nineteenth Century Economic History. The Old Northwest*. Ohio University Press, Athens, Ohio, pp. 3–34.

Parkman, F. (1892) *Discovery of the Great West*. Little, Brown, Boston.

Pearce, D. and McAdoo, H. (1981) *Women and Children: Alone and in Poverty*. Center for National Policy Review, Washington, DC.

Peet, R. (ed.) (1972) Geographical perspectives on American poverty, *Antipode*. Worcester, MA.

Peet, R. (1975) The geography of crime: A political critique, *Professional Geographer* **27**, 277–80.

Peet, R. (1983) Relations of production and the relocation of US manufacturing industry since 1960, *Economic Geography* **59**, 112–43.

Perry, D. C. and Watkins, A. J. (eds) (1977) *The Rise of the Sunbelt Cities*. Sage Publications, Beverly Hills, CA.

Perry, D. C. and Watkins, A. J. (1981) Contemporary dimensions of uneven urban development in the USA, in Harloe, M. (ed.), *City, Class and Capital*. Arnold, London, pp. 115–42.

Physician Task Force on Hunger in America (1985) *Hunger in America: The Growing*

Epidemic. Harvard University, School of Public Health, Cambridge, Mass.

Pierson, G. W. (1972) *The Moving American*. Alfred Knopf, New York.

Platt, R. H. (1984) The planner and nuclear crisis relocation, *Journal of the American Planning Association* **50**, 259–69.

Pope, C. (1984) Ronald Reagan and the limits of responsibility, *Sierra Club Bulletin* **69**, 3: 51–4.

Popper, F. (1982) Why we should care who owns the land, *American Land Forum* **2**, 1: 15–19.

Popper, F. (1983) LULUs, *Resources* (June), 2–4.

Popper, F. (1984) LULUs and their blockage: A new issue for national economic policy, *Looking Ahead* (July), 10–14.

Potter, J. (1965) The growth of population in America, 1700–1860, in Glass, D. V. and Eversley, D. C. (eds), *Population in History: Essays in Historical Demography*. London, pp. 678–98.

Pred, A. R. (1965) Industrialization, initial advantage and American metropolitan growth, *Geographical Review* **55**, 158–85.

Pred, A. R. (1966) *The Spatial Dynamics of US Urban–Industrial Growth, 1800–1914*. MIT Press, Cambridge, Mass.

Pred, A. R. (1974) *Major job-providing organizations and systems of cities*. Association of American Geographers, Resource Papers for College Geography, 27, Washington, DC.

Pred, A. R. (1977) *City-systems in Advanced Economies*. Hutchinson, London.

Pred, A. R. (1980) *Urban Growth and City Systems in the United States, 1840–1860*. Harvard University Press, Cambridge, Mass.

President's Commission for a National Agenda for the Eighties (1980) *Urban America in the Eighties: Perspectives and Prospects*. US Government Printing Office, Washington, DC.

Preston, S. H. (1984) Children and the elderly in the U.S., *Scientific American* **251**, 44–9.

Price, M. L. and Clay, D. C. (1980) Structural disturbances in rural communities: Some repercussions of the migration turnaround in Michigan, *Rural Sociology* **45**, 591–607.

Prunty, M. C. (1951) Recent quantitative changes in the cotton regions of the southeastern states, *Economic Geography* **27**, 202–7.

Prunty, M. C. (1955) The renaissance of the southern plantation, *Geographical Review* **45**, 459–91.

Pucher, J. (1983) Distribution of federal transport subsidies: cities, states and regions, *Urban Affairs Quarterly* **19**, 191–216.

Pyle, G. (1968) *The geography of disease in large cities, III: Geosocial pathology in Chicago*. Chicago Regional Hospital Study Working Paper IV. 4.

Pyle, G. and Rees, P. (1971) Modeling patterns of death and disease in Chicago, *Economic Geography* **49**, 344–56.

Radford, J. (1981) The social geography of the nineteenth century US city, in Herbert, D. T. and Johnston, R. J. (eds), *Geography and the Urban Environment. Progress in Research and Application, Vol. IV*. John Wiley, Ch. 8.

Raltz, K. (1979) Themes in the cultural geography of European ethnic groups in the United States, *Geographical Review* **69**, 79–94.

Reagan, M. (1982) *The New Federalism*. Oxford University Press, New York.

Reed, J. S. (1972) *The Enduring South: Subcultural Persistence in Mass Society*. Lexington Books, Lexington, MA.

Reed, J. S. (1982) *One South: An Ethnic Approach to Regional Culture*. Louisiana State University Press, Baton Rouge.

Rees, J. (1983a) Regional economic decentralization processes in the United States and their policy implications, in Hicks, D. A. and Glickman, N. J. (eds), *Transition to the 21st Century: Prospects and Policies for Economic and Urban–Regional Transformation*. JAI Press, Greenwich, Conn., pp. 241–78.

Rees, J. (1983b) Government policy and industrial location, in House, J. (ed.), *United States Public Policy*. Oxford University Press, London, pp. 213–62.

Reischauer, R. (1981) The economy and the federal budget in the 1980s: implications for the state and local sector, Bahl, R. (ed.), *Urban Government Finance: Emerging Trends*, Urban Affairs Annual Reviews,

Vol. 20. Sage, Beverly Hills, pp. 13–38.

Reps, J. (1965) *The Making of Urban America*. Princeton University Press, Princeton, NJ.

Richter, K. (1985) Nonmetropolitan growth in the late 1970s: the end of the turnaround?, *Demographics* **7**, 23–5.

Riis, J. A. (1890) *How the Other Half Lives*. C. Scribners and Sons, New York.

Robbins, J. (1984) Range war in Rosebud Valley, *New York Times Magazine* (6 May), 82–9.

Robertson, J. O. (1980) *American Myth, American Reality*. Hill and Wang, New York.

Robey, B. (1985) The not-so-huddled masses, *American Demographics* **7**, 44–6.

Robinson, I. (1986) Blacks move back to the South, *American Demographics* **8(6)**, 40–3.

Rogerson, P. and Plane, D. (1985) Monitoring migration trends, *American Demographics* **7**, 27–9, 49.

Rooney, J. F., Zelinsky, W. and Louder, D. R. (eds), (1982) *This Remarkable Continent: An Atlas of United States and Canadian Society and Culture*. Texas A & M University Press, College Station, TX.

Rose, H. (1971) *The Black Ghetto*. McGraw-Hill, New York.

Rose, H. (1985) The evolving spatial pattern of black America: 1910–1980, in McKee, J. O. (ed.), *Ethnicity in Contemporary America: A Geographical Appraisal*. Kendall Hunt, Dubuque, pp. 55–75.

Roseman, C. (1977) *Changing Migration Patterns Within the United States*. Resource Papers for College Geography, No. 772, Washington, DC.

Roseman, C. and Williams, J. (1980) Metropolitan to nonmetropolitan migration: a decision-making perspective, *Urban Geography* **1**, 283–94.

Rosen, G. (1958) *A History of Public Health*. MD Publications, Inc., New York.

Ross, P., Bluestone, H. and Hines, F. K. (1979) *Indicators of Social Well-Being for U.S. Counties*. Economic Development Division, Economics, Statistics, and Cooperative Services, US Department of Agriculture, Washington, DC.

Rowles, G., Hanham, R, and Bohland, J. (1985) Explaining changes in the regional concentration of the elderly in the U.S.A.

Paper presented at XIIIth International Congress of Gerontology, New York.

Rundquist, B. S. (1980) On the theory of political benefits in American public programs, in Rundquist, B. S. (ed.), *Political Benefits*. Lexington Books, Lexington, pp. 227–54.

Rundquist, B. S. (1983) Political benefits and public policy: interpretation of recent US studies, *Environment and Planning C, Government and Policy* **1**, 401–12.

Russell, L. (1982) *The Baby Boom Generation and the Economy*. Brookings Institution, Washington, DC.

Sauer, H. (1974) Geographic variation in mortality and morbidity, in Erhardt, C. and Berlin, T. (eds), *Mortality and Morbidity in the United States*. Harvard University Press, Cambridge, Mass, pp. 105–29.

Sawers, L. and Tabb, W. (eds) (1984) *Sunbelt/Snowbelt: Urban Development and Regional Restructuring*. Oxford University Press, New York.

Saxenian, A. (1983a) The genesis of Silicon Valley, *Built Environment* **9**, 7–17.

Saxenian, A. (1983b) The urban contradictions of Silicon Valley, *International Journal of Urban and Regional Research* **7**, 237–62.

Schafer, J. (1936) *The Social History of American Agriculture*. Macmillan, New York.

Schattschneider, E. A. (1960) *The Semi-Sovereign People*. Dryden, Hinsdale, Il.

Scherer, F. M. (1980) *Industrial Market Structure and Economic Performance* (2nd edn). Rand McNally, Chicago.

Schlesinger, A. M. (1971) *The Rise of the City*. Quadrangle Books, Chicago.

Schmitt, P. J. (1969) *Back to Nature: The Arcadian Myth in Urban America*. Oxford University Press, London.

Scully, V. J. (1955) *The Shingle Style and the Stick Style*. Yale University Press, New Haven.

Scully, V. J. (1975) *Pueblo: Mountain Village, Dance*. The Viking Press, New York.

Sennett, R. (1970) *The Uses of Disorder*. Penguin, London.

Seyler, H, and Lonsdale, R. (1979) Implications for nonmetropolitan development policy, in Lonsdale, R. and Seyler, H. (eds),

Nonmetropolitan Industrialization. V. H. Winston, Washington, DC, pp. 104–16.

Shalala, D. E. and McGeorge, J. A. (1981) The women and mortgage credit project: a governmental response to the housing problems of women, in Keller, S. (ed.), *Building for Women.* Lexington Books, Lexington, MA, pp. 39–45.

Shaw, R. P. (1975) *Migration Theory and Fact.* Regional Science Research Institute, Philadelphia.

Short, J. F. (1981) *The Social Fabric of the Metropolis.* University of Chicago Press, Chicago.

Shortridge, J. R. (1984) The emergence of 'Middle West' as an American regional label, *Annals, Association of American Geographers* **74**, 209–20.

Shortridge, J. R. (1985) The vernacular Middle West, *Annals, Association of American Geographers* **75**, 48–57.

Sinclair, V. (1905) *The Jungle.* The New American Library, New York, 1960.

Slater, C. (1985) The illegals, *American Demographics* **7**, 27–9.

Sloan E. (1966) *An Age of Barns.* Funk and Wagnalls, New York.

Smith, C. J. and Hanham, R. Q. (1982) *Alcohol Abuse: Geographical Perspectives.* Association of American Geographers, Washington, DC.

Smith, C. J. and Hanham, R. Q. (1985) Regional change and problem drinking in the U.S., 1970–78, *Regional Studies* **19**.

Smith, D. M. (1973) *The Geography of Social Well-Being in the United States.* McGraw Hill, New York.

Smith, D. M. (1977) *Human Geography: A Welfare Approach.* Edward Arnold, London.

Smith, D. M. (1979) *Where the Grass is Greener: Living in an Unequal World.* Penguin, Harmondsworth.

Smith, D. M. (1985) Inequality in Atlanta, Georgia, 1960–1980, *Occasional Paper* 25, Department of Geography and Earth Science, Queen Mary College, London.

Smith, E. Jr. (1980) America's richest farms and ranches, *Annals, AAG* **70**, 528–41.

Smith, H. N. (1950) *Virgin Land: The American West as Symbol and Myth.* Harvard University Press, Cambridge, MA.

Smith, N. (1979) Toward a theory of gentrification: A back to the city movement of capital not people, *Journal of the American Planning Association* **45**, 538–48.

Smith, N. (1984) Deindustrialization and regionalization: class alliance and class struggle, *Papers of the Regional Science Association* **54**, 113–28.

Smith, N. (1985) *Uneven Development.* Basil Blackwell, New York.

Smith, R. (1985) Residential patterns of female-headed households in U.S. metropolitan areas. Paper presented at Annual Meetings of Association of American Geographers, Detroit.

Smith, T. W. (1984) America's religious mosaic, *American Demographics* **6**, 6: 18–23.

Sokolow, A. (1981) Local politics and the turnaround migration: newcomer–oldtimer relations in small communities, in Roseman, C., Sofranko, A. and Cedal, W. J. (eds), *Population Redistribution in the Midwest.* Iowa State University, Ames, Iowa. pp. 169–190.

South, S. J. and Poston, D. L. Jr. (1982) The US metropolitan system: regional change 1950–1970, *Urban Affairs Quarterly* **18**, 187–206.

Stanback, T. M. Jr. and Noyelle, T. J. (1982) *Cities in Transition.* Allanheld, Osmun, Totowa, NJ.

Stanback, T. M. Jr., Bearse, P. J., Noyelle, T. J. and Karasek, R. A. (1981) *Services: The New Economy.* Allanheld, Osmun, Totowa, NJ.

Steinbeck, J. (1939) *The Grapes of Wrath.* Viking Press, New York.

Steinbeck, J. (1952) *East of Eden.* Viking Press, New York.

Steinbeck, J. (1962) *Travels with Charlie: In Search of America.* Viking Press, New York.

Steiner, M. C. (1983) Regionalism in the great depression, *The Geographical Review* **73**, 4: 430–46.

Stephens, J. D. and Holly, B. P. (1980) The changing patterns of industrial corporate control in the metropolitan United States, in Brunn, S. D. and Wheeler, J. O. (eds), *The American Metropolitan System: Present and Future.* V. H. Winston and Sons, New York, pp. 161–80.

Sternleib, G. and Hughes, J. W. (1977) New

regional and metropolitan realities of America, *Journal of the American Institute of Planners* **43**, 227–41.

Sternlieb, G. and Hughes, J. W. (1979) Back to the central city: Myths and realities, *Traffic Quarterly* **33**, 617–36.

Sternlieb, G. and Hughes, J. W. (eds) (1981) *Shopping Center: U.S.A.* Center for Urban Policy Research, New Brunswick.

Sternlieb, G. and Hughes, J. W. (1983) *The Atlantic City Gamble.* Harvard University Press, Cambridge, MA.

Sternlieb, G. and Hughes, J. W. (1984) *Income and Jobs: USA.* Center for Urban Policy Research, New Brunswick, N J.

Sternlieb, G., Hughes, J. W. and Hughes, C. O. (1982) *Demographic Trends and Economic Reality: Planning and Markets in the 80s.* Center for Urban Policy Research, New Brunswick.

Stilgoe, J. R. (1976) The puritan townscape: Ideal and reality, *Landscape* (Spring), 3–7.

Stilgoe, J. R. (1982) *Common Landscapes of America, 1580 to 1845.* Yale University Press, New Haven.

Stilgoe, J. R. (1983) *Metropolitan Corridor: Railroads and the American Scene.* Yale University Press, New Haven.

Stoler, P. (1982) Land sale of the century, *Time* (23 August), 26–32.

Storper, M. and Walker, R. (1984) The spatial division of labor: labor and the location of industries, in Sawers, L. and Tabb, W. K. (eds), *Sunbelt/Snowbelt.* Oxford University Press, New York, pp. 19–47.

Summers, G., Evans, S., Clemente, F., Beck, E. M. and Minkoff, J. (1976) *Industrial Invasion of Nonmetropolitan America.* Praeger, New York.

Suttles, G. D. (1968) *The Social Order of the Slum.* University of Chicago Press, Chicago.

Suttles, G. D. (1972) *The Social Construction of Communities.* University of Chicago Press, Chicago.

Suttles, G. D. (1975) Community design: the search for participation in a metropolitan society, in Hawley, A. H. and Rock, V. (eds), *Metropolitan America in Contemporary Perspective.* Halsted Press, pp. 235–98.

Tabb, W. K. (1984) Urban development and regional restructuring: an overview, in Sawers, L. and Tabb, W. K. (eds), *Sunbelt/Snowbelt.* Oxford University Press, New York, pp. 3–18.

Taylor, P. J. (1985) *Political Geography: World-Economy, Nation-State and Community.* Longman, London.

Terkel, S. (1980) *American Dreams: Lost and Found.* Pantheon Books, New York.

Thomas, J. (ed.) (1983) The Chicago School: the tradition and the legacy, *Urban Life* **11**, 387–511.

Thoreau, H. D. (1862) Walking, in Bode, C. (ed.), *The Portable Thoreau.* The Viking Press, New York, 1947.

Thornton, A. and Freedman, D. (1983) *The Changing American Family.* Population Reference Bureau, Washington, DC.

Thrower, N. (1966) *Original Survey and Land Subdivisions: A Comparative Study of the Farm and Effect of Contrasting Cadastral Surveys.* Association of American Geographers Monograph #4, Skokie, Il.

Tiebout, C. M. (1956) A pure theory of local expenditures, *Journal of Political Economy* **64**, 416–24.

Tocqueville, A. de (1864) *Democracy in America.* Oxford University Press, New York, 1947.

Toffler, A. (1970) *Future Shock.* Random House, New York.

Tonnies, F (1887) *Community and Society,* translated by Loomis, C. P. (1963). Harper, New York.

Trachte, K. and Ross, R. (1985) The crisis of Detroit and the emergence of global capitalism, *International Journal of Urban and Regional Research* **9**, 186–217.

Trees, J. (1981) Postwar trends in family size, *Demography* **18**, 321–34.

Trewartha, G. T. (1948) Some regional characteristics of American farmsteads, *Annals, Association of American Geographers* **38**, 196–225.

Trillin, C. (1978) *Alice, Let's Eat.* Random House, New York.

Turner, F. J. (1920) *The Frontier in American History.* Henry Holt and Co., New York.

Urban Resources (1983) Toward a new urban infrastructure, Special issue of *Urban Resources* **1**, 2.

US Bureau of Industrial Economics (1980) Evaluating the economic performance of US manufacturing industries, *Industrial Economic Review* 6–19.

US Bureau of the Census (1972) *General Demographic Trials for Metropolitan Areas, 1960 to 1970. U.S. Summary*. US Government Printing Office, Washington, DC.

US Bureau of the Census (1976) *The Statistical History of the United States. From Colonial Times to the Present*. Basic Books, New York.

US Bureau of the Census (1978) *Census of Agriculture: Graphic summary*. US Government Printing Office, Washington, DC.

US Bureau of the Census (1982a) *Population Profile of the United States: 1981*. Current Population Reports, Population Characteristics, Series P-20, No. 374, Washington, DC.

US Bureau of the Census (1982b) *Statistical Abstract of the United States: 1981*. US Government Printing Office, Washington, DC.

US Bureau of the Census (1982c) *Statistical Abstract of the United States: 1982*. US Government Printing Office, Washington, DC.

US Bureau of the Census (1982d) *Users' Guide, 1980*. US Government Printing Office, Washington, DC.

US Bureau of the Census (1983) *General Population Characteristics: U.S. Summary*. 1980 Census of the Population, US Government Printing Office, Washington, DC.

US Bureau of the Census (1984a) *Estimates of the Population of States by Age: July 2, 1981 to 1983*. Current Population Reports, Population Estimates and Projections, P-25, No. 951, Washington, DC.

US Bureau of the Census (1984b) *Geographical Mobility for Metropolitan Areas*. US Government Printing Office, Washington, DC.

US Bureau of the Census (1984) *Statistical Abstract of the United States, 1985*. Government Printing Office, Washington, DC.

US Bureau of the Census (1986) *Statistical Abstract of the United States: 1985*, US Government Printing Office, Washington, DC.

US Department of Agriculture (1981) *A Time to Choose*. US Government Printing Office, Washington, DC.

US Department of Commerce (1980) *Social Indicators III*. US Government Printing Office, Washington, DC.

US Department of Housing and Urban Development (1980) *The President's National Urban Policy Report, 1980*. US Government Printing Office, Washington, DC.

US Department of Housing and Urban Development (1982) *The President's National Urban Policy Report, 1982*. US Government Printing Office, Washington, DC.

Vance, J. E. Jr. (1970) *The Merchant's World: The Geography of Wholesaling*. Prentice-Hall, Englewood Cliffs.

Vedder, R. and Gallaway, L. (1971) Mobility of native Americans, *Journal of Economic History* **31**, 613–49.

Vedder, R. and Gallaway, L. (1975) Migration and the old Northwest, in Klingaman, D. and Vedder, R. (eds), *Essays in Nineteenth Century Economic History. The Old Northwest*. Ohio University, Athens, Ohio, pp. 159–76.

Vile, M. J. C. (1976) *Politics in the USA*. Hutchinson, London.

Vining, D. and Strauss, A. (1977) A demonstration that the current deconcentration of population in the United States is a clean break with the past, *Environment and Planning A* **9**, 751–8.

de Vise, P. (1973) *Misused and Misplaced Hospitals and Doctors*. Commission on College Geography, Association of American Geographers, Resource Paper #22, Washington.

Vogeler, I. (1981) *The Myth of the Family Farm: Agribusiness Dominance of U.S. Agriculture*. Westview Press, Boulder, CO.

Wald, M. (1984) The American dream is changing: A new outlook takes shape in shared housing, *New York Times* (28 October), Section 12, 1, 29.

Wallerstein, I. (1979) *The Capitalist World-Economy*. Cambridge University Press, Cambridge.

Ward, D. (1971) *Cities and Immigrants: A Geography of Change in Nineteenth Century America*. Oxford University Press, New York.

Wardwell, J. and Brown, D. (1980) Population redistribution in the United States during the 1970s, in Brown, D. and Wardwell, J. (eds), *New Directions in Urban–Rural Migration*. Academic Press, New York.

Warner, S. B. Jr. (1972) *The Urban Wilderness: A History of the American City*. Harper and Row, New York.

Warner, W. L. and Lunt, P. S. (1941) *The social life of a modern community*. Yale University Press, New Haven.

Warnes, A. M. and Law, C. M. (1984) The elderly population of Great Britain: Locational trends and policy implications, *Transactions of the Institute of British Geographers* **9**, 37–59.

Waslyenko, M. (1981) The location of firms: the role of taxes and fiscal incentives, in Bahl, R. (ed.), *Urban Government Finance: Emerging Trends*. Urban Affairs Annual Reviews, 20, Sage, Beverly Hills, pp. 185–90.

Watkins, A. J. and Perry, D. C. (1977) Regional change and the impact of uneven urban development, in Perry, D. C. and Watkins, A. J. (eds), *The Rise of the Sunbelt Cities*. Sage, Beverly Hills.

Watkins, C. M. (1976) The English heritage, in Marzio, P. C. (ed.), *A Nation of Nations*, Harper and Row, New York, pp. 36–51.

Watson, J. W. (1963) *North America, Its Countries and Regions*. Longman, London.

Watson, J. W. (1967) *Mental Images and Geographical Reality in the Settlement of North America*. University of Nottingham, England, Lecture, 22 pp.

Watson, J. W. (1969) The role of illusion in North American geography, *Canadian Geographer* **13**, 10–28.

Watson, J. W. (1970) Image geography: The myth of America in the American scene, *The Advancement of Science* **27**, 1–9.

Watson, J. W. (1974) The image of nature in America, in Mead, W. R. (ed.), *The American Environment*. The Athlone Press of the University of London, pp. 2–19.

Watson, J. W. (1976) Image regions, in Watson, J. W. and O'Riordan, T. (eds), *The American Environment: Perceptions and Policies*. Wiley, London, pp. 15–28.

Watson, J. W. (1979) *The Social Geography of the United States*. Longman, London.

Watson, J. W. and O'Riordan, T. (1976) Image and reality in the American scene, in Watson, J. W. and O'Riordan, T. (eds), *The American Environment: Perceptions and Policies*. Wiley, London, pp. 1–11.

Webb, W. P. (1931) *The Great Plains*. Ginn and Co., New York.

Webber, M. M. (1964) Culture, territoriality and the elastic mile, *Papers, Regional Science Association* **13**, 59–69.

Weinstein, B. L. and Firestine, R. E. (1978) *Regional growth and decline in the US: the rise of the sunbelt and decline in the Northeast*. Praeger, New York.

Weinstein, B. L., Gross, H. and Rees, J. (1985) *Regional Growth and Decline in the United States*. Praegon, New York.

Wells, R. (1985) *Uncle Sam's Family*. State University of New York Press, Albany.

Westoff, C. (1977) Fertility decline in the United States and its implications, in Cohen, W. and Westoff, C., *Demographic Dynamics in America*. The Free Press, New York, pp. 53–88.

Wheare, V. C. (1953) *Federalism*. The University Press, Oxford.

Wheeler, J. O. (1986) Corporate spatial links with financial institutions: the role of the metropolitan hierarchy, *Annals, Association of American Geographers* **76**, 262–74.

White, G. (1985) Geographers in a periously changing world, *Annals, Association of American Geographers* **75**, 4–10.

White, J. H. (1976) Railroads and the westward bound immigrant, in Marzio, P. C. (ed.), *A Nation of Nations*. Harper and Row, New York, pp. 178–92.

White, M. and White, L. (1962) *The Intellectual Versus the City: From Thomas Jefferson to Frank Lloyd Wright*. Harvard University

Press and the MIT Press, Cambridge, MA.

Whiteman, J. (1983) Deconstructing the Tiebout hypothesis, *Environment and Planning D, Society and Space* **1**, 339–53.

Whyte, W. F. (1956) *The Organization Man.* Simon and Schuster, New York.

Whyte, W. F. (1967) On 'Street Corner Society', in Burgess, E. W. and Bogue, D. J. (eds), *Urban Sociology*. Phoenix Books, Chicago, pp. 156–68.

Wigglesworth, M. (1662) God's Controversy with New England, *Proceedings of the Massachusetts Historical Society, 1871* **12**, 83–93.

Wilbanks, T. J. (1985) Geography and public policy at the national scale, *Annals of the Association of American Geographers* **75**, 4–10.

Williams, J. and Sofranko, A. (1979) Motivations for the immigration component of population turnaround in nonmetropolitan areas, *Demography* **16**, 239–56.

Winsberry, M. (1980) Concentration and specialization in United States agriculture, 1939–1978, *Economic Geography* **56**, 183–9.

Winthrop, J. (1629) Conclusion for the plantation in New England, *Old South Leaflets*, Boston, 1893, **2**, 50:5ff.

Wirth, L. (1938) Urbanism as a way of life, *American Journal of Sociology* **44**, 1–24.

Wohlenberg, E. H. (1976a) Interstate variations in AFDC programs, *Economic Geography* **52**, 254–66.

Wohlenberg, E. H. (1976b) Public assistance effectiveness by states, *Annals, Association of American Geographers* **66**, 440–50.

Wohlenberg, E. H. (1976c) An index of eligibility standards for welfare benefits, *The Professional Geographer* **26**, 381–4.

Wohlenberg, E. H. (1982) The geography of civility revisited: New York blackout looting, 1977, *Economic Geography* **58**, 29–44.

Wolpert, E. and Wolpert, J. (1974) From asylum to ghetto, *Antipode* **6**, 63–76.

Wolpert, J., Dear, M. and Crawford, R. (1975) Satellite mental health facilities, *Annals of the Association of American Geographers* **65**, 24–35.

Wolpert, J. and Wolpert, E. (1976) The relocation of released mental hospital patients into residential communities, *Policy Science* **7**, 31–51.

Wright, J. R. (1947) Terrae incognitae: The place of imagination in geography, *Annals of the Association of American Geographers* **37**, 1–15.

Yeates, M. (1965) Some factors affecting the spatial distribution of Chicago land values, 1910–1960, *Economic Geography* **40**, 57–70.

Zangwill, I. (1909) *The Melting Pot: A Drama in 4 Acts.* Macmillan, New York.

Zelinsky, W. (1961) An approach to the religious geography of the United States: Patterns of church membership in 1952, *Annals, Association of American Geographers* **51**, 139–93.

Zelinsky, W. (1971) The hypothesis of the mobility transition, *Geographical Review* **61**, 219–49.

Zelinsky, W. (1973) *The Cultural Geography of the United States.* Prentice-Hall, Englewood Cliffs, New Jersey.

Zelinsky, W. (1977) Coping with migration turnaround: The theoretical challenge, *International Regional Science Review* **3**, 175–8.

Zelinsky, W. (1980) North America's vernacular regions, *Annals of the Association of American Geographers* **70**, 1–16.

Zorbaugh, H. W. (1929) *The Gold Coast and the Slum.* University of Chicago Press, Chicago.

Zuiches, J. J. (1981) Residential preferences in the United States, in Hawley, A. H. and Mazie, S. M. (eds), *Nonmetropolitan America in Transition.* University of North Carolina Press, Chapel Hill, pp. 72–115.

Zysman, J. (1980) Research, politics and policy: regional planning in America, in OECD, *The utilization of the social sciences in policy-making in the USA.* OECD, Paris, pp. 121–58.

INDEX